DANIELS

v.

CANADA

DANIELS

V.

CANADA

IN AND BEYOND THE COURTS

EDITED BY NATHALIE KERMOAL
AND CHRIS ANDERSEN

UNIVERSITY OF MANITOBA PRESS

University of Manitoba Press
Winnipeg, Manitoba, Canada
Treaty 1 Territory
uofmpress.ca

Cataloguing data available from Library and Archives Canada
ISBN 978-0-88755-927-3 (PAPER)
ISBN 978-0-88755-931-0 (PDF)
ISBN 978-0-88755-929-7 (EPUB)
ISBN 978-0-88755-933-4 (BOUND)

Cover art: Christi Belcourt, *Flow*.
Cover and interior design by Jess Koroscil

Printed in Canada

The University of Manitoba Press acknowledges the financial support for
its publication program provided by the Government of Canada through
the Canada Book Fund, the Canada Council for the Arts, the Manitoba
Department of Sport, Culture, and Heritage, the Manitoba Arts Council,
and the Manitoba Book Publishing Tax Credit.

Funded by the Government of Canada | Canadä

CONTENTS

vii ACKNOWLEDGEMENTS

1 INTRODUCTION
NATHALIE KERMOAL AND CHRIS ANDERSEN

14 CHAPTER 1
Daniels in Context
TONY BELCOURT

21 CHAPTER 2
Harry Daniels and Section 91 (24) of the British
North America Act: A Blueprint for the Future
NATHALIE KERMOAL

44 CHAPTER 3
After the Hysteria: Understanding *Daniels v.
Canada* from a Métis Nation Perspective
JASON MADDEN

78 CHAPTER 4
Daniels v. Canada: A Framework for Redress
AREND J.A. HOEKSTRA AND THOMAS ISAAC

98 CHAPTER 5
The Other Declarations in *Daniels*: Fiduciary
Obligations and the Duty to Negotiate
CATHERINE BELL

116 CHAPTER 6
Racism, Canadian Jurisprudence, and the
De-Peopling of the Métis in *Daniels*
D'ARCY VERMETTE

148 CHAPTER 7

Daniels through an International Law Lens

BRENDA L. GUNN

169 CHAPTER 8

Daniels v. Canada beyond Jurisprudential
Interpretation: What to Do Once
the Horse Has Left the Barn

CHRIS ANDERSEN

188 CHAPTER 9

Outlining the Origins of "Eastern Métis" Studies

DARRYL LEROUX

210 CHAPTER 10

Making Kin in a Postgenomic World:
Indigenous Belonging after the Genome

RICK W. A. SMITH, LAUREN SPRINGS, AUSTIN W.
REYNOLDS, AND DEBORAH A. BOLNICK

233 CHAPTER 11

How We Know Who We Are: Historical
Literacy, Kinscapes, and Defining a People

BRENDA MACDOUGALL

268 CONCLUSION

The Multiple Lives of the *Daniels* Case

275 BIBLIOGRAPHY
309 CONTRIBUTORS
317 INDEX

Acknowledgements

We are indebted to a number of individuals and institutions for their help in bringing Daniels v. Canada: *In and Beyond the Courts* into being. The book's foundation was laid at a 2017 conference organized by the Rupertsland Centre for Métis Research in Edmonton, Alberta, entitled *Daniels: In and Beyond the Law.* The academic and non-academic participants and audience were all very inspirational during the conference. We gratefully acknowledge the funding received for the conference from the Ministry of Advanced Education, Government of Alberta, as well as the Métis Nation of Alberta, the Rupertsland Institute, and the Faculty of Native Studies at the University of Alberta. More specifically, we want to acknowledge the support of Audrey Poitras, Métis Nation of Alberta President; Aaron Barner, Métis Nation of Alberta Senior Executive Officer; and Lorne Gladue, Rupertsland Institute Chief Executive Officer.

We appreciate the support and advice of the anonymous reviewers, the University of Manitoba Press Editorial Board, Glenn Bergen, and David Larsen at the University of Manitoba Press (UMP). Jill McConkey, acquisitions editor at the UMP, skillfully and patiently guided us through the editorial stages of the book and Maureen Epp's copy-editing skills were invaluable to finalize the book. We are also extremely grateful to Chantal Roy Denis, Jenn Rossiter, Amanda Evans, and Leah Hrycun, who worked on the book at different stages of its development.

Introduction

NATHALIE KERMOAL AND CHRIS ANDERSEN

Of all the groups in Canada, the Métis have clearly suffered the most from an inflexible federalism that emphasizes provincial boundaries at the expense of nation-wide interests which transcend those boundaries. Because the federal government precludes any special status for national minorities and avoids the kind of legal responsibility for Métis that it jealously guards in relation to Indians, the onus for improving the socio-economic condition of hundreds of thousands of Métis has fallen to provincial governments. The individual provincial governments, however, have amply demonstrated they lack the will—to say nothing of the lack of administrative machinery and constitutional powers—to tackle the problems of the Métis which have been, and are, national in scope. . . . The basic problem, the fundamental issue at stake for Canada's Métis, is the unwillingness, inability, or incapacity of the federal government to deal with the Métis as an indigenous people, a national minority with a century-old claim to Aboriginal Rights.[1]

Over the past twenty years, the Supreme Court of Canada (scc) has played a major role in defining Métis rights. Though the Métis were recognized in the Constitution Act of 1982 as one of the Aboriginal peoples of Canada, the federal government continued to exclude them from the kinds of social programs and negotiation processes that First Nations had long been engaged with. For example, lawyer Joseph Magnet and his team discovered a number of government documents indicating that the federal government was very much aware of the fact that the Métis were "far more exposed to discrimination and other social disabilities. It is true to say that in the absence of Federal initiative in this field they are the most disadvantaged of all Canadian citizens."[2] This seems to corroborate findings reported in other government documents around housing needs for the Métis.[3] As early as 1969, for example, the Hellyer report on housing and urban renewal had noted the dire conditions in which Métis were living: "Indeed some of the housing conditions witnessed by the Task Force in Métis areas around Winnipeg ranked with the very worst one could encounter anywhere in Canada. These people require special assistance and should receive it."[4] Yet even though the government admitted in the 1980s to "possessing the power to legislate theoretically in all domains in respect of Métis and Non-Status Indians under Section 91(24) of the British North America Act,"[5] it consciously refused to do so.

With the failed Charlottetown Accord in 1992, the Métis lost (through no fault of their own) a chance to gain political traction through negotiation with the federal and provincial governments. Indeed, the proposed amendment package to the Canadian constitution would have enshrined an Aboriginal right to self-government for the Métis people, as outlined in the draft Métis Nation Accord. Access to programs and funding was central to the accord. In the section on the Métis, the 1996 report of the Royal Commission on Aboriginal Peoples (RCAP) emphasized that "Aboriginal collectivities claiming to be nations of Métis people should be recognized under the same recognition policy and using the same criteria as applied to all Aboriginal peoples."[6] The RCAP further recommended that "the government of Canada either (a) acknowledge that section 91(24) of the Constitution Act, 1867 applies to Métis people and base its legislation, policies and programs on that recognition; or (b) collaborate with appropriate provincial governments and with Métis representatives in the formulation and enactment of a constitutional amendment specifying that section 91(24) applies to Métis people. If it is unwilling to take either of these steps, the government of Canada make a constitutional reference to the Supreme Court of Canada, asking that court to decide whether section 91(24) of the Constitution Act, 1867 applies to Métis people."[7] Following their setback with the Charlottetown Accord, the Métis turned to the courts and more specifically to the SCC to advance their rights.

In 2003, *R. v. Powley* became the first major judicial breakthrough for the Métis people—this was perhaps especially notable given that First Nations and Inuit had been making use of the courts for the previous three decades. Hailed as a victory by Métis organizations, the *Powley* decision defined Métis rights as they relate to subsistence hunting. Through the "Powley test," the SCC clarified the boundaries and contours of Métis rights. Two subsequent SCC decisions involving Métis litigants followed: the Manitoba Metis Federation (MMF) case in 2013 and the *Daniels* decision in 2016. As Métis scholar Adam Gaudry explains, "In *MMF v. Canada* the court found that the federal government had failed in its constitutional obligation to protect Métis interests in the 1870s allocation of Manitoba lands. In effect, the court identified a duty to reconcile Métis interests in Manitoba lands and neces-sitated movement towards a bilateral relationship between the MMF and the Government of Canada."[8] In *Daniels v. Canada* the court determined that Métis and non–Status Indians were "Indians" under s. 91(24) of the Constitution Act, 1867. After years of federal government neglect, the SCC confirmed what the Métis had known all along: that the federal government possessed jurisdictional responsibilities vis-à-vis the Métis. The court ruled that the term "Indians" needed to be understood broadly and that Métis and non–Status Indians "are all 'Indians' under s. 91(24) by virtue of the fact that they are all Aboriginal peoples."[9]

On 14 April 2016, the SCC "put an end to a 17 year odyssey that began in 1999."[10] For Joseph Magnet, the *Daniels* decision is among the "most trans-formative indigenous constitutional cases, if not the most transformative case, of this generation."[11] The plaintiffs sought three declarations:

(1) that Métis and Non-Status Indians (MNSI) are "Indians" as defined in s. 91(24) of the Constitution Act, 1867;

(2) that the Crown owes a fiduciary duty to Métis and Non-Status Indians as Aboriginal peoples; and

(3) that Métis and Non-Status Indians have the right to be consulted and negotiated with by the federal government as to their rights, interests, and needs as Aboriginal peoples.[12]

The court granted only the first declaration, arguing that the other two had already been covered by previous jurisprudence.

At least formally, the *Daniels* decision puts an end to the federal government's politics of avoidance that have left the Métis in jurisdictional limbo. The signing of recent framework agreements by Métis organizations in Western Canada show how s. 91(24) has opened the door for the Métis Nation to forge a new relationship with Canada based on a "nation-to-nation," "government-to-government" dialogue, a foundation and accommodation that heralds the end of the political and administrative isolation of the Métis Nation.[13]

However, like all court decisions, *Daniels* is imperfect, particularly with respect to the SCC's comments on the nature of Métis identity. By dismissing a nationhood-based definition of "Métis," the court positioned the term in a racial "Métis-as-mixed" logic. This characterization has been seized by individuals as well as organizations as a means of validating their particular understanding of Métis history and Métis identity, a move that is deeply troubling for Métis people who see themselves not as a mixture of races but as distinctive political and cultural communities.[14]

An example of the broad cultural power law possesses in Canadian society, *Daniels* demonstrates the use of court decisions by people and organizations that look to them for validation of their identity. As Métis scholar Chris Andersen argued at the "*Daniels*: In and Beyond the Law" conference, held at the University of Alberta in 2017, courts can be "roadmaps to nowhere." At their best, they provide logics that help produce policy, guidelines to be used in the context of future litigation strategies and decision making in associated policies.[15] For example, the *Powley* decision not only affected subsequent court cases but also shaped the ways in which political relationships have developed between Métis organizations and provincial and federal governments. While SCC decisions can serve to clarify Aboriginal rights and establish legal tests to determine their scope and content, they are never just about the logics of the court cases themselves. Decisions—like those produced by the scc—nearly always hold broader political and social ramifications. Some of these ramifications are good, while some are not so good. As Andersen explains, "Court decisions—especially those written by the Supreme Court of Canada . . . are beginnings as much as they are endings. That is to say, court decisions must be understood as imparting important—if sometimes necessarily vague and often maddeningly contra-dictory—policy principles that have the power to enormously impact the dynamics of future policy relationships."[16] Court rulings can thus open a Pandora's box that further complicates matters. For many social actors, court decisions are important not for what they say but for what people *think* they say, and for what people *wish* them to say. Likewise, court decisions can also be important for certain actions they seem to encourage or discourage, and social actors often draw from a particular court decision the rationale to take those actions. People like to think that the logic of a scc decision is clearly laid out and will effectively "settle things once and for all," but that is rarely the case. Groups of people and governments isolate the sentences or paragraphs that fit their understanding of a given ruling. In this way, court decisions can hold different meanings for different people (we will return to this in the volume's conclusion).

At the heart of the question is the constitutive power of law. Andersen positions courts as a specific and generative form of juridical power that hold a particular forum of power in Canadian society. Indeed, they shape "the production of logics not only irreducible to the dynamics of other social fields but potentially resistant to them."[17] Courts are a generative form of juridical power, since they "produce a form of 'juridical capital' that rather than directly constituting social relations or (re)producing a 'grand hege-mony,' generates particular depictions and problematizations of social issues and classifications that can potentially shape the parameters within which subsequent political strategies and struggles ensue."[18] For Andersen, ordina-tions of "Métis" take a distinctively juridical form: "they refract, rather than reflect, broader forms of racialization according to logics that remain largely insulated from critique."[19]

Following Andersen, the authors in this volume pay close attention to the ways in which the *Daniels* decision affects the Métis people on questions of history, law, genomics, genealogy, and identity.[20] This book thus provides different perspectives, including on the legal outcomes of the case (good or bad), its policy ramifications, and its multiple interpretations by Métis and by Canadian society at large.

Overview of the Book

The first two chapters in the volume focus on history. Both pay tribute to the Métis politicians, including Harry Daniels, who fought the hard battles that set the stage for the recognition of Métis rights evidenced in *Daniels*. Up until 1982, there was no provision in Canada's constitution that recognized and affirmed the existing Aboriginal and treaty rights of Aboriginal peoples, no provision stating who the Aboriginal peoples of Canada are, no Equality Clause prohibiting discrimination on the basis of sex, and no SCC decisions confirming the existence of any Métis rights. Thus it is recent history that provides the contextualization crucial to understanding the importance of the *Daniels* decision for Métis communities.

In the post–Second World War period, poverty, shanty housing, and lack of education had become endemic among Métis and non–Status Indian populations. The federal government took the position that it only had jurisdictional responsibility for Status Indians registered under the Indian Act and largely refused responsibility for providing programs or services to Métis people. Any process to address Métis land claims was also denied. In response, Métis and non–Status Indian organizations formed the Native Council of Canada (NCC) in 1971. The NCC maintained that their constituents were "Indians" within the meaning of s. 91(24) of the British North America Act (now known as the Constitution Act, 1867). In Chapter 1, Tony Belcourt, one of the actors of the time, clearly expresses what was sought, what was achieved, and the consequences for Métis people today. His personal account provides a snapshot on the environment and the history that led to the *Daniels* decision.

With Chapter 2, Nathalie Kermoal adds to Belcourt's narrative by examining the social and political circumstances of the 1970s and '80s that put Métis leader Harry Daniels on the judicial path to contesting the federal government's narrow definition of s. 91(24) of the British North America Act. Her historical analysis gives voice to Daniels and identifies the intellectuals and political movements that influenced him in formulating a counter-narrative to Pierre Elliott Trudeau's concept of a "just society." This contextualization provides the necessary background to analyze the rhetoric Daniels used to position Métis people as one of the founding nations of Canada. The Métis rejected being seen as just another disadvantaged minority group, arguing that they were not an ethnic group but rather a historical national minority—just as Québécois nationalists had claimed in the 1960s and '70s—and consequently deserving of more recognition than the Trudeau government was willing to give them.

Harry Daniels, along with other leaders such as Tony Belcourt and Jim Sinclair, thus played a significant role in breaking through the conventional boundaries of Canadian politics and society by dedicating much of his political life to the advancement of his people's rights. The pressure that the Métis and other Indigenous groups (First Nations and Inuit) exerted on Trudeau's agenda eventually bore fruit, and they were included in the Constitution Act of 1982. The rhetoric that positioned the Métis as a "collectivity" or Nation rather than "ordinary citizens" helped reinforce the notion that they should have access to programs available to First Nations (Status Indians). Section 91(24) became the political avenue for making those indispensable social and political advances.

Following this consideration of the historical background to the 2016 *Daniels* decision 2016, Chapters 3 through 7 provide legal analyses of the scc decision itself, highlighting what the court said and, more importantly, what it should have said but did not.

In Chapter 3, Jason Madden analyzes the *Daniels* decision from a Métis Nation perspective. Providing an overview of the purpose and evolution of the case, the various decisions of the courts in *Daniels* as well as the case's role in the development of Métis law as a part of Aboriginal law in Canada, the author argues that *Daniels* joins the scc's judgements in *R. v. Powley*[21] and *Manitoba Metis Federation v. Canada*[22] to form a trifecta of Métis law. Together, these decisions have led to recent developments in Crown–Métis Nation negotiations and agreements related to Métis rights and self-government. While *Daniels v. Canada* was a unanimous decision, it is arguably one of the most confusing and misunderstood recent decisions from the court in the area of Aboriginal law. This has led to much erroneous media coverage, commentary, and analysis in relation to *Daniels*. Introducing ideas developed later in this volume by Darryl Leroux and Brenda Macdougall, Madden argues that *Daniels* does not create a new category of "Métis" who are owed any form of reconciliation from federal, provincial, or territorial governments, outside those already recognized within the meaning of s. 35 of the Constitution Act, 1982.

Arend J.A. Hoekstra and Thomas Isaac contend in Chapter 4 that the *Daniels* decision acts as a prominent signpost in the scc's journey of evolving judicial language. It introduced the noun "Indigenous" at a time when Canada was engaged in fundamental conversations regarding its history and its relationship with Indigenous peoples, following the inquiry into Indian residential schools. Through *Daniels*, the court introduced a novel framework for s. 91(24) of the Constitution Act, 1867 that contrasts with the well-defined s. 35 framework of the Constitution Act, 1982. Whereas s. 35 focuses on the prospective protection of Aboriginal communities through the constraint of the Crown, s. 91(24) focuses on the retrospective redress of harms to individuals that have resulted from Crown actions targeted at Indigenous peoples. In relying on a broad categorization of "Indigenous," this new framework encompasses not only those people with a shared culture and ancestry but also, potentially, those persons who are "Indigenous" by race or ancestry alone.

In Chapter 5, Catherine Bell focuses on the last two declarations of the *Daniels* decision. As previously mentioned, the plaintiffs in *Daniels* had asked for three judicial declarations, but only the first was granted.[23] Bell argues that the court's reasoning in refusing the second and third declarations creates potential confusion about duties flowing from honour of the Crown in two key ways: (1) the apparent conflation of the "fiduciary relationship" between the Crown and Indigenous peoples with fiduciary duties that flow from that relationship; and (2) the apparent conflation of the Crown's "context-specific duty to negotiate" with the duty to negotiate identification and definition of rights claims and fulfill constitutionalized promises aimed at reconciliation of Indigenous interests. This chapter also considers some of the challenges faced by Métis people seeking to negotiate through representatives of their choice, given the nature of contemporary Métis political organization.

Even without the challenges identified by Catherine Bell, D'Arcy Vermette argues in Chapter 6 that the *Daniels* case is not without its drawbacks. For Vermette, *Daniels* is not out of place among older and more obviously racist case law from both Canada and the United States. While the *Daniels* decision ushered in constitutional clarity by placing the Métis within federal jurisdiction as "Indians," Vermette's comparison of *Daniels* with an older case law, *Tronson* (a lower-level case in which Indian identity sat at the core of the legal dispute), demonstrates that the scc's determinations of Métis identity are functionally racist, since they define Métis identity in ways that undermine the very peoplehood of the Métis, which in turn diminishes their role as constitutional actors.

Brenda L. Gunn, in Chapter 7, discusses the *Daniels* decision in light of the rights of Indigenous peoples recognized in the United Nations Declaration on the Rights of Indigenous Peoples (UNDRIP). Gunn begins by reviewing the court decision and issues that have arisen as a result. For example, there has been an increase in self-proclaimed "Métis" groups who seek to exploit and appropriate what it means to be Indigenous (Métis) in Canada, while maintaining their white privilege (see also Darryl Leroux, Chapter 9 in this volume). International human rights have evolved over the past thirty years, including and especially with respect to the rights of Indigenous peoples. The chapter then considers how international human rights law, including UNDRIP, alleviates some of the concerns that have been raised, including through the potential expansion of the definition of Métis people. Gunn concludes with a brief description of the types of rights that could flow from the resolution of the jurisdictional issues, which it is hoped will encourage the federal government to engage in self-government negotiations with the Métis people.

The remaining four chapters examine some of the broader societal implications of the Daniels decision. The *Daniels* decision was meant to provide clarification on the meaning of s. 91(24) of the British North America Act of 1867. Only time will tell whether the scc's decision will achieve that goal. Still, the decision itself makes for an excellent starting point for thinking about the sometimes vast gulf between what jurisprudential scholars think about the merits of a given decision and how that decision gets put to use by a wide variety of social and political actors outside the comparatively narrow confines of the jurisprudential arena. In Chapter 8, Chris Andersen begins by exploring several core streams of logic contained within the court decision, then investigates the manner in which Indigenous political organizations in particular have claimed victory—despite their different and even oppositional understandings of terminology used in the decision—with an eye to understanding both the power of juridical discourse in contemporary Canadian society and the limitations of judicial interpretations of the decision's meaning(s).

As an example of the power of juridical discourse—and one that gives ammunition to different groups to claim Métis identity—Darryl Leroux explores in Chapter 9 the claims to Métis identity that have flourished in the Eastern provinces of Canada over the past decade as well as since *Daniels*, including through the emergence in the post-*Powley* period of nearly thirty separate organizations representing self-identified "métis" individuals. Alongside this remarkable political mobilization, a new historiography promoted primarily by French-language historians and anthropologists has emerged to challenge the land- and kinship-based terms for Métis peoplehood. Leroux analyzes two of the most common claims of this revisionist history: first, the argument for Eastern ethnogenesis, or the idea that Red River Métis ethnogenesis took place in seventeenth-century New France; and second, the idea, based on the normative French-English political cleavage in Canadian society, that the Métis are oppressing their French-speaking Eastern peers. Leroux carefully examines both these claims in relation to the countervailing understandings of Métis identity and belonging developed by Métis scholars themselves.

This revisionist history often bases its claims on DNA and genealogy. As Sisseton Wahpeton Oyate scholar Kim TallBear emphasized during the Daniels conference, "In the 21st century, new technological developments meet the old social technology of playing Indian. DNA ancestry testing conditioned by settler state racial formations has emerged to capitalize on actualized citizen consumers of DNA tests."[24] Many of the "métis" claims in Eastern Canada analyzed by Leroux illustrate settler colonial efforts to define Indigeneity in ways that rely too heavily on linear, biological descent and attend too lightly to Indigenous people's definitions of peoplehood.

In Chapter 10, Rick W.A. Smith, Lauren Springs, Austin W. Reynolds, and Deborah A. Bolnick present an overview of both conventional and emerging genomic ancestry technologies and map their limitations for defining Indigenous belonging. Genomics has emerged as a powerful but often problematic framework for producing notions of identity and belonging, and the ways that DNA is used to constitute certain relations are often set against the interests of Indigenous peoples' sovereignty and self-determination. In the context of the *Daniels* decision, which codifies long-standing misconceptions about Métis as a mixed-race category, non-Indigenous people are increasingly turning to commercial genetic ancestry tests for evidence of their Indigenous and European ancestry in order to claim Métis belonging. These genetic claims are frequently disengaged from Métis people and therefore lack recognition from the communities to which consumers of genetic ancestry tests seek entry, casting doubt on the legitimacy of DNA as an arbiter of belonging. Drawing upon publicly available genome data and interviews with consumers of genetic ancestry tests, the authors of this chapter further disrupt notions of Indigeneity as a genetically coherent category and support an understanding of Indigenous belonging that is produced in and through lived relations.

Brenda Macdougall addresses the limitations of genealogical research in Chapter 11, which arise—much like the limitations of DNA tests—from a focus on the individual rather than family or community. As demonstrated by Darryl Leroux, many new "métis" will rely on "an Indigenous ancestor born in the 1600s as the sole basis for their claim to indigeneity," but such a claim of a "long-ago Indigenous ancestry simply does not suffice as evidence of a distinct Métis community today."[25] At best, genealogical research is used to support a person's desire to explore their lineage; at worst, it encourages the individual to imagine that an ancestral reality equals their contemporary identity.

Macdougall points out that tracing family history as a primary methodological approach is not new to Métis scholarship. There has been a long-standing recognition of the conceptual importance of the family within the socio-economic history of the Métis. As such, when built for a community rather than an individual, genealogies become a reflection of social organization over time. By using genealogical reconstruction as a methodological tool in community, regional, and national studies, and then contextualizing that data with qualitative archival records (such as trade, mission, governmental, newspapers), insights into economic, social, and religious behaviours of Métis communities in specific spatial and temporal geographies are possible. If used dynamically, then, genealogical reconstructions are an important methodological tool to organize, interpret, and analyze wahkootowin—a kinscape of people's relatedness, framed within a specific socio-cultural world view.

Daniels v. Canada is indeed a multifaceted decision whose outcome has not yet been fully understood and whose effects will continue to reverberate across a wide variety of social, political, economic, and geographical contexts. By focusing on various impacts of the *Daniels* Supreme Court decision, this collection of essays makes a distinctive contribution to understanding the continued power of the courts in Canadian society and the manner in which Canada's colonial legacy continues to bedevil our attempts to come to terms with a peoplehood-based understanding of not just Métis identity but Indigenous identities more generally.

NOTES

1   Harry Daniels, *We Are the New Nation/Nous sommes la nouvelle nation* (Ottawa: Native Council of Canada, 1979), 6.

2   Joseph Magnet, "*Daniels v. Canada*: Origins, Intentions, Futures," *aboriginal policy studies* 6, no. 2 (2017): 28.

3   See Nathalie Kermoal, "Navigating Troubled Political Waters for Better Housing : The Canative Example," in *Métis Rising*, ed. Larry Chartrand and Yvonne Boyer (Vancouver: UBC Press, forthcoming).

4   Canada Mortgage and Housing Corporation, *Report of the Federal Task Force on Housing and Urban Development* (Ottawa: Task Force on Housing and Urban Development, 1969), 58. See also Evelyn Peters, Matthew Stock, and Adrian Werner, *Rooster Town: The History of an Urban Métis Community, 1901–1961* (Winnipeg: University of Manitoba Press, 2019).

5   Magnet, "*Daniels v. Canada*," 28–29.

6   Royal Commission on Aboriginal Peoples, *Perspectives and Realities*, vol. 4 of *Report of the Royal Commission on Aboriginal Peoples* (Ottawa: Libraxus, 1996), 187.

7   Ibid., 196.

8   Adam Gaudry, "Better Late Than Never? Canada's Reluctant Recognition of Métis Rights and Self-Government," *Yellowhead Institute*, Policy Brief Issue 10 (2018): 2.

9   Magnet, "*Daniels v. Canada*," 27.

10 Ibid., 26.

11 Ibid.

12 *Daniels v. Canada* (Indian Affairs and Northern Development), 2016 SCC 12.

13 For more information, see Janique Dubois, "The Emerging Policy Relationship between Canada and the Métis Nation," Institute for Research of Public Policy, https://on-irpp.org/2L-JOPgf; Gaudry, "Better Late Than Never?"; and "Métis Nation of Alberta–Canada Framework Agreement for Advancing Reconciliation," Métis Nation of Alberta, 16 November 2017, http://albertametis.com/wp-content/uploads/2017/02/MNA-GOC-Framework-Advancing-Reconciliation_SIGNED.pdf.

14 See the following for analyses of the Daniels decision: Chris Andersen and Adam Gaudry, "*Daniels v. Canada*: Racialized Legacies, Settler Self-Indigenization and the Denial of Indigenous Peoplehood," *TOPIA* 36 (2016): 19–30; Brenda Macdougall, "The Power of Legal and Historical Fiction(s): The *Daniels* Decision and the Enduring Influence of Colonial Ideology," *International*

Indigenous Policy Journal 7, no. 3 (2016): 1–6; Chelsea Vowel and Darryl Leroux, "White Settler Antipathy and the *Daniels* Decision," *TOPIA* 36 (2016): 30–42; Adam Gaudry and Darryl Leroux, "White Settler Revisionism and Making Métis Everywhere: The Evocation of Métissage in Quebec and Nova Scotia," *Critical Ethnic Studies* 3, no. 1 (2017): 116–42; Adam Gaudry, "Communing with the Dead: The 'New Métis,' Métis Identity Appropriation, and the Displacement of Living Métis Culture," *American Indian Quarterly* 42, no. 2 (2018): 162–90.

15 See Chris Andersen, "The Supreme Court Ruling on Métis: A Roadmap to Nowhere," *Globe and Mail*, 14 April 2016, https://www.theglobeandmail.com/opinion/the-supreme-court-ruling-on-metis-a-roadmap-to-nowhere/article29636204/.

16 Ibid.

17 Chris Andersen, *"Métis": Race, Recognition, and the Struggle for Indigenous Peoplehood* (Vancouver: UBC Press, 2014), 63.

18 Ibid.

19 Ibid.

20 This book focuses on the ramifications of the *Daniels* decision as it pertains to Métis people and does not examine its implications for non–Status Indian rights.

21 *R. v. Powley*, 2003 SCC 43.

22 *Manitoba Metis Federation Inc. v. Canada* (Attorney General), 2013 SCC 14.

23 *Daniels v. Canada* (Indian Affairs and Northern Development), 2016 SCC 12, 3.

24 *"Daniels*: In and Beyond the Law," Rupertsland Centre for Métis Research, University of Alberta, Edmonton, 26–28 January 2017, unpublished conference notes, 7.

25 Darryl Leroux, "Self-Made Métis," *Maisonneuve Magazine* (Fall 2018): 37.

CHAPTER 1

Daniels in Context[1]

TONY BELCOURT

I see the *Daniels* decision through the lens of a Métis person who grew up in what is known as the historic Métis community of Lac Ste. Anne, Alberta. I see it through the lens of someone who was active in the Métis Association of Alberta (MAA) in the late 1960s and became its vice-president in 1970. I see it through the lens of having moved to Ottawa as the founding president of the Native Council of Canada (NCC), now called the Congress of Aboriginal Peoples (CAP). I also see *Daniels* through the lens of a time before the Constitution Act, 1982 recognized the existing Aboriginal and treaty rights of the Aboriginal peoples of Canada, including the Métis people.

The fact is that I do not remember us using the term Métis very much when I was growing up in Lac Ste. Anne, Alberta, although the term was common in other areas, particularly in the "Métis settlements."[2] Many of us referred to ourselves as Nêhiyaw, which means "the people" in Cree. The Indians (as we referred to them then) thought of us as their "poor relatives, the Awp-ee-tow-Koosons,"[3] which in Cree means "half-people." Indians also referred to us as tipeyimisiwak, which means "the free people" or "their own boss." The federal government referred to us as half-breeds.[4] In Lac Ste. Anne and in other places throughout the West we adopted these names for ourselves.

Racism and discrimination were prevalent. So was poverty. In a personal letter to me dated 12 January 1989, my mother wrote about the time when I was growing up as a child: "And dad & I barely survived. he tried to get the old farm going[.] he trapped in the winter fish done odd jobs [*sic*]. I tell you it was hard. We were so poor at one point if it wasn't for Bill Solberg giving us fat to render for our bread we wouldn't have had anything."[5]

The goal of my parents was to get out of poverty and get a better life for their children. In 1951, when I was eight, we moved to Edmonton, where at one point my father worked three jobs from morning till night in order to put food on the table and pay the rent. My mom also worked full-time as a labourer at a glass company. I got my Grade 12 certificate, held various jobs, and eventually got involved in the M A A, first at the community level, and in 1969 as provincial vice-president. That is when I first met Harry Daniels, whom we hired as a fieldworker to organize our people at the community level.

I started doing a lot of research on our historic relationship with Canada. I saw that we were denied participation in the treaty process in 1885, when Métis representatives were told that commissioners were there for the full-bloods and that there would be commissioners who would come for the half-breeds. Instead of a treaty, the Métis were given scrip[6] that could be traded for land or money. I saw that the federal government had responsibility for "Indians and lands reserved for Indians,"[7] and that in the 1939 case of *Reference Re Eskimo*,[8] the Supreme Court determined that the federal government also had responsibility for the Inuit.

At Lac Ste. Anne, when people came from all over to attend pilgrimage every year,[9] talk around the campfires at night would be about Batoche. People would talk about the loss of our lands. Some lands had been set aside for Métis in what we called the "colonies" back then and are now called the Métis settlements. Not everyone wanted to, or could, move to them. I know that my dad and everyone of his age wondered what had happened to the lands that they thought were to be set aside for seven generations.

I knew we would never be able to address our issue of land unless we dealt with Ottawa.

On 7 November 1970, we decided to set up a presence in Ottawa. The leaders from the Manitoba Metis Federation, the Métis Society of Saskatchewan, the Métis Association of Alberta, and the British Columbia

Association of Métis and Non–Status Indians met in a small hotel room in
Victoria: Angus Spence from Manitoba, Jim Sinclair and Howard Adams
from Saskatchewan, Stan Daniels and me from Alberta, and Butch Smitheram
and Harry Lavallee from British Columbia.[10]

In those days our organizations also had members who identified as non–
Status Indian. When we formed the Native Council of Canada, we decided
to build an organization that would lobby both for the rights of the Métis
and for those who wanted to regain their Indian status.

Although our overarching goal was to get a process whereby we could
address our land claims, our initial focus in those days was first and foremost
dealing with the ravages of poverty, discrimination, and poor or inadequate
housing. Our people were living on road allowances[11] or in the bush, many
times in shacks with no insulation and oil barrels cut in half to use as stoves
to heat their place in the bitter cold of winter. Often, we would hear about
families being burned because the stoves blew up from overheating. Many
of our people were moving into the cities to try to get work and to make a
living. But often as not, if they had a brown face and the smoky sounds of
Cree in their voice, landlords would turn them away.

We wanted to get Ottawa to pay attention to these needs and to provide
programs and services that we desperately needed for health, housing, and
education. The avenue we saw was through section 91(24) of the Constitution
Act, 1867—the source of federal power to legislate for "Indians and lands
reserved for Indians." We took the position that we were "Indians" for purposes
of that federal authority and lobbied the federal government on that basis.

It's important to look back on those days and reflect on the fact that up to
that point, we had absolutely no profile at the national level. Métis were regarded
as having been done away with by the hanging of Louis Riel. We weren't even a
blip on the radar of the national media. There was some awareness of "Indians"
because the government of Prime Minister Pierre Trudeau had issued a White
Paper,[12] outlining a policy of assimilation that was loudly denounced by the chiefs.

My primary job then was to lobby for desperately needed programs and
services to deal with housing, health, welfare, and economic opportunity.[13]
But first we needed to create the awareness about who we were and what we
were seeking. It meant spending countless hours with national journalists who
scoffed at us, bureaucrats who stiff-armed us and told us to go see the provinces,
and federal ministers who had never given any thought to the issues we faced.

Thanks to the Honourable Bob Stanbury, Federal Minister for Citizenship, we were able to get core funding shortly after I moved to Ottawa in 1971. We set about to organize Métis and non–Status Indians in the rest of the provinces and the two northern territories. We produced some brochures and started a tabloid called *The Forgotten People*. In time I was able to meet with ministers, including the Honourable Jean Chrétien, who was Minister of the Department of Indian and Northern Affairs (DIAND), as well as Prime Minister Pierre Elliot Trudeau. We submitted briefs, made some noises, and eventually members of the media started to show up at our press conferences.

Again, without yet having the benefit of the Aboriginal Rights clause in the patriated constitution of 1982, we saw that our only way forward was to position ourselves as "Indians" for the purposes of the constitution at that time and to argue that therefore the federal government had a responsibility to us.

That was the theme of our first major written brief to the Honourable Gérard Pelletier, Secretary of State, on 6 June 1972.[14] Our opening paragraph reads in part as follows: "We speak to you Mr. Minister as the representatives of the non-status Indian and Métis people of Canada who number in excess of 400,000 Canadians, all of whom are of Indian ancestry. In the eyes of the dominant society we are Indians because for the most part we look like Indians, think like Indians, live like Indians and have a value system that is characteristic of the Indian way of life. . . . We are desperately poor with levels of ill-health, inadequate housing, unemployment and poverty that are a disgrace in the western world."[15] In our brief to the minister we sought to explain who we were and our circumstances: "Historically we have a greater claim to this country than does anyone in the dominant society because our ancestry can be traced, at least on one side, to pre-history."[16] We went on to say,

> When this country was put together more than one hundred years ago there were no artificial, legalistic definitions as to who was native and who was not. The first parliament of Canada in 1868 recognized the existence of "Indian people" which included all those persons of Indian ancestry, who were living an Indian way of life, who chose to remain such and all their descendants. Our people understood, accepted and supported that approach. Since then, however, both legislatively and administratively, successive federal governments have divided and dispersed our people. As

a result, at the present time, the vast majority of Canada's native people are shut out of special programs and services.[17]

We went on to describe how confusion and divisions were being sown by the federal government because of our position that the federal government had a responsibility to us through s. 91(24) of the British North America Act, 1867:

> You are well aware that for administrative convenience DIAND has consistently used a very narrow and legalistic definition of the term "Indian." As a result, the bulk of Canada's native people are not eligible for the special kind of help they need and want. . . .
>
> It is not our purpose to defend or destroy that department but only to indicate to you that the net effect of federal expenditures for native people through them has been to create division and disruption not only between the dominant society and the native people on the one hand but with the native groups themselves— some of whom are eligible for special services and others [who] have been told their Indianness cannot be recognized and they should seek help elsewhere. We are upset by this development because our registered Indian brother organizations are being led to believe that any help given to Métis and non-status Indians must necessarily result in loss of funds they would other otherwise get from DIAND. Their fears even go further to the point where they may suspect us of seeking to come under the umbrella of DIAND and to occupy Indian lands. This misunderstanding is one in which DIAND has done nothing to dispel but we think may even tacitly encourage and is serving to drive another wedge between us. . . .
>
> Regrettably there is a larger, more damaging side effect which is this: the public-at-large, the voluntary agencies, private industry and the majority of our political leaders, including some federal cabinet ministers, are unaware that the majority of native people are not receiving services.[18]

I think these quotes from our brief give a sense of what we were facing in the early 1970s and the tack we were taking to deal with them. In short, programs and services were desperately needed, the federal government was a source for them, and we were "Indians" and therefore they had an obligation to deal with us.

Although the federal government did not accept that the Métis came under its jurisdiction, we were nevertheless quite successful in accessing funds for various programs. In 1971, the federal government's Core Funding Program was changed to include funding for Métis and non–Status Indians. We lobbied for funding for native friendship centres, a court worker program and special ARDA (Agricultural and Rural Development) agreements in the Prairie provinces for Aboriginal economic development. Our greatest achievement in the early '70s was getting a commitment to build 50,000 new homes in five years through a Rural and Native Housing Policy we negotiated with Canada Mortgage and Housing.

The federal government never did accept any legal or legislative responsibility for us—not during my time nor during that of my successors, including the late Harry Daniels. Not even after we were included in the Constitution Act, 1982. We continued to be excluded from any process that would address Métis land entitlements.

Harry Daniels eventually succeeded me as president of the NCC in 1976. He served in that role from 1976 to 1981 and again from 1997 to 1999.

Daniels was flamboyant, charismatic, clever, and smart. In 1981, during the consultations on the patriation of Canada's constitution, he knew that unless the Métis were specifically mentioned in the proposed Aboriginal rights clause, the federal position would be that we were not included. The provision read: "The Aboriginal and Treaty rights of the Aboriginal peoples are hereby recognized and affirmed."[19] Daniels insisted that a sub-clause be added to identify who the Aboriginal peoples are. As a result of his deft manoeuvring, the prime minister finally agreed to add the following clause: "The Aboriginal peoples of Canada are the Indians, the Inuit and the Métis peoples."[20]

When the Honourable Jean Chrétien, then Minister of Justice, wrote a letter to the NCC to state categorically that the federal government had no responsibility for the Métis, and at the end of the round of the failed constitutional talks to elaborate the rights of the Aboriginal peoples in the constitution, Daniels in the 1980s had no choice but to take the federal government to court.

Did we succeed? Did we get what we want?

Not yet.

But the opportunity is now there, because we are finally recognized as "Indians" for the purposes of section 91(24) of the Constitution Act, 1867.

NOTES

1   Presented at "*Daniels*: In and Beyond the Law, conference," Rupertsland Centre for Métis Research, 26–28 January 2017.

2   The eight Alberta Métis settlements are the only recognized Métis land base in Canada. They were created in 1938 through the Métis Population Betterment Act.

3   Maria Campbell, *Halfbreed* (Lincoln: University of Nebraska Press, 1982).

4   See Library and Archives Canada, "Use of the Term 'Half Breed,'" updated 27 November 2013, http://www.bac-lac.gc.ca/eng/discover/aboriginal-heritage/metis/metis-scrip-records/Pages/term-half-breed.aspx.

5   Matilda (L'Hirondelle) Belcourt, letter to author, 12 January 1989.

6   Library and Archives Canada, "Métis Scrip Records," updated 1 March 2012, https://www.collectionscanada.gc.ca/metis-scrip/005005-3200-e.html.

7   British North America Act, 1867, s. 91(24).

8   Reference as to whether "Indians" in s. 91(24) of the BNA Act includes Eskimo inhabitants of the Province of Quebec, [1939] SCR 104.

9   "Lac Ste. Anne Pilgrimage," Wikipedia, https://en.wikipedia.org/wiki/Lac_Ste._Anne_(Alberta)#Lac_Ste._Anne_Pilgrimage (accessed 22 January 2020).

10 Meeting of Provincial Presidents and Representatives, Box 51, File 851, Métis Association of Alberta Fonds, Glenbow Library and Archives, Calgary, AB.

11 Stefan Dollinger and Margery Fee, eds., "Road Allowance People," in *DCHIP-2: A Dictionary of Canadianisms on Historical Principles*, 2nd ed., with the assistance of Baillie Ford, Alexandra Gaylie, and Gabrielle Lim (Vancouver: University of British Columbia, 2017), https://www.dchp.ca/dchp2/entries/view/Road%252520Allowance%252520People.

12 Indigenous and Northern Affairs Canada, Statement of the Government of Canada on Indian Policy (White Paper, 1969), updated 15 August 2010, https://www.aadnc-aandc.gc.ca/eng/1100100010189/1100100010191.

13 Minutes Emergency Meeting of NCC Executive Council, Box 72, File 861.3, Métis Association of Alberta Fonds, Glenbow Library and Archives, Calgary, AB.

14 Box 74, File 877, Métis Association of Alberta Fonds. Glenbow Library and Archives, Calgary, AB.

15 Native Council of Canada, Brief presented to the Honourable Gérard Pelletier, Secretary of State, by Native Council of Canada and its member associations, 6 June 1972 (Ottawa: Native Council of Canada, 1972), AMICUS No. 56078.

16 Ibid.

17 Ibid.

18 Ibid.

19 Constitution Act, 1982, s. 35(1).

20 Ibid., s. 35(2).

CHAPTER 2

Harry Daniels and Section 91 (24) of the British North America Act: A Blueprint for the Future

NATHALIE KERMOAL[1]

On 14 April 2016, the Supreme Court of Canada declared in the *Daniels* decision that Métis and non–Status Indians are "Indians" under section 91(24) of the Constitution Act, 1867 (formerly known as the British North America [BNA] Act), affirming federal responsibility for all Indigenous peoples in Canada. While section 35(1) of the Constitution Act, 1982, recognizes the "existing aboriginal and treaty rights" of "Indians, Inuit, and Métis peoples," it does not define them. As the court acknowledged, "both federal and provincial governments have, alternately, denied having legislative authority over non-status Indians and Métis. This results in these Indigenous communities being in a jurisdictional wasteland with significant and obvious disadvantaging consequences."[2] Calling their decision a "chapter in the pursuit of reconciliation and redress," the Supreme Court affirmed that "reading section 91(24) of the Constitution Act, 1867, as applicable to all Aboriginal peoples made sense in light of section 35 of the Constitution Act, 1982."[3]

In effect, the *Daniels* decision recognizes what the Métis have always asserted: they are a distinct Indigenous people with a special relationship with the Crown as partners in Confederation. Focusing exclusively on the Métis, this chapter examines the historical, social, and political circumstances that led Métis leader Harry Daniels and his co-plaintiffs to identify s. 91(24) of the BNA Act as an avenue for change after constitutional recognition failed to prompt government attention to long-standing Métis concerns. In particular, the chapter seeks to complicate narratives that focus on the economic disadvantages experienced by Métis communities by linking Harry Daniels's efforts to a Métis nationalism that extends back more than a century to its Red River origins.

A Historical Political Consciousness

During the nineteenth century, as Canadian expansionism pushed settlement westward, Métis nationalism coalesced in response to the increasingly invasive structures that threatened the economic livelihoods of the Métis and their control over the lands they lived on.[4] The Métis asserted their sovereignty against colonial encroachment, starting with the Pemmican Proclamation of 1814, which prohibited the export of pemmican and the Métis practice of running the buffalo. At the Battle of Seven Oaks (north of the forks of the Red and Assiniboine rivers), led by Métis leader Cuthbert Grant, on 19 June 1816, the Métis "resisted HBC's efforts to curb their livelihoods" and won. The battle—immortalized in Pierre Falcon's song "La bataille de la grenouillière"—was a response to the proclamation and to the escalating disputes between the two major fur trade companies of the time, the Hudson's Bay Company (HBC) and the North West Company (NWC).[5] The event strengthened the sense of nationhood among the Métis, and as "la nouvelle nation" they continued to assert their sovereignty in Red River by defying the HBC's trade monopoly (following its merger with the NWC in 1821). In 1849, when Guillaume Sayer and three other Métis traders were prosecuted for selling furs without HBC permission,[6] the Métis demonstrated their discontent in a display of force around the courthouse of Assiniboia.[7] While Sayer and the others were found guilty, the HBC had no way to enforce the decision.[8] The Métis display of unity effectively secured them the right to trade freely, opening up a new era of economic opportunities and extending the buffalo robe market to the United States.[9] According to Métis scholar Adam Gaudry, "the Red River Métis of the mid-nineteenth century typically viewed Company authority as an outside imposition of questionable legitimacy, and thus felt justified to act in ways that limited the reach of HBC governance into their daily lives."[10] While successful at asserting their political authority vis-à-vis the HBC, by the end of the 1860s the Métis were facing a much greater threat: the annexation of their homeland by Canada.

The land question escalated in 1869, when the HBC sold Rupert's Land to the new Dominion of Canada (created in 1867) without consulting the region's Indigenous peoples. Canada's aim was to open the Prairies to immigration, and the federal government rushed to send surveyors to Red River even before the transfer was complete.[11] Fearing that their land holdings were at stake, the Métis challenged the survey and organized a collective response. They formed a provisional government on 8 December 1869, composed largely of French Métis and English Métis and led by Louis Riel, to negotiate "with the Dominion government to enact the formal entry of Rupert's Land into the Canadian Confederation."[12] The Métis drafted several bills of rights that communicated the demands of the local population and later formed the basis of the Manitoba Act of 1870.[13] On 15 July 1870, Manitoba became a province, with equality provisions for language rights (French and English) and denominational schools (Catholic and Protestant), and 1,400,000 acres of land for the Métis.[14] As the Royal Commission on Aboriginal Peoples acknowledged, "Louis Riel and many Métis believed the Métis-related provisions of the Manitoba Act, supplemented by the other promises, to be the equivalent of a treaty."[15] They believed they had forged a new relationship and that the Dominion of Canada would honour the promises made to the Métis through the Manitoba Act.

Those gains, however, were short-lived. In August 1870, Canadian troops (originally dispatched to quell the 1869–70 Resistance) arrived in Red River. Driven by anti-Métis sentiments, the soldiers terrorized the population,[16] pushing Louis Riel into exile for fear of his life.[17] Canada delayed implementing the promised Métis land base, and the arrival of new immigrants hungry for lands in the 1870s and '80s shifted the balance of power and led to the dispersal and the dispossession of the Métis people from Red River.[18] Half of the Métis families left Manitoba to find kin and economic opportunity across the Prairies and into British Columbia, the North-West Territories, and the United States.[19] Yet before long, in these other parts of the Métis homeland, too, the disappearance of the buffalo and the influx of new settlers hastened the need of the Métis to secure formal titles to their lands as a way of avoiding further land dispossession.

By 1884, many settlers and English-speaking "half-breeds" in the North-West Territories had secured formal title to their lands; however, French-speaking Métis had not. When sympathetic white neighbours questioned the federal government's agent, Mr. W. Pearce, he stated that he "could not speak French and as the Employment of an interpreter would have entailed expense, no enquiry was made in to special grievances of the French [Métis]."[20] On 4 June 1884, the Métis from Batoche and surrounding areas persuaded Louis Riel to leave his exile in Montana to negotiate with the Canadian government. Once more, the Métis formed a provisional government. This time, however, their bill of rights and petitions were ignored, and the federal government prepared to intervene.[21] Aided by the new railway, the Dominion of Canada quickly deployed a military force to Saskatchewan. After winning several initial battles, the Métis were defeated at the Battle of Batoche and fighting ceased on 12 May 1885.[22] Riel surrendered, went to trial, and was hanged on 16 November 1885.[23] In his address to the court in 1885, Riel insisted that "the troubles of the Saskatchewan are not to be taken as an isolated fact. They are the result of fifteen years' war. The head of that difficulty lies in the difficulty of Red River. . . . They [the Dominion of Canada] made the treaty with us. As they made the treaty, I say they had to observe it and did they observe the treaty? No."[24]

As Métis scholar Chris Andersen has maintained elsewhere, "the seeds of a continuing nationalism were sown [in 1870 and 1885] by the very dispossession ostensibly intended to destroy it."[25] The Métis Nation did not die with Louis Riel, but the aftermath of 1885 brought many hardships to Métis people. Stigmatized as "rebels,"[26] many hid their Métis heritage.[27] The disappearance of bison herds and with them the trade in buffalo robes, the decline of overland freighting activities due to railway and steamboat competition, and the fraudulent scrip system left the Métis, for the most part, landless as well as politically, socially, and economically marginalized.[28]

Toward a Politics of Recognition

Dispossessed of their lands, many Métis families lived on road allowances[29] or on the edges of towns and cities in makeshift communities in Manitoba, Saskatchewan, and Alberta (Ste. Madeleine and Rooster Town in Manitoba; Little Chicago and Round Prairie in Saskatchewan, to name a few).[30] Perceived as a "problem" by settler society in the early twentieth century and frequently referred to as "the forgotten people,"[31] these families lived in poverty and in poor health. Since children were often not allowed to attend school if their parents did not pay taxes, educational opportunities were scarce.[32] Job opportunities did exist, but as Métis scholar and activist Howard Adams explains, "When I sought jobs in the St. Louis area [near Batoche] from White employers, they were always manual, dirty, hard work. Most of the Métis men worked only those jobs. My Dad worked out most every fall. He was employed only in unskilled, casual dirty jobs. I never saw him work in a clean, secure job where there was [any] promotion. All jobs for the Métis were low status jobs."[33] Métis families who did manage to acquire small plots of land often did not have the capital to buy equipment and "were forced out of business by larger farm operation[s]."[34] Métis families who relied on fishing to support themselves similarly faced strong competition from larger operations and, over time, were also forced out.[35] As a result, many Métis found they were unable to support themselves and their families.

These dire social and economic circumstances spawned a political revival in the 1920s and '30s. Métis leaders and activists such as Jim Brady, Malcom Norris, and Peter Tomkins formed the Association des Métis d'Alberta et des Territoires du Nord-Ouest in 1932 to press governments into action on Métis concerns.[36] These leaders asserted the inherent rights of the Métis to land, resources, education, and health care. They also denounced the pernicious influence of colonialism on their communities.[37] Their main objective was to acquire land, which they hoped would provide economic opportunities. In Alberta, this led to the creation of twelve Métis settlements in 1938 (of which only eight remain today) through the Métis Population Betterment Act.[38] Before then, "there was no recognition of the Métis in law other than a few hunting regulations that permitted half-breeds to hunt and fish."[39] The settlements provided Alberta Métis with a land base with which to pursue economic activities. Their success spurred the organization of Métis across the Prairies, and soon other communities formed their own associations. The Saskatchewan Métis Society was founded in 1937, followed by the Saskatchewan Métis Association in 1943, while Métis in northern Manitoba mobilized throughout the 1930s via the Northern Halfbreed Association.[40] Their efforts led to some gains; however, these were primarily local and provincial.

By the late 1960s, intergenerational poverty had pushed many Métis families to move—for some, to move back—to cities such as Winnipeg, Saskatoon, and Edmonton in hopes of finding work. But a lack of skills and education combined with societal prejudice meant that people often could not find decent jobs, and housing was a major issue. As Tony Belcourt recalls in Chapter 1, "Many of our people were moving into the cities to try to get work and to make a living. But often as not, if they had a brown face and the smoky sounds of Cree in their voice, landlords would turn them away."[41] Gene Rhéaume, a Métis from Grouard, Alberta, who was instrumental in forming the Native Council of Canada (NCC) and helped found the Native Housing Task Force (1970), believed that poor housing conditions were "a primary obstacle to the optimal use of other programs for educational, health, economic, and cultural upgrading. Indeed, without decent housing, millions of dollars spent annually by government agencies on other programs are wasted."[42] Rhéaume's task force affirmed that there was clearly "a lack of an integrated, co-ordinated approach by various federal agencies to the problem of Aboriginal housing, as a pre-requisite to raising their standard of living."[43] This was also true at the provincial level, where programs geared toward the Métis were disparate and often conflicting, creating "administrative inefficiency and a frightening waste of desperately needed housing funds."[44] "Ineffective government policies, bureaucratic red tape, lack of opportunity to guide programming, ill-timed release of funds (winter stalls), and poor coordination between Métis residents and the federal and provincial governments" hindered the development of effective social programs.[45]

Meanwhile, the Métis still had no voice in Ottawa. Claims that had been brought forward as far back as the nineteenth century remained largely unresolved in the middle of the twentieth century. The urgent need for government action and the growth of decolonizing movements around the world, particularly the American Indian Movement (AIM) and the Black Power Movement, reinvigorated Indigenous political action in Canada and prompted the Métis to reorganize older associations and create new ones.[46] In 1967, the two Saskatchewan associations amalgamated to become the Métis Society of Saskatchewan and the Métis in Manitoba reorganized to create the Manitoba Metis Federation.[47] Elsewhere, the Ontario Métis and Non-Status Indian Association and the Lake Nipigon Métis Association formed in 1965, and the British Columbia Association of Non-Status Indians came into being in 1968. These organizations adopted strategies such as marches, boycotts, and sit-ins to publicize their discontent with the status quo.[48] In 1971, they joined forces as the Native Council of Canada (NCC). As noted by Tony Belcourt in the previous chapter, the move to create a national organization began in Victoria on 16 November 1970—the eighty-fifth anniversary of the hanging of Louis Riel—by leaders of the Métis and Non-Status Indian associations of the Prairies and British Columbia.[49] They met again in Ottawa in 1971, and according to Belcourt, "It was at this meeting that we decided to form a national organization and to call it the Native Council of Canada (Métis and Non-Status Indians). We made a deliberate and collective decision to build a national organization that would include both Métis and Non-Status Indians for two reasons: first, because it reflected the reality of the membership of all organizations at the time; and, second, because we shared the same goals and were in basically the same position, landless and without federal recognition."[50]

This national Indigenous political vitality opened up new possibilities and new directions for leaders and intellectuals to frame oppositions, demands, and protests against centuries of colonization and imperialist subjugation. One of the most prominent and influential Métis thinkers of the time was Howard Adams, president of the Métis Society of Saskatchewan from 1969 to 1970. Adams put into writing a discourse on the Métis and colonialism and provided a language of decolonization that the political leadership could draw on. Born into poverty in 1921 in St. Louis, Saskatchewan, Adams completed a BA degree in sociology at the University of British Columbia while working full time. In 1957, after obtaining a teaching diploma from the University of Toronto, he taught high school in Coquitlam, British Columbia, until enrolling in a PhD program at the University of California Berkeley in 1962. In 1966, he became the first Canadian Métis to acquire a PhD.[51] Adams's years at Berkeley had a huge impact on his intellectual and political development. Beyond learning tactics of civil disobedience, he was greatly inspired by Malcolm X on the topic of African American nationalism and by Martin Luther King on the topic of civil rights struggles for freedom. After hearing Malcolm X speak, Adams "thought how and where nationalism fitted in with the Indians and the Métis back home in Canada."[52] And after hearing Martin Luther King, his "thoughts turned more and more to the subjugated Métis and Indians at home, and their horrible state of impoverishment and power-lessness."[53] Having identified the Métis as a colonized group, Adams thought the time was ripe to recommit to self-determination and push to end discrimi-nation for his people in Canada. Back in Saskatchewan, he became a professor in the Community Studies Department at the University of Saskatchewan, working closely with Métis and First Nations communities. As he visited these communities, he "talked about politics and the discrimination against them. They were anxious to discuss possible plans to challenge the semi-apartheid rule [of the White colonizers]."[54]

In his seminal book, *Prison of Grass: Canada from a Native Point of View*, Adams recalls the painful denial of his own identity. Having once rejected his Métis heritage because of a deep sense of shame and inferiority, Adams confesses that his greatest desire in life had been to blend into white Canadian society; however, his time in Berkeley awoke in him a pride he had never felt before.[55] He recounts the story of his great-grandfather Maxime Lépine, who fought with Louis Riel and Gabriel Dumont against Canadian troops during the 1885 conflict in Batoche: "In my childhood, I often stayed on the old farm of Maxime Lépine in Batoche. I did not realize at the time that I was tramping in the footprints of a noble guerilla warrior. Maxime's spirit was not there, not felt at all. Of the many games we halfbreed kids invented, none was related to the struggle of 1885. This history was hidden from us because our grandparents and parents were defeated generations."[56]

According to Adams, the Métis defeat at Batoche had "left a vacuum [instead of] a proud heritage. . . . The federal government and media imposed this monstrous Métis guilt, which became an everlasting oppression."[57] For Adams, to overcome this guilt, the Métis—much like other colonized peoples in the world—needed to reclaim their histories of resistance and launch their own liberation movement.[58] As Métis scholar Ron Laliberté notes, "Adams' aggressive political leadership style during the late 1960s and early 1970s symbolized the Indigenous struggle for decolonization and self-determina-tion."[59] Adams's theoretically informed anti-imperialist and anti-colonialist discourse laid a foundation for Harry Daniels, who became president of the NCC in 1976, to build upon.

Harry Daniels was born in Regina Beach, Saskatchewan, on 16 September 1940, to Henry and Emma Daniels. At age seventeen he joined the navy, and after a couple of years he went to work for the Company of Young Canadians, a short-lived organization inspired by the U.S. Peace Corps that was created in the mid-1960s by the federal government. In the late 1960s, the Métis Association of Alberta hired Daniels as coordinator of field workers, which meant travelling throughout the province, often to remote northern regions, to help spread information and foster community organization. Most people remember him as a mobilizer.[60] According to Tony Belcourt, Daniels "was just an absolute outstanding presence of a person when he walked in the room. You just couldn't help but notice Harry when he walked into the room . . . he just had that kind of commanding personality."[61]

Like Adams, Daniels was interested in the African American liberation movement. In November 1969, he met with Fred Hampton, deputy chairman of the Chicago Chapter of the Black Panther Party, at the University of Saskatchewan campus in Regina. According to labour historian Bryan Palmer, the "Black Panther spokesmen received a warm welcome among Native activists in the Canadian west, where they were embraced as fellow revolutionaries."[62] Soon after his visit to Regina, "Hampton was shot dead by Chicago police during a raid at his home. On 12 December 1969, more than 100 people, including Harry Daniels, held a torchlight parade in downtown Regina in memory of Fred Hampton."[63] While we do not know what Hampton and Daniels shared during their encounter, Daniels—much like Adams—saw resonances between the plight of African Americans and the colonialist and racist attitudes Métis were forced to contend with in Western Canada. The Black Power Movement provided a language and a frame of reference for political actions to confront white supremacy and assert self-determination and sovereignty, helping to shape the Métis response to federal ambitions for assimilation, multiculturalism, and constitutional reform.

More Than Citizens Like Any Other

This same era of political activism saw Pierre Elliott Trudeau elected prime minister on his "just society" platform in the spring of 1968, and a year later, his government's White Paper provided a new target for Indigenous political mobilization. The White Paper proposed to fundamentally change the basis of the relationship between the Canadian state and Indigenous peoples (though it was largely targeted toward First Nations). The government planned to eliminate reserves, invalidate the treaties, remove Indians' legal status by abolishing the Indian Act, and dissolve the Department of Indian Affairs,[64] declaring that "Canada cannot seek the just society and keep discriminatory legislation on its statute books."[65] Under this plan, the mandate for Indian Affairs would be transferred to the provinces, which would assume "the same responsibility for services to Indian residents as they do for services to others."[66]

Although the Métis did not fall under the Indian Act, they knew too well what it meant to be nominally considered "citizens like any other"[67] and to suffer under provincial responsibility. Even though the Métis had asserted their sovereignty and secured land and language rights when they negotiated the entry of Manitoba into Confederation, Métis lawyers Jean Teillet and Carly Teillet have shown that the federal government believed "that their Aboriginal rights had been extinguished through land grants and scrip,"[68] thus severing their ties with the Crown. As Teillet and Teillet note, the Métis "suffered greatly from a legal regime that persistently refused to acknowledge them,"[69] which "prevent[ed] them from reaching their full potential in Canadian society,"[70] as the *Daniels* decision recognized. Jean Teillet further stresses that "the practical result of this jurisdictional avoidance was to leave Métis and non-status Indians vulnerable and marginalized, lacking access to federal programs and services available to 'status' Indians or Inuit. They have been denied access to federal processes to address their rights and claims."[71] Even the federal government admitted internally that "in absence of Federal initiative in this field [Métis and non–Status Indians] are the most disadvantaged of all Canada citizens."[72] The jurisdictional confusion and buck-passing by various levels of governments was at the heart of Harry Daniels's fight. He was deeply committed to putting an end to this "political football."[73]

Concurrent with the government's push for assimilation, Pierre Trudeau's nascent multiculturalism policy also threatened to countermand Indigenous rights and sovereignties. It recognized a Canada with two official languages and a plurality of cultures—"a multicultural policy within a bilingual framework"[74] that, like the White Paper, discounted the fundamental role of

Indigenous nations as partners in Confederation. In the midst of their fight for recognition, Métis intellectuals and leaders saw the conflation of political and ethnic identity as a renewed threat. They stressed the importance of recognizing the Métis as a distinct Indigenous people with a unique history, collective identity, and a political relationship with the Crown rooted in the Manitoba Act rather than as individual members of a "mixed-blood" ethnic group.[75] More specifically, the Métis employed anti-imperialist rhetoric to remind the federal government of their historic relationship. In their 1979 Declaration of Métis and Indian Rights, the Native Council of Canada proclaimed:

> When the Métis Nation under the leadership of Louis Riel
> brought the West into Confederation, it did so on the
> understanding that it was a partner in Confederation. What else
> could our ancestors believe after they opened up the West to trade
> and development, upheld law and order on the plains and resisted
> offers to join the United States? We came into Confederation as
> partners and believed that this was confirmed by the Manitoba
> Act. Since then we have seen our special rights in the Manitoba Act
> ignored if not wiped out by a stroke of the pen. We will no longer
> accept this non-recognition. We know what our contributions are
> to this country and on what terms we entered Confederation.[76]

By emphasizing the Métis as a self-determining nation of people that joined Canada on its own terms through the Manitoba Act (1870), Daniels and other Métis leaders deconstructed the dominant narrative that justified the denial of Métis rights with a rhetorical strategy that harkened back to the sovereign assertions of their nineteenth-century Red River ancestors.

For Daniels, "Native peoples feel that the policies of bilingualism and multiculturalism assume that those who have a culture tied to this land and whose roots are in this land are inferior."[77] After he became president of the NCC in 1976, Daniels reminded the federal government that the Métis were more than "citizens like any other."[78] In *We Are the New Nation*, for example, he eloquently deconstructed the concept of the two founding nations as well as Canada's multiculturalism policy.[79] As Métis policy advisor John Weinstein notes, "the upsurge of nationalism in Quebec during this period undoubtedly played a role in Métis political revival. Quebec's demands on the federal state and Ottawa's response to them—the Royal Commission on Bilingualism and Biculturalism and 'equal partnership between two founding races'—had a telling effect on many Métis who believed that, as a founding people, their nation had as much right to special status as Quebec."[80] Daniels believed that cultural harmony and national unity were impossible until Canadians made efforts to accept that Canada had an Aboriginal heritage. For Daniels, the Manitoba Act was "the Métis cornerstone of Confederation and confirmation of their role as a founding nation but one that proved to be an empty guarantee," since the promises of land and language rights had gone unfulfilled.[81] Yet the fact that the Métis had negotiated the terms of entry of a colony into the Canadian union made them "a historical national minority with a right to special status in Confederation" and "the right to remain separate and distinct from both English and French Canada and to develop as a people according to [their] own destiny."[82] The federal government's limited recognition of Métis as mixed individuals rather than as a historically rooted Indigenous people meant that they had had little to no voice in their own governance. As Daniels observed, "It is clear that Métis people still wish to participate in the Canadian political system but feel that in order for them to be truly integrated into the larger society they must be guaranteed participation as a collectivity in the political life of the country. This includes participation in representative assemblies as well as in government functions."[83] Daniels's goal was to challenge Canada to accept Métis people as partners in Confederation, as it had in 1870: "We are a people who take pride in our past and hope in our future. We refuse to remain the 'forgotten people.' We are the New Nation."[84]

Trudeau's desire to patriate the constitution presented a critical opportunity for Indigenous peoples across Canada to successfully campaign for consultation and inclusion, and for Métis and non–Status Indians to rearticulate their position and renew calls for recognition.[85] According to Weinstein, Daniels entered the constitutional talks "fixated on the status of the NCC participation in the patriation process."[86] Concerned that the Métis would be left out of the political exercise, that Aboriginal rights would not be included in the constitutional reform, and that governmental delays would continue to preclude Indigenous issues from those constitutional discussions, Daniels launched his own initiative: the Métis and Non–Status Indian Constitutional Review Commission.[87] Following an agreement with the federal government, the NCC formally established the commission in July 1980. Chaired by Daniels, the commission travelled across Canada (stopping in Ottawa, Sault Ste. Marie, Moncton, Kikino [Alberta], Winnipeg, and Quebec City) to listen to what Métis and non–Status Indians had to say about the constitution.[88] During the hearings, participants reiterated that "there hasn't been an acknowledgement by the federal government that Métis and non–status Indians are within its jurisdiction," and that "core funding [for programs] has been provided for Métis . . . in much the same way that funding has been given to ethnic organizations through the multiculturalism program."[89] The testimonies Daniels heard in the context of the commission supported his belief that the non-recognition of the Métis as a founding nation implied that the Métis had to start "at the bottom of the ladder, like immigrants just off the boat, and move [their] way up."[90] He further denounced the idea that the Métis "had to deal with government departments like multiculturalism which merely offer to buy advertisement space in ethnic newspapers. Culture cannot be preserved in a jar."[91] In 1979, he declared that "the government continues to feed us the two founding nations myth while tossing in some Ukrainian Easter eggs, Italian grapes, or Métis bannock for some extra flavor."[92] Daniels was adamant that "special status" for the Métis needed to be addressed. Campaigning across Canada, Daniels and the NCC were ultimately successful in their quest for a seat at the constitutional talks, with the result that the Constitution Act of 1982 formally recognizes the "aboriginal and treaty rights of . . . the Indian, Inuit, and Métis peoples of Canada."[93] Even so, that recognition failed to secure government attention to Métis concerns.

On 17 February 1981, Minister of Indian Affairs John Monroe told the House of Commons "that even though the aboriginal rights of the Métis people were affirmed in the patriation resolution, the federal government did not intend to assume responsibility for the provision of services to Métis."[94] Prime Minister Pierre Elliott Trudeau, in his opening statement to the 1983 First Ministers' Conference on Aboriginal Constitutional Matters several years later, reiterated that "the provincial governments are mainly responsible for the Métis. While in the view of the federal government they do not fall within the definition of the word 'Indian' in section 91(24) of the Constitution Act, 1867, the federal government accepts a measure of responsibility to them as disadvantaged people."[95]

According to Métis lawyer and negotiator Mark Stevenson, these views became "authoritative statements by the federal government with respect to the issue of which level of government has jurisdiction over the Métis."[96] The government stood its ground even though, according to secret documents obtained by constitutional law professor Joseph Magnet and his team, it recognized in 1980 that it "possessed the power to legislate theoretically in all domains in respect of Métis and Non-Status Indians under Section 91(24) of the BNA Act."[97] As Magnet shows, the government was fully aware that the Métis "must cope with severe disadvantage" and "desperate circumstances," which a cabinet memo called "intolerable judged by the standards of Canadian society."[98] While the Government of Canada recognized that remedies were needed to fight the widespread poverty in Métis communities, Ottawa held off any decision to extend Indian programs to the Métis and Non-Status Indians because it did not want to foot the bill.[99] Ultimately, Daniels and the Métis turned their attention to s. 91(24) of the BNA Act in order to push the federal government to acknowledge its responsibility toward them.[100]

Section 91(24): A Blueprint for the Future

Section 91(24) of the BNA Act (1867) gave the federal government jurisdiction over "Indians and the lands reserved for Indians." While it did not define the term "Indian," earlier legislation had. The Act for the Better Protection of the Lands and Property of the Indian in Lower Canada (1850) had included a set of requirements for a person to be considered a legal Indian:

First—All persons of Indian blood reputed to belong to the particular Body or Tribe of Indians interested in such lands, and their descendants;

Secondly—All persons intermarried with any such Indians and residing amongst them, and the descendants of all such persons;

Thirdly—All persons residing among such Indians, whose parents on either side were or are Indians of such Body or Tribe, or entitled to be considered as such; and

Fourthly—All persons adopted in infancy by any such Indians; and residing in the Village or upon the lands of such Tribe or Body of Indians, and their descendants.[101]

People of mixed ancestry were clearly included in this definition, but, under the new Dominion of Canada of 1867, the federal government chose to restrict its authority (and spending) to registered (Status) Indians and exclude other Indigenous peoples. The report of the Métis and Non–Status Indian Constitutional Review Commission emphasized the fact that the government's narrow definition of Indian should be broader, pointing to the Supreme Court's recognition in 1939 that Inuit people were "Indians" within the meaning of the BNA Act, s. 91(24), as precedent for a more expansive interpretation.[102]

Harry Daniels's conviction that Métis should be considered Indians under s. 91(24) of the BNA Act predates the *Daniels* case by more than twenty years. Section 91(24) was effectively a bright light at the end of a century-long tunnel: it held the potential to recognize Métis as a partner in Confederation and put an end to the jurisdictional limbo between federal and provincial powers that the Métis had long endured. Daniels's deconstruction of the idea that Métis were "citizens like any other" demonstrated his rhetorical ability to position the Métis as one of the founding nations of Canada. Such recognition, he hoped, would extend federal jurisdiction to the Métis, resulting in access to much-needed social investments and processes to address Métis land claims. Yet the federal government still rejected their responsibility after the Constitution Act of 1982.[103]

In 1983, feeling increasingly unrepresented because of a focus on non–Status Indian issues, the Métis withdrew from the NCC to form the Métis National Council (MNC), representing associations in Manitoba, Saskatchewan, Alberta, British Columbia, and Ontario.[104] However, Daniels remained connected to the NCC. During the 1992 Charlottetown Accord negotiations, the MNC drafted a Métis Nation Accord, which sought the inclusion of an amendment "to the Constitution Act, 1982 recognizing the inherent right of self-government of the Aboriginal peoples of Canada and the coming into force of section 91A of the Constitution Act, 1867, clarifying that all of the Aboriginal peoples of Canada are included in section 91(24)."[105] The rejection of the Charlottetown Accord by a national referendum pushed the Métis to resort to litigation and pursue recognition in the courts. Daniels, with co-plaintiffs the Congress on Aboriginal Peoples and Leah Gardner, an Anishinaabe non–Status woman from Ontario, launched their suit in 1999. It would be seventeen years before the Supreme Court ruling; sadly, Harry Daniels passed away in 2004 and did not live to see it.

Court actions such as *R. v. Powley*, *Manitoba Metis Federation v. Canada*, and *Daniels v. Canada*, along with Thomas Isaac's report "A Matter of National and Constitutional Import,"[106] continued to challenge the idea that Métis were merely a provincial responsibility and provided opportunities for the Métis to advance their rights and governance agenda at both provincial and federal levels.[107] As Isaac states in his report, "It is in the best interests of Canada that it designate programs and services, or parts thereof, as may be appropriate, as Métis-specific so as to be able to track success on the road to reconciliation with Métis peoples and treat Métis as distinct Section 35 rights-bearing peoples."[108] The *Daniels* decision was consolidated several months later by Isaac's recommendations, forcing the federal government finally to revise its position toward the Métis.

The decision provided a clear declaration of federal responsibility to and for Métis people. One year after the *Daniels* decision, on 13 April 2017, the Government of Canada and the MNC signed the Canada–Métis Nation Accord, which promises to "establish a process for co-development and negotiation" to "uphold the special constitutional relationship that the Métis Nation has with the Crown as partners in Confederation and as recognized and affirmed in section 35 of the Constitution Act, 1982"; to "renew the Métis Nation–Crown relationship on a nation-to-nation, government-to-government basis"; and to "advance reconciliation."[109] As Jason Madden notes in Chapter 3, "there is room for optimism, and it will be extremely challenging for Canada to pull back from these negotiation processes."[110] This long-sought development in the Métis-Canada relationship owes a great deal to the political dedication and activism of Harry Daniels and his commitment to the political ideals of his nineteenth- and early twentieth-century Métis forebears.[111]

NOTES

1 I would like to thank the anonymous reviewers, Dr. Chris Andersen, and Dr. Nancy Van Styvendale for their constructive comments on earlier drafts of this chapter, as well as my graduate student Leah Hrycun for her help in finalizing and formatting this chapter.

2 *Daniels v. Canada*, 2016 SCC 12, 1.

3 Keith Bergner, Shailaz Dhalla, and John Olynyk, "The *Daniels* Decision: All Aboriginal Peoples, Including Métis and Non-Status Indians, Are 'Indians' under Section 91(24) of the Constitution Act, 1867," Lawson Lundell *Project Law Blog*, 15 April 2016, https://www.lawsonlundell.com/project-law-blog/the-daniels-decision-all-aboriginal-peoples-including-metis-and-non-status-indians-are-indians-under-section-9124-of-the-constitution-act-1867 (accessed 18 May 2018).

4 For more details on the imprint the Métis left in Canadian history, see, among others, Nicole St-Onge, Carolyn Podruchny, and Brenda Macdougall, eds., *Contours of a People: Metis Family, Mobility, and History* (Norman: University of Oklahoma, 2012); Brenda Macdougall and Nicole St-Onge, "Rooted in Mobility: Metis Buffalo Hunting Brigades," *Manitoba History* 71 (2013): 21–32; and Adam Gaudry, "Kaa-tipeyimishoyaahk—'We are those who own ourselves': A Political History of Métis Self-Determination in the North-West, 1830–1870" (PhD diss., University of Victoria, 2014).

5 On the Battle of Seven Oaks, see Gerhard J. Ens, "The Battle of Seven Oaks and the Articulation of a Metis National Tradition, 1811–1849," in *Contours of a People*, ed. St-Onge, Podruchny, and Macdougall, 93–119; Lyle Dick, "The Seven Oaks Incident and the Construction of a Historical Tradition, 1816–1970," *Journal of the Canadian Historical Association* 2 (1991): 91–113; and Gaudry, "Kaa-tipeyimishoyaahk."

6 Alexander Ross, *The Red River Settlement: Its Rise, Progress, and Present State; With Some Account of the Native Races and Its General History to the Present Day* (London: Smith, Elder and Co., 1856), 372.

7 According to court records, "'A great number of armed halfbreeds' waited outside the courthouse"(Provincial Archives of Manitoba. District of Assiniboia Court Records. 17 May 1849, 151 quoted in Laudicina, "The Rules of Red River: The Council of Assiniboia and Its Impact on the Colony, 1820–1689," *Past Imperfect* 15 (2009): 58; Alexander Ross states that "the French Canadians, as well as half-breeds, began to move from all quarters, so that the banks of the river, above and below the fort, were literally crowded with armed men, moving to and fro in wild agitation, having all the marks of a seditious meeting, or rather a revolutionary movement. . . . who no sooner reached the west bank of the river, than they drew together about Fort Garry and the court-house. . . . 377 guns were counted; besides, here and there, groups armed with other missiles of every description" (Ross, *The Red River Settlement*, 373–74).

8 For further details on the Battle of Seven Oaks and the Sayer trial, see *Indigenous Peoples Atlas of Canada*, "Métis" (Ottawa: Royal Canadian Geographical Society, 2016). For further details on the inability of the HBC to enforce its authority, see Doug Owram, "Conspiracy and Treason: The Red River Resistance from an Expansionist Perspective," *Prairie Forum* 3, no. 2 (1978): 157–74; and Gaudry, "Kaa-tipeyimishoyaahk."

9 Gerhard J. Ens, *Homeland to Hinterland: The Changing Worlds of the Red River Metis in the Nineteenth Century* (Toronto: University of Toronto Press, 1996), 6.

10 Gaudry, "Kaa-tipeyimishoyaahk," 169.

11 Olive P. Dickason, "Metis," in *Aboriginal Peoples of Canada: A Short Introduction*, ed. Paul Robert Magocsi (Toronto: University of Toronto Press, 2002), 200; Gerald Friesen, *The Canadian*

Prairies: A History (Toronto: University of Toronto Press, 1987), 117; Douglas Sprague, *Canada and the Métis, 1869–1885* (Waterloo, ON: Wilfrid Laurier University Press, 1988), 40.

12   *Indigenous Peoples Atlas of Canada*, "Métis," 32.

13   Kelly L. Saunders, "No Other Weapon: Métis Political Organization and Governance in Canada," in *Métis in Canada: History, Identity, Law, and Politics*, ed. Christopher Adams, Gregg Dahl, and Ian Peach (Edmonton: University of Alberta Press, 2013), 345.

14   Manitoba Act, 1870.

15   Royal Commission on Aboriginal Peoples, *Perspectives and Realities*, vol. 4 of *Report of the Royal Commission on Aboriginal Peoples* (Ottawa: Libraxus, 1997), 208.

16   Owram, "Conspiracy and Treason," 171. See also Jean Teillet, *The Northwest Is Our Mother: The Story of Louis Riel's People, the Métis Nation* (Toronto: HarperCollins, 2019); and Nathalie Kermoal, "Les rôles et les souffrances des femmes Métisses lors de la Résistance de 1870 et de la Rébellion de 1885," *Prairie Forum* 19, no. 2 (1994): 153–68.

17   Sprague, *Canada and the Métis*, 74.

18   For a discussion on how the promised land base was delayed through bureaucratic administration and how the balance of power shifted to favour new settlers, see Doug N. Sprague, "The Manitoba Land Question, 1870–1882," *Journal of Canadian Studies/Revue d'études canadiennes* 15, no. 3 (1980): 74–84.

19   *Indigenous Peoples Atlas of Canada*, "Métis," 33.

20   Donald McLean, "1885: Métis Rebellion or Government Conspiracy," in *1885 and After: Native Society in Transition*, ed. F. Laurie Barron and James B. Waldram (Regina: Canadian Plains Research Center, 1986), 84.

21   Ibid., 97.

22   John Weinstein, *Quiet Revolution West: The Rebirth of Métis Nationalism* (Saskatoon: Fifth House Publishers, 2007), 15.

23   Ibid., 15.

24   "Address to the Court, Regina," in Louis Riel, *The Collected Writings of Louis Riel/Les écrits complets de Louis Riel*, vol. 3, ed. Thomas Flanagan et al. (Edmonton: University of Alberta 1985), 541–42.

25   Chris Andersen, *"Métis": Race, Recognition, and the Struggle for Indigenous Peoplehood* (Vancouver: UBC Press, 2014), 116.

26   Diane Payment, "Batoche after 1885: A Society in Transition," in *1885 and After: Native Society in Transition*, ed. F. Laurie Barron and James B. Waldram (Regina: Canadian Plains Research Center, 1986), 179.

27   Patrick C. Douaud, "Genesis," in *The Western Métis: Profile of a People*, ed. Patrick C. Douaud (Regina: Canadian Plains Research Center, 2007), 11; Weinstein, *Quiet Revolution West*, 22.

28   For more details on the impact of colonization and the marginalization of the Métis in Western Canada, see *Indigenous Peoples Atlas of Canada*, "Métis." Regarding the scrip process, see Frank J. Tough and Kathleen Dimmer, "'Great Frauds and Abuses': Institutional Innovation at the Colonial Frontier of Private Property: Case Studies of the Individualization of Maori, Indian and Métis Lands," in *Settler Economies in World History*, ed. C. Lloyd, J. Metzer, and R. Sutch (Leiden: Brill, 2013), 205–49; Frank Tough and Erin McGregor, "'The Right to the Land May Be Transferred': Archival Records as Colonial Text—A Narrative of Métis Scrip," in *Natives and*

Settlers, Now and Then: Historical Issues and Current Perspectives on Treaties and Land Claims in Canada, ed. Paul W. DePasquale (Edmonton: University of Alberta Press, 2007), 33–63; and "Métis Scrip in Alberta," Rupertsland Centre for Métis Research (Edmonton: Rupertsland Centre for Métis Research and Métis Nation of Alberta, 2018).

29   A road allowance is Crown land set aside for the building of roads. See *Indigenous Peoples Atlas of Canada*, "Métis," "Road Allowance People."

30   For more information on the "road allowance people," see ibid., 40–41; Ken Zelig and Victoria Zelig, *Ste. Madeleine: Community without a Town; Metis Elders in Interview* (Winnipeg: Pemmican Publications, 1987); David Burley, "Rooster Town: Winnipeg's Lost Métis Suburb, 1900–1960," *Urban History Review/Revue d'histoire urbaine* 42, no. 1 (2013): 3–25; Evelyn Peters, Matthew Stock, and Adrian Werner, *Rooster Town: The History of an Urban Métis Community, 1901–1961* (Winnipeg: University of Manitoba Press, 2019); Bill Waiser, "History Matters: Round Prairie Métis Made Saskatoon Their Home in Early 20th Century," *Saskatoon Star Phoenix*, April 25, 2017, https://thestarphoenix.com/opinion/columnists/history-matters-round-prairie-metis-made-saskatoon-their-home-in-early-20th-century; and Carolyn Podruchny, Jesse Thistle, and Elizabeth Jameson, "Women on the Margins of Imperial Plots: Farming on Borrowed Land," *Journal of the Canadian Historical Association* 29, no. 1 (2018): 158–81.

31   See D. Bruce Sealey and Antoine S. Lussier, *The Métis: Canada's Forgotten People* (Manitoba Metis Federation, 1975).

32   *Indigenous Peoples Atlas of Canada*, "Métis," 40–41. However, some Métis children did attend school. See Peters, Stock, and Werner, *Rooster Town,* 131.

33   Hartmut Lutz, Murray Hamilton, and Donna Heimbecker, *Howard Adams: Otapamy! The Life of a Métis Leader in His Own Words and in Those of His Contemporaries* (Saskatoon: Gabriel Dumont Institute, 2005), 9.

34   Peters, Stock, and Werner, *Rooster Town*, 11.

35   Ibid.

36   Kelly L. Saunders and Janique Dubois, *Métis Politics and Governance in Canada* (Vancouver: UBC Press, 2019), 31.

37   See Murray Dobbin, *The One-and-a-Half Men: The Story of Jim Brady and Malcolm Norris, Metis Patriots of the Twentieth Century* (Vancouver: New Star, 1981).

38   Ibid. The Métis Population Betterment Act (1938) is available at https://www.canlii.org/en/ab/laws/astat/sa-19382-c-6/latest/sa-19382-c-6.html.

39   Jean Teillet and Carly Teillet, "Devoid of Principle: The Federal Court Determination That Section 91(24) of the Constitution Act, 1867 Is a Race-Based Provision," *Indigenous Law Journal* 13, no. 1 (2016): 12.

40   Saunders and Dubois, *Métis Politics and Governance in Canada*, 31–32.

41   See Tony Belcourt, Chapter 1 in this volume, 16. It should be noted that in 1969, Paul Hellyer, then minister of transportation under the Trudeau government, had been appointed to lead a housing task force. After travelling across the country, he released the *Report of the Federal Task Force on Housing and Urban Development* (Ottawa: Task Force on Housing and Urban Development, 1969). The Hellyer report noted that the Métis were living in very dire conditions and recommended that "special housing programs and pilot projects for Canada's Indian, Eskimo and Métis peoples be carefully evaluated after a fair trial and, if found successful, be vigorously pursued to meet the special needs of these groups." Hellyer, *Report of the Federal Task Force on Housing and Urban Development*, 59). See also Kermoal, "Canative"; and Kermoal, "Navigating Troubled Political Waters."

42 Gene Rhéaume, *Housing for Native People: A Low Income Housing Policy for 1971* (Ottawa: CMHC Policy Planning Group, 1970), 16. Rhéaume was the national chairman of the Native Housing Task Force. Funded by the Canada Mortgage and Housing Corporation (CMHC) when Walter Rudnicki was its executive director (1969–73), the task force was responsible for building and repairing thousands of homes in needy communities.

43 Ibid., 17.

44 Ibid.

45 Amanda Linden, "The Advocate's Archive: Walter Rudnicki and the Fight for Indigenous Rights in Canada, 1955–2010" (MA thesis, University of Manitoba/University of Winnipeg, 2016), 28.

46 Weinstein, *Quiet Revolution West*, 30.

47 Saunders and Dubois, *Métis Politics and Governance in Canada*, 32.

48 For details about the era, see Brian Palmer, *Canada's 1960s: The Ironies of Identity in a Rebellious Era* (Toronto: University of Toronto Press, 2009).

49 According to Tony Belcourt, "The leaders met in a small hotel room in Victoria, British Columbia: Angus Spence, President of the Manitoba Metis Federation (MMF); Jim Sinclair, Vice-President of the Association of Métis and Non-Status Indians of Saskatchewan (AMNSIS); Stan Daniels, President of the Métis Association of Alberta (MAA); myself as Vice-President of the Métis Association of Alberta; and Butch Smitheram, President of the BC Association of Non-Status Indians (BCANSI). We chose to meet in Victoria so we could also attend the First Annual General Assembly of BCANSI, which was also taking place at the time." Belcourt, "For the Record . . . On Métis Identity and Citizenship within the Métis Nation," *aboriginal policy studies* 2, no. 2 (2013): 128–41.

50 Ibid.

51 For more information on Harold Adams, see Deborah Simmons, "In Tribute to Howard Adams," *Studies in Political Economy* 68 (2002): 5–12.

52 Lutz, Hamilton, and Heimbecker, *Howard Adams: Otapamy!*, 165. This book is a compilation of Adams's writing based on an unfinished autobiographical project he was working on before he passed away on 8 September 2001.

53 Ibid.

54 Ibid.

55 Howard Adams, *Prison of Grass: Canada from a Native Point of View* (Saskatoon: Fifth House Publishers, 1975, 1989), 98.

56 Ibid., 98.

57 Lutz, Hamilton, and Heimbecker, *Howard Adams: Otapamy!*, 11.

58 Adams, *Prison of Grass*; see chap. 2.

59 Ron Laliberté, "Howard Adams, 1921–2001," *Indigenous Saskatchewan Encyclopedia*, https://teaching.usask.ca/indigenoussk/import/adams_howard_1921-2001.php (accessed 5 December 2019).

60 Daniels was president of the Native Council of Canada in 1967 and again between 1997 and 2000, by which time it was called the Congress of Aboriginal Peoples. On the international front, he called on the United Nations to pressure Canada to meet its obligations to the country's Indigenous peoples. He also participated in various UN initiatives and served as a director of the World Council of Indigenous Peoples. When Pope John Paul II made his historic visit to

the Northwest Territories in 1984, Daniels greeted him in Yellowknife. In a gesture of welcome, he took off his jacket and gave it to the pope as a gift. Daniels was also a television and stage actor, playing Gabriel Dumont in a historical miniseries called *Big Bear*, which aired on CBC television in the late 1990s. Daniels died in September 2004 at age sixty-three. Harry Daniels, *We Are the New Nation/Nous sommes la nouvelle nation* (Ottawa: Native Council of Canada, 1979).

61 Cheryl Petten, "Friends Say Goodbye to Harry Daniels," *Alberta Sweetgrass* 1, no. 10 (2004): 2.

62 Palmer, *Canada's 1960s*, 400.

63 Dawn Rae Flood, "A Black Panther in the Great White North: Fred Hampton Visits Saskatchewan, 1969," *Journal for the Study of Radicalism* 8, no. 2 (2014): 39.

64 Indigenous and Northern Affairs Canada, Statement of the Government of Canada on Indian Policy (White Paper, 1969), updated 15 August 2010, https://www.aadnc-aandc.gc.ca/eng/1100 100010189/1100100010191, 6.

65 Ibid., 8; Dale Turner, *This Is Not a Peace Pipe: Towards a Critical Indigenous Philosophy* (Toronto: University of Toronto Press, 2006), 16, 20.

66 Indigenous and Northern Affairs Canada, Statement of the Government of Canada, 6.

67 Harry Daniels, *Native People and the Constitution of Canada: The Report of the Métis and Non-Status Indian* (Ottawa: Mutual Press, 1981), 20. This expression was used by the people who were consulted during the hearings of the Métis and Non-Status Indian Constitutional Review Commission established in July 1980 and chaired by Harry Daniels. According to the letter of transmittal, this commission was established to "canvas the views of Métis and non-status Indians across Canada on the subject of a new constitution."

68 Teillet and Teillet, "Devoid of Principle," 13.

69 Ibid.

70 *Daniels v. Canada*, 2013 FC 6 (F.C.T.D.), para. 108.

71 Jean Teillet, *Métis Law in Canada* (Vancouver: Pape Salter Teillet, 2013), 119.

72 Ibid.

73 See *Daniels v. Canada*, 2013 FC 6 at paras. 86, 107.

74 John English, *Just Watch Me: The Life of Pierre Elliott Trudeau*, vol. 2, *1968–2000* (Toronto: Vintage Canada, 2010), 624.

75 For an analysis on Canada's inability to differentiate between Métis as a form of mixedness and Métis imagined nationally, see Chris Andersen, "*Métis.*"

76 Native Council of Canada (with commentary by Harry Daniels), *Declaration of Métis and Indian Rights* (Ottawa: Native Council of Canada, 1979), 8.

77 Daniels, *Native People and the Constitution of Canada*, 43.

78 Ibid., 20.

79 Daniels, *We Are the New Nation*.

80 Weinstein, *Quiet Revolution West*, 29.

81 Ibid., 38–39.

82 NCC, *Declaration of Métis and Indian Rights*, 18. See also Daniels, *We Are the New Nation*, 5–11; and Daniels, *Native People and the Constitution of Canada*, 29.

83 Daniels, *We Are the New Nation*, 11–12; and Daniels, *Native People and the Constitution of Canada*, 30.

84 NCC, *Declaration of Métis and Indian Rights*, 18.

85 See Weinstein, *Quiet Revolution West*; and *Indigenous Peoples Atlas of Canada*, "Métis," "Métis and the Constitution."

86 Weinstein, *Quiet Revolution West*, 40.

87 Ibid., 40–41. According to Weinstein, Daniels received a letter on 11 August 1980 from Prime Minister Trudeau stating "that constitutional discussions of Aboriginal issues would have to wait until late 1980 or early 1981."

88 See Daniels, *Native People and the Constitution of Canada*, App. 2, p. 95.

89 Daniels, *Native People and the Constitution of Canada*, 20–21.

90 Daniels, *We Are the New Nation*, 51.

91 Ibid., 52.

92 Ibid., 51–52.

93 Constitution Act, 1982, sec. 35(1, 2)

94 Daniels, *Native People and the Constitution of Canada*, 30.

95 Opening statement of Prime Minister Trudeau at the First Ministers' Conference on Aboriginal Constitutional Matters, (Ottawa, 8–9 March 1983). Cited in Mark Stevenson, "Section 91(24) and Canada's Legislative Jurisdiction with Respect to the Métis," *Indigenous Law Journal*, no. 1 (2002): 243–44.

96 Ibid., 244.

97 *Daniels v. Canada*, Trial Record, in Joseph Magnet, "*Daniels v. Canada*: Origins, Intentions, Futures," *aboriginal policy studies* 6, no. 2 (2017): 29.

98 Ibid., 30.

99 Ibid.

100 Tony Belcourt, "What Brought It On—And Did We Get What We Wanted?," Presentation at "*Daniels*: In and Beyond the Law" unpublished conference notes, 33. See also Daniels, *Native People and the Constitution of Canada*, 3; Native Council of Canada (with commentary by Harry Daniels), *Declaration of Métis and Indian Rights*, 11.

101 The Act for the Better Protection of the Lands and Property of the Indian in Lower Canada (1850). See also Daniels, *Native People and the Constitution of Canada*, 3. For further discussion on the definition of the term "Indian," see Clem Chartier, "'Indian': An Analysis of the Term as Used in Section 91 (24) of the British North America Act, 1867," *Saskatchewan Law Review* 43 (1978–79): 37–80.

102 Daniels, *Native People and the Constitution of Canada*, 3.

103 Ibid.

104 Belcourt, "For the Record," 131–32; Saunders and Dubois, *Métis Politics and Governance in Canada*, 73.

105 Métis Nation Accord, 1992, http://www.metismuseum.ca/media/document.php/148925. Worsley77.pdf (accessed 18 May 2018), 3.

106 Thomas Isaac, "A Matter of National and Constitutional Import: Report of the Minister's Special Representative on Reconciliation with Métis: Section 35 Métis Rights and the Manitoba Metis Federation Decision," Indigenous and Northern Affairs Canada, June 2016, http://www.aadnc-aandc.gc.ca/eng/1467641790303/1467641835266.

107 Janique Dubois and Kelly Saunders, "Explaining the Resurgence of Métis Rights: Making the Most of 'Windows of Opportunity,'" *Canadian Public Administration* 60, no. 1 (2017): 48–67. See also Saunders and Dubois, *Métis Politics and Governance in Canada*; and Adam Gaudry, "Better Late Than Never? Canada's Reluctant Recognition of Métis Rights and Self-Government," *Yellowhead Institute*, Policy Brief Issue 10 (2018): 1–5.

108 Isaac, "A Matter of National and Constitutional Import," 25.

109 Canada–Métis Nation Accord between the Government of Canada Canada–Métis Nation Accord between the Government of Canada and the Métis Nation as represented by the MNC and Its Governing Members, 13 April 2017, https://pm.gc.ca/eng/canada-metis-nation-accord.

110 See Jason Madden, Chapter 3 in this volume.

111 It should be noted that even though Harry Daniels was forceful in portraying "Métis distinctive-ness as vested in Métis political activism at the time of Canadian Confederation," in later years, according to Jennifer Adese, "he put forth a view that Métis existed throughout Canada and what made them Métis was their mixedness." See Adese, "A Tale of Two Constitutions: Métis Nationhood and Section 35(2)'s Impact on Interpretations of *Daniels*," *TOPIA* 36 (2016): 14. As well, Jason Madden and Darryl Leroux note in their respective chapters in this book that the *Daniels* decision has reinvigorated the "Métis-as-mixed" paradigm, especially as more groups in Eastern Canada perceive themselves as métis.

CHAPTER 3

After the Hysteria: Understanding *Daniels v. Canada* from a Métis Nation Perspective

JASON MADDEN[1]

On 16 April 2016, the Supreme Court of Canada (scc) released its judgement in *Daniels v. Canada* (*Daniels*).[2] In the *Daniels* decision, the scc issued the following relatively straightforward declaration that: "Non-status Indians and Métis are 'Indians' under s. 91(24) of the Constitution Act, 1867."[3] As this chapter and others in this book detail, however, nothing is really that straightforward when it comes to *Daniels*. Despite the judgement being short (it is only fifty-eight paragraphs) and unanimous (written on behalf of "the Court" by Justice Rosalie Abella), *Daniels* is arguably one of the most confusing and misunderstood recent decisions from the scc in the area of Aboriginal law.[4] Jokingly, I have compared *Daniels* to a Rorschach inkblot test because everyone who reads it can see what they want within it.[5]

This confusion about what *Daniels* means has led to much erroneous, and in some cases hysterical, media coverage, commentary, and analysis. For example, following the release of the judgement, the Canadian Broadcasting Corporation (cbc) initially published a story that Métis were now included as "Indians" under the federal Indian Act. Wrong. Other media outlets wrote that Métis were immediately eligible for federal benefits in the areas

of health, education, and housing totalling billions of dollars. Wrong again.
Some Métis leaders, commentators, and academics have expressed concern
that the Métis were now under the "control" of the federal government.
Wrong. Wrong. Wrong.

In this chapter, I attempt to explain *Daniels* from a Métis Nation perspective. I refer to the Métis Nation as the distinct Indigenous people that emerged
in the early 1800s in the historic North-West with a shared history, language,
culture, and collective consciousness. Its historic homeland includes large
parts of what are now known as the Prairie provinces, extending into parts
of Ontario, British Columbia, the Northwest Territories and the northwest
United States. The Métis Nation is comprised of the citizens and communities that were recognized and identify as being a part of it historically as well
as those individuals and communities who are accepted as being a part of the
people today. In contemporary times, the Métis Nation, for the most part, is
represented by democratically elected Métis governments such as the Métis
Nation of Ontario (MNO), the Manitoba Metis Federation (MMF), the Métis
Nation of Saskatchewan (MNS), the Métis Nation of Alberta (MNA), and the
Métis Nation of British Columbia (MNBC).[6] Collectively, these Métis governments come together to mandate the Métis National Council (MNC) as a
body to represent the Métis Nation at the national and international levels.[7]

I write this chapter based on my experiences in representing individual
Métis harvesters, the Métis governments noted above, as well as the MNC
and specific Métis communities from Ontario westward in the courts and in
negotiations with the Crown,[8] my involvement in the *Daniels* litigation,[9] and
my personal perspective as a citizen of the Métis Nation.[10] I do not address
what *Daniels* means for non–Status Indians.[11] Nor do I address *Daniels* in
the context of mixed-ancestry individuals, or groups who now claim to be
"Métis" for the purpose of s. 91(24) but do not connect to a historic Métis
community or the Métis Nation. As I explain further in this chapter, I argue
that despite the SCC's confusing reasons, *Daniels* does not create a new category of "Métis" that requires reconciliation in any way.

In order to explain *Daniels*, this chapter is organized in three parts. The
first part provides an overview of some of the history and context for the
case: the parties, the procedural history, the declarations sought, and the
political and legal backdrop for the litigation, including the Métis Nation's
participation within it. The second part provides an overview of s. 91(24),

including its history, evolution, and relevance today, as well as reviews of the Federal Court of Canada (Federal Court), Federal Court of Appeal (FCA), and SCC decisions in *Daniels*. The third part provides an analysis of the legal and practical implications of *Daniels*, including significant developments in Crown–Métis Nation negotiation processes on lands, rights, and self-government since the judgement.

Background and Overview of the Case

The Parties

In 1999, the original statement of claim in *Daniels* was filed in the Federal Court. The original three plaintiffs in the case were Harry Daniels, Leah Gardner, and the Congress of Aboriginal Peoples (CAP). Harry—a charismatic Métis leader originally from Regina Beach, Saskatchewan, and the president of CAP at the time—was the individual "Métis plaintiff." Leah Gardner—an "Anishanabe without status"[12] living in northwestern Ontario—was the individual "non–Status Indian plaintiff."[13] CAP—as a national Aboriginal advocacy organization that claims to represent Métis, non–Status Indians, and status Indians living off-reserve throughout Canada—was the third original plaintiff. The statement of claim was filed against Canada.

The Procedural History of the Litigation

As in most Aboriginal law litigation, Canada advanced a series of preliminary motions in an attempt to avoid and delay the trial of the matter, which were all unsuccessful.[14] In 2005, Harry's son Gabriel (Harry had passed away in 2004) and Terry Joudrey—a Mi'kmaq from Nova Scotia—were added as plaintiffs.[15] In 2011, the plaintiffs brought a successful motion seeking advanced costs against Canada in order to bring the case to trial.[16] When the trial finally began in May 2011, Harry, Gabriel, Leah, Terry, and CAP were the five named plaintiffs (referred to in this chapter as the Plaintiffs).

Justice Phelan of the Federal Court (the trial judge) heard evidence and argument for thirty-one days, spanning six weeks. In total, five experts and five other witnesses testified. The evidentiary record in *Daniels* included 800 exhibits extracted from over 15,000 documents.[17] It is likely the most comprehensive record on contemporary Métis politics leading up to the enactment of s. 35 of the Constitution Act, 1982 and following Métis inclusion in s. 35. The trial ended on 30 June 2011.

The Declarations Sought in the Litigation
The final amended statement of claim in *Daniels* sought the following declarations: (1) that Métis and non–Status Indians are "Indians" within the meaning of s. 91(24) of the Constitution Act, 1867; (2) that the federal government owes a fiduciary duty to Métis and non–Status Indians; and (3) that Métis and non–Status Indians have the right to be consulted and negotiated with, in good faith, by the federal government on a collective basis through representatives of their choice.

Declarations are a common court remedy sought in legal proceedings dealing with Aboriginal law in Canada. A court is asked to declare "the law" in relation to a dispute between governments and Aboriginal peoples. The parties are then expected to change their behaviour to be consistent with or to address the judiciary's statement of "the law."

In *Daniels*, the Plaintiffs advanced a three-pronged declaratory relief strategy with the goal of spurring long-denied federal negotiations and action on Métis and non–Status Indians issues. The first declaration sought clarity that Métis and non–Status Indians are included within the term "Indians" in s. 91(24). At its core, however, all this declaration did was provide clarity that Parliament *could* enact laws in relation to Métis and non–Status Indians under s. 91(24).[18] So, why did the Plaintiffs believe clarity on this issue mattered? Because whether logical, legally sound, believable or not, Métis and non–Status Indian leaders had heard from Canada—for generations— that uncertainty on this issue was a reason to not deal with the people and communities they represented; and the Plaintiffs had evidence to show that this excuse (as absurd as it was) had directly caused these people and communities significant harm. Further, contemporary history had shown them that when jurisdiction was clarified for other Indigenous peoples (i.e., the Inuit), Canada spent federal dollars on the Inuit as well as initiated negotiations and reached agreements.[19] When viewed from this perspective, the Plaintiffs had nothing to lose and a lot to gain from this declaration.

The first declaration's acknowledged permissiveness, however, is why the second and third declarations in *Daniels* were just as important to the Plaintiffs' litigation strategy. The second declaration's statement that Canada owed a fiduciary duty to Métis and non–Status Indians would arguably require concrete action by Canada to discharge this duty. The third declaration also sought a judicial statement that consultation and negotiations were owed—as a right—to Métis and non–Status Indians on subject matters such as lands, self-government, and rights. Similar to the second declaration, this declaration sought to have positive obligations imposed on Canada.

The Métis Nation and the Litigation

In order to understand the Métis Nation's perspective and involvement in *Daniels* (as well as its lack of involvement at trial),[20] it is necessary to understand why and how Aboriginal law related to the Métis—as a separate area of Canadian Aboriginal law that is distinct from Métis Nation law and legal orders and law—has developed, as well as to know something of contemporary Métis Nation politics. These legal and political issues were present in both the background and foreground of *Daniels*, particularly in relation to the dispute between the Métis Nation, the Plaintiffs, and ultimately the courts over who are the "Métis" in s. 91(24), as the litigation worked its way up through the courts.

The dispute about who are the "Métis" for the purposes of Canada's constitution is not new. The starting point is the fact that the Métis Nation is a distinct Indigenous people. Before Canada became Canada in 1867, the Métis Nation had emerged in the historic North-West with its own language (Michif), laws, and self-government, culture, relationships with other Indigenous peoples, territory, and, most importantly, a repeatedly demonstrated collective consciousness as a distinct Indigenous people.[21] By any definition, whether in international or domestic law, the Métis Nation meets the threshold for peoplehood.[22] The conclusions of the Royal Commission on Aboriginal Peoples (RCAP), which released its final report in 1996, remain helpful and apt in framing these issues today:

> Although there are differences of opinion about precisely how far the Métis Nation extends beyond its prairie core, there is wide agreement that it includes some portions of Ontario, the Northwest Territories and British Columbia.
>
> It is not for the Commission to say which Métis communities in the disputed areas form part of the Métis Nation and which do

not. These are matters to be determined by the Métis Nation and the communities themselves. What we can say is the Métis Nation is the most significant Métis collectivity in Canada. It unquestionably constitutes an Aboriginal people within the meaning of section 35 of the *Constitution Act, 1982* and an Aboriginal nation for purposes of negotiations with other governments.[23]

It is also important to recognize that the Métis Nation's dispute with others over the use of the term "Métis" is not merely a political one among competing "organizations." The dispute arises because the word "Métis," unlike the term "Indian" that was ascribed to a multitude of Indigenous peoples by colonizers,[24] was historically used by the Métis Nation to describe itself as an Indigenous people. The Métis Nation does not consider the term to be an adjective or "catch all" term of art like the word "Indian" that others can now try to fit their identities into. For the Métis Nation, the word "Métis," for Canadian constitutional purposes, is a noun and the proper name of an Indigenous people. It rejects the premise that the dictionary definition of the term *métis*, which points to the French and Latin words for "mixed," is a legally defensible or acceptable way to identify an Indigenous people generally or the "Métis" for the purpose of s. 35 or s. 91(24).

With that said, one of the trade-offs that came with Métis inclusion in s. 35 and with advancing litigation on Métis inclusion in s. 91(24) is that Canadian courts ultimately get to define what the term means for the purposes of Canada's constitution, not what it means based on Métis laws, legal orders, or world view. For example, despite repeated arguments advanced by Métis Nation communities, Canadian courts have refused to undertake a peoplehood-based analysis to identify the Métis or Métis rights holders for the purpose of s. 35.[25] While Canadian court decisions can never change what these terms may mean from the Métis Nation's perspective or Métis legal orders and law, these judicial definitions influence, and in some ways, can infect Métis perspectives and law on identity issues.[26]

In some respects, what Canadian courts are doing is similar to what Parliament did with the Indian Act in 1876. The Indian Act does not define who are the citizens of Indigenous peoples such as the Cree, Dene, or Haida. It only defines who Parliament determines are "Indians" for the purposes of its own legislation. Based on international law and common sense, Canada can never tell Indigenous peoples who they are and who are a part of them (i.e., their citizens). Today, while First Nations face challenges in untangling themselves from the Indian Act's colonial web, it is uncontroversial to say that the Indian Act does *not* define the full citizenship of the Indigenous peoples it applies to. In the same way, judicial interpretations related to Métis rights for the purposes of Canada's constitution can never define the Métis Nation, including who belongs to it from a community or citizenship perspective. Only the Métis Nation—as an Indigenous people—holds this inherent right.[27]

The case law relating to Métis s. 35 rights as well as s. 91(24) interprets who is "Métis" for the purposes of Canada's constitution and which groups or individuals have recognized rights in Canadian law. The distinction— between what Canadian courts are doing and what only an Indigenous people can do—is often lost in reactions to and analyses of court decisions, including those by both Métis and non-Métis academics (as evidenced in some of the chapters of this book). In all of my legal representations, the Métis Nation has consistently maintained that it will never accept a Canadian court's defining who the nation is or who is a citizen of the Métis Nation, and that a Canadian judge has no authority in that core area of Métis jurisdiction. This remains true to this day. Unfortunately, as is the case in *Daniels*, courts do not acknowledge this distinction and often carelessly veer into Indigenous identity issues without regard to what they may be doing.

This context informs the Métis Nation's political representation today as well as the ongoing dispute about the term "Métis." In *Daniels*, the trial judge acknowledged some of this history: "CAP (previously known as the Native Council of Canada or NCC) had a serious internal dispute over Métis issues and representation. In March 1983, the prairie Métis either left or were expelled from the [Native Council of Canada] and formed their own organization—the Métis National Council [MNC]. Thereafter, at the various constitutional discussions involving native issues, the MNC were present along with the NCC/CAP. Although the MNC were not involved in this litigation, the Court is cognizant of the fact that CAP is not the sole recognized voice of Métis."[28]

The evidence in *Daniels* also documented that one of the main reasons for the MNC-NCC split in 1983 was the dispute over the definition of "Métis." This has not gone away. It remained a live issue in the constitutional conferences held in the 1980s and it remains an issue today: "There is a serious dispute between MNC and the NCC [now CAP] as to which organization is the legitimate representative of the Métis people. In part, this turns on the definition of the term 'Métis'; the MNC argue for a definition based on the historical or geographic evolution of Métis.... The NCC would accommodate all individuals of mixed ancestry throughout Canada."[29] This ongoing debate was front and centre in *Daniels*. In their statement of claim, the Plaintiffs put forth the usual NCC/CAP's all-encompassing definition of "Métis."[30] Despite the Métis Nation's concerns with the definition being advanced by the Plaintiffs in *Daniels*, the MNC and its Governing Members did not become involved in the case at trial. The main reason for this decision was limited financial resources to participate, combined with the Métis Nation's alternative strategic litigation approach, which focused on the establishment of Métis rights and claims in the courts based on s. 35 rather than concentrating on s. 91(24).

Informing the Métis Nation's strategic litigation approach were the three legal issues identified by the RCAP as central to overcoming the denial and challenges Métis faced with governments: (1) the judicial recognition of Métis rights, including Métis title, harvesting rights, etc., as s. 35 "aboriginal" rights; (2) the recognition of outstanding Métis claims against the Crown, particularly in relation to Métis lands; and (3) clarity on Métis inclusion in s. 91(24).[31] In particular, the Métis Nation focused on the first and second legal issues noted above on the assumption that the establishment of specific Métis rights and claims would provide more legal leverage to ultimately secure negotiations and agreements with governments. The strategy also recognized that, following 1982, the SCC and Aboriginal law generally would be far more focused on s. 35, instead of s. 91(24).[32]

Aligned with this strategy, the MNO advanced *R. v. Powley*[33]—the first case to deal with Métis s. 35 rights—all the way to the SCC. The MMF advanced its land claim–related litigation against Canada based on sections 31 and 32 of the Manitoba Act, 1870 all the way to the SCC as well in *MMF v. Canada*.[34] Both *Powley* and *MMF* provide legal frameworks for other Métis communities to advance s. 35 rights and claims. Based on these frameworks, other Métis rights test cases have been advanced from Ontario westward based on s. 35 and Métis land-related claims, which have led to negotiations or litigation that is still before the courts.

Although neither the MNC nor any of its Governing Members became a party or intervener in *Daniels* at trial, the Métis Nation did intervene at both the FCA and SCC levels in order to make its voice heard. Helpfully, by the time *Daniels* went to trial and proceeded to subsequent appeals, the courts had to grapple with the legal precedents set in *Powley* and *MMF*, which had been advanced by the Métis Nation and challenged the "Métis-as-mixed" paradigm. With that said, it was also clear in *Daniels* that since the Plaintiffs were able to solely shape the trial judge's impressions of the term "Métis"—without any Métis Nation participation—CAP's "Métis-as-mixed" definition is deeply embedded in *Daniels* and contributes to the case's controversy and confusion.

The Court Decisions in *Daniels*
Understanding Section 91(24)
In order to truly appreciate *Daniels*, it is important to understand what s. 91(24) is and, just as importantly, what it is not. This requires some historical context. When Canada was created in 1867, its original constitution set out which subject matters Parliament and provincial legislatures would each have "exclusive Legislative Authority" over in sections 91 and 92. Specifically, the Constitution Act, 1867 states:

> It shall be lawful for the Queen, by and with the Advice and
> Consent of the Senate and House of Commons, to make Laws for
> the Peace, Order, and good Government of Canada, in relation
> to all Matters not coming within the Classes of Subjects by this
> Act assigned exclusively to the Legislatures of the Provinces; and
> for greater Certainty, but not so as to restrict the Generality of
> the foregoing Terms of this Section, it is hereby declared that
> (notwithstanding anything in this Act) the exclusive Legislative
> Authority of the Parliament of Canada extends to all Matters
> coming within the Classes of Subjects next hereinafter enumerated;
> that is to say. . .

> 24. Indians, and Lands reserved for the Indians.[35]

The list of provincial powers in s. 92 is generally concerned with more local or provincial matters that are not national or interprovincial in scope.

Provincial heads of power included direct taxation within a province, management and sale of public lands, incorporation of companies, property and civil rights, administration of justice, and all matters of a merely local or private nature. The list of federal powers in s. 91 is generally concerned with nation-wide and international matters. Federal heads of power included unemployment insurance, postal service, the census, the military, navigation and shipping, sea coast and inland fisheries, banking, weights and measures, and patents.

At their simplest, sections 91 and 92 grant legislatures the authority to pass laws in relation to the identified subjects matters in each list, including an essential component within each subject matter that the other level of government cannot impair. These subject matters are interchangeably called constitutional "heads of power," "jurisdictions," "responsibilities," "authorities," or the "division of powers." Despite the compulsory-sounding nature of some of these terms, legislatures are not obligated to pass laws in these subject matters. Nor do these heads of power—in and of themselves—compel government action.

For the most part, much of the division of powers litigation since 1867 has been disputes between Canada and the provinces with respect to protecting their jurisdictions. In more recent years, division of powers litigation has decreased somewhat, and the courts have also endorsed an approach that promotes "cooperative federalism" among governments. Within this overall division of powers discourse, s. 91(24) is unique in four ways:

1. It is the only head of power that includes peoples (i.e., "Indians") as opposed to things (e.g., national defence, civil and property rights, currency and coinage, etc.).

2. Implicit within the division of powers lies the faulty "assumption of Crown sovereignty" over Indigenous peoples and their lands, and that all "jurisdictions" in Canada are allocated between the federal government and the provinces, as opposed to the reality that Indigenous jurisdictions and laws stand independent and in their own right. This elephant in the room has never been directly addressed by the scc.[36]

3. Section 91(24)'s initial and perverted use led to the Indian Act as a means to assimilate "Indians," treat "Indians" as wards of the state, and attempt to control the lives of "Indians" from cradle to grave. This colonial legacy and the flawed assumption that s. 91(24) grants control over "Indians" runs deep among First Nations based on their experience. For many, this head of power is seen as a prison into which no Indigenous people would want to seek entry.

4. While in earlier SCC jurisprudence, s.91(24) this provision was recognized as "special" and included additional protective powers and obligations owing to "Indians," in more recent SCC jurisprudence this recognized uniqueness has waned, been ignored, or overturned.

All of these realities, myths, and contradictions are projected onto and lie within s. 91(24). In contemporary times, the SCC has never set out a coherent, comprehensive, and consistent judicial approach to s. 91(24) that fully explains its scope, how it reconciles with pre-existing Indigenous land, jurisdiction and laws, the obligations inherited from the Imperial Crown, the royal prerogative, the treaty-making power, its interplay with government action, or the SCC's jurisprudence. Instead, the judicial ground continues to shift in relation to s. 91(24). In 2014, for example, long-standing SCC precedent, which had previously confirmed that Aboriginal rights, including Aboriginal title, lie in the "core" of s. 91(24), therefore providing additional protection to these rights from provincial laws through the operation of constitutional doctrines, was overturned.[37] In *Tsilhqot'in Nation*, the SCC held that

> the guarantee of Aboriginal rights in s. 35 of the *Constitution Act, 1982*, like the *Canadian Charter of Rights and Freedoms*, operates as a limit on federal and provincial legislative powers. The *Charter* forms Part I of the *Constitution Act, 1982*, and the guarantee of Aboriginal rights forms Part II. Parts I and II are sister provisions, both operating to limit governmental powers, whether federal or provincial. Part II Aboriginal rights, like Part I *Charter* rights, are held *against* government—they operate to *prohibit* certain types of regulation which governments could otherwise impose. These

limits have nothing to do with whether something lies at the core of the federal government's powers.[38] (Emphasis in original.)

In the same way, s. 91(24)'s previously recognized special protective role of providing "primary constitutional responsibility for securing the welfare of Canada's aboriginal peoples"[39] to the federal government has been whittled down to simply looking to the division of powers to see which level of government's law may be infringing on an Aboriginal right.[40] As further discussed below, the above-noted unaddressed issues, combined with the SCC's dramatic changes with respect to s. 91(24)'s interpretation, are not clarified or addressed in any way by *Daniels*.

The Trial Decision

The trial judge's reasons for judgement in *Daniels* were released on 8 January 2013. Justice Phelan granted the following declaration to the Plaintiffs: "that Métis and non-status Indians are 'Indians' within the meaning of the Constitution Act, 1867, s 91(24)."[41] In arriving at this conclusion, the trial judge noted that the historical records showed that in order to achieve the objectives of Canadian Confederation (creating a country from coast to coast, settling the North-West, building a national railway, etc.), Canada needed s. 91(24) so that it could deal with all of the different Aboriginal peoples, including the Métis, it encountered along the way.[42] This required the "Indian" head of power to be "sufficiently broad that the federal government could address a wide range of situations . . . covering a diverse composition of native people."[43]

From Ontario westward, the evidence showed that Canada used this power in relation to the Métis in many ways, including the inclusion of Métis (Half-breeds)—as individuals—in the treaties negotiated with Indians in and around the Upper Great Lakes,[44] in negotiating the Half-breed Adhesion to Treaty 3 in northwestern Ontario,[45] in enacting s. 31 of the Manitoba Act in the old "postage stamp" province of Manitoba,[46] and in passing the Dominion Lands Act that established the Métis scrip system that spanned the Prairies and parts of northeastern British Columbia and the North-West Territories.[47] The trial judge concluded that these federal actions, among others, showed that s. 91(24) has been used historically to deal with Métis.[48]

The trial judge also noted that historically, wherever non–Status Indians and Métis were discriminated against or treated differently than non-Aboriginal peoples by the federal government (i.e., residential schools, liquor laws), it was because non–Status Indians and Métis could be dealt with under the "Indian" head of power.[49] Justice Phelan noted that the distinguishing feature of both non–Status Indians and Métis is that their "Indianness"— not language, religion, or connection to European heritage—brought them within s. 91(24).[50] He held that the term "Indian" in s. 91(24) is broader than the term "Indian" in the Indian Act and that while Canada may be able to limit the number of Indians it recognizes under the Indian Act, that cannot have an effect on the determination of who is within s. 91(24).[51]

In order to craft a definition of Métis for the purposes of s. 91(24), the trial judge rejected the approach used in *Powley* because s. 35 rights were not at issue and a definition on a national scale was needed. He ultimately defined the Métis and non–Status Indians that were included in his declaration as "a group of native people who maintained a strong affinity for their Indian heritage without possessing Indian status."[52] Justice Phelan refused to grant the second and third declarations sought. Regarding the second declaration (that the Crown owes a fiduciary duty), he acknowledged that the Crown's relationship with the Métis was fiduciary in nature, but "the Court [was] not prepared to make some general statement concerning fiduciary duty"[53] when specific facts giving rise to such a duty were not before the court. Regarding the third declaration (the right to consultation and negotiation), he refused to grant it because "absent better particulars of what is at issue to consult on or negotiate, the Court can offer no guidance. The duty to consult and negotiate depends on the subject matter, the strength of the claim and other factors not before the Court."[54]

The Federal Court of Appeal Decision
Canada appealed the trial judge's decision to the FCA. The FCA heard the appeal in October 2013. The appeal court's judgement was released on 17 April 2014.[55] In the appeal, several new parties intervened, including the MNC, MMF, MNO, Métis Settlements General Council, and Gift Lake Métis Settlement. These interveners all supported the trial judge's determination that Métis were included in s. 91(24), but raised concerns about the definition of Métis for the purposes of s. 91(24). In addition, the Alberta

government intervened, arguing that Métis and non–Status Indians were not included in s. 91(24).

On appeal, Canada argued that the trial judge had made three errors in granting the declaration because (1) the declaration that Métis and non–Status Indians are within s. 91(24) lacked practical utility; (2) the declaration was unfounded in fact and law; and (3) the declaration defined the core meaning of the constitutional term "Indian" in the abstract.[56]

The FCA rejected all of Canada's submissions that the declaration lacked practical utility[57] with respect to the Métis.[58] The appeal court went on to agree with Canada, however, that the declaration with respect to non–Status Indians was redundant because Canada conceded it could legislate with respect to non–Status Indians, but it had just chosen not to legislate.[59] On this basis, the FCA declined to make a declaration that non–Status Indians are within s. 91(24).[60]

Canada also argued that by adopting a definition of Métis that was contrary to history and the jurisprudence of the SCC on Métis, the trial judge erred in law.[61] As noted above, Justice Phelan described Métis in s. 91(24) as "a group of native people who maintained a strong affinity for their Indian heritage without possessing Indian status."[62] Canada argued that this definition was inconsistent with the SCC's recognition of the Métis as a distinct Aboriginal people, related to, but different from, their Indian forebearers. In Canada's view, recognition that Métis are culturally different from Indians led to the conclusion that Métis are not "Indians" in s. 91(24).[63]

The FCA agreed that the trial judge's definition of Métis was problematic[64] but did not agree that this led to Métis being excluded from s. 91(24). In holding that Métis are within s. 91(24), the appeal court explained the trial judge's definition was correct and that when the trial judge used the phrase "Indian heritage," he meant Indigenousness or Aboriginal heritage.[65] The FCA also noted that in several cases, including *Powley*, the SCC had rejected the notion that the term Métis encompassed all individuals with mixed Indian and European heritage, instead finding that the term referred to a distinctive group of people who developed separate and distinct identities.[66] According to the FCA, it did not matter whether these comments had been made with reference to s. 35 or s. 91(24), because "individual elements of [Canada's] constitution are linked to one another and must be interpreted by reference to the structure of the Constitution as a whole."[67]

Having clarified the confusion caused by the trial judge's definition, the
FCA went on to conclude that it did not need to define the term "Métis" in
order to determine whether Métis people fall within the scope of s. 91(24).[68]
The FCA noted that Canada's constitution did not define "Indian" and the
SCC did not define "Eskimos" when it determined that they were included in
s. 91(24) in 1939.[69] It held that it was sufficient to say that the term "Métis"
was not defined in a manner that is contrary to the jurisprudence of the SCC.[70]
On this point, the FCA accepted the MMF's submission that the declaration
be reformulated as follows: "that the Métis are included as 'Indians' within
the meaning of section 91(24) of the Constitution Act, 1867."[71]

While the FCA issued a reformulated first declaration (to apply to the
Métis but not to non–Status Indians), it also held that the trial judge did not
err in denying the issuance of the second and third declarations with respect
to the Crown's fiduciary duty and duty to negotiate and consult with Métis.[72]

The Supreme Court of Canada Decision

Following the FCA's decision, the Plaintiffs appealed to the SCC to have
the declaration with respect to non–Status Indians reinstated and to have
the second and third declarations issued. Canada cross-appealed, seeking to
have the FCA's declaration with respect to Métis inclusion in s. 91(24) overturned. On 20 November 2014, the SCC agreed to hear the appeals of both
the Plaintiffs and Canada in the *Daniels* case. It granted intervener status to
the MNC, the MSGC, and the Gift Lake Métis Settlement. It also granted
intervener status to the Assembly of First Nations, several other First Nation
and non–Status Indian groups as well as other groups who claimed to represent "Métis" from coast to coast to coast. The Alberta and Saskatchewan
governments also intervened.

On appeal, Canada argued—again—that all of the declarations had no
practical utility. With respect to the first declaration, the SCC held it had
practical utility, because even though Métis and non–Status Indian inclusion in s. 91(24) "does not create a duty to legislate," "it has the undeniable
salutary benefit of ending a jurisdictional tug-of-war in which these groups
were left wondering about where to turn for policy redress" and "would
guarantee both certainty and accountability" for these groups through resolv-
ing "a long-standing jurisdictional dispute."[73] The court relied on the trial
judge's findings that "the political/policy wrangling between the federal and

provincial governments [about this issue] has produced a large population of collaterally damaged [Métis and non–Status Indians]" as proof that the declaration would have practical utility and they would now know "it is the federal government to whom they can turn."[74]

With respect to the purpose of s. 91(24), the SCC upheld the trial judge's findings that the expansion of "British North America across Rupert's Land and the North-West Territories," including the building of a national railway, underpinned it.[75] In order to "protect the railway from attack" and facilitate "the westward expansion of the Dominion," Canada had to have the jurisdiction to deal with the "large and diverse Aboriginal population, including many Métis" who occupied the land sought to be brought into Confederation.[76]

The SCC then proceeded to determine whether Métis are included in s. 91(24). It began with the statement that "there is no consensus on who is considered Métis or a non-status Indian, nor need there be."[77] The SCC went on to note, in *obiter dictum* (i.e., said in passing by the Court, but not upholding a finding of fact or specific legal conclusion necessary to the Court's ultimate determination that Métis, "however ... defined"[78] are included in s. 91[24]), that "Métis" can refer to the historic Métis community in Manitoba's Red River Settlement, or it can be used as a general term for anyone with mixed European and Aboriginal heritage, with "some mixed-ancestry communities identify[ing] as Métis, others as Indians."[79] As explained above, and, elaborated on in other chapters of this book, this "Métis-as-mixed" sentiment is rejected by the Métis Nation, but embraced by others who believe the term to simply mean any individual or group with mixed Indigenous ancestry.

The SCC ultimately concluded that these "definitional ambiguities" about Métis and non–Status Indians do not preclude a determination with respect to whether they are in s. 91(24) because a consideration of the "historical, philosophical, and linguistic contexts" for the term "Indians" in s. 91(24) includes *all* Aboriginal peoples, Métis and non–Status Indian alike.[80] The Court relied on various findings of the trial judge that demonstrated Canada had long acted on the basis of Métis inclusion in the broad purpose of s. 91(24).[81] With respect to the Métis Nation specifically, Justice Abella cited the writings of Professor John Burrows that "the Métis Nation was ... crucial in ushering in western and northern Canada into Confederation and in increasing the wealth of the Canadian nation by opening up the prairies to agriculture and settlement. These developments could not have occurred without Métis intercession and legal presence."[82]

The scc then went on to reconcile s. 91(24) with s. 35 with respect to Métis inclusion. While s. 35 does not define s. 91(24)'s scope, the scc held that s. 91(24) and s. 35's "grand purpose" of "reconciliation between Aboriginal and non-Aboriginal Canadians in a mutually respectful long-term relationship" should be "read together."[83] This results in "Indians" in s. 91(24) being interchangeable with the term "aboriginal peoples of Canada" in s. 35, which includes First Nations, Métis, and Inuit. The scc also noted that it would be "constitutionally anomalous" for Métis to be included within s. 35, but then be the only Aboriginal people excluded from s. 91(24).[84]

The scc's existing jurisprudence was also relied upon to support the conclusion that Métis are included in s. 91(24). Justice Abella cited *Re Eskimo* and *Attorney General of Canada v. Canard*[85] as support for the conclusion that intermarriage and mixed ancestry do not preclude groups from inclusion in s. 91(24).[86] The scc relied on these two precedents to support the finding that the Métis—who have also been recognized as a distinct Aboriginal people in cases such as *Powley* and *MMF*—can also be included within s. 91(24) without undermining their distinctiveness in any way. The Court also distinguished its decision in *R. v. Blais*.[87]

Since *Daniels* was not about whether specific Métis communities possess Aboriginal rights or claims protected by s. 35, the scc found "there is no need to delineate which mixed-ancestry communities are Métis and which are non-status Indians" at this determination of jurisdiction stage.[88] It held that all of these groups are included in s. 91(24) "by virtue of the fact that they are all Aboriginal peoples."[89] Determining whether "particular individuals or communities" are in s. 91(24) "is a fact-driven question to be decided on a case-by-case basis in the future."[90] As such, at the jurisdiction stage, "community acceptance" is not required because s. 91(24) includes *all* Aboriginal peoples, including "people who may no longer be accepted by their communities because they were separated from them as a result, for example, of government policies such as Indian Residential Schools."[91]

The scc, however, went on to emphasize that Métis or non–Status Indian inclusion in s. 91(24) is not the same as being recognized as a rights-bearing community or rights-holder for the purpose of s. 35.[92] Section 91(24) serves "a very different constitutional purpose" than s. 35. In effect, s. 91(24) casts a wide net and deals with Parliament's "relationships" with *all* Aboriginal peoples. Section 35, on the other hand, protects "historic community-held rights" and calls for the just settlement of rights and claims.[93] Aboriginal rights and definitional issues are answered *downstream* from jurisdiction, and the legal requirement in *Powley* must still be met to establish Métis rights.[94]

In reinstating the trial judge's original declaration that Métis and non–Status Indians are in s. 91(24), the Court reconfirmed that it is the federal government to whom these groups can turn.[95] With respect to the second declaration on finding a Crown-Métis fiduciary relationship, the Court refused to issue it because it would just be "restating settled law."[96] On the third declaration, the scc refused to issue it because "*Haida Nation v. BC*, *Tsilhqot'in Nation v. BC* and *Powley* already recognize a context-specific duty to negotiate" exists "when Aboriginal rights are engaged."[97]

The Implications of the *Daniels* Case

The Legal Implications of Daniels

As discussed above, despite all the public and media hoopla post-*Daniels*, the only declaration issued by the scc—that Métis and non–Status Indians are in s. 91(24)—simply provides judicial clarity that Parliament *may* pass laws in relation to these groups under this head of power. This does not create *any* duty to legislate. With respect to what had changed for the Plaintiffs, the scc repeatedly focused on the idea that with this constitutional question answered, these groups now know "it is the federal government to whom they can turn" for "policy redress."[98] Nowhere within its reasons, however, does the Court explain the interplay or corollary obligations (if any) between Parliament being able to pass laws in relation to Métis and non–Status Indians and what Canada must do with the policy issues brought forward by these groups.

While the scc held that this declaration will have "enormous practical utility" and will "guarantee both certainty and accountability," it failed to explain what happens if, after these groups turn to Parliament or the federal government, Canada ultimately decides to do nothing. Behind the Court's robust rhetoric, it is difficult to discern exactly what new legal or specific constitutional levers the Plaintiffs actually gained from the first declaration, aside from the potential passing of laws related to the Métis or non-Status

Indians by Parliament (that even the Plaintiffs acknowledged was permissive), knowing whose door to go knock on (as they had been for generations) or possible additional political and moral suasion based on the SCC's passionate call to arms.

In *Daniels*, the SCC notably avoids its own language from less than twenty years earlier that s. 91(24) brings with it "primary constitutional responsibility for securing the welfare of Canada's aboriginal peoples,"[99] which would have clearly assisted the Plaintiffs in arguing that Canada has a positive obligation to secure the welfare of Métis and non–Status Indian groups as well. Instead, s. 91(24)'s purpose is now described as merely being about "the federal government's relationship with Canada's Aboriginal peoples," without any discussion about what that "relationship" requires or whether any additional protective measures and obligations lie within this head of power. While disappointing, this ongoing cutting down of s. 91(24)'s previously recognized unique protective powers is aligned with other recent SCC cases, including *Tsilhqot'in* and *Grassy Narrows*.[100]

With that said, however, I would argue that the SCC's treatment of the third declaration, dealing with the Crown's duty to negotiate is the potential "sleeper hit" in *Daniels* and provides the necessary legal and constitutional leverage for Métis and non–Status Indian groups to force Canada's hand if steps to change the status quo are not taken. Specifically, the SCC held that *Haida, Tsilhqot'in*, and *Powley* "already recognize a context-specific duty to negotiate when Aboriginal rights are engaged."[101] While the SCC wrote that this was "a restatement of the existing law,"[102] it was far from clear based on this case law that there was a stand-alone, legally enforceable, constitutional duty to negotiate (related to but not the same as the Crown's duty to consult and accommodate) that could be relied upon if the Crown refused negotiations where established or credibly asserted rights were engaged.[103] As discussed above, this issue—governments refusing to negotiate with Métis on substantive rights issues—had been one of the most challenging for even the Métis Nation and its communities to crack.

Based on the SCC's articulation of the Crown's duty to negotiate as settled law, a Métis or non–Status Indian group could now arguably advance judicial review against a government that refused to negotiate after a formal request was brought forth, detailing an asserted Aboriginal right or claim or pointing to relevant case law that had recognized a right in a regulatory or civil litigation context. Alternatively, the group could commence an action seeking a declaration and/or order from the court directing negotiations. Time will tell how this duty is ultimately used and interpreted, and what it will accomplish, but it appears to provide a helpful new constitutional "stick" that could spur negotiations with Métis and non–Status Indian groups with established or credibly asserted s. 35 rights or claims. Clearly, this duty is particularly helpful to the Métis Nation and its communities, which, as noted above, have successfully pursued a litigation strategy that has established Métis rights and claims from Ontario westward. Frankly, I believe this duty, if properly advanced, has the potential to be a game changer for Métis and non–Status Indian groups with credibly asserted claims who have historically been denied negotiation processes.

For example, this duty could be particularly helpful if Métis Nation communities had to challenge Canada's current comprehensive and specific claims policies, which provide opportunities for negotiations with First Nations and Inuit based on rights and claims but exclude the Métis (either expressly or by design).[104] The fact that Métis communities with recognized s. 35 rights have absolutely no place to go within the federal system would likely trigger the duty to negotiate. This is particularly so given that the FCA identified this issue as being relevant to the *Daniels* litigation: "the respondents' claim extended beyond a claim to programs and services available under the federal spending power. The claim put in issue, among other things, the failure of the federal government to negotiate or enter treaties with respect to unextinguished Aboriginal rights, or agreements with respect to other Aboriginal matters or interests analogous to those treaties and agreements which the federal government has negotiated and/or entered into with status Indians."[105] With respect to definitional concerns about a new class of "Métis" being created within s. 91(24), the first declaration's permissiveness, combined with the reality that in order to access the Crown's duty to negotiate "Aboriginal rights [need to be] engaged," may, in a likely unintended but helpful way, address these challenges in *Daniels*. While *Daniels* unfortunately reinvigorates the troubling "Métis-as-mixed" proposition for the purposes of s. 91(24), it also reaffirms that *Powley* remains as the legal test for the purpose of establishing Aboriginal rights under s. 35.[106] This requires rights-bearing Métis communities to have emerged with their own distinct identity and culture prior to effective control and the members of those communities to self-identify as Métis, be ancestrally connected to the historic Métis community at issue, and be accepted by the modern-day Métis community.[107] As such, individuals with some Indigenous ancestry but no connection to a rights-bearing Aboriginal collective cannot access this duty to negotiate. Nor can mixed Aboriginal ancestry groups who cannot either meet the *Powley* test for Métis rights or the test laid out in *R. v. Van der Peet*[108] for Indian communities.

These individuals and groups claiming new "Métis" status under s. 91(24) are similarly excluded from the SCC's vigorous call to arms "that reconciliation with *all* of Canada's Aboriginal peoples is Parliament's goal."[109] In *Haida*, the SCC held that "reconciliation is not a final legal remedy in the usual sense. *Rather, it is a process flowing from rights guaranteed by s. 35(1) of the* Constitution Act, 1982. This process of reconciliation flows from the Crown's duty of honourable dealing toward Aboriginal peoples, which arises in turn from the Crown's assertion of sovereignty over an Aboriginal people and *de facto* control of land and resources that were formerly in the control of that people" (emphasis added).[110] This constitutionally mandated process is owed to the Indigenous peoples, nations, and communities who actually have "rights guaranteed by s. 35(1) of the *Constitution Act, 1982.*" In order to possess s. 35 rights related to lands, self-government, and resources, these groups needed to be on the—as collectives—prior to contact (for First Nations and Inuit) or effective control (for Métis). *Daniels*, through s. 91(24), cannot create new classes of self-identifying Indigenous individuals or groups who are now owed this process of reconciliation independent from pre-existing Indigenous communities, nations, or peoples that collectively hold rights and interests.

While s. 91(24) "includes people who may no longer be accepted by their communities because they were separated from them as a result, for example, of government policies such as Indian Residential Schools . . . [and] there is no principled reason for presumptively and arbitrarily excluding them from Parliament's protective authority on the basis of a 'community acceptance' test,"[111] implicit within this statement is the recognition these individuals must still ancestrally connect to the historic Indigenous communities or peoples that occupied Canada *prior to* the relevant dates set out above. Any constitutionally mandated reconciliation owing to these individuals who have been separated from their communities would necessarily flow from their being a part of these historic Indigenous collectives. If, as the SCC stated, "this case represents another chapter in the pursuit of reconciliation and redress in . . . Canada's relationship with its Indigenous peoples,"[112] reconciliation is advanced by these individuals finding their way back to their family, kin, communities, and nations, not by creating some new "Indigenous" collectives to seek individual or separate policy redress independent from the rights-bearing Indigenous collectives who are actually owed reconciliation.

This is unquestionably a contentious aspect of *Daniels* that has the potential to undermine reconciliation and embolden self-Indigenizing individuals and groups if not properly understood and implemented by governments. The SCC's desire to be rightly compassionate and inclusive of individuals separated from their Indigenous nations and communities—through no fault of their own—is commendable. It is important to note, however, that the reasons for the separations that the SCC noted (e.g., residential schools, the Indian Act, etc.) were not the creations of Indigenous peoples. It is the government with the s. 91(24) authority that created these divisions. The idea that in the ongoing process of reconciliation, the Indigenous collectives, who were harmed and undermined by these unilaterally imposed federal policies, would have no role in determining who ultimately belongs to them—and that this would be left to the federal government's exercise of its s. 91(24) authority again—is a sort of colonization redux. Such an approach would fly in the face of the constitutionally mandated reconciliation demanded by s. 35.

Clearly, much care and thought is required to ensure that the SCC's stated goal of reconciliation is not thwarted through new federal government–created approaches under s. 91(24) in this area, which would simply make new divisions among Indigenous peoples and possibly prop up illegitimate self-Indigenizing individuals and groups. Ironically, real Indigenous peoples and communities now need to rely on Canada's long-standing inaction, which they have faced for generations, to ensure that the interests of these self-Indigenizing individuals and groups are not addressed.

The Practical Implications of Daniels to Date

For the Métis Nation, *Daniels* completed what I have often referred to as the "trifecta of Métis law" and what the RCAP had previously identified as the three key outstanding Métis legal issues. As noted above, *Powley* (2003) and *MMF* (2013) respectively set out a new legal frameworks for advancing Métis s. 35 right and claims. *Daniels* (2016) confirmed the missing legal piece; namely, that Canada has jurisdiction under s. 91(24) to advance "relationships" with the Métis as well.

As discussed above, it is very likely that if Canada had refused to begin negotiations with Métis governments that represent rights-bearing communities and component parts of the Métis Nation, the combination of the judicial recognition of established Métis s. 35 rights, established or credible Métis claims against the Crown, federal jurisdiction for Métis, and the Crown's duty to negotiate would likely have been put together to seek an order from the courts for negotiations.[113] Prior to the release of *Daniels*, however, other political developments contributed to further softening the ground for substantive Crown–Métis Nation negotiations.

In June 2015, the minister of Indian and Northern Affairs (under the then Conservative government) appointed Tom Isaac, a lawyer practising in Aboriginal law, to act as a Ministerial Special Representative on Métis issues. Mr. Isaac was specifically tasked with looking at and providing recommendations to Canada on two issues: (1) Métis s. 35 rights; and (2) a response to the SCC's decision in *MMF*. In June 2016, less than two months after the *Daniels* decision was released, Mr. Isaac's report was released, recommending formal negotiation processes be established between Canada and the MMF in relation to the SCC's decision in *MMF* as well as negotiations with rights-bearing Métis communities from Ontario westward, as represented by some of the MNC's Governing Members.[114]

During the federal election campaign of fall 2015, the Liberal Party released a Métis Nation–specific reconciliation plan. This plan included commitments to "immediately" establish a negotiations process with the MMF to "settle the outstanding land claim of the Manitoba Métis community, as recognized by the [SCC] in [*MMF*]" and to "work with Métis groups, as well as the provinces and territories, to establish a federal claims process that recognizes Métis self government and resolves outstanding claims."[115] In November 2015, following the election of a Liberal government, Prime Minister Trudeau mandated the newly appointed Minister for Indigenous Affairs to "work, on a nation-to-nation basis, with the Métis Nation to advance reconciliation and renew the relationship, based on cooperation, respect for rights, our international obligations, and a commitment to end the status quo."[116]

These political developments, combined with the above-noted "trifecta of Métis law," led to a series of exploratory discussion agreements being signed between Canada and the MNC's Governing Members, as well as the MSGC based the premise that these discussions would assess the existence of rights-bearing Métis communities within these respective regions as the representativeness of these entities in relation to these communities. Notably, these types of agreements were not signed with groups claiming "Métis" rights in the East Coast and Quebec, where claimants seeking to establish "Métis" rights in these regions have repeatedly failed.[117] These discussions were "exploratory" in nature because it was recognized that Canada's existing policies excluded or did not adequately address the distinctiveness of Métis claims, and that unique federal Cabinet mandates would need to be crafted. These exploratory discussions ultimately led to framework agreements that established formal negotiations processes between Canada and some of the MNC's Governing Members where Canada was satisfied that the MNC Governing Member in question was authorized to represent a rights-bearing Métis community or communities in a given provincial boundary for the purpose of s. 35 Métis rights, including, self-government.[118]

On 15 November 2016, the MMF signed the first of these framework agreements, representing a breakthrough for Métis communities south of the 60th parallel. Similar framework agreements for negotiations on Métis self-government, lands, rights, and outstanding claims were signed with the MNA (November 2017), MNO (December 2017), and MNS (July 2018).[119] At the time of writing this chapter, framework agreements had not yet been signed with MNBC, the MSGC, or other groups claiming to represent "Métis." Ironically, these framework agreements were exactly what the previous Office of the Federal Interlocutor for Métis and Non–Status Indians (OFI), as the body officially tasked with advancing Métis issues in the federal system, warned that Canada should guard against.[120]

More recently, specific federal Cabinet mandates have been secured under these framework agreement negotiations. In September 2018, Canada and the MMF announced a $154.3 million "interim reconciliation plan" that includes the following components: (1) investments in MMF-identified priority areas to improve the social and economic well-being of the Manitoba Métis Community; (2) negotiation of the recognition of the MMF as the Manitoba Métis Community's self-government; and (3) support for the transition of MMF from a corporation to a self-governing Indigenous government.[121]

In June 2019, the MNO, MNA, and MNS each signed a Métis Government Recognition and Self-Government Agreement (MGRSA).[122] These agreements, also approved by a co-developed federal Cabinet mandate, provide a level of immediate recognition for these Métis governments.[123] The MGRSAS set out mutually agreeable processes, similar to the processes followed in modern-day treaty making with First Nations and Inuit, for the formal recognition of these Métis governments in Canadian law through federal legislation.[124] The MGRSAS also include commitments related to the development and ratification of constitutions and the negotiation of intergovernmental and fiscal agreements, as well as the passage of a core set of laws by each Métis government.

Significantly, the MGRSAS also contemplate upfront implementation legislation to provide a legislative framework for the transition of these Métis governments from their current corporate structures, as opposed to relying on a federal policy that may be subject to political whim.[125] Other key MGRSA provisions include that the honour of the Crown applies to their implementation; that there is an obligation to negotiate; and Canada's acknowledgement that participation in these negotiation processes do not undermine existing Métis self-government in any way: "Notwithstanding the recognition provided for and the processes set out in this Agreement, the MNA maintains its position that it is already a Métis government that is mandated by Métis Nation within Alberta based on the inherent right of self government. Nothing in this Agreement will be interpreted, used, or relied upon to undermine the position held by the MNA on this issue."[126]

Each of the MGRSAS also contemplate that they may be constitutionally protected, as a treaty or modern-day land claims agreement in the future: "This Agreement is not a treaty or a land claims agreement within the meaning of section 35(3) of the *Constitution Act, 1982*, however, the Parties agree to consider the potential constitutional protection of this Agreement under section 35(3) of the *Constitution Act, 1982* in the future."[127]

In this same period of time, a national accord between Canada, the MNC, and its Governing Members was signed in April 2017 (the Canada-Métis Nation Accord).[128] While Métis s. 35 rights-related issues, including self-government as well as outstanding Métis land-related claims, are being negotiated by some of the MNC's Governing Members, as Métis governments, through their respective framework agreements, the Canada-Métis Nation Accord established a Permanent Bilateral Mechanism which involves annual meetings between the prime minister, members of the federal Cabinet, and the Métis Nation's leadership. This national process has resulted in a series of Métis-specific investments—topping well over $1 billion over the next decade—in the 2017, 2018, and 2019 federal budgets.[129] These types of direct Métis-specific investments in areas such as housing, education, and child care were previously unheard of.

Conclusion

Time will tell whether these types of Métis-specific investments will be sustained over the long term, and whether these new Crown-Métis Nation negotiations will ultimately lead to lasting settlements and formal Métis self-government recognition in Canadian law. While significant progress has been made on these fronts, more contentious issues such as Métis land rights and scrip as well as outstanding Métis claims remain unresolved. That said, there is room for optimism, and it will be extremely challenging for Canada to pull back from these now established negotiation processes or ignore the need to address Métis land-related issues for much longer.

It is debatable whether all of these relatively recent Canada–Métis Nation developments are solely attributable to *Daniels*; however, the SCC decision has been successfully leveraged by the Métis Nation to push Canada into processes, negotiations, and investments that would have previously been unthinkable. While there are significant dangers in *Daniels* for the Métis Nation (i.e., the reinvigoration of the "Métis-as-mixed" paradigm) and the case has unquestionably emboldened self-Indigenizing individuals and groups, it has also smoothed the way for the Métis Nation and rights-bearing Métis communities to finally secure federal negotiation processes that were previously elusive. Who knows—after all the confusion, contradictions, and hysterics, *Daniels* may simply fall into simply playing its supportive role in completing the trifecta of modern Métis law in Canada. Nothing more. Nothing less.

NOTES

1   Co-managing partner, Pape Salter Teillet LLP. The opinions expressed in this chapter are my own, and may not necessarily reflect those of my Métis or other clients. I would like to thank John Wilson for his assistance in finalizing this chapter.

2   *Daniels v. Canada* (Indian Affairs and Northern Development), 2016 SCC 12.

3   Ibid., at para. 50.

4   Throughout this chapter, I refer to "Aboriginal law" as the law developed by Canadian courts in relation to Indigenous peoples, including their "rights" that are recognized as a part of section 35 of the Constitution Act, 1982. Aboriginal law is different, and is often truncated and more limiting than "Indigenous law," which is a body of law in its own right based on the lands, inherent rights, jurisdictions, and the laws of Indigenous peoples as peoples. Métis Nation law, legal orders and customs are Indigenous law, and should not be confused with modern Métis law related to section 35 that is a component of Aboriginal law.

5   Jason Madden, "*Daniels v. Canada*: Understanding the Inkblot from a Métis Nation Perspective," in *Key Developments in Aboriginal Law 2019*, ed. Thomas Isaac (Toronto: Thomson Reuters, 2019), 85–114. This chapter is based on my previous writings on *Daniels*.

6   I refer to Métis governance structures such as the MNA, MNS, MMF, and MNO as "Métis governments" because they represent rights-bearing Métis communities and components of the Métis Nation. Admittedly these Métis governments currently use provincial legislation to establish "associations," "secretariats," and "corporations" to act as their legal and administrative arms, however, their legitimacy comes from the mandates they receive from their citizens, their democratic elections and their longstanding representative roles. While federal law may not yet formally recognize them as Indigenous governments, they are unquestionably Indigenous "representative institutions" as recognized in the *United Nations Declaration on the Rights of Indigenous Peoples*, arts. 19 & 32. Moreover, I have always personally believed that their legitimacy as governments comes from their longevity and credibility in the eyes of the Métis citizens and communities they represent, not from ultimately being recognized by other governments. It should also be noted that parts of the Métis Nation within Canada are represented by the eight Métis Settlements in Alberta and the Northwest Territories Métis Nation, which are not currently a part of the MNC.

7   The Métis governments and governance structures that form the MNC are known as its "Governing Members."

8   Over the last seventeen years, I have been involved in much of the Métis harvesting rights litigation from Ontario westward, including: *R v. Laviolette*, 2005 SKPC 70; *R v. Goodon*, 2008 MBPC 59; *R. v. Belhumeur*, 2007 SKPC 11; *R. v. Hirsekorn*, 2010 ABPC 385, 2011 ABQB 682, 2013 ABCA 242, as well as in negotiating Métis harvesting agreements in Ontario (2004 and 2018), Manitoba (2012), and Alberta (2019). I have also appeared for Métis clients in all of the SCC cases that have dealt with Métis-specific legal issues since 2003. I currently represent the MNO and MNA in their self-government negotiations with Canada and was counsel for the MMF in their negotiations with Canada on the implementation of *MMF v. Canada* that led to an incremental reconciliation plan worth $154.3 million being announced in September 2018.

9   In *Daniels*, I represented the intervener MMF at the Federal Court of Appeal and the intervener MNC at the SCC.

10 I am a citizen of the Métis Nation and a descendant of the "Halfbreeds of Rainy Lake and River" in northwestern Ontario who collectively adhered to Treaty 3 in 1875. I am a white-passing Métis who has been involved in Métis Nation politics since I was a teenager. As a lawyer, I have collectively spent over a year of my life sitting in courtrooms listening to historians, qualified experts on

Métis language, music, genealogy/kinship/mobility, and, most importantly, Métis Nation elders, citizens, and elected leadership testify about their lived experiences as well as their families and communities. This unique vantage point and experience as well as my own personal experiences inform my understandings set out in this chapter.

11 I use the term "non–Status Indians" to refer to the members of First Nations, or "Indian" peoples (i.e., Cree, Dene, etc.), who have not been registered as "Indians" under section 5 of the Indian Act, RSC, 1985 c I-5.

12 *Daniels v. Canada* (Minister of Indian Affairs and Northern Development), 2013 FC 6 at para. 36.

13 Ibid., at paras. 34–36.

14 *Daniels v. Canada* (Minister of Indian Affairs and Northern Development), 2002 FCT 295; *Daniels v. Canada* (Minister of Indian Affairs and Northern Development), 2008 FC 823.

15 *Daniels v. Canada* (Minister of Indian Affairs and Northern Development), 2005 FC 699, affirmed in 2005 FC 1109.

16 *Daniels v. Canada* (Minister of Indian Affairs and Northern Development), 2011 FC 230.

17 See note 12, at para. 70.

18 Through the *Daniels* litigation, even the Plaintiffs acknowledged that this declaration would not require Parliament to pass *any* laws in relation to them. See Appellants' Factum, 1 April 2015, at para. 51, https://www.scc-csc.ca/WebDocuments-DocumentsWeb/35945/FM010_Appellants_ Harry-Daniels-et-al.pdf.

19 In *Reference re: British North America Act, 1867* (UK), s. 91, [1939] SCR 104,] the SCC confirmed Inuit were "Indians" in s. 91(24). This decision, along with federal policies that responded to the SCC's decision in *Calder v. British Columbia* (Attorney General), [1973] SCR 313, led to federal negotiations and treaty making with Inuit. Today, Canada has achieved four modern-day land claim agreements and the creation of Nunavut through negotiations with the Inuit.

20 While Harry and Gabriel Daniels are undeniably citizens of the Métis Nation, they were plaintiffs in their personal capacities as Métis individuals seeking judicial declarations, not acting in a representative capacity on behalf of a Métis community or the Métis Nation as a whole. Neither the Métis Nation nor authorized representatives of the Métis Nation or Métis communities participated in *Daniels* at the trial level.

21 Royal Commission on Aboriginal Peoples, *Perspectives and Realities*, vol. 4 of *Report of the Royal Commission on Aboriginal Peoples* (Ottawa: Libraxus, 1997), Part 5: "Métis Perspectives," 204–37.

22 While there is no universally accepted definition of a "people," domestic and international jurisprudence has generally taken a very broad view of the term. Without being exhaustive, elements can include common language, history, culture, kinship, race or ethnicity, way of life, and territory. In addition, a subjective element is necessary, whereby a "people" identifies itself as such. For a discussion on these issues, see *Reference re: Secession of Quebec*, [1998] 2 SCR 217 at paras 123–25; Royal Commission on Aboriginal Peoples, *Restructuring the Relationship*, vol. 2 of *Report of the Royal Commission on Aboriginal Peoples* (Ottawa: Communication Group, 1996), Part 1, 169–78, 184. The Métis Nation easily meets any indicia required for peoplehood. It is debatable whether any other "Métis" community or group in Canada would meet these peoplehood criteria.

23 Royal Commission on Aboriginal Peoples, *Perspectives and Realities*, vol. 4 of *Report of the Royal Commission on Aboriginal Peoples*, Part 5: "Métis Perspectives," 216–17.

24 For example, the proper names for other Indigenous peoples are the Cree, the Dene, the Haida. These groups were all called "Indians" by outsiders, but none tie their origin stories or identity to the term "Indian" or being recognized as "Indian" by colonial powers.

25 See *R. v. Belhumeur*, note 8, 2007 SKPC 11: "The Crown submits that the [SCC] clearly contemplated that Metis rights are possessed by individual Metis communities which make up the Metis Nation or the Metis people, not the Nation or the people themselves. . . . I agree with the position of the Crown. *Powley* makes it clear that rights are possessed by '*individual*' communities that may make up a nation." See also *R v. Hirsekorn*, ABAC, note 8, 2013 ABCA 242 at para. 64: "I decline to make a determination with respect to whether there was only one, prairie-wide Métis community during the relevant time period."

26 For example, since 2003, when I attend Métis Nation assemblies or conferences, frequently an individual will proudly identify themselves to me as a "*Powley*-compliant Métis." These sorts of statements demonstrate the powerful and dangerous role courts play in shaping Métis identity and belonging, as opposed to connection to Métis family, kin, community, or the Métis Nation.

27 The United Nations Declaration on the Rights of Indigenous Peoples recognizes the inherent right of Indigenous peoples to define their own membership in Article 33: "Indigenous peoples have the right to determine their own identity or membership in accordance with their customs and traditions."

28 See note 2, at paras. 45–47.

29 Evidence in *Daniels*, Canada Briefing Note for Constitutional Conference, 1984 (Appeal Book, Vol. 35, 1431, Trial Exhibit P52 at 1435).

30 The statement of claim in *Daniels* included the following definition of Métis: "(a) Any person having maternal or paternal Aboriginal ancestors, genetic or otherwise, who were recognized as Metis (or 'Métis,' 'half-breeds,' 'liviers,' or 'settlers'); (b) Any person having only paternal ancestors in category (a) above; (c) Any person having only maternal ancestors in category (a) above; (d) any person who identifies himself or herself as Metis (or as 'Métis') and is accepted as such by the Métis community or locally-organized community branch, chapter or council of a Métis association or organization with which the person wishes to be associated." In contrast, in 2002, the MNC adopted a national definition of "Métis" for citizenship within the Métis Nation, which reads: "'Métis' means a person who self-identifies as Métis, is distinct from other Aboriginal peoples, is of historic Métis Nation Ancestry and who is accepted by the Métis Nation."

31 See RCAP, *Perspectives and Realities*, Part 5: "Métis Perspectives," 217–20, 245–49, 209–10.

32 Since the 1990s, s. 91(24)'s importance in Aboriginal law has significantly diminished. Prior to 1982, s. 91(24) and interjurisdictional immunity were often the only constitutional tool available to protect the lands and interests of the "Indians" from provincial legislation or executive action. Since 1982, s. 35's protection of "aboriginal and treaty rights" provides a constitutional shield that can be used against both federal and provincial legislation that unjustifiably infringes aboriginal or treaty rights. As discussed later in this chapter, the SCC in *Tsilhqot'in Nation v. British Columbia*, 2014 SCC and *Grassy Narrows First Nation v. Ontario (Natural Resources)*, 2014 SCC 48 largely neutered the application of s. 91(24) and interjurisdictional immunity and pointed to s. 35 and the SCC's infringement test as the preferred constitutional tool to protect the lands and interests of the "Indians" (i.e., Aboriginal peoples).

33 *R. v. Powley*, 2003 SCC 43. For other Métis s. 35 harvesting cases advanced by the Métis Nation, see *R. v. Morin & Daigneault*, [1998], 159 Sask R 161 1 CNLR 182 (SKQB), aff'g [1996] 3 CNLR 157 (SKPC); *R v. Goodon*, note 8, 2008 MBPC 59; *R v. Laviolette*, note 8, 2005 SKPC 70; *Belhumeur*, see note 8; *Hirsekorn*, *ABCA*, note 8, aff'g 2011 ABQB 682, and 2010 ABPC 385.

34 *Manitoba Metis Federation Inc v. Canada (Attorney General)*, 2013 SCC 14.

35 Constitution Act, 1867 (UK), 30 & 31 Vict, c 3, S.S. 91 and 92, reprinted in RSC 1985, Appendix II, No 5.

36 For example, see *Campbell v. British Columbia* (AG), 2000 BCSC 1123, and *Sga'nism Sim'augit (Chief Mountain) v. Canada* (AG), 2013 BCCA 49. Both cases challenged the Nisga'a treaty as being unconstitutional because the distribution of powers between s. 91 and s. 92 was exhaustive. In *Campbell* the court found that not all legislative powers fell under ss. 91 and 92, and an Aboriginal right to self-government akin to a legislative power to make laws survived (at paras 65, 81). In *Chief Mountain* the court concluded that it was unnecessary to decide whether the Nisga'a Nation's jurisdiction was derived from an inherent self-government power or delegated authority (at paras 8, 45–46). No appeal of *Campbell* was pursued; the SCC denied leave to appeal the decision in *Chief Mountain*.

37 *Delgamuukw v. British Columbia*, [1997] 3 SCR 1010 at paras. 178, 181.

38 *Tsilhqot'in Nation v. British Columbia*, 2014 SCC 44, note 32, at para. 142.

39 *Delgamuukw*, note 37, at para. 176.

40 *Grassy Narrows First Nation v. Ontario (Natural Resources)*, 2014 SCC 48, note 32 at para. 53.

41 See note 12, at para. 619.

42 Ibid., at paras. 151, 351.

43 Ibid., at para. 318.

44 Ibid., at para. 311.

45 Ibid., at para. 428.

46 Ibid., at para. 399.

47 Ibid., at para. 415.

48 Ibid., at para. 410.

49 Ibid., at para. 532.

50 Ibid., at para. 532.

51 Ibid., at para. 113.

52 Ibid., at para. 117.

53 Ibid., at paras. 607–9.

54 Ibid., at paras. 611, 614.

55 *Canada (Indian Affairs) v. Daniels*, 2014 FCA 101.

56 Ibid., at para. 3.

57 The FCA rejected Canada's arguments that the first declaration had no practical utility because there needed to be proposed legislation to answer a jurisdiction question based on Canada's constitution (paras. 68–69); that a finding of jurisdiction created no obligation to legislate (para. 70) and that this was really about federal spending priorities, not a jurisdictional issue (para. 72).

58 See note 55, at paras. 73, 151.

59 Ibid., at para. 76.

60 Ibid., at para. 79.

61 Ibid., at para. 81.

62 See note 12, at para. 117.

63 See note 55, at para. 85.

64 Ibid., at para. 88.

65 Ibid., at para. 100.

66 Ibid., at para. 97.

67 Ibid., at para. 98.

68 Ibid., at paras. 110.

69 Ibid., at para. 110.

70 Ibid., at para. 111.

71 Ibid., at para. 159.

72 Ibid., at paras. 159, 156–58.

73 See note 2, at para. 15.

74 Ibid., at paras. 14, 50.

75 Ibid., at paras. 4–5, 10,.25.

76 Ibid., at para. 25.

77 Ibid., at para. 17.

78 Ibid., at para. 19.

79 Ibid., at para. 17.

80 Ibid., at para. 19.

81 Métis were considered "Indians" for the purposes of pre-Confederation treaties such as the Robinson Treaties of 1850 (para. 24); many post-Confederation federal statutes included Métis (paras. 24, 27); the federal government's residential school policy encompassed Métis (paras. 28–30); the issuance of Métis scrip and moving Métis in and out of the Indian Act (paras. 31–32).

82 See note 2, at para. 26. The SCC also noted that the Métis blocked surveyors and prevented Canada's expansion if "they were unhappy with the Canadian government," which necessitated Canada being able to have the jurisdiction to deal with Métis demands.

83 Ibid., at paras. 34–37.

84 Ibid., at para. 35.

85 *Re Eskimo*, see note 19; *Attorney General of Canada v. Canard*, [1976] 1 SCR 170.

86 See note 2, at para. 41.

87 In *R. v. Blais*, 2003 SCC 44, the SCC held Métis were not included as "Indians" in Manitoba's Natural Resources Transfer Agreement, 1930. The SCC distinguished that *Blais* was about whether Métis were included in a specific constitutional agreement, while *Daniels* was about jurisdiction in Canada's constitution.

88 See note 2, at para. 46.

89 Ibid., at para. 46.

90 Ibid., at para. 47.

91 Ibid., at paras. 46–49.

92 Ibid., at para. 49.

93 Ibid., at paras. 34, 49; *Haida Nation v. British Columbia (Minister of Forests)*, 2004 SCC 73 at paras. 20, 25.

94 See note 2, at paras. 48–49.

95 Ibid., at para. 50.

96 Ibid., at para. 53. In *Delgamuukw* (see note 37), the SCC confirmed that the Crown is in a fiduciary relationship with all Aboriginal peoples as well as Métis specifically (*MMF*, see note 34).

97 See note 2, at para. 56.

98 Ibid., at para. 50.

99 See note 37, at para. 176.

100 See note 32; note 41.

101 See note 2, at para. 56.

102 Ibid.

103 On the contrary, several lower courts had previously recognized that the Crown maintains absolute discretion on if and when to negotiate with Indigenous groups (*Huron-Wendat Nation of Wendake v. Canada*, 2014 FC 1154 at para. 121; *Aundeck Omni Kaning v. Canada*, 2014 SCTC 1 at para. 87; *Mohawks of the Bay of Quinte v. the Minister of Indian Affairs and Northern Development*, 2013 FC 669 at para. 45; *Chemainus First Nation v. British Columbia Assets and Lands Corporation*, [1999] 3 CNLR 8 at paras. 25, 26).

104 The Specific Claims Policy and Specific Claims Tribunal Act, SC 2008, c 22 is expressly limited to "First Nations" which are defined (in section 2 of the Act) as a band under the Indian Act, or a group of persons that was but is no longer a band and has retained the right to bring a specific claim. On its face, this definition excludes the Métis as a distinct Aboriginal people who were not and are not Indian "bands." Likewise, Canada's Comprehensive Claims Policy has a number of outdated assumptions within it that act as barriers to Métis claims, including the use of "pre-contact" language and citing only the test for s. 35 Indian rights in *R v. Van der Peet*, [1996] 2 SCR 507, as opposed to mentioning *Powley* for Métis rights claims.

105 See note 55, at para. 72.

106 See note 2, at paras. 48–49.

107 *Powley*, see note 33.

108 *Van der Peet*, see note 104.

109 See note 2, at para. 37.

110 *Haida,* see note 93, at para. 32 (emphasis added).

111 See note 2, at para. 49.

112 Ibid., at para. 1.

113 For example, the Manitoba Métis, as represented by the MMF, already had established s. 35 Métis rights in Manitoba (*Goodon*, note 8) a judicially-recognized claim against the federal Crown (*MMF*, note 35) and were expressly acknowledged in *Daniels* as a distinct Métis community that fell within s. 91(24)'s scope (*Daniels,* note 2, at para. 42).

114 Thomas Isaac, "A Matter of National and Constitutional Import: Report of the Minister's Special Representative on Reconciliation with Métis: Section 35 Métis Rights and the *Manitoba Metis Federation* Decision," Indigenous and Northern Affairs Canada, June 2016, http://www.aadnc-aandc.gc.ca/eng/1467641790303/1467641835266.

115 Liberal Party of Canada, "Liberals Announce Reconciliation Plan for the Métis Nation," 29 September 2015, https://www.liberal.ca/liberals-announce-reconciliation-plan-for-the-metis-nation/.

116 Prime Minister Justin Trudeau, Mandate letter to Dr. Carolyn Bennett, Minister of Indigenous and Northern Affairs, 2015, last modified 12 November 2015, https://pm.gc.ca/eng/minister-indigenous-and-northern-affairs-mandate-letter_2015.

117 In May 2016, the MMF and Canada signed the first of these Memorandums of Understanding on Advancing Reconciliation (MOUs). Other MOUs were signed between Canada and the MNO, MNA, MNS, MNBC and the MSGC between May 2016 and December 2017.

118 The MMF-Canada Framework Agreement is unique when compared to other framework agreements signed with Métis groups because it also contemplates addressing the SCC's decision in *MMF*.

119 Notably, the MNO's framework agreement includes the province of Ontario as a signatory, and a separate bilateral agreement was signed between Canada and the Métis community in northwestern Ontario to attempt to find a shared solution in relation to the 1875 Adhesion to Treaty #3 signed with the "Halfbreeds of Rainy Lake and River." Both the MNA and MNS framework agreements include commitments to address Métis scrip as well as a process to address the MNS's Aboriginal title claim that was filed in the courts in 1994.

120 In *Daniels*, the evidence disclosed showed that the OFI warned other departments internally that the pursuit of negotiations with the Métis in the Northwest Territories "may be interpreted as an acknowledgement of Métis rights [that] . . . would be problematic in that it would be difficult for the federal government to deny a similar process for Métis South of 60." This letter urged Canada to not pursue negotiations with the Métis north of the 60th parallel bilaterally, because it "would set a troublesome precedent for both provincial and federal governments." In reading this evidence, I was reminded of the saying "with friends like that, who needs enemies?" See letters from Claude Rocan, Director, OFI, to Philippe Doré, Senior Negotiator, Department of Indian Affairs and Northern Development (Appeal Book, Volume 43, Trial Exhibit P156 at 2954–2955 and Exhibit P158 at 2961–2965).

121 Manitoba Metis Federation, "Manitoba Metis Federation and Government of Canada Announce Joint Action Plan on Advancing Reconciliation," 22 September 2018, https://www.newswire.ca/news-releases/manitoba-metis-federation-and-government-of-canada-announce-joint-action-plan-on-advancing-reconciliation-694047101.html.

122 Métis Nation of Alberta, "After 90 Years, Métis Nation within Alberta Achieves Federal Recognition of Its Self-Government—Métis Nation of Alberta and Canada Sign Historic Agreement in Ottawa," 27 June 2019, http://albertametis.com/wp-content/uploads/2019/07/MNA-MGRSA-FAQ-DOCUMENT-V7.pdf; Métis Nation of Ontario, "Métis Nation of Ontario and Canada Sign Breakthrough Agreement on Self-Government," 27 June 2019, http://www.metisnation.org/media/655331/2019-06-27-metis-government-recognition-and-self-government-agreement.pdf; and Métis Nation of Saskatchewan, "Métis Nation-Saskatchewan Signs Historic Self-Governance Agreement with the Government of Canada," 27 June 2019, https://metisnationsk.com/wp-content/uploads/2019/06/M%C3%A9tis-Government-Recognition-and-Self-Government-Agreement-.pdf.

123 For example, Chapter 3 of the Canada-MNA MGRSA provides: "Upon signing of this Agreement, Canada recognizes that: (a) the MNA is mandated to represent the Métis Nation within Alberta; (b) the Métis Nation within Alberta has an inherent right to self-government over their internal governance that is protected by sections 25 and 35 of the Constitution Act, 1982; and, (c) the MNA has been mandated by the Métis Nation within Alberta to implement its

inherent right to self-government that is protected by sections 25 and 35 of the Constitution Act, 1982." Similar clauses are included in both the MNO and MNS MGRSAs.

124 For the most part, modern-day treaties or land claims agreements, as contemplated by section 35(3) of the Constitution Act, 1982, are negotiated between: (1) the Executive branch of the federal government based on the royal prerogative and/or s. 91(24), (2) representatives from the Executive branches of relevant provincial and/or territorial governments (where appropriate or required), and (3) the modern-day representatives of Indigenous peoples *before* ratification and/ or execution by the citizenship and/or political representatives of the Indigenous treaty nation or collective as well as the relevant Executive branches of public governments. Similar to international treaties, these agreements are then "approved, given effect and declared valid and [have] the force of law" through implementation legislation adopted by Parliament (and in some situations similar provincial legislation), which binds third parties and becomes a part of the Canadian law. For example see, Tlicho Land Claims and Self-Government Act, SC 2005, c 1, s. 3(1). Uniquely and strategically, the MGRSAs contemplate this type of federal implementation legislation being adopted *prior to* all aspects of these Métis self-government negotiations being finalized. The rationale for this reverse engineered approach in the Métis context was that the upfront implementation legislation would anchor these negotiations as well as the commitments in MGRSAs, as opposed to Métis self-government negotiations being subject to political whim and/or ever-changing Aboriginal policies at the federal level.

125 Canada-MNA MGRSA, Chapter 5. The same chapter is included in both the MNO and MNS MGRSAs.

126 Canada-MNA MGRSA, s. 3.03. A similar clause is included in both the MNO and MNS MGRSAs.

127 Canada-MNA MGRSA, s. 28.02. A similar clause is included in both the MNO and MNS MGRSAs.

128 Canada–Métis Nation Accord, 13 April 2017, https://pm.gc.ca/en/canada-metis-nation-accord.

129 See Métis-specific commitments in the federal budgets for the years 2016, 2017, 2018, and 2019, at https://www.canada.ca/en/department-finance/services/publications/federal-budget.html.

CHAPTER 4

Daniels v. Canada: A Framework for Redress

AREND J.A. HOEKSTRA AND THOMAS ISAAC[1]

The Supreme Court of Canada (SCC) has a long, and at times confusing, history of evolving the language it uses to refer to Indigenous peoples. Some of this evolution, such as substituting "Inuit" for "Eskimo" and "Métis" for "Half-breed," matched the language of section 35 of the Constitution Act, 1982[2] and addressed obviously objectionable terminology. Other changes, such as the occasional adoption of the term "Native" and regular use of the term "First Nation," have arisen in response to other factors, including evolving legislative terms, and political and social practices.

The SCC took decades to transition from using "Indian" toward the constitutionally defined term "Aboriginal." This transition started before the Constitution Act, 1982. In *Kruger et al. v. The Queen*[3] (1978) and *Paulette et al. v. The Queen*[4] (1977), the SCC referred to "aboriginal rights" while still referring to Indigenous peoples as "Indians." In the years following the enactment of the Constitution Act, 1982, "Indian" was still the predominantly used term; however, the SCC increasingly employed "aboriginal" when referring to broader groups and rights. Finally, in *Native Women's Assn. of Canada v. Canada* [1994],[5] the SCC adopted the use of the capitalized noun "Aboriginal" to refer to both Indigenous peoples and their associated rights. However, *Native Women's Assn. of Canada* did not mark a completed transition, and over the following years, the SCC continued to use the lower-case "aboriginal" and even occasionally "Indians."

The transition to "Aboriginal" occurred during a period of limited comment on Aboriginal rights by the SCC. By 1990, when the landmark decision of *Sparrow*[6] was delivered, "Aboriginal" had been fully adopted as the appropriate descriptor for s. 35 Aboriginal and treaty rights. By 1996, a landmark year for SCC decisions on Aboriginal law—which included such decisions as *Gladstone*,[7] *Van der Peet*,[8] and *Badger*,[9]—the SCC had fully replaced the use of "Indian" with "Aboriginal."

In understanding the perspectives, objectives, and direction of the SCC, it is reasonable to consider the precise language applied by the court. The jurisprudence that has evolved from s. 35 of the Constitution Act, 1982, in particular, has relied on the precise and careful use of language to provide substantial and applicable direction for an imprecise constitutional clause. In considering Daniels and s. 91(24) of the Constitution Act, 1867,[10] such reliance on the precise language of the court is also both reasonable and necessary.

The evolution of language is an important element of *Daniels*.[11] *Daniels* concerns s. 91(24) of the Constitution Act, 1867, specifically whether Métis are "Indians" for the purposes of s. 91(24). In its analysis, the SCC considered the 1939 Reference as to whether "Indians" includes "Eskimo"[12] and historic laws relating to the treatment of "half-breeds." In making its decision, the SCC did more than simply expand the legal definition of an antiquated but constitutionally enshrined term; the SCC also added a new term to Canadian Aboriginal legal discourse: "Indigenous."

However, *Daniels* is about more than language. *Daniels* is about the examination of identity and the search for redress. Prompted, potentially, by the *Final Report of the Truth and Reconciliation Commission*, the SCC appears to use *Daniels* to create a conceptual framework around s. 91(24) that contrasts with s. 35. Where s. 35 focuses on the prospective constitutional protection of the rights of Aboriginal peoples through the constraint of Crown authority, the s. 91(24) developed by the SCC in *Daniels* focuses on the retrospective redress of harms to individuals that resulted from Crown actions targeted at Indigenous peoples. This new framework relies on a broad categorization of "Indigenous" and a nuanced understanding of "redress" focused on political and moral responsibility.

Who Are "Aboriginal Peoples"?

The definition of "Aboriginal peoples" is set out in s. 35(2) of the Constitution Act, 1982: "in this Act, 'aboriginal peoples of Canada' includes the
Indian, Inuit and Métis peoples of Canada."[13] "Indians," for the purposes of
s. 35, comprise those Indigenous peoples more commonly known as First
Nations and represents those communities of peoples who predate the assertion of British sovereignty over Canada. "Inuit" are those peoples who occupied in 1867, as they do now, the northern littoral of the North American
continent from Alaska to Labrador.[14] Finally, Métis refers to those distinctive peoples who, in addition to having mixed Indian or Inuit and European
heritage, "developed their own customs, way of life, and recognizable group
identity separate from their Indian or Inuit forebears."[15]

The SCC has never examined the meaning of the word "includes" in the
sentence "'aboriginal peoples of Canada' *includes*" (emphasis added). This
word suggests that the peoples protected by s. 35 may be more expansive
than just Indian, Inuit, and Métis peoples. This phrasing raises an important
question: Who, besides those listed expressly in s. 35(2), could be considered
Aboriginal for the purposes of s. 35?

In *Powley*, the SCC set out a three-part test for determining whether
an individual was Métis for the purposes of s. 35. First, the claimant must
self-identify as a member of a Métis community.[16] Second, the claimant must
present evidence of an ancestral connection to a historic Métis community
by birth, adoption, or other means.[17] Third, the claimant must demonstrate
that he or she is accepted by the modern community whose continuity with
the historic community provides the legal foundation for claimed s. 35 rights.
This requires ongoing participation in a shared culture and in those customs
and traditions that constitute the Métis community's unique identity.[18]

In *Daniels*, the SCC modified the *Powley* test for those qualifying as s.
91(24) "Indians." To qualify as Métis under s. 91(24), claimants would no
longer need to show participation in, and acceptance by, the community.
While the court expressly stated that this modified test applied to s. 91(24)
peoples and not to s. 35 peoples,[19] it demonstrates the flexibility the court has
employed in categorizing Indigenous peoples for constitutional purposes.[20]

Who Are "Indigenous Peoples"?

At the time of writing, with nearly two years having passed following the delivery of *Daniels*, the SCC's intended use of the term "Indigenous" is clearer than when *Daniels* was first delivered. The SCC's subsequent use of the term in *Chippewas of the Thames First Nation*[21] and *Clyde River (Hamlet)*[22] provide additional insights into the SCC's new preference for the term "Indigenous" instead of "Aboriginal." However, the SCC's choice to use the term in the unique circumstances presented in *Daniels* continues to raise uncertainty with regard to its full meaning as a noun. Prior to *Daniels*, the SCC had only used the term "Indigenous" in an Aboriginal law context eight times.[23] In these instances, the word was used as an adjective and never as a capitalized noun.

The SCC's Clear Intention

Prior to *Daniels*, the SCC had consistently used the term "Aboriginal" with regard to both s. 35 rights and peoples holding those rights, and had almost no history of using "Indigenous" in any form. To practitioners of Aboriginal law, prior to *Daniels*, "Indigenous" as a legal term referred to the United Nations Declaration on the Rights of Indigenous Peoples and, more broadly, to the protection of the rights of Indigenous peoples in the international context.[24]

The SCC's use of "Indigenous" within *Daniels* was significantly restrained, appearing only five times in the decision.[25] "Indigenous" appears almost entirely at the beginning of the decision, and there is no occurrence of the word in the second half, including in any of the analytical discussion. Instead, the analysis and conclusions heavily use "Aboriginal" in reference to both rights and peoples. This restraint in the use of "Indigenous" and the continued reliance on the term "Aboriginal" alludes to the court's potential concern about creating uncertainty within the law.

The SCC's restraint should not be construed as a lack of intent or purpose in using the term "Indigenous." The SCC used the term in its opening paragraph when it set the tone for the remainder of the decision: "As the curtain opens wider and wider on the history of Canada's relationship with its Indigenous peoples, inequities are increasingly revealed and remedies urgently sought. Many revelations have resulted in good faith policy and legislative responses, but the list of disadvantages remains robust. This case represents another chapter in the pursuit of reconciliation and redress in that relationship."[26] This intention to employ "Indigenous" was further evidenced by how the court summarized the decisions of the Federal Court and the Court of Appeal. In two instances, the SCC incorporated the term "Indigenous" while rephrasing the findings of the lower courts, despite the fact that neither employed "Indigenous" as a proper noun. As will be discussed later in this chapter, the SCC's continued and increased use of the term "Indigenous" within the 2017 decisions *Clyde River (Hamlet)* and *Chippewas of the Thames First Nation* further evidence its intentional deployment of the noun.

The Meaning of "Indigenous"

While the SCC's intention to use "Indigenous" as a term is clear, the meaning of the term is less clear. The most reasonable interpretation of the term "Indigenous," given the context of *Daniels*, is that it is intended to encompass all peoples covered by s. 91(24) rather than just those peoples possessing s. 35 rights. This interpretation is supported by the way "Indigenous" is used within *Daniels*, being prefaced by the word "all" in three of the five times it occurs. The broad interpretation is also supported by the SCC's expansion of the *Powley* test for the purposes of s. 91(24), which appears to create a distinction between "Aboriginal" Métis possessing s. 35 rights, and those Métis who are subject only to federal legislative authority under s. 91(24).

This broad interpretation is challenged by the SCC's use of language when referring to the modified *Powley* test. The SCC states: "Section 91(24) serves a very different constitutional purpose. It is about the federal government's relationship with Canada's *Aboriginal peoples*" (emphasis added).[27] The use of "Aboriginal peoples" in this context is challenging to explain. Given the clear intention of the SCC to use the noun "Indigenous," it is unclear why this occurrence of "Aboriginal" appears within the broad context of s. 91(24). Not only does the quote challenge any purposeful interpretation of "Indigenous," it also unnecessarily conflates those peoples possessing s. 35 rights with those subject to s. 91(24).

This problematic language may be testament to the novel use of the term "Indigenous." As will be seen elsewhere, the SCC's initial use of "Indigenous" has not been consistent, and raises important questions about the nature of identity, rights, reconciliation, and redress.

Culture and Race

The extent to which "Indigenous" may categorize peoples other than Aboriginal peoples is not clear from *Daniels*. The SCC's modification of the *Powley* test results in the only specifically identifiable difference between those peoples included in s. 35 and those included in s. 91(24). The expansion of the *Powley* test raises important questions and possibilities around the confluence of s. 35, s. 91(24), race/ancestry, and culture.

To date, the SCC has always framed Aboriginal rights in terms of both race/ ancestry and community. In *Van der Peet*, the SCC found that "the doctrine of aboriginal rights exists, and is recognized and affirmed by s. 35(1), because of one simple fact: when Europeans arrived in North America, aboriginal peoples *were already here*, living in communities on the land, and participating in distinctive cultures, as they had done for centuries" (emphasis in original).[28]

The SCC has likewise framed Aboriginal rights as specific rights held by a society. Aboriginal rights are derived from social practice: they are practices, customs, or traditions that form a central and significant part of the society's distinctive culture.[29] These activities are more than just the incidental activities common to every culture and society. Instead, they are what "*made the society what it was*" (emphasis in original).[30]

Though more broad than other Aboriginal rights, Aboriginal title is likewise a communal right, limited by communal constraints: "Aboriginal title cannot be held by individual aboriginal persons; it is a collective right to land held by all members of an aboriginal nation. Decisions with respect to that land are also made by that community."[31]

The SCC has been clear that claiming s. 35 Aboriginal rights on the basis of Inuit or First Nation ancestry alone is insufficient. Though the SCC has not examined whether Inuit and First Nations peoples can exercise asserted rights outside of their communities, other courts have found that a modern connection to a historic community is essential.[32]

The test set out in *Powley* for Métis rights followed the SCC's approach to Aboriginal rights generally. To reiterate, the test set out in *Powley* and summarized in *Daniels* "for defining who qualifies as Métis for the purposes of s. 35(1) [is]:

Self-identification as a Métis;

An ancestral connection to an historic Métis community; and

Acceptance by the modern Métis community."[33]

The *Powley* test sets out clearly what is implied by the SCC generally with regard to Aboriginal rights: Aboriginal rights require both a racial/ancestral element and a distinct societal one. The racial/ancestral element is explicit in s. 35: not all societies are protected by s. 35, only Aboriginal societies. The societal element has been made clear through consistent jurisprudence: the objective of reconciliation is not with individuals but rather between the Crown and Aboriginal communities and, more broadly, societies.[34]

The SCC's approach in *Daniels* suggests that this convergence of race/ancestry and culture may not necessarily apply to the "Indigenous" categorization for the purposes of s. 91(24). As noted, the amended *Powley* test, which removed the requirement for current acceptance by a modern Métis community, leaves the test as a predominantly racial/ancestral test for the purposes of s. 91(24), whereby an applicant must show that they have a connection to a "historic Métis community by birth, adoption, or other means."[35] The court justifies this amendment by stating that "there is no principled reason for presumptively and arbitrarily excluding them from Parliament's protective authority on the basis of a "community acceptance test."[36]

By modifying the *Powley* test, the SCC has created the opportunity for other individuals with Aboriginal ancestry to be included under s. 91(24). Such individuals may include those who have disassociated from their ancestral community, or who discover their Aboriginal ancestry later in life. While s. 91(24) appears broader than s. 35, the scope of those impacted by s. 91(24) or with recourse thereto will depend on the functional purpose of s. 91(24).

Redress and Reconciliation

The pursuit of "redress" forms a significant theme within *Daniels*. The need for redress is highlighted, both in the introductory paragraph and again when the SCC explains the implications of inclusion under s. 91(24). As the SCC states, "finding Métis and non-status Indians to be 'Indians' under s. 91(24) does not create a duty to legislate, but it has the undeniably salutary benefit of ending a jurisdictional tug-of-war in which these groups were left wondering about where to turn for policy *redress*" (emphasis added).[37] This focus on redress does not occur in isolation within *Daniels*. Instead, the need for redress and the subjects of redress themselves provide a context for understanding the scc's framework of "Indigenous peoples," s. 91(24), and redress.

While the term "redress" is only employed twice in *Daniels*, it is necessary for understanding the decision. The scc implies that s. 91(24) is intended to provide a form of relief for those seeking a declaration.[38] The scc also affirms that s. 91(24) does not create a duty to legislate.[39] Besides "redress," the scc provides no other alternatives for what remedies Indigenous peoples can procure from the federal government on account of s. 91(24).

Redress as a concept contrasts with the scc's oft-stated desire for "reconciliation." Reconciliation as a concept is fundamentally connected with s. 35 and the associated Aboriginal peoples. As the scc stated in *Tsilhqot'in*: "Section 35 of the Constitution Act, 1982 represents 'the culmination of a long and difficult struggle in both the political forum and the courts for the constitutional recognition of Aboriginal rights.'[40] It protects Aboriginal rights against provincial and federal legislative power and *provides a framework to facilitate negotiations and reconciliation of Aboriginal interests with those of the broader public*" (emphasis added).[41] Reconciliation does not occur individually, but rather between the Crown and Aboriginal communities. This reconciliation is focused on the coexistence of different cultures and different legal systems. As the scc quoted in *Delgamuukw*, "[the] basic purpose of s. 35(1)—is 'the reconciliation of the pre-existence of aboriginal societies with the sovereignty of the Crown.' Let us face it, we are all here to stay."[42] While reconciliation at times allows for the peaceful coexistence of practices and communities, when s. 35 rights come into conflict with other laws, it can also require the restraint of the Crown and Parliament's laws. Section 35 "protects Aboriginal rights against provincial and federal legislative power and provides a framework to facilitate negotiations and reconciliation of Aboriginal interests with those of the broader public."[43] In *Sparrow*, the scc noted that "the best way to achieve that reconciliation is to demand the justification of any government regulation that infringes upon or denies Aboriginal rights."[44]

Reconciliation and the classification of "Aboriginal people" holding s. 35 rights share common attributes. They are focused on a collective social existence. Aboriginal rights are collectively held rights and inalienable except to the Crown.[45] Reconciliation allows for the continued exercise of those distinct communal and cultural activities that predate the assertion of Crown sovereignty. Reconciliation acts as a double-edged sword, cutting into Aboriginal rights and the Crown's sovereign powers depending on the nature of the overlap.

Reconciliation is conceptually focused on societies and in practice it is only possible on a societal level. Reconciliation in practice is burdensome. It requires the production of evidence and ongoing dialogue. The Crown is obligated to inform itself of the rights and interests of those it seeks reconciliation with, and where appropriate, to temper its sovereign authority. Given this burden, reconciliation is most effective when sought in relation to larger social groups with specific, identifiable, and locatable rights. Larger communities are more likely to have the capacity to communicate effectively with the Crown. They are also better equipped to bring forth evidence of rights, and to identify and evaluate the potential implications of the Crown's actions.

The process of reconciliation, as contemplated by the SCC, does not occur at the individual level, although individuals may very well be affected by it. The Crown cannot effectively communicate with individual rights holders, and even if it could, individuals are not sufficiently equipped to effectively engage in reconciliation. The possibility of reconciling with the Crown on an individual basis is also inconsistent with the very principle of reconciliation, as the Crown would be so burdened by individual rights as to effectively undermine its sovereign power.

Whereas s. 35 seeks reconciliation between the Crown and Aboriginal communities, "section 91(24) serves a very different constitutional purpose."[46] Section 91(24) addresses Canada's relationship with Canada's Indigenous people generally. As the court notes, "this includes [individual] people who may no longer be accepted by their communities because they were separated from them as a result, for example, of government policies such as Indian Residential Schools."[47]

It is within the context of examining s. 91(24) that the SCC introduced the concept of redress, which contrasts with reconciliation in s. 35. As the court notes, "s. 91(24) does not create a duty to legislate"[48] but instead provides an avenue "for policy redress."[49] While reconciliation is focused on the sustainable coexistence and accommodation of conflicting interests, redress appears focused instead on the amelioration of individual harms and events. While reconciliation is focused on preserving communally held rights, redress within the context of *Daniels* does not depend on the existence or preservation of a community.

Redress and "Indigenous"

The SCC's use of "Indigenous" may be partially an attempt to capture those *individuals* needing redress, and may provide an indication of those individuals categorized as "Indigenous." While reconciliation can protect cultural practices with impacted Aboriginal peoples, it is ineffective at addressing specific harm caused by the Crown's actions toward individuals.

One example of harm caused by the Crown against individuals, and which the court focuses on exclusively, is the Indian residential school system and its legacy. The SCC in *Daniels* referred to Indian residential schools on four separate occasions,[50] and mentioned that "the federal government has since acknowledged and apologized for wrongs such as Indian Residential Schools."[51] The court notes that despite s. 91(24) only referring to "Indians," Métis were included in the Indian Residential School system.[52] This reference by the court to "Métis" people, given its amendment to the *Powley* test, could apply to both s. 35 Métis peoples and non-Métis peoples of mixed ancestry.

Within this context, it appears that the SCC is not only attempting to encompass Aboriginal peoples within the definition of "Indigenous" but also those persons who were impacted by the Crown's actions because the Crown *perceived them* to be Indigenous persons. Such a definition would encompass not only those peoples with a shared culture and ancestry but also those persons who are "Indigenous" by race/ancestry alone.

The Uncertainty of Redress

The SCC's use of the term "redress" within *Daniels* produces uncertainty, both internally and within a broader legal framework. Redress appears to suggest a process of amelioration defined and limited in scope and duration. For those individuals subjected to the Indian Residential School system, redress may have been accomplished through the Truth and Reconciliation Commission and the associated settlements. Such efforts are, in their application, retrospective, attempting to cure historic or ongoing harms.

This model of redress is challenged by the court's suggestion that s. 91(24) offers an avenue "for policy redress."[53] Policy, in practice, is prospective. It looks to address current structural harms and offences and tends to be neither limited in scope nor in duration. "Policy redress" suggests instead a form of continuing reconciliation, an undertaking by the Crown to prospectively modify its behaviour and constrain its actions. The court's use of Indian residential schools as an example for redress does not alight with this call for "policy redress" and leaves unclear the intentions of the court.

A second challenge with the concept of redress is with its practical obtainment. The court states that "s. 91(24) does not create a duty to legislate. . . . [instead] it has the undeniably salutary benefit of ending a jurisdictional tug-of-war in which these groups were left wondering about where to turn for policy redress."[54] Using the court's example of survivors of Indian residential schools, it is unclear how s. 91(24) provides a meaningful remedy for the abuses that occurred. Survivors have a right to claim damages against those who harmed them and those who were complicit in their harm. Section 91(24) provides no additional avenue of *legal* redress.

It is possible that redress is not intended to be legal, but instead, moral, and political, as we have suggested elsewhere.[55] The Indian residential school settlement and Parliament's apology were the result of political and moral forces. By assigning responsibility to Parliament for past harms to Indigenous peoples and ending the "tug-of-war" between provinces and the federal government, the court may be directing and focusing political pressure on the federal government, while also informing Parliament of its moral obligations. This interpretation is relevant with regard to the legacy of Indian residential schools but may have limited practical value for other Indigenous peoples who are not able to attract the same level of political sympathy and engagement.

A third challenge with the court's focus on redress is its origin. While the SCC states that s. 91(24) is about redress, the historical evidence it considers shows that in relation to non–First Nations peoples, s. 91(24) was predominantly a tool for supporting the expansionist ambitions of the federal government[56] and efforts of cultural integration.[57] The more readily apparent interpretation is that s. 91(24), which allocates a federal power under the Constitution Act, 1867, is about the allocation of responsibility and, potentially, specific obligations, though the court reduces the effectiveness of such an assertion by confirming that s. 91(24) does not create a duty to legislate.[58] Instead, the court's introduction of "redress" appears to be a novel purpose for an otherwise empty constitutional bucket (at least as it relates to mixed ancestry and Métis peoples).

A fourth challenge with the SCC's focus on redress relates to the beneficiaries of redress. As noted earlier, *Daniels* diverges from the language typically used in relation to s. 35 in finding that the categorization of "Indigenous peoples" does not require a cultural or community element, and instead can be determined on race or ancestry alone. In practice, this suggests that s. 91(24) is intended to address harms to specific Indigenous individuals who are not members of Aboriginal groups and who may never be subject to the Crown's efforts for reconciliation. It is unclear why the federal government should have a specific "constitutional responsibility"[59] with regard to offering redress to specific individuals based on ancestry or race alone. The federal government has, over the years, allowed for harm to be caused to many groups of people, including through the internment of Japanese Canadians and the charging of a "head tax" on certain immigrants. These harms may have been long-lasting and some have been the subject of Parliamentary apologies. To distinguish some on the basis of race or ancestry alone raises questions about the equality of Canadians.

As with the challenges of "policy redress" noted earlier, the focus on providing redress to the broad scope of "Indigenous peoples" appears in practice to be a modified, less constricted form of s. 35 reconciliation. Where s. 35 has always focused on the prospective coexistence of the Crown and Aboriginal communities, the Court's use of s. 91(24) appears as an attempt, at least partly, to address historic grievances and encourage dialogue.

Redress and the Truth and Reconciliation Commission

The SCC referred to Canada's history of Indian residential schools on four separate occasions within *Daniels*. In addition, the concept of redress was associated solely with the Indian Residential School system; the Court provided no other examples of the ills and harms that its framework of "Indigenous," s. 91(24), and redress could address.

The *Final Report of the Truth and Reconciliation in Canada*,[60] which explored the history of Canada's Indian residential schools, was released in July 2015, shortly before the 8 October hearing date for *Daniels*. It is clear that the SCC gave consideration to the report when formulating its decision. The court made specific reference to the *Final Report* in five paragraphs and twice quoted it directly. At the time of its release, the *Final Report* was the subject of significant public discourse, discourse that often related to Canada's historic and continuing treatment of Indigenous peoples. Prior to *Daniels,* the SCC was absent from this discourse, though Chief Justice McLachlin had, less than two months prior to the release of the *Final Report*, stated that

Canada had attempted to commit "cultural genocide" through such programs as Indian residential schools.[61]

Given this context, it is possible that the broad approach the court took in *Daniels*—which, based on the requested declaration "that Métis and non-status Indians are 'Indians' under s. 91(24),"[62] did not require the language of "Indigenous" or "redress," or the expansion of the *Powley* test—was intended to provide a framework for addressing the harms identified in the *Truth and Reconciliation Commission Report*.

The Future of Redress

A challenge with the SCC's focus on the Indian Residential School system is whether the framework set out in *Daniels* has jurisprudential value. When considering factors requiring redress, the court focused exclusively on the Indian Residential School system, a matter that was settled in 2007.[63] The 1982 enactment of s. 35 provided Aboriginal peoples with protection against efforts to culturally assimilate Indigenous peoples. The Canadian Charter of Rights and Freedoms[64] was enacted at the same time, constraining the Crown's ability to adversely impact all Canadians, including non-Aboriginal Indigenous peoples. The last of the Indian residential schools were closed when these constitutional enactments were in their infancy.[65]

While a legacy of unredressed harm may still exist, s. 35 and the Canadian Charter of Rights and Freedoms should limit the causation of new harms. So long as "redress" remains focused on the amelioration of past harms, it is conceivable that the framework set out in *Daniels* may not be needed in the future.

Conclusions on the *Daniels* Framework

Within the context of *Daniels*, "Indigenous" appears to be used to define a broad category of people who, by ancestry or race, are connected with those Aboriginal peoples who occupied Canada before European settlement. Though the breadth of both the "Indigenous" classification and s. 91(24) appears expansive, the purpose of s. 91(24), as suggested by the court, significantly limits those who in practice are impacted by s. 91(24). If the purpose of s. 91(24) is to provide an avenue for redress, those potentially impacted by *Daniels* and s. 91(24) are Indigenous individuals who, as a consequence of their identity as an Indigenous person, have been harmed by the Crown.

Within this context, s. 91(24) provides a framework that includes Indigenous peoples and the concept of redress. This s. 91(24) framework sits in contrast with the s. 35 framework, which impacts Aboriginal peoples and focuses on reconciliation. Though not clearly elucidated by the court, it appears that these two frameworks are complementary tools intended to help address both the retrospective and prospective relationship between the Crown, Aboriginal peoples, and Indigenous individuals.

As will be discussed below, the effectiveness of this conceptual structure for Indigenous peoples and s. 91(24) depends on how the structure is implemented by the court in subsequent decisions. The novel concept of redress introduced in *Daniels* is especially dependent on repetition, as it lacks a foundation in evidence or logical necessity. Without the court's conscious adoption of the principles set out in *Daniels*, *Daniels* risks becoming orphaned jurisprudence, seeming to highlight a moral obligation within the context of the recently delivered report of the Truth and Reconciliation Commission, while leaving the Crown and Indigenous peoples without meaningful legal guidance.

The Legacy of *Daniels*

In July 2017, the SCC released two decisions: *Clyde River (Hamlet)* and *Chippewas of the Thames First Nation*. These were complementary decisions that explored the Crown's duty to consult and the power of regulators to fulfill the Crown's consultation obligations. The decisions also represented the court's first examination of s. 35[66] since its release of *Daniels*. As a result, *Clyde River (Hamlet)* and *Chippewas of the Thames* provide additional guidance on the court's use of "Indigenous" and suggest the extent to which the court intends to carry forward the conceptual frameworks developed in *Daniels*.

While the court's initial adoption of the noun "Indigenous" was tempered within *Daniels*, only appearing five times, the term was fully embraced by the SCC in *Clyde River (Hamlet)* and *Chippewas of the Thames*, being used over twenty times in each. In addition to the expansion of use, the context in which the term "Indigenous" was used also materially changed with the

2017 decisions. While in *Daniels* "Indigenous" appears within a framework of redress and s. 91(24), in *Clyde River (Hamlet)* and *Chippewas of the Thames* the term is used as a synonym for "Aboriginal peoples."

The court's intention to adopt "Indigenous peoples" as a synonym for "Aboriginal peoples" is made clear through its rephrasing of previous jurisprudence. In both decisions, the court restated text from *Haida Nation* and *Rio Tinto*[67] describing the duty to consult, substituting the word "Indigenous" for the word "Aboriginal." For example, where the scc in *Rio Tinto* stated that "the duty seeks to provide protection to Aboriginal and treaty rights while furthering the goals of reconciliation between *Aboriginal* peoples and the Crown" (emphasis added).[68] In *Clyde River (Hamlet),* the scc restated the jurisprudence as "the duty to consult seeks to protect Aboriginal and treaty rights while furthering reconciliation between *Indigenous* peoples and the Crown" (emphasis added).[69] Similarly, while *Haida Nation* stated that "the duty to consult and accommodate, as discussed above, flows from the Crown's assumption of sovereignty over lands and resources formerly held by the *Aboriginal* group" (emphasis added),[70] the same language was restated within *Clyde River (Hamlet)* as "[the duty to consult] is based in the Crown's assumption of sovereignty over lands and resources formerly held by *Indigenous* peoples" (emphasis added).[71]

The scc's substitution of "Indigenous" for "Aboriginal" within *Clyde River (Hamlet)* and *Chippewas of the Thames* is consistent, repetitive, and implemented with a nuanced attention to broader jurisprudence. The scc in both decisions continues to refer to "Aboriginal rights" and "Aboriginal claims" but substitutes "Indigenous peoples" and "Indigenous groups" for the language of "Aboriginal peoples" and "Aboriginal groups" that was in common use by the scc before *Daniels.*

The scc's consistent application of language within the 2017 decisions is relevant to the interpretation of *Daniels.* The conceptual framework introduced in *Daniels* is dependent on the consistent application of language, including the language that *Daniels* introduced.

Inconsistencies with Daniels

The scc's employment of "Indigenous" as a synonym for "Aboriginal" within *Clyde River (Hamlet)* and *Chippewas of the Thames* contrasts with the language found in *Daniels,* possibly undermining the conceptual framework that *Daniels* set out. In *Daniels*, "Indigenous" was cast broadly, allowing for non-Aboriginal people to access redress. This interpretation may not survive *Clyde River (Hamlet)* and *Chippewas of the Thames*.

The SCC's restatement of the Crown's s. 35 consultation obligations using the term "Indigenous" in *Clyde River (Hamlet)* and *Chippewas of the Thames* may constrict the meaning of "Indigenous" to "Aboriginal," an outcome inconsistent with *Daniels*. In *Clyde River (Hamlet)*, the Court mostly refers to the Crown's duty to consult "Indigenous group[s]";[72] however, in *Chippewas of the Thames* the SCC on several occasions refers to the Crown's duty to consult "Indigenous peoples."[73] The former is consistent with *Daniels*, since "groups" acts as a constraint, reintroducing the societal requirement of s. 35. The broader "peoples" is more expansive and does not *necessarily* connote a social requirement. By stating that "it is the Crown that owes a constitutional obligation to consult with potentially affected Indigenous peoples"[74] the Court's language implies that Indigenous peoples are subject to a section 35 obligation, by necessity limiting those who can be described as "Indigenous."

While not every substitution of "Indigenous" for "Aboriginal" within the context of *Clyde River (Hamlet)* and *Chippewas of the Thames* necessitates a constricted interpretation of "Indigenous," the repeated use, even if unintentional, encourages conflation by readers and users of the court's jurisprudence.

As discussed, *Daniels* created a framework for s. 91(24), redress, and an expansive understanding of "Indigenous" peoples. These concepts were introduced by *Daniels*, and their successful jurisprudential adoption will take time and repetition. Equating "Aboriginal" and "Indigenous" moves away from an expansive, individual-focused interpretation toward the collective, community-focused approach to s. 35. Shifting the focus to s. 35 may similarly shift the objective to reconciliation rather than redress.

Conclusions on *Daniels*

Daniels acts as a prominent signpost on the SCC's journey of evolving judicial language. It introduced the noun "Indigenous" at a time when Canada was engaged in deep conversation regarding its history and relationship with Indigenous peoples following the inquiry into Indian residential schools. At a time when the federal government was providing compensation for tens of thousands of Indian residential school attendees, the court highlighted the history of harm caused to Indigenous individuals and emphasized the need for redress.

The SCC, through *Daniels*, introduced a novel framework for s. 91(24) that contrasted with the well-defined s. 35 framework. Whereas s. 35 focused on the prospective protection of Aboriginal communities through the constraint of the Crown, s. 91(24) focused on the retrospective redress of harms to individuals that had resulted from Crown actions targeted at Indigenous peoples. This new framework relied on a broad categorization of "Indigenous" and a nuanced understanding of "redress," focused on political and moral responsibility.

While *Daniels* may survive as a marker of the SCC's historic change in language, the s. 91(24) framework risks becoming orphaned jurisprudence. The issue of the Indian residential schools that the SCC chose to focus on is, in some ways, a matter of the past. For Aboriginal peoples, s. 35 provides protection against historic efforts of cultural integration. All Canadians, including non-Aboriginal Indigenous peoples, are now protected by the rights granted under the Canadian Charter of Rights and Freedoms, an instrument that was in its infancy when the last of the Indian residential schools were closed. The SCC's individual focus on Indian residential schools, many suggest, limited apparent opportunities for further redress. So long as "redress" remains retrospective, it is reasonable to assume that the need for individual redress, rather than reconciliation, will pass, perhaps soon.

The SCC's intentions from *Clyde River (Hamlet)* and *Chippewas of the Thames* seem clear: going forward, "Indigenous" is intended to be synonymous with "Aboriginal." This marks an evolution rather than an innovation in jurisprudential language. Whether the SCC's delicate framework of redress, "Indigenous," and s. 91(24) can survive this shift in language depends on the future writings of the SCC and the continuing need for redress.

NOTES

1 Authors' note: The material in this chapter has also been reviewed in Thomas Isaac and Arend Hoekstra, "Identity and Federalism: Understanding the Implications of *Daniels v. Canada*," *Supreme Court Law Review* 81 (2017): 27–51.

2 Constitution Act, 1982, being Schedule B to the Canada Act 1982 (UK), 1982, c 11.

3 *Kruger et al. v. The Queen*, [1978] 1 SCR 104, 75 DLR (3d) 434.

4 *Paulette et al. v. The Queen*, [1977] 2 SCR 628, 72 DLR (3d) 161.

5 *Native Women's Assn. of Canada v. Canada*, [1994] 3 SCR 627, 119 DLR (4th) 224.

6 *R v. Sparrow*, [1990] 1 SCR 1075, 70 DLR (4th) 385.

7 *R v. Gladstone*, [1996] 2 SCR 723, 137 DLR (4th) 648.

8 *R v. Van der Peet*, [1996] 2 SCR 507, 137 DLR (4th) 289.

9 *R v. Badger*, [1996] 1 SCR 771, 133 DLR (4th) 324.

10 Constitution Act, 1867 (UK), 30 & 31 Vict, c 3, reprinted in RSC 1985, Appendix II, No 5.

11 *Daniels v. Canada* (Indian Affairs and Northern Development), 2016 SCC 12, [2016] 1 SCR 99.

12 Reference as to whether "Indians" in s. 91(24) of the BNA Act includes "Eskimo," [1939] SCR 104, 1939 CanLII 22 (SCC).

13 Constitution Act, 1982, s. 35(2).

14 Reference as to whether "Indians" includes "Eskimo."

15 *R v. Powley*, 2003 SCC 43 at para. 10, [2003] 2 SCR 207.

16 Ibid., at para. 31.

17 Ibid., at para. 32.

18 See note 15, at para. 33.

19 See note 11, at para. 49.

20 As the authors have noted elsewhere, expanding the definition of *Powley* appears to do away with community-based rights and identity and move toward a framework based solely on ancestral connection (be it by "birth, adoption, or other means"). This is a material alteration of the definition of Métis, not only because it may significantly increase those included in the category, but also because it may become significantly more difficult to establish or dismiss claims of inclusion. The availability of 'other means' by which ancestry can be demonstrated, in tandem with eliminating a requirement for continuity with a historic community, creates the possibility of additional difficult-to-disprove claims of Métis identity and the potential for a significant expansion of the category of Métis. This definition of Métis appears to run counter to the definition in *Powley*, where it was noted that Métis are not all mixed-ancestry people, but rather peoples who have, in addition to their mixed ancestry, "developed their own customs, way of life, and recognizable group identity separate from their Indian or Inuit and European forebears," and has the potential of materially expanding the number of individuals included under the term "Métis."

21 *Chippewas of the Thames First Nation v. Enbridge Pipelines Inc.*, 2017 SCC 41, 411 DLR (4th) 596.

22 *Clyde River (Hamlet) v. Petroleum Geo-Services Inc.*, 2017 SCC 40, 411 DLR (4th) 571.

23 See *Mitchell v. Minister of National Revenue*, 2001 SCC 33, [2001] 1 SCR 911; *R. v. Marshall*, 2005 SCC 43, [2005] 2 SCR 220; *Tsilhqot'in Nation v. British Columbia*, 2014 SCC 44, [2014]

2 SCR 256; *R v. Côté,* [1996] 3 SCR 139, 1996 CanLII 170 (SCC); *R. v. Van der Peet,* see note 8; *R v. Kapp,* 2008 SCC 41, [2008] 2 SCR 483; *Calder v. British Columbia* (Attorney General), [1973] SCR 313, 34 DLR (3d) 145 (SCC); *Manitoba Metis Federation Inc. v. Canada* (Attorney General), 2013 SCC 14, [2013] 1 SCR 623.

24   United Nations Declaration on the Rights of Indigenous Peoples.

25   See note 11.

26   Ibid., at para. 1.

27   Ibid., at para. 49.

28   See note 8, at para. 30.

29   Ibid., at para. 55.

30   Ibid., at para. 55.

31   *Delgamuukw v. British Columbia,* [1997] 3 SCR 1010 at para. 115, 153 DLR (4th) 193.

32   See *Hopper v. R.,* 2008 NBCA 42, 331 NBR (2d) 177.

33   See note 15, at para. 48.

34   See note 8, at para. 31.

35   See note 15, at para. 32.

36   See note 11, at para. 49.

37   Ibid., at para. 15.

38   Ibid., at paras. 1, 49, and 50.

39   Ibid., at para. 15.

40   See note 6.

41   *Tsilhqot'in,* 2014 SCC 44, [2014] 2 SCR 256 at para. 118.

42   See note 31, at para. 186, 153 DLR (4th) 193.

43   *Haida Nation v. British Columbia* (Minister of Forests), 2004 SCC 73, [2004] 3 SCR 511 at para. 118.

44   See note 6.

45   See note 8, at para. 55.

46   See note 11, at para. 49.

47   Ibid., at para. 49.

48   Ibid., at para. 15.

49   Ibid., at para. 15.

50   Ibid., at paras. 28, 30 and 49.

51   Ibid., at para. 30.

52   Ibid., at paras. 28 and 30.

53   Ibid., at para. 15.

54   Ibid., at para. 15.

55   Isaac and Hoekstra, "Identity and Federalism."

56   See note 11, at paras. 25 and 26.

57 Ibid., at para. 30.

58 Ibid., at para. 15.

59 Ibid., at para. 15.

60 Truth and Reconciliation Commission of Canada, *Final Report of the Truth and Reconciliation Commission of Canada* (Truth and Reconciliation Commission of Canada, 2015), www.trc.ca.

61 Sean Fine, "Chief Justice Says Canada Attempted "Cultural Genocide" on Aboriginals," *Globe and Mail,* 28 May 2015, https://beta.theglobeandmail.com/news/national/chief-justice-says-canada-attempted-cultural-genocide-on-aboriginals/article24688854/?ref=http://www.theglobeandmail.com&.

62 See note 11, at para. 1.

63 Sean Fine, "Indigenous Peoples Can Decide Fate of Residential-School Settlement Records, Supreme Court Rules," *Globe and Mail*, 6 October 2017, https://beta.theglobeandmail.com/news/national/records-of-residential-school-abuse-can-be-destroyed-supreme-court/article36511037/?rcf=http://www.theglobeandmail.com&.

64 Canadian Charter of Rights and Freedoms.

65 "Although most of the schools had closed by the 1980s, the last federally supported residential schools remained in operation until the late 1990s." TRC, *Final Report*, 3.

66 *Musqueam Indian Band v. Musqueam Indian Band* (Board of Review), 2016 SCC 36, [2016] 2 SCR 3.

67 *Rio Tinto Alcan Inc. v. Carrier Sekani Tribal Council*, 2010 SCC 43, [2010] 2 SCR 650.

68 Ibid.

69 See note 22, at para. 19.

70 *Haida Nation,* 2004 SCC 73, [2004] 3 SCR 511 at para. 53.

71 See note 22, at para. 19.

72 Ibid., at paras. 22, 23, 31, 32, 39, and 41.

73 See note 21, at paras. 1, 19, 33, 34, and 63.

74 Ibid., at para. 34.

CHAPTER 5

The Other Declarations in *Daniels*: Fiduciary Obligations and the Duty to Negotiate

CATHERINE BELL[1]

Section 91(24) of the Constitution Act, 1867 provides that the federal government has jurisdiction in relation to "Indians and lands reserved for the Indians."[2] In *Daniels*, the plaintiffs asked for three declarations from the Supreme Court of Canada (scc): (1) that Métis and non–Status Indians are within the constitutional definition of "Indian" in s. 91(24); (2) that the federal Crown owes a fiduciary duty to Métis and non–Status Indians; and (3) that Métis and non–Status Indians have the right to be consulted and negotiated with, in good faith, by the federal government on a collective basis through representatives of their choice.[3]

Courts may grant declarations to resolve disputes or clarify the law, but a declaration will not be given if it has no practical utility—for example, because a question of law is already considered answered or "settled" in a given area. As other chapters in this volume elaborate, the scc decided that granting the first declaration had practical utility, because evidence presented at trial demonstrated that denial of jurisdiction by both federal and provincial governments acted as a barrier to policy responses, negotiation, and settlement of Métis claims. There are, of course, some exceptions. For example, before judicial recognition of Métis Aboriginal harvesting rights in *R v. Powley*,[4] some provincial governments had entered into agreements with Métis communities and political organizations, typically in relation to initiatives to improve cultural, economic, or social well-being, or as frameworks for negotiation in these and other areas, including delegated powers of governance. The most comprehensive agreement was in Alberta.[5] However, these arrangements did not respond to or recognize s. 35 Métis constitutional rights. Neither Alberta's Métis settlement legislation[6] nor Saskatchewan's Métis Act[7] expressly recognize or accommodate s. 35 Métis constitutional rights.[8]

The SCC denied the second two declarations—that the federal government owes a fiduciary obligation to Métis, and has a duty to consult and negotiate with representatives of their choice—on the basis that such declarations have no practical utility because they restate "settled" law.[9] However, the reasoning offered by the SCC for denying these declarations creates confusion in the law of Crown constitutional obligations to Aboriginal peoples. It does this by (1) the apparent conflation of the "fiduciary relationship" between the Crown and Aboriginal peoples with enforceable "fiduciary duties" that flow from that relationship; and (2) the apparent conflation of the Crown's "context-specific duty to negotiate"[10] with the duty to identify, define, and consult on matters affecting comprehensive land or other Aboriginal rights-based claims. This confusion has contributed to disagreement concerning responsiveness of government policy to the ruling in *Daniels*, including in relation to access to federal programs and services, the duty to negotiate credibly asserted constitutional rights, and proof of representative capacity by Métis political organizations to assert, negotiate, and resolve claims.

The Second Declaration: Fiduciary Duty or Relationship?

Speaking for a unanimous court, Justice Abella gave the following reasons for refusing to declare that the federal government has a fiduciary obligation to the Métis: "The second declaration sought is to recognize that the Crown owes a *fiduciary duty* to Métis and non-status Indians. *Delgamuukw* . . . accepted that Canada's Aboriginal peoples have a *fiduciary relationship* with the Crown and *Manitoba Metis Federation* accepted that such a relationship exists between the Crown and Métis. As a result, the declaration lacks practical utility because it is restating settled law" (emphasis added).[11]

Justice Abella's failure to clearly distinguish between "fiduciary duty" and "fiduciary relationship" has resulted in at least two significantly different interpretations of her reasons by legal scholars and practitioners. The first is that *Daniels* expands current law concerning Crown obligations to First Nations, Inuit, and Métis by recognizing a general fiduciary duty to act in their best interests at all times in dealings with them.[12] The second interpretation is that her reference to "settled law" and agreement with the lower courts should be viewed as affirming previous judicial decisions concerning the Crown-Métis "fiduciary relationship."

Both interpretations find some support in Justice Abella's agreement with "the trial judge and the Federal Court of Appeal that neither the second nor third declaration should be granted."[13] At trial, Justice Phelan refused the second declaration on the basis there is no general federal fiduciary duty to act in the best interest of First Nations, Métis, or Inuit because of federal jurisdiction in relation to them.[14] The Federal Court of Appeal (FCA) refused the declaration for other reasons. It thought it was being asked to consider the existence of a fiduciary relationship between the federal government and the Métis.[15] It concluded that because the SCC already ruled in favour of the existence of such a relationship in *Manitoba Metis Federation* (*MMF*),[16] a declaration should not be granted.[17] The matter was "settled law."[18]

In *MMF*, the SCC clarified that the fiduciary relationship between the Crown and Aboriginal peoples, in and of itself, does not generate a corresponding fiduciary obligation to act in the best interests of Inuit, First Nations, or Métis peoples. However, the fiduciary nature of the Aboriginal-Crown relationship does engage honour of the Crown. The legal principle of honour of the Crown is concerned with reconciling the rights and interests of "Aboriginal peoples of Canada," including with the sovereign imposition of a "legal system that they did not share" and taking of lands and resources formerly in their control.[19] It "gives rise to different duties in different circumstances,"[20] including fiduciary duties, the duty to consult, and the duty to diligently and purposively fulfill constitutional promises aimed at reconciliation.[21]

After Confederation in 1867, Canada began implementing a policy of western expansion, including through settlement in the western territories. This included Rupert's Land and the Red River area in southern Manitoba, part of the Métis Nation homeland. The purpose of the Manitoba Act, 1870 was to bring this area peaceably into Confederation and address the concerns of Métis and other settlers in possession of Manitoba lands.[22] It included promises to allocate 1.4 million acres of land to Métis children as well as additional land grants to Métis and other settlers in possession of land. The promise to the Métis children was included in s. 31 of the Manitoba Act and to Métis and other settlers in s. 32. However, errors and delays in implementing these sections, insufficient legislative response, instances of federal facilitation of land scrip speculation, and other frauds and abuses resulted in many Métis not receiving the land grants promised.[23]

The Manitoba Metis Federation (the Federation) sought three declarations: (1) that the federal government had breached its fiduciary duty in implementing sections 31 and 32 of the Manitoba Act; (2) that the federal government had failed to implement these sections in a manner consistent with the honour of the Crown; and (3) that certain legislation enacted to implement these provisions was outside the jurisdiction of the province of Manitoba.[24] The SCC held that the claim based on s. 32 was not established. On s. 31 of the Manitoba Act, the Court held that

> [it] constitutes a constitutional obligation to the Métis people of Manitoba, an Aboriginal people, to provide the Métis children with allotments of land. The immediate purpose of the obligation was to give the Métis children a head start over the expected influx of settlers from the east. Its broader purpose was to reconcile the Métis' Aboriginal interests in the Manitoba territory with the assertion of Crown sovereignty over the area that was to become the province of Manitoba. The obligation enshrined in s. 31 of the Manitoba Act did not impose a fiduciary or trust duty on the government. However, as a solemn constitutional obligation to the Métis people of Manitoba aimed at reconciling their Aboriginal interests with sovereignty, it engaged the honour of the Crown. This required the government to act with diligence in pursuit of the fulfillment of the promise. On the findings of the trial judge, the Crown failed to do so and the obligation to the Métis children remained largely unfulfilled.[25]

In reaching this conclusion, the SCC confirmed that the relationship between the Métis and the Crown is fiduciary in nature, but also distinguished
this relationship from enforceable fiduciary trust obligations to act in the
best interest of a beneficiary.[26] The Court outlined two situations in which
fiduciary obligations arise. The first is when the Crown assumes discretion-
ary control over specific collective Aboriginal interests. The Court provided
that "the interest (title or some other interest) must be distinctly Aboriginal," defined as "a communal Aboriginal interest in land that is integral to
the nature of the . . . distinctive community and their relationship to the
land."[27] A fiduciary duty may also arise where there is (1) "an undertaking
by [an] alleged fiduciary to act in the best interests of the alleged beneficiary"; (2) "a person vulnerable to a fiduciary's control"; and (3) "a legal or
substantial practical interest of the beneficiary . . . that stands to be adversely
affected by the alleged fiduciary's exercise of discretion or control."[28] For
such undertaking to give rise to a fiduciary obligation, it must be one of
"loyalty to act in the beneficiaries' best interests" by forsaking "the interests
of all others in favour of those of the beneficiary, in relation to the specific
legal interest at stake."[29]

Conflating fiduciary obligations with fiduciary relationships is not only
contrary to *MMF* (which Justice Abella cited in her reasons in *Daniels*) but
also to other SCC cases that indicate fiduciary obligations do not arise in all
dealings between Aboriginal peoples and the Crown. As elaborated in the
following comment on *Daniels* by the Aboriginal and Environmental Law
Unit at McMillan LLP,

> it is not easy to see this case [*MMF*] as authority for the proposition
> stated [by Justice Abella in *Daniels*]. That case seems to indicate
> that a fiduciary duty exists only when the Crown has assumed
> discretionary control over specific aboriginal interests. Other
> cases, like *Haida Nations v. British Columbia (Minister of Forests)*
> also expressly rejected the "fiduciary" concept as the overarching
> basis for Crown/aboriginal relations. In *Haida* the Court said
> this at paragraph 18. As explained in *Roberts*, at para. 81, the term
> "fiduciary duty" does not connote a universal trust relationship
> encompassing all aspects of the relationship between the Crown
> and Aboriginal peoples. . . .

In any case, the Court [scc in *Daniels*] declined to make the second requested declaration regarding this fiduciary relationship, noting it "lacks practical utility because it is restating settled law." This is an incredibly powerful statement that opens up all kinds of questions as to what the fiduciary duty entails, when and how it may have been breached in the past, and who has the right to bring cases going forward regarding damages for historic breaches. It will, once again, surely spawn more litigation.[30]

For these reasons, the reference to "settled law" by Justice Abella in denying the second declaration suggests *Daniels* is best understood as affirming the federal Métis fiduciary relationship, not as recognizing a general fiduciary duty to always act in the best interests of the Métis.[31] This interpretation is also consistent with the evolution of legal counsel's argument over the years and through the various levels of court. In 1999, when the *Daniels* litigation was commenced, the law on fiduciary obligations and the constitutional principle of honour of the Crown were just developing in Canadian law. The distinction between fiduciary duties and the overarching Crown-Aboriginal fiduciary relationship was not yet clearly drawn. As this distinction emerged in Canadian jurisprudence, the Congress of Aboriginal Peoples (the CAP) indicated before the FCA that the substance of their request was for affirmation of the *fiduciary relationship* and application of the standard of honourable conduct that such a relationship engages in Crown dealings with the Métis.[32]

These different interpretations of *Daniels* contribute to disagreement about the practical implications of Métis inclusion in s. 91(24)—in particular whether inclusion imposes a duty on the federal government to legislate, negotiate, or enact policy in the best interest of the Métis, for example through provision of programs and services in health and education similar to those offered to status Indians. Canadian constitutional law draws a distinction between jurisdiction (the power to enact law) and the responsibility to legislate or otherwise act in the best interest of Aboriginal peoples.[33] For this reason, although Métis are similarly situated with First Nations and Inuit under federal s. 91(24) jurisdiction, it is unlikely the scc will rule that the federal government has a legal duty to deliver programs and services in any given area absent some other constitutional basis, such as inequality of treatment of Aboriginal peoples under s. 15 of Canada's Charter of Rights and Freedoms.[34]

For example, some of the arguments accepted by the Canadian Human Rights Tribunal with respect to equality rights and discrimination faced by First Nations communities in relation to child and family services delivered on and off reserves have parallels to delivery of benefits to status Indians and Métis, and have fuelled federal policy reform.[35] As with the debates concerning jurisdiction in relation to Métis, debates over jurisdiction and financial responsibility led to disparities between the quantity and quality of programs and services offered to First Nations children on reserve and those available to other children. Canada argued unsuccessfully in *First Nations Child and Family Caring Society of Canada* that because child welfare is a matter of provincial jurisdiction, the federal government has no legal obligation to provide child welfare services, but does so as a matter of policy to help ameliorate some of the differences in treatment between provinces. The Human Rights Tribunal held that this position ignores federal s. 91(24) jurisdiction over Indians.[36] Delegating child welfare to the province through the Indian Act[37] also did not relieve the federal government of its constitutional responsibility flowing from the honour of the Crown under s. 91(24).[38] It is this reading of *Daniels* within a wider constitutional context that gives rise to enforceable obligations on the Crown.

Another area where this has significant practical implications is participation in government claims negotiation processes. Read together, *MMF*, *Haida, Daniels,* and *Tsilhqot'in Nation v. British Columbia*[39] also stand for the proposition that Métis should be included in federal and provincial processes.[40] As a consequence, it is unsurprising that Douglas Eyford's 2015 report on Canada's comprehensive claims negotiation policy,[41] Tom Isaac's more recent report on the implications of *MMF* and reconciliation with Métis,[42] and Brenda Gunn's analysis of *Daniels* in an international context in Chapter 7 all call on the Crown to engage with Métis representative bodies in consultation and negotiation of s. 35 rights and other Crown obligations. There is now a framework for negotiations with the Federation.[43] Although the Federation is the primary beneficiary of the ruling in *MMF*, the implications of these and other SCC decisions are much broader.[44] However, as elaborated below, debate continues about the existence of a legal duty to negotiate with Métis and the representative authorities of Métis local and regional bodies in relation to their provincial and national organizations for this and other purposes.[45]

The Third Declaration: Consultation and/or Negotiation?

Among the specific duties flowing from honour of the Crown are fiduciary duties, the duty to consult, the duty to "act in a way that accomplishes [the] intended purposes of treaty and statutory grants to Aboriginal peoples,"[46] and the duty to diligently and purposively fulfill constitutional promises aimed at reconciliation of Aboriginal interests. Debate exists among legal practitioners and scholars about adding a duty to enter good faith negotiations to this list. The nature of the third declaration sought in *Daniels* and the reasons for its denial add to the complexity of this debate.

The CAP sought a declaration "that Métis and non-status Indians have the right to be consulted and negotiated with, in good faith, by the federal government on a collective basis through representatives of their choice."[47] In response, the SCC said:

> The claim is that the First Ministers' conferences anticipated by ss. 37 and 37.1 of the Constitution Act, 1982 did not yield the hoped-for results in identifying and defining Aboriginal rights. The subsequent lack of progress implies that the federal government has not fulfilled its constitutional obligations.[48]
>
> However, *Haida Nation v. British Columbia (Minister of Forests)*, [2004] 3 S.C.R. 511, *Tsilhqot'in Nation v. British Columbia*, [2014] 2 S.C.R. 257, and *Powley* already recognize a context-specific duty to negotiate when Aboriginal rights are engaged. Because it would be a restatement of the existing law, the third declaration too lacks practical utility.[49]

Some argue that Justice Abella's reference above to the "context-specific duty to negotiate" is to a duty to negotiate accommodations if consultation obligations are triggered.[50] Others argue there is no duty to negotiate within or outside of consultation. For example, the SCC has held that the process of consultation can be completed and accommodations imposed through a regulatory process created by the provinces.[51] As the following legal opinion of McCarthy Tetrault LLP elaborates,

> The SCC's use of the term "negotiate" appears to be used interchangeably with "consult" since none of *Haida, Tsilhqot'in, Powley* or other SCC decisions impose a distinct "duty to negotiate"

in the context of consultation with Aboriginal groups. Since *Haida*,
the SCC has consistently held that the Crown owes a duty to
consult, and where appropriate, accommodate Aboriginal peoples
when their rights may be affected by a Crown action or decision.
Such duties do not impose a requirement on the Crown to reach
agreement with Aboriginal groups, nor do they grant a veto to
Aboriginal groups. . . . It does not require the Crown to negotiate
any terms upon which its decision or action will proceed.

In our view, the use of the term "negotiate" is not appropriately
applied in the context of consultation, and [*Daniels*] could be
wrongly interpreted as imposing additional duties or obligations
on the Crown than what the law of the duty to consult, and where
appropriate, accommodate, presently requires.[52]

Yet others say Justice Abella's reasons affirm the principle that honour of
the Crown gives rise to an independent duty to negotiate, in good faith, s.
35 and other constitutional obligations flowing to Aboriginal peoples. As
argued in the following legal opinion,

> The Court reaffirmed based on *Haida Nation v. BC*, *Tsilhqot'in
> Nation v. BC* and *Powley* that "a context-specific duty to negotiate"
> exists "when Aboriginal rights are engaged." This duty is not
> triggered by mere inclusion in s. 91(24), however; it applies
> where Métis or non-status Indian communities have credible or
> established s. 35 rights or claims. Again, the Court did not issue
> a declaration on this issue because to do so would have been "a
> restatement of the existing law" (para. 56).
>
> This is a particularly significant development for Métis
> communities from Ontario westward whose s. 35 rights and/or
> claims have already been recognized by courts and/or provincial
> government but who yet find that the federal government does not
> have any negotiation processes with them and they are excluded
> from Canada's specific and comprehensive claims policies. Further,
> this clear statement from the Court that there is a duty to negotiate
> (related to but distinct from the Crown's duty to consult and
> accommodate) will be helpful to all Aboriginal peoples.[53]

Although the scc has upheld the ability of the Crown to impose accommodations following adequate consultation, and that the duty to consult does
not provide Aboriginal peoples with a veto,[54] it does not necessarily follow
that there is no duty to negotiate in good faith. To argue that there is a duty
to negotiate s. 35 rights claims is not the same as arguing that there is a duty
to agree. Indeed, the cases cited by Justice Abella in *Daniels* and by McCarthy Tetrault above discuss a duty to negotiate within, and independent of,
consultation processes. As the scc explains in *Haida*:

> Where treaties remain to be concluded, the honour of the Crown
> requires negotiations leading to a just settlement of Aboriginal
> claims: *R. v. Sparrow*, [1990] 1 S.C.R. 1075, at pp. 1105–6. Treaties
> serve to reconcile pre-existing Aboriginal sovereignty with assumed
> Crown sovereignty, and to define Aboriginal rights guaranteed
> by s. 35 of the Constitution Act, 1982. Section 35 represents a
> promise of rights recognition, and "it is always assumed that the
> Crown intends to fulfill its promises" (*Badger, supra*, at para. 41).
> This promise is realized and sovereignty claims reconciled through
> the process of honourable negotiation. It is a corollary of s. 35 that
> the Crown act honourably in defining the rights it guarantees and
> in reconciling them with other rights and interests. This, in turn,
> implies a duty to consult and, if appropriate, accommodate.[55]

And later in the same decision:

> Put simply, Canada's Aboriginal peoples were here when
> Europeans came, and were never conquered. Many bands
> reconciled their claims with the sovereignty of the Crown through
> negotiated treaties. Others, notably in British Columbia, have
> yet to do so. The potential rights embedded in these claims are
> protected by s. 35 of the Constitution Act, 1982. The honour of
> the Crown requires that these rights be determined, recognized
> and respected. This, in turn, requires the Crown, acting
> honourably, to participate in processes of negotiation. While this
> process continues, the honour of the Crown may require it to
> consult and, where indicated, accommodate Aboriginal interests.[56]

Despite these passages and the fact that Canadian governments negotiate
with various levels of Métis political organization, federal and provincial
governments may still assert that such negotiations are a matter of government policy and not a constitutional right. However, a recent decision of
the SCC suggests this is too narrow an understanding of the Crown's legal
obligations. In *Tsilhqot'in*, an important Aboriginal title case decided in
2015, the SCC stated there is a duty on the Crown to negotiate in good
faith the resolution of "claims to ancestral lands."[57] The SCC also affirmed
in *MMF* that the duty to negotiate applies to treaty making and implementation "leading to requirements such as honourable negotiation and the avoidance of the appearance of sharp dealing."[58]

The CAP argued in *Daniels* that there is a duty to negotiate with Métis
arising from failure of "the First Ministers' conferences anticipated by ss. 37
and 37.1 of the Constitution Act, 1982 [to] ... yield the hoped-for results in
identifying and defining Aboriginal rights" and that continued "lack of progress implies that the federal government has not fulfilled its constitutional
obligations."[59] Progress has been delayed for many reasons. Before the *Powley*
decision in 2003, debates and uncertainty about the nature and scope of Métis
rights, the legal effects of scrip, Métis constitutional identity, federal and
provincial jurisdiction, and the role of various levels of Métis political organizations in rights litigation and negotiation created barriers to consultation
and negotiation. In *Powley*, the SCC was clear that these alleged uncertain-
ties do not relieve governments of their obligation to make "a serious effort
to deal with the question of Métis rights" or enable them to simply deny the
existence of such rights.[60] The CAP drew on these arguments, the honour
of the Crown, the duty to negotiate articulated in *Haida*, and the duty to
fulfill constitutional promises affirmed in *MMF* to argue that there is a federal
duty to negotiate identification of s. 35 Métis rights flowing from failure of
the s. 37 constitutional negotiation processes. Arguably, refusal to negotiate in good faith and to exclude Métis from negotiation processes aimed at
reconciliation is a breach of the duty to negotiate and a persistent pattern of
indifference and inaction giving rise to breach of the duty of purposive fulfill-
ment of constitutionalized promises analogous to the breach found in *MMF*.

The Third Declaration: Choice of Representation

Justice Abella and the other members of the SCC in *Daniels* did not speak to the second part of the declaration that the Métis have the right to be negotiated and consulted with "through representatives of their choice."[61] This is likely because the SCC decided it was unnecessary to define who Métis are for the purpose of s. 91(24) and that the *Powley* criteria for establishing rights-bearing Métis communities continue to apply to s. 35 claims. However, the SCC did recognize the standing of the Manitoba Metis Federation to represent the individual Manitoba Métis scrip claims in a manner analogous to a class action, and the Federation has been recognized as the appropriate representative for negotiating these and s. 35 Métis rights-based claims in Manitoba.[62]

The issue of representative authority continues to block progress on Métis consultation and other issues for negotiation in some provinces. For example, a recent issue before Alberta courts was whether the province had the duty to consult a Métis local, known as the Fort Chipewyan Métis Nation of Alberta Local 125 (FCM Local), concerning a mining development.[63] The bylaws of the Métis Nation of Alberta (MNA) set out three levels of government—local, regional, and provincial councils. Although the MNA's mandate is to advance their collectively held Métis rights and interests, disagreement exists over which level of Métis government should be engaged in consultation.[64] The court held that the FCM Local had to establish that it represented a s. 35 rights-bearing community. Ultimately, the court determined that the FCM Local did not demonstrate that its members were part of a rights-bearing Métis community, nor that the Local had the authority to engage in consultation on behalf of its members.[65] In reaching its conclusion, the court held that insufficient evidence was led to establish the existence of a rights-bearing community, but also that Alberta's Métis Harvesting Policy established "a *prima facie* basis that the Fort Chipewyan Métis Community is a rights-bearing community within a 160 km radius of Fort Chipewyan."[66] However, the court also commented on the size of the rights-bearing community in the area of Fort Chipewyan in comparison to the membership in the FCM Local,[67] the fact that other organizations had claimed to represent this community in other consultations,[68] and that there was no other credible evidence of representative capacity (e.g., clear membership criteria, bylaws, and constitution). Only legal entities "whose *source of authority* and *nature of . . . representation* are demonstrably determinable would have the appropriate legal standing to speak for the . . . Aboriginal collective right-bearer."[69]

Viewed from one perspective, this ruling is consistent with the principle that Aboriginal peoples have the right to authorize political organizations or governments to represent them. However, reasons for denying representativeness in this case place burdens on Métis political organizations and governments not borne by First Nation, Inuit, or non-Aboriginal Canadian governments. These include emphasis on the gap between the size of the population represented and membership, and failure to recognize nuances in Aboriginal governance that have parallels in federal, provincial, and municipal relations—that various levels of political organization (local, regional, provincial, and national) may represent peoples for different purposes at different times. The case also creates additional hurdles for Métis to prove consultation rights and fails to recognize that the difficulty of identifying Métis representative authorities among competing claimants is not sufficient justification for failure to find a means to recognize and negotiate their rights.[70]

Conclusion

While confusion arising from the second declaration can be resolved to some degree by looking at other SCC decisions, the duty to negotiate in good faith within and outside of the consultation process, and with whom, remains contentious. Since the decision in *Daniels*, Canada has endorsed the United Nations Declaration on the Rights of Indigenous Peoples (UN-DRIP)[71] and elaborated principles for its implementation to guide the review of Canadian laws and policies.[72] Regardless of the areas of legal ambiguity raised by *Daniels*, what is clear is that consultation and unilaterally imposed accommodation represent the minimum standard for developing relationships between Aboriginal peoples and the Crown in a policy environment purported to be grounded in reconciliation and the UNDRIP. However, principles contained in the UNDRIP, together with Canada's interpretation of them, support the existence of a higher standard and a duty to negotiate in good faith.

The UNDRIP contains numerous articles on consultation,[73] and specifically calls for the implementation of free, prior, and informed consent,[74] including on projects affecting Indigenous lands, territories, and resources.[75]

Canada has acknowledged that meaningful engagement with First Nations, Inuit, and Métis grounded in these principles and Canada's constitution includes recognition of the right to participate in decision making in matters that may affect Aboriginal rights, including to their lands, territories, and resources; the need to consult and cooperate in good faith; and the importance of securing free, prior, and informed consent prior to taking any actions that may affect Aboriginal rights.[76] Canada has also recognized the "inherent right of self-government," including "jurisdiction and legal orders of Indigenous nations" as "the starting point of discussions" and that reconciliation requires "involving Indigenous peoples in the effective decision making and governance of our shared home" and "processes for negotiation and implementation of treaties, agreements and other constructive arrangements."[77] Thus, while the SCC may be unclear in *Daniels* whether and when the Crown has an obligation to negotiate, Canada's own interpretation of the UNDRIP principles[78] calls for collaboration and negotiation.[79] For these reasons it is not surprising that following the *Daniels* decision, the government entered into framework agreements with other provincial Métis governments, including the MNA.[80] However, Canada's position is also clear that it does not interpret the UNDRIP as requiring consent of Aboriginal peoples when it takes actions that impacts their rights or Canada's constitutional obligations to them.

If, as part of this process, agreements are reached that are inclusive of a wider community of Aboriginal people than may meet strict tests of representative capacity, or that purportedly extend rights and accommodations beyond those anticipated by s. 35, such agreements are not necessarily unconstitutional.[81] However, despite the ruling in *Tsilhqot'in* and *Grassy Narrows* that federal and provincial governments have jurisdiction and a role in resolution of s. 35 claims, it remains unclear how provincial governments can enter agreements that recognize, abrogate, or affect in other ways Métis Aboriginal rights and title that bind future governments with any degree of legal certainty, without the involvement of the federal Crown and protection in the Canadian constitution.

NOTES

1   This research was supported by a grant from the Social Sciences and Humanities Research
     Council and the Métis Treaties Research Project, http://www.metistreatiesproject.ca/, and by
     research assistance from Nicholas Kunysz and Caitlin Heit.

2   Constitution Act, 1867, (UK), 30 & 31 Vict, c 3, reprinted in RSC 1985, Appendix II, No 5.

3   Daniels v. Canada (Minister of Indian Affairs and Northern Development), 2016 SCC 12, [2016]
     1 SCR 99.

4   The term "Aboriginal" is used in this chapter as defined by the Constitution Act, 1982, being
     Schedule B to the Canada Act, 1982 (UK), 1982, c 11, s. 35(2). Subsection 35(1) recognizes and
     affirms "existing aboriginal and treaty rights of the Indigenous peoples of Canada" and s. 35(2)
     defines Aboriginal peoples as the "Indian, Inuit and Métis peoples of Canada."

5   R. v. Powley, 2003 SCC 43, 2 SCR 207.

6   Métis Settlements Act, R.S.A. 2000, c M-14; Métis Settlements Lands Protection Act, S.A. 1990,
     c M-14.8; Métis Settlements Accord Implementation Act, S.A. 1990, c M-14.5; and Constitution
     of Alberta Amendment Act, 1990, R.S.A. 2000, c C-24, Preamble.

7   Métis Act, S.S. 2001, c M-14.01, Preamble.

8   Since the SCC's recognition of Métis Aboriginal rights to hunt, fish, gather, and trap for food in
     Powley (see note 5, at para. 53), some provinces have also negotiated agreements and amended
     provincial laws to accommodate these rights. The geographical scope of these rights, the binding
     nature of accommodation agreements on future provincial governments, and whether contempo-
     rary self-identifying Métis communities, such as Alberta's Métis settlements, are entitled to exercise
     them as a matter of constitutional law rather than as provincial policy continue to be debated and
     litigated. See for example R v. Hirsekorn, 2011 ABQB 682, 520 AR 60; L'Hirondelle v. Alberta,
     2013 ABCA 12, 542 AR 68.

9   See note 3, at paras. 53, 56.

10   Ibid., para. 56.

11   Ibid., at para. 53 (relying on) Delgamuukw v. British Columbia, [1997] 3 SCR 1010 at para. 162,
     153 DLR (4th) 193.

12   See Pamela Palmater, "Don't Partake in Celebrations over New Supreme Court Ruling on Métis Just
     Yet," Rabble.ca (blog), 15 April 2016, http://rabble.ca/blogs/bloggers/pamela-palmater/2016/04/
     dont-partake-celebrations-over-new-supreme-court-ruling-on-m%C3%A9.

13   See note 3, at para. 52.

14   Daniels v. Canada (Minister of Indian Affairs and Northern Development), 2013 FC 6 at paras.
     602–609, [2013] FCJ No 4.

15   Daniels v. Canada (Minister of Indian Affairs and Northern Development), 2014 FCA 101 at
     paras. 156–157, 371 DLR (4th) 725.

16   Manitoba Metis Federation Inc. v. Canada (Attorney General), 2013 SCC 14, [2013] 1 SCR 623.

17   See note 15, at para. 157.

18   See note 3, at para. 53.

19   See note 16, at para. 67. The honour of the Crown is engaged in a variety of other contexts,
     including where there is a fiduciary duty arising from "discretionary control over specific
     Aboriginal interests" (at para. 49) in treaty making and settlement, and in the "intended purposes
     of treaty and statutory grants to Aboriginal peoples" (at para. 4).

20 *Haida Nation v. British Columbia* (Minister of Forests), 2004 SCC 73 at para. 18, [2004] 3 SCR 511.

21 Ibid., at paras. 16 and 18.

22 Manitoba Act, 1870, RSC 1985, App II, No 8, s. 31.

23 See note 16.

24 Ibid., at para. 7.

25 Ibid., at para. 9.

26 Ibid., at paras. 47–49.

27 Ibid., at para. 53; also see *Powley*, 2003 SCC 43, 2 SCR 207 note 15, at para. 37. [see note 5]

28 See note 16, at para. 60, (relying on) *Elder Advocates of Alberta Society v. Alberta*, 2011 SCC 24 at para. 36, [2011] 2 SCR 261.

29 See note 16, at para. 61.

30 Robin M. Junger, Timothy John Murphy, and Brent Ryan, "A Thunderbolt Decision on Métis Rights: *Daniels v. Canada* (Indian Affairs and Northern Development)," McMillan LLP, April 2016, http://www.mcmillan.ca/A-Thunderbolt-Decision-on-Metis-Rights-Daniels-v-Canada-Indian-Affairs-and-Northern-Development (accessed 23 January 2018).

31 See Jason Madden, Nuri Frame, Zachary Davis, and Megan Strachan, "'Another Chapter in the Pursuit of Reconciliation and Redress . . .': A Summary of *Daniels v. Canada* at the Supreme Court of Canada," Pape Salter Teillet LLP, 19 April 2016, http://www.metisnation.org/media/652855/pst-llp-summary-daniels-v-canada-scc-april-19-2016.pdf, 6.

32 See note 15, at paras. 154, 371 DLR (4th) 725, the FCA described the CAP's argument as follows: "It was an error . . . [for the trial judge] to refuse the second declaration because the terminology used . . . [fiduciary duty vs fiduciary relationship] has changed over time. Essentially, they argue that at the time the claim was framed [1999], there was no distinction between a fiduciary duty and a fiduciary relationship. In turn, the Judge is said to have failed to properly consider the substance of what was requested: *a declaration that the Métis and non-status Indians are in a fiduciary relationship with the Crown*" (emphasis added).

33 Kerry Wilkins, "*R. v Morris:* A Shot in the Dark and Its Repercussions," *Indigenous Law Journal* 7, no. 1 (2008): 31–32.

34 Canadian Charter of Rights and Freedoms.

35 *First Nations Child and Family Caring Society of Canada v. Attorney General of Canada* (for the Minister of Indian and Northern Affairs Canada), 2016 CHRT 2 at para. 78, [2016] 2 CNLR 270.

36 Ibid.

37 Indian Act, RSC 1985, c I-5, s 88.

38 See note 35, at para. 78, [2016] 2 CNLR 270 at para. 83.

39 *Tsilhqot'in Nation v. British* Columbia, 2014 SCC 44, [2014] 2 SCR 256; *Grassy Narrows First Nation v. Ontario* (Natural Resources), 2014 SCC 48, [2014] SCR 447. In *Tsilhqot'in*, the SCC suggests that whichever government is potentially implicating Aboriginal rights has the duty to consult. See also Bruce McIvor, "The Downside of Tsilhqot'in Decision," *First Peoples Law*, 19 October 2016, https://www.firstpeopleslaw.com/index/articles/286.php%3E.

40 *Tsilhqot'in*, ibid., at paras. 77–88.

41   Douglas R. Eyford, "A New Direction: Advancing Aboriginal and Treaty Rights," Indigenous and Northern Affairs Canada, April 2015, http://www.aadnc-aandc.gc.ca/eng/1426169199009 /1426169236218 (accessed 23 January, 2018).

42   Thomas Isaac, "A Matter of National and Constitutional Import: Report of the Minister's Special Representative on Reconciliation with Métis: Section 35 Métis Rights and the Manitoba Metis Federation Decision," Indigenous and Northern Affairs Canada, June 2016, http://www.aadnc-aandc.gc.ca/eng/1467641790303/1467641835266.

43   Indian and Northern Affairs, Memorandum of Understanding on Advancing Reconciliation.

44   Isaac, "A Matter of National and Constitutional Import," 34. See also Bell and Seaman, "A New Era for Métis Constitutional Rights?" regarding potential implications of *MMF* for Alberta Metis. Since the writing of this chapter, the federal government has entered into framework agreements with other Métis political bodies, including the MNA. The MNA-Canada Memorandum of Understanding on Advancing Reconciliation contemplates arriving at a formal MNA-Canada framework agreement for negotiations on issues such as self-government, Métis rights, outstanding Métis claims against the federal Crown, health, and housing, among many other priorities. In 2018 and 2019 the MNA signed several agreements, among them a Self-Government Agreement with Canada that acknowledges the MNA is authorized to represent the Métis Nation within Alberta in implementing the inherent right to self-government, a Housing Accord, and a Consultation Agreement. See Métis Nation of Alberta, "Governance," http://albertametis.com/governance/.

45   See *Fort Chipewyan Métis Nation, Local 125 v. Alberta* (Minister of Indigenous Relations), 2016 ABQB 713.

46   See note 16, at para. 73.

47   See note 3, at para. 2.

48   Ibid., at para. 55.

49   Ibid., at para. 56.

50   See note 20, at para. 41, [2004] 3 SCR 511.

51   For example, by a regulatory agency that has conducted adequate consultation. See *Chippewas of the Thames First Nation v. Enbridge Pipelines Inc*, 2017 SCC 41 at para. 32, 411 DLR (4th) 596; *Clyde River (Hamlet) v. Petroleum Geo-Services Inc*, 2017 SCC 40 at para. 30, 411 DLR (4th) 571.

52   Stephanie Axmann, "Métis and Non–Status Indians No Longer in a 'Jurisdictional Wasteland,' SCC Confirms," McCarthy Tétrault LLP, 11 May 2016, http://www.mccarthy.ca/article_detail. aspx?id=7258#utm_source= Mondaq& utm_medium=syndication&utm_campaign=inter-article–link (accessed 23 January 2018).

53   Madden, Frame, Davis, and Strachan, "'Another Chapter,'" 6.

54   See note 45, at para. 59, 411 DLR (4th) 596, (relying on)note 20, at para. 48, [2004] 3 SCR 511.

55   See note 20, at para. 20, [2004] 3 SCR 511.

56   Ibid., at para. 25, [2004] 3 SCR 511.

57   See note 40, at para. 18.

58   See note 16, at para. 73 (relying on) *R v. Badger*, [1996] 1 SCR 771 at para. 41, 133 DLR (4th) 324.

59   See note 3, at para. 55.

60   *R v. Powley*, 196 DLR (4th) 221 (Ont CA) at para. 166, aff'd 2003 SCC 43, 2 SCR 207.

61 See note 3, at para. 2.

62 Ibid., at para. 43, (relying on) note 16, at para. 91.

63 See note 45, at para. 121.

64 Métis Nation of Alberta, "Bylaws," http://albertametis.com/governance/bylaws/ (accessed 23 January 2018).

65 See note 45, at paras. 421–23.

66 Ibid., at para. 365.

67 Ibid., at para. 411.

68 Ibid., at para. 423.

69 Ibid., at para. 397. Following this case, the MNA entered an agreement in principle with the Government of Alberta that adopted a regional approach supported by many Métis locals. However, the agreement is on hold and has not been finalized or implemented since the change from an NDP to Conservative government in 2019. Disagreements remain between the MNA and Metis Settlements General Council (MSGC) regarding representative authority for s. 35 and scrip claims relating to settlement members. The MSGC has entered a separate Framework Agreement for Advancing Reconciliation with the federal government and has entered its own hunting, consultation and other agreements. See Metis Settlements General Council, Framework Agreement for Advancing Reconciliation, between MSGC and Canada.

70 See note 5, para. 50. For a critique of *Fort Chipewyan Métis Nation, Local 125 v. Alberta*, see Jason Madden, Zachary Davis, and Megan Strachan, "Recent Legal Developments on Métis Consultation in Alberta—A Case Summary of MNA Local #125 v Alberta," Pape Salter Teillet LLP, 7 March, 2017, http://albertametis.com/wp-content/uploads/2017/03/PST-LLP-Summary-MNA-125-Local-v-Alberta-Feb-2017-2.pdf.

71 United Nations General Assembly, Declaration on the Rights of Indigenous Peoples, GA Res 61/295, UN Doc A/RES/61/295 (2007).

72 Department of Justice, "Principles Respecting the Government of Canada's Relationship with Indigenous Peoples," Government of Canada, last modified 4 October 2017, http://www.justice.gc.ca/eng/csj-sjc/principles-principes.html.

73 UNDRIP, GA Res 61/295, UN Doc A/RES/61/295 (2007), Preamble (para. 2), Annex (para. 19), arts. 15(2), 17(2), 30(2), 32(2), 36(2), 38.

74 Ibid., at arts. 10, 11(2), 19, 28, 29(2), 30(2).

75 Ibid., at art. 32(2).

76 Department of Justice, "Principles Respecting . . . Indigenous Peoples."

77 Ibid.

78 Indian and Northern Affairs, United Nations Declaration on the Rights of Indigenous Peoples, last modified 3 August 2017, http://www.aadnc-aandc.gc.ca/eng/1309374407406/130 9374458958.

79 Department of Justice, "Principles Respecting . . . Indigenous Peoples," 1–3.

80 See notes 44 and 69.

81 See *R v. Kelley*, 2007 ABCA 41 at paras 63–64, 413 AR 269.

CHAPTER 6

Racism, Canadian Jurisprudence, and the De-Peopling of the Métis in *Daniels*

D'ARCY VERMETTE

Legal histories (those written by courts in legal judgements) are written in a particular context for a particular purpose. We can analyze these decisions from within that context or from outside of that context. The internal perspective often focuses on legal doctrine and tends not to stray too far from an examination of the case law itself. This perspective helps to illustrate the ways in which legal historical characterizations impact the development of law. The histories that are created by courts in order to justify judicial reasoning are tied directly to rights that allow Aboriginal peoples to live their ways of life and/or demand obedience to the colonial state. In that context, the histories found in Aboriginal law in Canada seem to have a potentially high consequence for how Aboriginal peoples are seen as legal rights holders. For example, if a court was to characterize an Indigenous community as an "independent nation," we would expect that court to issue much more liberating legal doctrine than a court that described them merely as an "organized society."[1] This chapter examines the problems with Aboriginal histories as they are set out in Canadian law, primarily by examining the legal decisions in the *Daniels* cases.[2] The primary problem with the *Daniels* case law is that the Métis as a People seem to disappear as the case moves from trial to the Supreme Court of Canada (scc). I begin by examining legal history and method so as to justify my approach for the analysis that follows. Then I discuss racism so as to deploy a framework that goes beyond choices made by judges and allows us to examine how racism functions within legal discourse to encourage or maintain dispossession of Indigenous peoples. Moving into case law, I follow the characterization of the Métis in legal histories in order to illustrate how they support legal doctrine that is firmly rooted in racist ideology. These roots run deep and go beyond Métis issues. In order to make this argument, I will compare *Daniels* to a rather obscure case called *Tronson*,[3] which will help draw out similar themes from a different Aboriginal legal context.

Legal History and Method

Courts produce history, in part, to outline the factual basis upon which judicial decisions are made. Showing how facts meet law becomes important for understanding the bounds of the applicability and doctrinal development of law. Imagine a situation where a court decision is issued without any reference to how judges perceived the facts or what legal doctrines were applied. This lack of transparency would undermine the function and legitimacy of the court, in part because it would remove the public vindication that state rules receive through law.[4] Without legal decisions that present a justification of legal decision making, the law would appear arbitrary and courts would run the risk of losing public faith.

We should hesitate to conflate, however, the *legal* authority of the courts with an authority (or competence) to write histories in general. Indeed, there is much to criticize about the way in which a court gains access to historical "facts."[5] The most obvious critique would be the adversarial process itself.[6] With both sides seeking advantage on points of law, histories can be presented in isolation of broader social factors,[7] and context can be lost in favour of a literalist interpretation of official historical sources.[8] There is a very good reason for this. A legal dispute will often turn on one or several key interpretations of fact dependent entirely upon which *legal* question becomes central to the determination of the case. For example, if the key legal question is one of Aboriginal title to land, the social and economic orientations of a group of people might serve as interesting background but would not be nearly as interesting for a court as whether that group occupied the land in a particular way.[9] That is to say that when a decision is issued in an Aboriginal title case, the history presented by the court will emphasize things like hunting sites, fishing sites, village sites, and the like. Therefore, legal histories must be taken with a grain of salt and an appreciation of the limited context and purposes out of which they arise.

To get at the histories and logics of the court I will primarily analyze the written judgements of several cases. For the purposes of this chapter, it is not beneficial to follow a method that analyzes the discourses involved in the legal process, such as through factums. Chris Andersen, for example, undertook a detailed examination of the *Powley*[10] decision by looking beyond case law.[11] His explanation for this broader method was that "entire cases rather than simply decisions must be analyzed in order to glean the entirety of the discourses that comprise them."[12] The reality, however, is that no particular method can get at the entirety of a discourse that makes up the outcome (in almost any context). If a researcher is to take account of the factums, a critique could be made that they are simply relocating the focus of analysis to the point of discussion rather than the point of judgement. Another critique could be made that this broader discourse analysis fails to consider the oral arguments (either by not looking at them, or by only looking at transcripts, which fail to capture the nuance in discussions between judge and lawyer). Even if those things are considered, if we want to grasp the entirety of a discourse in a legal case, we should seek a transcript of the discussions the judges had in chambers, or an account of the legal education conference the judges attended, or the factums and oral arguments of other precedential case law that the lawyers in the case under study were relying upon. After all, if we are being thorough, we should be aware of the background discussion of the points of fact or discussions that are used to support our current discussion. And on and on it goes. However, we can draw a line because the appropriateness of method is only validated by the questions that the researcher has set out to answer.

This chapter goes straight to the case law because it aims to examine the racist ideologies embedded in Canadian jurisprudence. There is no better way to do this than to analyze the ways in which courts justify their decision making. As such, the primary focus must be the written justifications offered by the courts. Andersen cautions that "court decisions rarely come with operator manuals,"[13] noting that decisions alone are not predictive of how governments will respond to the decision. This is true, yet I would not agree that an analysis that focuses primarily on legal decisions necessarily "oversells the constitutive power of court decisions,"[14] or that such analysis "undersells the complexity of the various social fields and areas of competency that embody 'law' in Canada today."[15] Method does not, in itself, over- or undersell anything without consideration of the purpose for which it was deployed. The question with any method is whether it is appropriate for what is being studied. Studying the arguments made to the court are not necessary to develop an understanding of the internal logics of the court itself. It may help us understand the confines of legal argumentation, but the court is responsible for presenting its decisions in a way that responds to common sense and, at the very least, for presenting a logic that is internally consistent with legal doctrine. As such, legal decisions remain the best way to look at the internal logics of the court. After all, as I have stated elsewhere, "colonialism isn't only about confiscating lands; it is also about controlling mind and spirit. This is accomplished by controlling the rules, venue, issues and decision makers in the debates."[16] Legal decisions are a great way to see how these factors play out (although, to come back to Andersen's caution, we should not think that a legal decision represents the end of a larger debate). I am pursuing a case law method here because I believe that by placing legal decisions in the forefront of this study, we can get to the heart of the racist ideologies that guide Canadian law on Aboriginal issues.

To understand the impact of legal logics it is important to recognize, as F.C. DeCoste wrote, that "reasonable people in societies such as ours think that their societies are societies governed by law, rather than by the will or whimsy of government."[17] This law consists of "prescriptive" rules that "constrain the activities of those to whom they apply" as well as those "who are entrusted with their application."[18] The logics that are used to explain legal reasoning and authority should be scrutinized for fairness, biases, and internal consistency. Courts do not have to be expert historians in explaining this logic, but judges should set out the reasons for arriving at particulat decisions in ways that give people trust in the thoroughness and justice of the prescriptive rule they are creating or explaining. Indeed, as Andersen explains, "the real power of the law is in the extent to which we, as citizens, view the rulings of decisions . . . as legitimate and binding."[19] Both the layperson and the legal actor see the law as authoritative, and this is why studying the internal logic of legal decisions is so important.

Racism: Seeking a Definition

Racism seems to be a largely misunderstood concept. When I ask the students in my introductory courses what racism is, the most common responses revolve around the idea that racism involves a particular race of people treating another race poorly. This poor treatment, my students explain, is because one race thinks it is superior to the other race. In these initial responses, the idea of "race" is rarely challenged. It is important to remember that this idea exists precisely because it has a function. Racism functions by providing a justificatory framework that allows those who claim full humanity (and the property interests that come along with it) to distinguish themselves from those who are dehumanized (and thus not able to claim property in the same ways).[20] It is this function that makes the grouping of people into categories based primarily on skin colour useful, despite the obvious lack of a biological basis and attendant logical flaws.[21] Because race is a social construct, it is necessary to appreciate its social purpose before delving into how the court has used these notions in its decision making. I will now work to set out a conception of racism that I can use to help measure the rationalizations of legal reasoning.

The philosopher Harry Bracken has stated that his perception of racism includes "the doctrine which a group may articulate in order to justify their oppressing another group by appealing to some putative flaw in the human essence, in recent times usually interpreted as the biological constitution of the members of the oppressed group."[22] Bracken identifies "different forms of racism—e.g. based on color, language, religion, and nationality," with "color racism" being "the most widespread" and "the most fundamental."[23] To illustrate how racism relates to power, Bracken notes that "there is nothing *inferior* about Flemish, or Yiddish, Catalan or Gaelic, Basque or Breton [languages]—except the political power of their speakers!" (emphasis in original).[24] Another explanation defines the function of racism as "an ideology of dehumanization designed to conceal or deny the material content of dispossession, discrimination, and prejudice."[25] This approach to racism, which is complementary to Bracken's, has four main parts. Let's examine each of these parts in turn.

First, racism is an *ideology*. An ideology is "a set of ideas and concepts deriving from systematically motivated, but unintended, distortions of reality" and is "rooted in a class-based interest in maintaining the status quo."[26] This means that ideology can be ingrained or unconscious beliefs, as well as conscious beliefs. As a result, ideology can be found in the foundation of society and not only in those notions harboured by a few deviants.

Second, racism *dehumanizes*. This is a necessary process that can take many gradients. It can involve likening a group of people to "savages," "brutes," or "wild beasts." Or it can be as simple as denying that group of people an aspect of humanity that other groups (usually the group[s] in power) hold for themselves—for example, the right to self-govern, the right to speak their language in school, or the right to educate their own children.[27]

Third, racism *conceals or denies*. In the belief that a group of people is less than, entitled to less, deserving of less, racist people and institutions find ways to justify their norms and beliefs. Those justifications serve to conceal the fact that things are being taken from the oppressed group.

This leads to the fourth aspect of racism. Racism conceals or denies the *material content of dispossession, discrimination, and prejudice*. This gets to the heart of the function and impact of racism. Racism serves to take things from the targeted group. A racism that works well and is deployed with sufficient power will distribute the taken things (like land, governance power, wealth, freedom) to the group that uses those things to dominate others and enrich itself. In other instances, racism serves to destroy things like equal opportunity, fair access, and so on. Both of these approaches to dispossession, discrimination, and prejudice are deployed, often unconsciously, to maintain the status quo wherein certain freedom-seeking groups are kept oppressed.

The effects of that oppression come to be seen as inherent traits of the oppressed group. The dehumanization that was successfully deployed becomes emboldened by the conditions that it created. Similarly, racism creates the conditions to verify its own ideology. This is why I have previously stated that "the dehumanization of Aboriginal peoples is both a result of and justification for colonizing actions."[28] When examining jurisprudence, it is important to ask how the reasoning articulated by the court supports a continuation of the racism upon which the law was built.

Racism: Carving Out Distinctions

Notions of race and legal identity merge when the legal identity in question is a racially classified group of people. "Indian" is one such legal identity. An "Indian" can be defined as someone who has "status" under the Indian Act. A "status" Indian is an example of a legal identity that has clear utility. By "utility," I do not mean to imply that having status is only a positive thing. I simply mean that there can be strategic reasons for choosing (when available) to be a "status" Indian, just as there can be strategic reasons for how government legislators choose to allow (or disallow) "status" to be passed on through generations.[29] The legislation that determines who an Indian is can change and has changed over the years.[30] But the constitution does not change with the whims of politics in the way that legislation does. As a result, we have seen the more robust definition of "Indian" found in the constitution to be altered through legal interpretation rather than through amendment of the constitution itself.

In 1939, in a case called *Reference Re: Eskimo* (*Re: Eskimo*), the Supreme Court of Canada (SCC) decided that the "Eskimo" in Quebec were "Indians" according to section 91(24) of the British North America Act, 1867 (BNA).[31] Section 91(24) reserved to the federal Parliament power to legislate over "Indians, and Lands Reserved for Indians."[32] The *Re: Eskimo* decision was marked by historical inquiry into the meaning and scope of the word "Indian" as it was understood at the time that the constitution was drafted. Maps, census data, Hudson's Bay Company records, prior dictionary definitions, and even the French-language translation of the BNA were consulted in three separate but concurring judgements. The one notable absence from the case was the involvement of the "Eskimo" themselves.[33] The lack of inclusion is one of the dominant characteristics of early Aboriginal law jurisprudence in Canada.[34] But the point here is more about the utility of the racial designation itself. Whether to include "Eskimo" under the constitutional definition of "Indian" is really an argument between provincial and federal powers over which level of government has to pay for the services that are provided to the "Eskimo" in Quebec. The central debate then, has very little to do with the "Eskimo" themselves, or even whether they see themselves as "Eskimo." As Constance Backhouse has stated, the case paid no attention to whether the "Eskimo" wanted to be "Indians," or if they wanted to be under federal or provincial jurisdiction.[35] The wisdom of a law should not interfere with the function of a court in interpreting that law.[36] In recognizing that the law is not concerned with broad social issues and/or the arrangements of colonial power in Canada, we are able to view the law as a tool rather than as a major force of social change.

Blais (2003) was a similar case to *Re: Eskimo*, in which the SCC determined that the Métis were not "Indians" as that term was found in the Natural Resource Transfer Agreements (NRTAS) of 1930.[37] Although still a constitutional matter, *Blais* did not involve the division of powers.[38] In the *Blais* decision, the SCC consulted historical documentation to develop the context of the time, and from that determined that the Métis were always understood to be distinct from Indians. However, in the *Blais* decision the SCC referred to the Métis' view of themselves as distinct from Indians in order to help justify the conclusion that was reached. This is bizarre, because there is no indication that the Métis were involved in drafting the terms of the NRTAS. As such, the court seems to have taken a decontextual approach in its historical interpretation. The court gave no indication that the inclusion of a Métis perspective was designed to overcome the overtly colonial interpretations that might be obtained without such inclusion. If that had been the case, we would expect a more nuanced treatment that included a thorough explanation of colonialism and reasons why including Métis perspective at this late stage could counter the impacts of colonialism. Instead of doing that, the court simply included a Métis perspective as if it were part of the context for the NRTAS (which it was not). The court gave the illusion of Métis participation, but only used it to help reinforce the views of colonial officials.

In both *Re: Eskimo* and *Blais*, we can see that racial categories in law have had an impact upon the actual living conditions of the groups being defined. In *Re: Eskimo*, the "Eskimo" would now have to deal with the federal government rather than the provincial government. In *Blais*, the decision of the SCC left the Métis without the hunting protections that might have been offered through the NRTAS. In both cases, it was race that was the key feature of the decision making, rather than nationality, peoplehood, or some other concept that imparts a level of political and legal distinctiveness upon the group(s) being defined. That is what is really being denied here in these histories. By not including the "Eskimo" at all in the decision making the court made them into malleable objects. By pretending the Métis were involved in drafting the NRTAS, the court cast the illusion that Métis acknowledgement of their distinctiveness from Indians applies in all contexts. And as the *Daniels* litigation shows, Métis understanding of their distinctiveness from Indians is a historical fact, not necessarily a legal fact.

It is one thing to say that law defines categories on the basis of race and that such decisions have an impact upon those "races" of people. It is another step, albeit a small one, to argue that law exhibits and reinforces racist ideology in those decisions. In the first instance the law could be stuck, beholden to a time gone by, and if that were the case, we would see the law only engage racist ideology as much as was absolutely necessary.[39] Yet it might also be possible to show that the law chooses to engage race-based decision making, and that those choices lead to rather predictable outcomes for the people being defined.

Even in some instances where race is not the primary feature of analysis, the racism in a case can seem obvious. An example can be found in a case called *Syliboy* (1929).[40] In that case, Acting County Court Judge Patterson referred to Mikmaq people as "savages" (dehumanization), which helped to justify (conceal or deny) a direct denial of their peoplehood and treaty rights (dispossession). All of this was done because Patterson carried an ideology, a sort of unconscious belief system, that included "savages" as a feature of common knowledge. The actual words of Patterson were that "the Indians were never regarded as an independent power. A civilized nation first discovering a country of uncivilized people or savages held such country as its own until such time as by treaty it was transferred to some other civilized nation. The savages' rights of sovereignty even of ownership were never recognized."[41] Patterson's overtly racist statements in *Syliboy* show that the racism was probably conscious as well as unconscious.

This type of overt racism seems to be an increasingly rare phenomenon in legal decisions. Despite that, racism that uses accepted norms to continue to dispossess groups of people with less social power is still quite common. This latter type of racism is common because it is *normal*, it is structural, it requires no acts that are abhorrent to the prevailing ideology. People can act as good, reasonable, considerate individuals while still operating exclusively within a system that excludes, objectifies, and dehumanizes groups of people. The ideologies of racism are embedded in systems which can operate without a conscious intervention to maintain those ideals. To help illustrate this, we can look at a few other examples of history in case law.

One example of this embedded racism in law can be found in a case called *Paulette* (1973), which appeared in the Northwest Territories Supreme Court.[42] In *Paulette* an application was made by "sixteen Indian chiefs representing the various Indian bands present in the area."[43] The total area being claimed was 400,000 square miles of land in the Northwest Territories. Despite what might have seemed like a grandiose claim for the time, the application was taken seriously by the trial judge, Justice Morrow, who tried to construct a history of treaty relations in the area. The implication coming out of Morrow's search for facts was that there was significant doubt that the numbered treaties in the area actually transferred title to the land from First Nations at the treaty negotiations to the Crown.[44] However, upon appeal, the Federal Court and later the scc both failed to deal with the substantive issues and instead merely denied that a proper application had been made. The history in this case was divorced from the legal reasoning rather than used to support it. The overall lesson from this case is that Aboriginal people do not make the rules through which they are required to protect their interests. Aboriginal people are denied the very human capacity of building and creating and interpreting. As Paulo Freire states, "the oppressors attempt to destroy in the oppressed their quality as 'considerers' of the world. Since the oppressors cannot totally achieve this destruction, they must mythicize the world. In order to present for the consideration of the oppressed and subjugated a world of deceit designed to increase their alienation and passivity, the oppressors develop a series of methods precluding any presentation of the world as a problem and showing it rather as a fixed entity, as something given—something to which people, as mere spectators, must adapt."[45] Accordingly, the Aboriginal people in *Paulette* are dehumanized, and as a consequence they are also dispossessed, not just of their humanity but of their property. Judges can avoid the moral responsibility for the outcome of such cases because they did not create the rules; they are simply operating the machinery that they were given.[46] That legal machinery has instructions for proper operation. To allow an improperly formed claim to proceed would violate those instructions, or legal principles.[47]

This is similar to one of the foundational cases on Aboriginal title in common law, *Cherokee Nation v. Georgia* (1831), where Justice Marshall of the United States Supreme Court found that Native Americans were "domestic dependent nations."[48] In reaching that decision, however, Justice Marshall

talked about both the independent nature of Indians and their warlike, savage
nature. In highlighting these two attributes, Justice Marshall acknowledged
the peoplehood of Indians while at the same time denying them the quintessential aspect of that peoplehood in the legal characterization of their
nationhood. In this case, even more than in *Paulette*, we can see a court dehumanize Indians and as a result deny their material interests. It is, in short, a
very functional use of racist ideology. I would submit, however, that this
same ideology would have revealed itself even if Marshall had not characterized Indians with such disparaging language. In denying their nationhood,
in subsuming it under the state of the colonizer, Marshall found a way to
dispossess the Illinois and the Piankeshaw nations of their peoplehood. He
did this under cover of law. The law is not neutral in this case. The denial
of Indigenous peoplehood serves to justify the very existence of the colonial state, which in turn justifies the claims (to both territory and control)
that those states make over Indigenous peoples. Law relating to Indigenous
peoples is crafted to uphold the foundation and legitimacy of the state itself.
Doing that requires the dehumanization of Indigenous peoples who make
claims that challenge that asserted sovereignty.

Ideological power backed by institutions is central to a functional operation of racism. A shared ideology is going to be more effective than an
ideology only carried by a few persons. A shared ideology that is backed by
the dominant language of a colonial authority, that is backed by the force
of the state, that is reinforced in other venues such as schools and media is
much more powerful yet. The ideologies that inform legal decision making
are backed by the coercive power of the law, which substantially enhances
the influence of those value systems and ways of thinking. The law carries
the ability to effectively use "rational" discourse to dehumanize Indigenous
peoples in a way that conceals the dispossession, discrimination, and prejudice taking place. Indeed, through the refinement of legal discourse, the
dispossession of Indigenous peoples can appear to be just part of a process.
To help draw this out a bit more I will examine a rather obscure case called
R. v. Tronson. This case helps illustrate how racism is at play in the seemingly
mundane operation of the law. It appears mundane because the dispossession,
discrimination, and prejudice brought about by racism becomes customary
through institutional norms.

R. v. Tronson

The *Tronson* case (1931) is clearly indicative of an earlier social and legal era. Still, I would argue that this case is actually quite consistent with the kind of historical narratives that courts continue to perpetuate about Aboriginal peoples. In this case, Tronson was charged and ultimately convicted under s. 115 of the Indian Act, which makes it illegal for persons other than "Indians of the band" to reside on reserve without the authority of the Superintendent General. It was submitted in this case that Tronson was not an "Indian of the band" and, as is evident from the presence of the charge, he obviously did not have permission from the Superintendent General to live on reserve.

The most central aspect of the charge brought against Tronson was that of band membership. While it is true that Tronson could be identified as a non-Indian (which would preclude him from band membership), he could be an "Indian" and still not be a member of that particular band. Band membership is a simpler route to answering the charge, because whether he was an "Indian" or not, being excluded from the band membership would mean that he was unlawfully residing. The status of band membership, we would expect, could have been easily proven by simply checking a government list of band members. His name would, or would not, be on the list. And in the absence of Tronson illustrating a bookkeeping error, the case would be concluded. Tronson could have paid his fine, and everyone involved could have grabbed a sandwich and had a laugh about how easy that case was.

Yet that is not how the court wrote its reasons in the case. Even though the reasons are not long, the court seemed to spend an inordinate amount of time trying to decide if Tronson was an "Indian." To do this, the court first turned to the definition of "Indian" found in the Indian Act, which requires one to be a male person of Indian blood and belonging to a band, or to be the child or current or former spouse of such a man.[49] This definition of "Indian" focuses on genetics (Indian blood) and carries status through the male descent. As we can see, these criteria are both sexist and racist.

The other thing we can see is that those who crafted this legislation loved kids' stories. There is often some magic in kids' stories: people are turned into frogs or other creatures and magically transformed back into humans, often by fairies with magical wands. But magic wands are hard to bring into real life. So as an alternative to a magic wand, the legislators used the penis. Through these laws that were created by men, which focused on the power of men and served to remove meaning from the actions of women, men were able to magically transmit cultural and community attachment and indeed, racial designation (and corresponding legal rights) to their spouses.

What makes this legislation even more tragic—tragedy being another key aspect of kids' stories—is that Tronson appeared to have had an Indian mother and grandmother. It would seem that his own racial categorization was changed by his white father. And, the case reveals, as if to make the loss even more impactful, Tronson, who was now legally non-Indian, had used his magic wand to remove his spouse's Indian status and thus her own ability to reside on what was clearly her reserve. As the reasons make clear, her mother was living and dying there on their home reserve. We can see that there is more at stake here than some random racist law that Canada is now ashamed of. This is an example of the types of family disconnection that is created through such laws, over generations.

If the legislation that determined Indianness was so straightforward, how then did the court manage to discuss it in such length? Here the court created a narrative of Tronson's own behaviour and how that reflected his own impression of his Indianness. The court reviewed evidence that Tronson was a non-Indian by consulting the following sources:

official band lists[50]

statements of the Indian Agent[51]

Tronson's father was a white man[52]

corroboration from RCMP[53]

applications Tronson had made for land and voting rights.[54]

In contrast, the evidence the court reviewed that Tronson was an Indian included the following:

an "old Indian woman" (eighty-two years old), who said that she remembered Tronson's birth on an Indian reserve[55]

another witness who stated that Tronson's grandmother was an Indian and that Tronson was born on a reserve[56]

Tronson's indication that he stayed on reserve at the request of the community.[57]

Other evidence that undermined Tronson's defence included a revelation that Mrs. Tronson's own residency application was denied (even though her mother resided on the reserve). This denial should not be a surprise if by virtue of the aforementioned identity provisions—by marrying Tronson—she became a non-Indian. The judge also noted that there was evidence that residents of the reserve had asked Tronson not to leave.[58] One witness assumed that Tronson enjoyed privileges of both a white man and an Indian.[59] This mistaken impression was something that the court seemed eager to clarify.

When the court found that Tronson had applied for and was granted land under the Land Act, and that Tronson had applied to be on the voters list, a finding that he was non-Indian was inevitable. As the court noted, "No Indian is Permitted to so apply" for these privileges; they can simply not be obtained by an Indian.[60] Rather than seeing this application as the response of a rational person trying to navigate a situation in which they were denied access to their community, the court viewed the application as a sort of dishonesty on Tronson's part. As the court put it: "Tronson cannot blow hot and blow cold. He cannot in one breath say in effect that he is a white man, and in the next say he is an Indian."[61] Here the court seems to take Tronson's actions as some sort of validation of his lack of Indian status. As the court put it: "Tronson had his name placed on the voters' list.... This is absolutely fatal to the position Tronson now takes before this Court, that he is entitled to the rights and privileges of an Indian under the Indian Act."[62] It should be remembered that Tronson did not create the process or legislation that denied him status, and he did not seem to have any recourse to appeal of that status. Yet despite this, there is evidence that he continued to try to maintain his Indian relations. Having been denied his Indianness, Tronson had to go on living his life and so he sought the privileges that went along with being non-Indian (as any rational person would do in that situation).

From what is presented in the case, there is very little recognition of Tronson's actual desires and agency. Tronson admitted at the start of the case that he did not have permission to be on the reserve.[63] Tronson also let the community speak for him. The residents had asked him to stay and he followed their wishes. The witnesses both attested to his Indian family, his birth in an Indian community. What happened in the reasons of this case and what happened in reality is that the Crown *told* Tronson he was a white man. He was told that because his Indian heritage resided in family members of the wrong gender. If your identity and community is denied through law, you adapt to your circumstances. In so adapting, individuals are not endorsing the colonial law that has severed their family connections. By using Tronson's actions to validate his non-Indianness, the court has concealed what is really going on. The reasoning of the court substitutes the decision making of an individual affected by legislation for the decision making of those who actually crafted the legislation. By placing "fatal" interpretive weight on Tronson's decision to apply for land and voting rights, the court conceals the actual decision-making power of the Indian agent and the government who held the official band lists. It is a tactic that operates through entrenched systems of domination that are deployed to conceal the true source of Tronson's dehumanization.

There are claims being staked in this case that go beyond the specific identity issues. One claim is clearly that the official line of evidence carries much more weight than "an old Indian woman" or the actions of residents who asked Tronson to stay. What is more disturbing is that Tronson's claims and motivations are wholly characterized by the actions of outsiders. To state it simply, Tronson's claims are actually a reflection of how he is being manipulated in law. The fact that the law operates, in its blind application, to dehumanize the "Indian" is enough to carry the charge that it is operating within a racist ideology. There do not need to be overtly racist characterizations from judges such as those seen above in *Syliboy* or *Cherokee Nation*. In fact, that is why racism operates so well in law. The dispossession, discrimination, and prejudice that it produces is normalized through official channels of discourse. This allows individual judges to divest themselves of responsibility (because they never fully hold it anyway), perhaps musing, "I just apply the law; I don't create it."

What does this have to do with the Métis and the *Daniels* case? Well, saying in one instance that you are Indian and in the other that you are a white man is something much more descriptive of the Métis experience. As the court made clear in its characterization of evidence in *Daniels*, there was no room for the Métis Nation in such political discourse. More importantly, similarly to how the court in *Tronson* used colonial law to undermine Tronson's argument, the court in *Daniels* used colonial law to justify Métis identity *as Indians*. With *Tronson* clearly being a "loss" and *Daniels* a "win," it might seem odd that I am comparing these cases. But despite the win, as I will illustrate below, the narrative in *Daniels* is even more disturbing than the narrative in *Tronson*, because it has the effect of confirming federal government jurisdiction over the Métis while at the same time almost completely silencing the Métis in the decision. This silencing (a form of dehumanization), I will argue below, is illustrative of the embedded racist ideology in Canadian courts.

Daniels v. Canada[64]

When the Supreme Court of Canada confirmed that the Métis are, legally speaking, "Indians" for the purpose of the division of powers, it did so by relying on evidence that "mixed-blood" Indians are Indians and used very little evidence that *Métis* are Indians. This might not seem like a big difference to those who see Métis as some mishmash of other cultures or genetics.[65] But as scholars such as Andersen have clearly articulated, the "Métis-as-mixed" narrative is problematic.[66] This argument is also furthered in this volume by Brenda Gunn in Chapter 7 and Darryl Leroux in Chapter 9. Here, however, I want to go back slightly further in scholarship and emphasize some points articulated by Paul Chartrand and Larry Chartrand about Métis peoplehood,[67] community, and culture. Those arguments locate the Métis as a People and not merely as a collection of randomly associated "mixed-blood" persons. To begin, I will look at the evidence that the Supreme Court does rely upon.

In setting up its argument for the inclusion of the Métis into the definition of "Indian" in s. 91(24), the scc pointed to evidence of government agency. This was done, primarily, by looking at the government's understanding of the words used in the Constitution Act, 1867,[68] examining the government's purpose in establishing the constitution,[69] and reviewing legislation that was targeted toward Métis people (here it refers primarily to "mixed" people).[70] In contrast, the court identified Métis agency by looking at the fact the Métis asked for the declaration in the case,[71] that the Métis had been a threat to Canada's expansion,[72] and that the Métis were builders of Confederation[73]—although the court does not specify how the Métis were builders of Confederation. Beyond these points, virtually all of the evidence used to justify the scc reasoning treats the Métis as mixed-blood Indians.[74]

To illustrate why this is problematic (beyond the "Métis-as mixed" arguments), it can be shown that the scc understood that the Métis are a People.

For example, the court cited with approval the following passage from John Borrows: "The Métis Nation was . . . crucial in ushering western and northern Canada into Confederation and in increasing the wealth of the Canadian nation by opening up the prairies to agriculture and settlement. These developments could not have occurred without Métis intercession and legal presence."[75] Here, Borrows nails it when he writes of the Métis "Nation" and its "legal presence." Both of these attributes are embodiments of a People. It is the peoplehood of the Métis that makes them an entity to negotiate with in the first place. Yet in order to carry this characterization of Métis agency into the decision itself, the SCC would have had to look toward evidence that the Métis "Nation" dealt with the federal government in a way that met the purpose of section 91(24). Fortunately, there is evidence of this. Unfortunately, the SCC did not rely upon that evidence.

The John Borrows quotation is a general value statement in that it is an assessment of the impact or meaning of history. What it does not do, at least in the way the SCC used it, is actually present that history. It was not used by the SCC to incorporate any specific acts by the Métis that would help the court interpret the constitution, despite the fact that the quotation creates a perfect set-up for that incorporation. The court ended up acknowledging that the Métis contributed something without specifically acknowledging anything that actually contributed to this nation building.

Instead of running with the nation-building argument, the court relied upon evidence that the federal government acted in ways that would incorporate Métis people as Indians through their mixedness. Here are some examples:

> "The government frequently classified Aboriginal peoples with mixed European and Aboriginal heritage as Indians."[76]

> "The federal government amended the Indian Act in 1894 to broaden the ban on the sale of intoxicating liquor to Indians or any person 'who follows the Indian mode of life,' which included Métis."[77]

> The federal government policy for residential schools was amended to include "even those children of mixed-blood."[78]

Referring to past case law, the court noted that "intermarriage
and mixed-ancestry do not preclude groups from inclusion under
s. 91(24)."[79]

These examples are illustrative of the belief that the Métis are "mixed." While
the court focuses rather inappropriately on the simple notion of mixing, the
reality is that the Métis as a People might also fit within the court's conception of mixedness (the full parameters of that are still unclear).[80] So, the idea
that the court might recognize Métis peoplehood is not necessarily lost by
the mixedness arguments upon which the court situated its decision making. Perhaps, the SCC is attempting to adopt a definition of Métis that goes
beyond the historical nexus of the Métis people.[81] There are good reasons
for doing this. Because law is decided on a case-by-case basis, the historical
knowledge upon which the law is built can also only develop incrementally.
While the SCC might be fully aware that there is a Métis Nation (in addition to the Borrows quotation, this is spelled out more clearly by the court
elsewhere),[82] it may not know whether or not there are other "métis" people.
Indeed, there are many claims to Métisness being made that rely only on
some distant ancestor or DNA discovery.[83] A bigger problem, then, is not
that the court conceives of Métis as "mixed," it is that the court does not give
any agency to the Métis People who are *obviously* Métis. This can only be
done through the use of express examples.

Paul Chartrand's work on the Manitoba Métis is helpful here.[84] Chartrand
presents a Métis conception of the Manitoba Act that clearly outlines how
the different provisions of the act were meant to operate to protect the Métis
community. The Manitoba Act had an eye to the future by protecting both
current and future land holders. That act, and the promises that it was built
upon, is characterized as a treaty by Chartrand.[85] That conception of the
agreement was also held by Riel, who wrote in 1874: "The bottom line is
that our cause has moved forward. I realized that in '69, we started defending our rights with a handful of men; a few months later, half of the colony
was already on our side; in March 1870, the entire colony was actively corrob-
orating our cause; and eight months following the serious beginning of our
fight, we obtained the sanction of all our rights by way of a treaty that became
law."[86] That "treaty" was negotiated directly with the federal government
and contained a provision that land would be granted to the Métis children

by virtue of the "Indian title" that they held. The Manitoba Act, as both a treaty and later as a constitutional document, represents the kind of evidence that the SCC could have used to recognize the federal government interacted with the Métis People and not merely with "mixed" persons. That is, it is evidence of the way that the federal government carried out its jurisdiction under s. 91(24) toward "Indians," but did so in relationship with the Métis People.[87] This can only be seen as a much stronger argument than an argument centered on mixedness, because by focusing on Métis peoplehood, the court can be assured that the entirety of its rationalization will not crumble once it is acknowledged that mixedness is a lousy way to identify Métis People (or any People for that matter).

Larry Chartrand also makes Métis peoplehood a central feature of his argument, contending that it is the political dimension of Aboriginal rights that is being negated in Aboriginal rights jurisprudence.[88] The implication of this lack of recognition of the political dimension is that Aboriginal rights are only seen as rights to use something and/or do something (a practice, custom, or tradition). This framework denies, by definition, the responsibility of Aboriginal peoples to decide, determine, and control things (jurisdiction and resources). The things that are denied to Aboriginal peoples under the courts' rights framework are the same types of things that help distinguish how one People distinguishes itself from another People. Chartrand states this clearly when he explains that past legal decisions have implicitly denied "that Aboriginal peoples are political societies with their own forms of social control."[89] This includes the ability to govern, to regulate an Indigenous right, and even the ability to determine who from the community gets to access the resources (like provinces might with licensing schemes). Chartrand developed his critique in 2001. I would argue that, today, the political dimension of Aboriginal rights is still negated by courts. Indeed, as *Daniels* illustrates, the political *identity* of the Métis is underplayed by the court.

Incorporating the political dimension of Aboriginal rights goes beyond empowering Aboriginal peoples in a rights context. In any historical interpretation (and Aboriginal rights are decidedly historical in nature),[90] the courts make choices about whether to view Aboriginal people as a designated conglomeration of persons or as distinct Peoples. Choosing whether or not to reinforce, validate, or otherwise acknowledge the political dimension of a People is the point at which the court validates or avoids Aboriginal peoplehood. To avoid this recognition is to not so subtly reinforce Crown authority over Aboriginal peoples. Without the court finding ways of incorporating this political dimension, we are left with doctrine that does not match rhetoric such as "nation-to-nation."[91]

The closest that the SCC has come to acknowledging the political dimension of Aboriginal rights is in the tangential aspects of Aboriginal title articulated in *Tsilhqot'in*. However, even as the court determined that the Tsilhqot'in have the right to decide how the land is used (which implies they had political interest over the land), it also reaffirmed provincial jurisdiction to regulate activities on those lands.[92] This regulatory power is in addition to the power to infringe upon the Tsilhqot'in title interest.[93] By limiting the political dimension in this way, the court secures a nation-to-subject approach of Aboriginal rights. This is problematic for Aboriginal peoples who continue to advocate for their rights as Peoples (including such variations as sovereignty, self-government, self-determination, land title, ownership, jurisdiction, etc.).[94] There appear to be some regular and predictable trends with how the law characterizes Aboriginal peoples, both within rights discourse and outside of it.

In addition to the rights-based concerns raised by Chartrand, I have previously discussed how Canadian law has created a situation where the nationhood of an Aboriginal group can be completely swallowed by the application of administrative law principles.[95] To uphold the distinctiveness of an Aboriginal People would pose a threat to current Canadian law because it would require a challenge to the default authority that is granted to the Crown. This is evidenced in part by the various statements of legal vacuums that the court has assumed when dealing with Aboriginal issues.[96] One situation where a legal vacuum would be present is when there is no authority to legislate over a matter. But Chartrand explains this is not the case in Aboriginal rights claims: "The problem with Justice Cory's understanding of Aboriginal rights, however, is that the alternative to responsible regulation is not anarchy as he would seem to suggest, but rather Aboriginal government control by the collective that 'owns' the right."[97] This reasoning by the SCC shows that it does not see Aboriginal peoples as a self-determining People capable of legislating over their internal affairs.

With such implications coming from legal reasoning, it is even more concerning that the Métis People have such a low visibility in a decision that was meant, in part, to help them find a negotiating partner. Without recognizing Aboriginal peoples as People, the government can choose any negotiating partner it wants or simply legislate over these "mixed" persons and call it a day. It can apply Canadian law and jurisdiction as a default, leaving Aboriginal Peoples having to *prove* their jurisdictional authority. Knowing what is at stake, it is apparent that *how* the court constructs Métisness is important. I am willing to concede, if only for purposes of this chapter, that there may be a good judicial reason for the court to envision Métis as more than the Nation, that is, the People that emerged in the West primarily out of Red River. That vision might allow the court to include groups of People that do not so easily fit that definition (whoever they may be). But certainly, any notion of Métis cannot proceed without recognition of the Métis People. To do so is to do real damage to Métis standing in legal discourse.

I have listed above instances where the court focuses on the presence of "mixed" persons to imply that that included Métis people. I have criticized this approach for its lack of recognition of Métis peoplehood. But it would be unfair to suggest that the SCC completely avoids any recognition of Métis peoplehood. Unfortunately, the recognition it did offer was quite weak.[98] It was brought to my attention that the reason for the lack of Métis agency in the *Daniels* ruling was because the Métis National Council and the Manitoba Metis Federation refused to participate in the litigation. However, a quick look at the reasoning of the trial decision illustrates how this argument does not stand up to scrutiny, because if we look at the trial level, we can see that the Federal Court (FC) did acknowledge the Métis People in its reasoning (even if only briefly). And it did so in ways that illustrated the political power and responsibility of the Métis People.

The recognition of Métis agency at the FC focused on the constitutional negotiations that produced the Manitoba Act, 1870. Here the FC looked at how the Métis at Red River established a provisional government,[99] and how this provisional government made claim to territory[100] and negotiated directly with Canada, resulting in the creation of Manitoba.[101] The FC also examined the circumstances of Treaty 3 and the "half-breed" Adhesion.[102] Each of these avenues of discourse could have been used by the SCC in its reasoning. Yet none were used in the SCC reasoning in *Daniels*. The only instance where the SCC identified legislation that targeted the Métis in a direct way was in regard to the residential school at St. Paul des Métis.[103] There were more powerful examples that embodied Métis peoplehood that could have been used.

Indeed, if we look at the way in which the FC discussed these issues, we can clearly see Métis agency acknowledged in the reasoning. Not only did the FC use these examples, but they explained how Métis *as a People* were treated as Indians for constitutional purposes. For example, the FC wrote: "The Red River Métis, as reflected by these negotiators, were 'Fathers of Confederation' and if not treated equally with whites, it is reasonable to conclude that they had a status akin to an enfranchised Indian. An enfranchised Indian was considered 'civilized' and avoided the strictures of the *Indian Act* but was nevertheless an Indian for constitutional purposes."[104] This is presented in the context of explaining that the Métis sent delegates to Ottawa to negotiate with Canada.[105] This type of organization and representation is something that a People does. It is not reflective of "a bunch of individuals bumping into each other . . . devoid of responsibility and the rule of law."[106]

And of the Treaty 3 Adhesion, the FC explained: "The Treaty 3 Adhesion is an instance where the federal government treated the half-breeds/Métis group as if it had a claim to Indian title."[107] Treaties are important in recognizing agency and peoplehood because, as was stated in *Campbell* in regards to a modern treaty in British Columbia, "the fact that the Crown in right of Canada and the Crown in right of British Columbia have entered into these negotiations, and concluded an Agreement, illustrates that the Crown accepts the Nisga'a Nation has the authority to bargain with the State and possesses rights which are negotiable."[108] The failure of the SCC to acknowledge these obvious instances of Métis agency should not be surprising, considering the courts' history with the issue of "Indian title." Indeed, if the SCC was to work the above examples into its reasoning, it would undercut years of downplaying Métis agency, interests, and Indigeneity in the courts. I will explore some examples of this below.

First, in *Blais*, the SCC showed little difficulty in overriding the express terminology of the constitution (the Manitoba Act, 1870) when it effectively wrote out the connection between half-breeds and "Indian title" in favour of words that were spoken in Parliament fifteen years after the Manitoba Act was created. The SCC justified the dismissal of the constitution as follows:

The *Manitoba Act, 1870* used the term "half-breed" to refer to the
Métis, and set aside land specifically for their use: *Manitoba Act,
1870*, S.C. 1870, c. 3, s. 31.... While s. 31 states that this land is
being set aside "towards the extinguishment of the Indian Title to
the lands in the Province," *this was expressly recognized at the time
as being an inaccurate description* [emphasis added]. Sir John A.
Macdonald explained in 1885:

    "Whether they [the Métis] had any right to those lands or not
was not so much the question as it was a question of policy to make
an arrangement with the inhabitants of that Province.... 1,400,000
acres would be quite sufficient for the purpose of compensating
these men for what was called the extinguishment of the Indian
title. That phrase was an incorrect one, the half-breeds did not
allow themselves to be Indians."[109]

The FC in *Daniels* also notes this passage from Macdonald but provides
the context to the quotation and ultimately finds that it is not persuasive
in undermining the constitutional wording. The FC explains: "The context in which Macdonald made his July 1885 statement was, as pointed out
by Jones, in response to an opposition motion accusing the Conservative
government of having caused the 1885 Riel Rebellion by neglect, delay and
mismanagement. At this time Riel was awaiting trial. Macdonald had been
subject to a seven-hour speech by the Opposition Leader attacking him for
the delay in implementing scrip outside Manitoba which was authorized
under the *Dominion Lands Act 1879* (*An Act to amend and consolidate the
several Acts respecting the Public Lands of the Dominion*, 42 Vict c 31)."[110]
More important than the reasoning of Macdonald's explanation of the Manitoba Act were his own contrary words which actually confirmed the wording of the Act and reinforced the "Indian title" of the "half-breeds." On this
point, the FC wrote: "While there was confusion among some opposition
members as to the scrip system, twice in the 2 May 1870 debate, Macdonald
referred to the allocation of lands to the half-breeds as being 'for the purpose
of extinguishing the Indian title.'"[111] This deeper dive into historical context
contradicts the earlier, somewhat flippant reasoning of the SCC in *Blais*. For
the SCC to rely upon the more detailed findings of fact produced by the
FC in *Daniels* would be to undermine its previous interpretation in *Blais*.
Rather than acknowledging the error and improving its historical narrative,

the scc simply ignored this line of evidence in crafting its own reasoning in *Daniels*. In so doing, the scc also excluded Métis peoplehood from the interpretation.

Acknowledging its error from *Blais* would also require the scc to question its neglect of constitutional language in the reasons of *MMF v. Canada*.[112] In *MMF*, the scc decided to contradict the fact that the constitution stated as fact that the half-breeds have "Indian title." In place of that wording, the scc wrote: "In summary, the words of s. 31 do not establish pre-existing communal Aboriginal title held by the Métis. Nor does the evidence: the trial judge's findings of fact that the Métis had no communal Aboriginal interest in land are fatal to this contention. It follows that the argument that Canada was under a fiduciary duty in administering the children's land because the Métis held an Aboriginal interest in the land must fail. The same reasoning applies to s. 32 of the Manitoba Act."[113] And with that, the scc found another way to disregard the plain wording of the constitution. These interpretations deny Métis Indigeneity, effort, and sacrifice in confederating with Canada. With this jurisprudential history, it should not come as a surprise that Métis peoplehood is underplayed by the scc in *Daniels*. With these interpretive decisions, the Métis People have virtually no interpretive impact in *Daniels* at the scc. Instead, the court favours a broad understanding of mixedness, within which distinct communities may or may not appear.

Conclusion: Back to Racism

The scc has a history of undermining Métis agency. This history, I would argue, dehumanizes the Métis People. It reduces their historical role, unilaterally alters their negotiated claims, and negates their peoplehood. The decisions of the court serve to provide a seemingly neutral decision-making process on Métis history and peoplehood that nevertheless dispossesses the Métis, not only as considerers of the world[114] but also of their "stuff" ("Indian title"). In examining a series of cases that involve determining who the Métis are and what they have access to, it is hard to explain this consistent denial of their peoplehood as being empowered by something other than a deeply entrenched racism. Judges do not have to be consciously thinking like racist bigots to exercise this type of structural racism. Instead, because the roots of the law run deep with decision making that has denied Aboriginal people's interests, judges merely have to apply the law and uphold Crown power to carry out racism. The individual culpability of particular judges can be set aside if we think about the full implication from this statement by Gordon Christie: "It is the imposition of the European vision to which Aboriginal peoples were, and continue to be, vulnerable."[115] That vision works better if it appears to be just part of *the* process. It works best if those carrying out *the* process do not recognize their role or their interpretive decisions as being linked to this racist vision. It is in that imposition that Aboriginal peoples continue to suffer, because even when Aboriginal peoples "win" their intended legal rights or declarations, the Aboriginal community has to rise against the narratives produced in those decisions.

If we return to a quotation from *Tronson*, it turns out that you can "blow hot and blow cold"—if you are the Crown. The court can claim that the Métis are a People *and* it can claim that they are "mixed." The Crown can claim that the Métis have "Indian Title" *and* its courts can assert that the Métis do not have "Indian Title" (or worse, that the Métis do not even have "Aboriginal title"). The court can claim that the Métis are builders of Confederation *and* it can avoid giving interpretive weight to that peoplehood where this might undermine its earlier case law. Just as in *Tronson*, where the court favoured the agency of the Crown, the SCC favours Crown agency in *Daniels*. Just as in *Tronson*, where the court discounts the agency of Indians in claiming their own, so too does the SCC discount the agency of the Métis in contributing to constitutional interpretation. It is important to keep in mind what was "won" in *Daniels*. The Métis "won" the privilege of being declared a legislative responsibility of the federal government, a situation that arose because neither provincial nor federal levels of government wanted to acknowledge a responsibility to deal with the Métis as an Aboriginal People of Canada. In both legal and government processes, the ideology that favours dehumanizing Aboriginal peoples holds sway. That dehumanization serves as a prejudice against the responsibilities that Métis people carry as a People, it serves to discriminate against them, and it serves to dispossess Aboriginal people of their claims to land. This is institutional racism, and it runs deep in Canadian jurisprudential reason.

NOTES

1   This characterization can be found in past case law in Canada. See, for example, *Baker Lake v. Minister of Indian Affairs and Northern Development*, [1980] 1 F.C. 180 at para. 80, where the court set out the features for proving Aboriginal title, one of which was: "That they and their ancestors were members of an organized society."

2   *Daniels v. Canada* (Indian Affairs and Northern Development), 2016 SCC 12.

3   *R. v. Tronson*, [1931], 57 C.C.C. 383, (1932).

4   See Frederick Charles DeCoste, *On Coming to Law: An Introduction to Law in Liberal Societies*, 2nd ed. (Markham, ON: LexisNexis Canada, 2007), 18–19, where he explains: "Legal rules are backed by the state through its own institutions, especially and typically through its court system. . . . That legal rules may be vindicated through public institutions means that legal rules, unlike all other rules, apply comprehensively. Where they apply, they regulate the whole of our conduct, even when such conduct might otherwise be the subject of some other, non-legal prescriptive rule. Law, in this way, 'defines the basic structure in which the pursuit of all other activities takes place,' because all other rules and associations are subordinate to it. Legal rules, then, add to the compulsiveness which is definitive of rules more generally, not merely because they are rules which the state endorses, but more specifically because public vindication of that sort means that state rules have priority over all other rules by which men and women attempt to guide the conduct of their lives."

5   See Arthur J. Ray, *Telling It to the Judge: Taking Native History to Court* (Montreal: McGill-Queen's University Press, 2012).

6   The court in *R. v. Sparrow* [1990] 1 S.C.R. 1075 at para. 59 noted, "The relationship between the Government and aboriginals is trust-like, rather than adversarial, and contemporary recognition and affirmation of aboriginal rights must be defined in light of this historic relationship." Clearly, if these relationships are being fought over in an adversarial court system, they have lost the fiduciary aspect.

7   It would seem that this is the point of creating Aboriginal histories in court. As McLachlin explains, in *R. v. Marshall*; *R. v. Bernard*, 2005 SCC 43 at para. 48, those histories (perspectives) that help explain an Aboriginal practice are meant to be "translated" into a "modern legal right."

8   See *Manitoba Metis Federation Inc. v. Canada (Attorney General) et al.* [2008] 2 C.N.L.R. 52; Stephen E. Patterson, "Land Grants for Loyalists: A Report Prepared for the Department of Justice Canada," File no. CI 81-01-01010, Winnipeg, 31 October 2005. Also note Patterson's take on Peace and Friendship treaties in Patterson, "Eighteenth-Century Treaties," *Native Studies Review* 18, no. 1 (2009): 25–52. I offer a critique of other similarly oriented scholarship in D'Arcy Vermette, "Rejecting the Standard Discourse on the Dispossession of Métis Lands in Manitoba," *Aboriginal Policy Studies* 6, no. 2 (2017): 87–119.

9   See the oral arguments in *Tsilhqot'in Nation v. British Columbia*, [2014] SCC 44 at Supreme Court of Canada (website), "Webcast of the Hearing on 2013-11-07," Case number 34986, where Justice Rothstein and counsel for the Tsilhqot'in had the following exchange. Justice Rothstein: "Is there any land that was included because of legal as opposed to physical occupation?" Mr. Rosenberg: "I think not." This helped clarify that the proof for Aboriginal title is through physical occupation rather than a broader political jurisdiction.

10   *R. v. Powley*, 2003 SCC 43.

11   Chris Andersen, *"Métis": Race, Recognition, and the Struggle for Indigenous Peoplehood.* (Vancouver: UBC Press, 2014), 137–51; see note 10.

12　Andersen, *"Métis,"* 136.

13　Ibid., 135.

14　Ibid.

15　Ibid.

16　D' Arcy Vermette, "Colonialism and the Process of Defining Aboriginal People," *Dalhousie Law Journal* 31, no. 1 (2008): 238.

17　DeCoste, *On Coming to Law*, 12.

18　Ibid., 17.

19　Chris Andersen, "Mixed Ancestry or Métis?," in *Indigenous Identity and Resistance: Researching the Diversity of Knowledge*, ed. Brendan Hokowhitu et al. (Dunedin, NZ: University of Otago Press, 2010), 34.

20　Helpful in examining these issues are Ronald Sanders, *Lost Tribes and Promised Lands: The Origins of American Racism* (Boston: Little, Brown and Company, 1978); and Robert A. Williams Jr., *The American Indian in Western Legal Thought: The Discourses of Conquest* (New York: Oxford University Press, 1990).

21　Robert Wald Sussman, *The Myth of Race: The Troubling Persistence of an Unscientific Idea* (Boston: Harvard University Press, 2016).

22　Harry M. Bracken, "Essence, Accident and Race," *Hermathena*, no. 116 (1973): 81.

23　Harry M. Bracken, "Philosophy and Racism," *Philosophia: Philosophical Quarterly of Israel* 8 (1978): 242.

24　Ibid.

25　Roland Chrisjohn, transcript of presentation, "Racism: Back to the Basics," http://www.native-studies.org/native_pdf/Racismbacktobasics.pdf (accessed 25 July 2011).

26　William Ryan, *Blaming the Victim*, rev. ed. (New York: Vintage Books, 1976), 11. Here Ryan is referring to the work of Karl Mannheim.

27　See Andrea Bear Nicholas, "Linguicide," *Briarpatch Magazine*, March/April 2011; and Tove Skutnabb-Kangas and Robert Phillipson, "Submersion Education and the Killing of Languages in Canada: Linguistic Human Rights and Language Revitalization in the USA and Canada," in *Language Rights*, vol. 3, *Language Endangerment and Revitalisation; Language Rights Charters and Declarations*, ed. Tove Skutnabb-Kangas and Robert Phillipson (London and New York: Routledge, 2017).

28　Vermette, "Colonialism and the Process of Defining," 216.

29　Indian Act R.S., 1985, c. I-5, s. 88. A historical overview can be found in James S. Frideres, *First Nations in the Twenty-First Century*, 2nd ed. (Don Mills, ON: Oxford University Press, 2016).

30　See Vermette, "Colonialism and the Process of Defining."

31　Reference as to whether "Indians" in s. 91(24) of the BNA Act includes Eskimo inhabitants of the Province of Quebec, [1939] S.C.R. 104.

32　British North America Act, 1867, 30 and 31 Victoria, c. 3 (U.K.) s. 133, in *A Consolidation of The Constitution Acts 1867 to 1982*.

33　Full comment on this case can be found in Constance Backhouse, "'Race' Definition Run Amuck: 'Slaying the Dragon of Eskimo Status' before the Supreme Court of Canada, 1939," in *Law, History, Colonialism: The Reach of Empire*, ed. Dianne Kirkby and Catharine Coleborne

(Manchester: Manchester University Press, 2001), 65. I have also written about this case previously, in Vermette, "Colonialism and the Process of Defining," 235–39.

34 See *St. Catherine's Milling and Lumber Company v. The Queen*, (1888), 14 A.C. 46 (P.C.) where the Privy Council sets out the features of Aboriginal title. A collection of older case law (1763–1910) can be found in Brian Slattery, *Canadian Native Law Cases*, vol. 1, *1763–1869*. (Saskatoon: Native Law Centre, 1980); Brian Slattery, *Canadian Native Law Cases*, vol. 2, *1870–1890* (Saskatoon: Native Law Centre, 1981); and Brian Slattery and Linda Charlton, *Canadian Native Law Cases*, vol. 3, *1891–1910* (Saskatoon: Native Law Centre, 1985).

35 Backhouse, "'Race' Definition Run Amuck," 73–74.

36 "Whether such laws are wise or unwise is of course a much-controverted question, but it is not relevant to their constitutional validity." P.W. Hogg, as referred to in *Delgamuukw, v. British Columbia* (1991), 79 D.L.R. (4th) 185 (B.C.S.C.), as cited in Mary Ellen Turpel, "Home/Land," *Canadian Journal of Family Law* 10, no. 1 (1991): 29.

37 See *R. v. Blais*, 2003 SCC 44, where the court discusses the Manitoba Natural Resources Act, S.C. 1930, c. 29.

38 This distinction was pointed out in *Reference re Same-Sex Marriage*, [2004] 3 S.C.R. 698, 2004 SCC 79, para. 30, where the court explained that "it is submitted that the intention of the framers should be determinative in interpreting the scope of the heads of power enumerated in ss. 91 and 92 given the decision in *R. v. Blais*, [2003] 2 S.C.R. 236, 2003 SCC 44 (CanLII). That case considered the interpretive question in relation to a particular constitutional agreement, as opposed to a head of power which must continually adapt to cover new realities. It is therefore distinguishable and does not apply here."

39 See *Mabo and Others v. Queensland* (No. 2), (1992) 175 CLR 1, where the court notes that there is a limit in how far the law can be pushed: "In discharging its duty to declare the common law of Australia, this Court is not free to adopt rules that accord with contemporary notions of justice and human rights if their adoption would fracture the skeleton of principle which gives the body of our law its shape and internal consistency."

40 *Rex v. Syliboy*, [1928] 1 D.L.R. 307.

41 Ibid.

42 *Re Paulette et al. and Registrar of Titles* (No.2), 42 D.L.R. (3d) 8, [1973] 6 W.W.R. 115 (N.W.T.S.C.).

43 Ibid.

44 Ibid. Justice Morrow summarized some of the testimony as follows: "Most witnesses were firm in their recollection that land was not to be surrendered, reserves were not mentioned, and the main concern and chief thrust of the discussions centred around the fear of losing their hunting and fishing rights."

45 Paulo Freire, *Pedagogy of the Oppressed*, 20th anniversary ed., transl. Myra Bergman Ramos (New York: Continuum, 1997), 120.

46 DeCoste, *On Coming to Law*, 17, notes that this division of decision making is part of the normal working of law: "*prescriptive rules are devices for allocating power to, and limiting the power of, decision-makers*" (emphasis in original). For a more thorough examination of the power of divesting responsibility through individual, bureaucratic action see Zygmunt Bauman, *Modernity and the Holocaust* (Ithaca, NY: Cornell University Press, 1989).

47   *Calder v. British Columbia* (Attorney-General), [1973] S.C.R. 313. The tie in *Calder* was also
     broken this way when Justice Pigeon decided to dismiss the case on the technicality that the
     Nishga were not entitled to sue the provincial government of British Columbia because they had
     not received permission to sue. This permission can only be given by the provincial government.

48   *Cherokee Nation v. Georgia*, (1831) 30 U.S. (5 Pet.) 1 at 17. For a look at how this case fits in with
     another seminal case written by Justice Marshall, *Johnson v. M'Intosh*, 21 U.S. 543 (1823) which
     discusses the doctrine of discovery, see Williams, *The American Indian*, 312–17.

49   See note 3, at 387, where these criteria are set out as follows: "'Indian' means – (i) Any male
     person of Indian blood reputed to belong to a particular band, (ii) any child of such person, (iii)
     any woman who is or was lawfully married to such person."

50   See note 3, at 390.

51   Ibid., at 389.

52   Ibid., at 389.

53   Ibid., at 387.

54   Ibid., at 390–91.

55   Ibid., at 391.

56   Ibid., at 391.

57   Ibid., at 387.

58   Ibid., at 387.

59   Ibid., at 391.

60   Ibid., at 391.

61   Ibid., at 390.

62   Ibid., at 391.

63   Ibid., at 388.

64   For more details on the background of the *Daniels* litigation that includes a different take on
     the limitations of the decision, see Signa A. Daum Shanks, "Commentary: The Wastelander
     Life: Living Before and After the Release of *Daniels v Canada*," *Osgoode Hall Law Journal* 54
     (2017): 1341–58.

65   For a clear articulation of the problems with "race-based" reasoning in *Daniels*, see Jean Teillet and
     Carly Teillet, "Devoid of Principle: The Federal Court Determination That Section 91(24) of the
     Constitution Act, 1867 Is a Race-Based Provision," *Indigenous Law Journal* 13, no. 1 (2016): 12,
     which focuses on the reasoning up to the Federal Court of Appeal. For another take on some of
     the issues I am discussing in this chapter, see Brenda L. Gunn, "Defining Métis People as a People:
     Moving Beyond the Indian/Métis Dichotomy," *Dalhousie Law Journal* 38, no. 1 (2015): 413–46.

66   Andersen, *"Métis."*

67   Ibid., 19, provides a nice use of "peoplehood" that reflects the use I am aiming at for the purposes
     of this chapter: "I use 'peoplehood' as a political entity to distinguish it from the more typical,
     locally based geographical use of the term 'community.' In particular, the ability of peoples to
     produce formal political relationships with other peoples both distinguishes and elevates people-
     hood above other kinds of community" (references omitted).

68   See note 2, at para. 25.

69   Ibid., at para. 25.

70 Ibid., at paras. 18, 24.

71 Ibid., at paras. 11–15.

72 Ibid., at para. 26.

73 Ibid., at para. 26.

74 Ibid., at paras. 4, 17, 18, 23, 24, 28, 32, 41. Larry N. Chartrand in "The Failure of the Daniels Case: Blindly Entrenching a Colonial Legacy," *Alberta Law Review* 51, no. 1 (2013): 181–89, argues for a more expansive interpretation of s. 91(24) informed by contemporary human rights and the honour of the Crown in recognition of the need for a decolonizing relationship with Aboriginal peoples.

75 *Daniels*, 2016 SCC 12 at para. 26, where the court cites John Borrows, *Canada's Indigenous Constitution* (Toronto: University of Toronto Press, 2010), 87–88.

76 *Daniels*, 2016 SCC 12, at para. 24.

77 Ibid., at para. 27.

78 Ibid., at para. 28.

79 Ibid., at para. 41.

80 The SCC tried to clarify Métis identity in *R. v. Powley*, 2003 SCC 43 at paras. 29–35.

81 This would seem to be the case. The court in *Daniels*, 2016 SCC 12, writes at para. 46: "there is no need to delineate which mixed-ancestry communities are Métis and which are non-status Indians. They are all 'Indians' under s. 91(24) by virtue of the fact they are all Aboriginal peoples."

82 See note 2, at para. 42.

83 See Darryl Leroux, "'We've Been Here for 2,000 Years': White Settlers, Native American DNA and the Politics of Indigeneity," *Social Studies of Science* 48, no. 1 (2018): 80–100.

84 Paul L.A.H. Chartrand, *Manitoba's Métis Settlement Scheme of 1870* (Saskatoon: Native Law Centre, University of Saskatchewan, 1991).

85 This treaty argument was updated in my doctoral thesis. See D'Arcy Vermette, "Beyond Doctrines of Dominance: Conceptualizing a Path to Legal Recognition and Affirmation of the Manitoba Métis Treaty" (PhD diss., University of Ottawa, 2012).

86 Riel to Dubuc, May 27, 1874, Exhibit 1-1001, as cited in *Manitoba Metis Federation Inc. v. Canada* (Attorney General) et al. [2008] 2 C.N.L.R. 52, File No.: CI 81-01-01010. Manitoba Metis Federation, Plaintiff's Final Argument, 1026.

87 This does not necessarily have to be a s. 91(24) issue. The only government that could have negotiated with the Métis was the federal government. However, we are assuming here that the SCC could have used stronger evidence to support its conclusion that the Métis are Indians. Certainly, whether by default or due to the actual promises that were brought into the act, the federal government did negotiate the "Indian" interests of the Métis People at Red River.

88 Larry N. Chartrand, "The Political Dimension of Aboriginal Rights" (LLM thesis, Queen's University, Faculty of Law, 2001).

89 Ibid., 27.

90 The test used to identify Aboriginal rights can be found in *R. v. Van der Peet*, [1996] 2 S.C.R. 507. I have critiqued aspects of this decision in D'Arcy Vermette, "Dizzying Dialogue: Canadian Courts and the Continuing Justification of the Dispossession of Aboriginal Peoples," *Windsor Yearbook of Access to Justice* 29, no. 1 (2011): 55–72.

91 *Mitchell v. Minister of National Revenue*, 2001 SCC 33, per Binnie at para. 130, where the Two-Row Wampum is used to justify assimilation of Aboriginal peoples into the body politic of Canada.

92 See note 9, at paras. 101–6.

93 Ibid., at paras. 24–50.

94 This does not always work out so well. See *R. v. Pamajewon*, [1996] 2 S.C.R. 821, where self-government was denied by definition; and *Mitchell*, note 91, per Binnie, where sovereignty was denied through assimilation of interests.

95 *Beckman v. Little Salmon/Carmacks First Nation*, 2010 SCC 53. This case is discussed in Vermette, "Dizzying Dialogue," 57.

96 Chartrand, "The Political Dimension," 88, is helpful in this regard. He notes *R. v. Nikal*, [1996] 1 S.C.R. 1013 and *R. v. Gladstone*, [1996] 2 S.C.R. 723 as two examples (pp. 25–30).

97 Chartrand, "The Political Dimension," 27.

98 See note 2, at para. 42, for example, where the court states that there "is no doubt that the Métis are a distinct people." The examples the court uses to display this are gutted of Métis agency and instead, the findings of the court are emphasized along with the duties and responsibilities of the Crown. This gives the impression that there are no competing polities in these situations.

99 See note 2, at para. 387.

100 Ibid., at paras. 388 and 395.

101 Ibid., at para. 395. See more generally paras. 392–424.

102 Ibid., at paras. 424–36.

103 Ibid., at para. 29.

104 Ibid., at para. 398.

105 Ibid., at paras 392–401.

106 Chartrand, "The Political Dimension," 26, characterizes the errors in the SCC's denial of the political dimension of Aboriginal rights.

107 See note 2, at para. 434.

108 *Campbell v. British Columbia* (Attorney General), [2000] B.C.J. 1524 at para. 33.

109 *R. v. Blais*, 2003 SCC 44 at para. citation where the court cites *House of Commons Debates*, July 6, 1885 at p. 3113, cited in Thomas Flanagan, "The History of Métis Aboriginal Rights: Politics, Principle, and Policy," *Canadian Journal of Law and Society* 5 (1990): 74. *Campbell v. BC* at para. 399 quotes s. 31 of the Manitoba Act as follows: "31. And whereas, it is expedient, *towards the extinguishment of the Indian Title* [my emphasis] to the lands in the Province, to appropriate a portion of such ungranted lands to the extent of one million four hundred thousand acres thereof, for the benefit of the families of the half-breed residents, it is hereby enacted that under regulations to be from time to time made by the Governor General in Council, the Lieutenant-Governor shall select such lots or tracts in such parts of the Province as he may deem expedient, to the extent aforesaid, and divide the same among the children of the half-breed heads of families residing in the province at the time of the said transfer to Canada, and the same shall be granted to the said children respectively in such mode and on such conditions as to settlement and otherwise, as the Governor General in Council shall from time to time determine."

110 See note 2, at para. 416.

111 See note 2, at para. 407.

112 *Manitoba Metis Federation Inc. v. Canada* (Attorney General), 2013 SCC 14.

113 Ibid., at para. 59.

114 Freire, *Pedagogy of the Oppressed*.

115 Gordon Christie, "Justifying Principles of Treaty Interpretation," *Queen's Law Journal* 26, no. 1 (2000): 143–224.

CHAPTER 7

Daniels through an International Law Lens

BRENDA L. GUNN

Under section 91(24) of division of powers in the Canadian constitution, the federal government has jurisdiction over "Indians and lands reserved for Indians." As discussed in previous chapters of this volume, in *Daniels v. Canada*, the Supreme Court of Canada (SCC) resolved the long-running dispute over whether it is the federal or the provincial governments that have a constitutional responsibility for Métis people and non–Status Indians under the constitution.[1] Previously, both governments had denied jurisdiction over Métis and non–Status Indians, claiming they had no legislative authority, with the federal government arguing it only had jurisdiction over Indians and Inuit, and many provinces arguing that Métis fell under s. 91(24).[2] The refusal of both levels of government placed Métis and non–Status Indians in a "jurisdictional wasteland" where they were denied material benefits, programs, and services because no government would take responsibility.[3] This denial of jurisdiction and responsibility increased the difficulty of the Métis people in succeeding in self-government negotiations, as no government believed it had jurisdiction or responsibility to enter into such negotiations.

With the hope of addressing this jurisdictional wasteland and promoting self-government, Harry Daniels, a Métis leader of the Congress of Aboriginal Peoples, joined by Leah Gardner, a non-Status Anishinaabe woman, and Terry Joudrey, a non-Status Mi'kmaq man, brought a claim to the Federal Court of Canada.[4] The plaintiffs sought three declarations, namely that (a) Métis and non–Status Indians fall under federal jurisdiction as "Indians" under s. 91(24); (b) the federal Crown owes a fiduciary duty to Métis and non–Status Indians; and (c) Métis and non–Status Indians have the right to be consulted and negotiated with, in good faith, by the federal government on a collective basis through representatives of their choice, respecting all their rights, interests, and needs as Aboriginal peoples.[5]

Ultimately, the Supreme Court of Canada held that Métis people do fall within the federal jurisdiction over "Indians and lands reserved for Indians."[6] Many have welcomed the *Daniels* decision and celebrate the end of the uncertainty and the lack of accountability faced by Métis people at the hands of the federal and provincial governments. However, the decision has also faced a lot of criticism.[7] One unfortunate consequence of *Daniels* has been a rise in self-declared Métis people who are claiming Indigeneity because of the Supreme Court's statements that Métis "can be used as a general term for anyone with mixed European and Aboriginal heritage."[8] While the court was attempting to ensure that the federal government's responsibility was clearly extended to all those who had been inappropriately excluded, the concern is that the court may have diminished the recognized distinctiveness of the Métis people as well as undermined Métis peoples' right to determine who is Métis.[9] As a result of *Daniels*, there has been an increase in self-proclaimed "Métis" groups who are seeking to exploit and appropriate what it means to be Indigenous (Métis) in Canada, while maintaining their white privilege.[10]

International human rights have evolved over the past thirty years, including and especially with respect to the rights of Indigenous peoples. This body of international law, especially the standards set out in the UN Declaration on the Rights of Indigenous Peoples, provides a useful lens through which to view the problem of the new "Métis" groups arising post-*Daniels*. The UN Declaration is the "most comprehensive and advanced of international instruments dealing with indigenous peoples' rights," as it recognizes a full range of Indigenous peoples' inherent civil, political, economic, social, cultural, and environmental rights.[11] The UN Declaration recognizes the inherent rights of

Indigenous peoples as grounded in their own customs, laws, and traditions. It is unique in that it identifies and protects both individual and collective rights, and imposes obligations on states, international organizations, and intergovernmental bodies to uphold those rights.[12] The rights recognized within the UN Declaration establish the minimum standards that all states must adhere to in order to protect Indigenous peoples around the world.[13]

The UN General Assembly adopted the Declaration on the Rights of Indigenous Peoples on 13 September 2007.[14] A majority of 144 states voted in favour of the UN Declaration, eleven states abstained, and four states, including Canada, voted against it. Canada initially resisted the UN Declaration's application in Canada, stating that it was inconsistent with the Canadian constitution and had no legal effect in Canada.[15] More recently, Canada has endorsed the UN Declaration and committed to implementing it. Shortly after Prime Minister Justin Trudeau took office, he mandated Carolyn Bennett, Minister of Indigenous and Northern Affairs, "to support the work of reconciliation, and continue the necessary process of truth telling and healing, work with provinces and territories, and with First Nations, the Métis Nation, and Inuit, to implement recommendations of the Truth and Reconciliation Commission, starting with the implementation of the United Nations Declaration on the Rights of Indigenous Peoples."[16] Following this, on 10 May 2016 Carolyn Bennett released a long-overdue news statement that Canada is now an unqualified supporter of the UN Declaration.[17] The difficult work of implementing the declaration in Canada now lies ahead. While the benefits of implementing the UN Declaration are many, one of the most relevant is the way in which it addresses the issue of new groups claiming to be Métis post-*Daniels*.

This chapter discusses the *Daniels* decision in light of the rights of Indigenous peoples recognized in the UN Declaration on the Rights of Indigenous Peoples. It begins by reviewing the court decision and issues that have arisen as a result of the *Daniels* decision. While previous chapters in this volume have discussed the case, the background is reiterated here to identify aspects of the decision that have been identified as problematic by other authors. The chapter then attempts to provide insight into how international human rights law, including the UN Declaration, alleviates some of the concerns that have been raised, including the potential expansion of the definition of Métis people. The chapter concludes with a brief description of the types of rights that could flow from the resolution of the jurisdictional issues, which will hopefully encourage the federal government to engage in self-government negotiations with the Métis people.

The *Daniels* Decision and the Subsequent Fallout

As discussed in other chapters, the issue in *Daniels* was whether the federal government or provincial levels of government had jurisdiction and responsibility for Métis people. In order for the court to consider this question, the issue needed to be phrased as whether "Métis people" were "Indians" for the purposes of s. 91(24) of the Constitution Act, 1967. Basically, this question asked whether it was possible to interpret the term "Indians" in s. 91(24) to include Métis people, similar to the decision that the term "Indians" included federal responsibility over "Inuit." While the *Daniels* decision finally put to rest the jurisdictional issues confronting the Métis people, in reaching its decision, the court made several statements that may have opened up questions as to who can be considered "Métis" for this federal jurisdiction. This section discusses some of the issues that have arisen since the *Daniels* decision before providing an analysis and response to those issues based on international human rights law.

An unfortunate outcome of the *Daniels* decision is a rise in self-declared Métis groups who aim to capitalize on perceived benefits of being Indigenous in Canada.[18] These groups seem to have latched on to the statement that "Métis can refer to the historic Métis community in Manitoba's Red River Settlement or it can be used as a general term for anyone with mixed European and Aboriginal heritage."[19] As Darryl Leroux demonstrates in Chapter 9 of this volume, the new groups that have arisen post-*Daniels* have designed their membership policies around whether a potential member can genealogically verify they have a single Indigenous ancestor, and therefore the group does not represent a specific Indigenous peoples, community, or nation of origin.[20] For example, the Communauté Mikinak de la Montérégie, Quebec, founded in December 2015, grew in the months following the *Daniels* decision from thirty-seven members to over 400.[21] To gain membership, a potential member need only provide genealogical evidence of at least one Indigenous ancestor from some point in history, from anywhere in Canada.[22] Once membership is gained, a member card is provided claiming that the bearer has harvesting

rights, transborder trade, and treaty rights.[23] The Mikinaks claim that they
were forced to hide their ancestral Indigenous cultures for generations and
seek redress through what they perceive as benefits provided to Indians by
the federal government.[24] New groups seek tax exemptions, hunting rights,
and university assistance while ignoring Indigenous peoples' existing legal
processes for determining who belongs to Indigenous communities.[25]

The identity reclamation tactic employed by these new groups amounts
to a type of "self-Indigenization," where groups utilize their white privilege
to appropriate Indigeneity.[26] This tactic has also been referred to as "settler
nativism."[27] While *Daniels* may not have caused a desire to erase Indigenous
peoples by taking their place, to feel a sense of belonging on stolen lands, or
to obtain perceived benefits of being Indigenous, the case has emboldened
self-proclaimed Métis groups to claim Indigenous identity and the rights
associated with it.[28]

These new claims after *Daniels* connect to issues where the court
comments on the term "Métis." The Supreme Court tried to refrain from
defining who is Métis for the purposes of the federal government's jurisdiction under s. 91(24).[29] While the issue before the court did not require it to
determine the legal definition of Métis or non–Status Indian, Justice Abella,
on behalf of the court, recognized that the name "Métis" has been used to
refer to different groups, including where she wrote that "'Métis' can refer to
the historic Métis community in Manitoba's Red River Settlement or it can
be used as a general term for anyone with mixed European and Aboriginal
heritage."[30] Unfortunately, there is a lack of precision in her phrasing, which
has led to confusion as to whether or not Justice Abella condoned both uses
of the term, or was simply stating the fact that the term has been used in both
contexts. An interpretation of "Métis" that emphasizes a "Métis-as-mixed"
definition, rather than recognizing the Metis as a distinct peoplehood has
long been criticized by Métis people.[31] The "Métis-as-mixed" definition is also
one that the court has clearly rejected in determining who can assert Métis
rights under s. 35(1) of the Constitution Act, 1982: "The term 'Métis' in s.
35 does not encompass all individuals with mixed Indian and European heritage; rather, it refers to distinctive peoples who, in addition to their mixed
ancestry, developed their own customs, way of life, and recognizable group
identity separate from their Indian or Inuit and European forebears."[32]

This problem of a "Métis-as-mixed" definition is compounded by the court's statement that the community acceptance requirement may not be necessary to prove in order for the federal government to have jurisdiction over Métis peoples.[33] Recognizing the multiple ways in which the colonial process in Canada has separated Indigenous peoples, including Métis people, from their communities (for example, via the residential school system), the court indicated that the federal government may still have jurisdiction and responsibility for Métis people who are no longer accepted by their community as a result of colonial policies.[34] Since the Canadian government was responsible for causing the separation of many Indigenous individuals from their communities, the court did not want to allow the federal government to escape responsibility for a problem it had created.[35] The court aimed to ensure the government's responsibility was sufficiently broad to prevent individuals from falling into a jurisdictional wasteland. As such, the constitutional purpose of s. 91(24) is to highlight the federal government's (protective) responsibility to Aboriginal peoples, and the court found no principled reason to exclude individuals on the basis that Métis communities no longer accepted them.[36] When making this statement, the court was discussing the scope of the federal responsibility under s. 91(24), not attempting to change the standard to assert Métis rights under s. 35(1) of the Constitution Act, 1982.

Further criticism surrounds the court's conclusion that "since s. 91(24) includes all Aboriginal peoples, including Métis and non-status Indians, there is no need to delineate which mixed-ancestry communities are Métis and which are non-status Indians." The concern is that the failure to delineate between the two groups may blur the line between Métis people (as a distinct nation) and non–Status Indians (people with First Nations ancestry who lost status, including for marrying non–Status Indians).[37] Blurring this line between Métis and non–Status Indians, it is argued, may further reinforce ideas that the definition of "Métis" includes anyone with a single Indigenous ancestor, or that Métis people are simply a mix of European and Indigenous ancestry. However, a more appropriate interpretation of the court's reasoning here is that rather than conflating the two groups, the court simply determined it was not necessary to define each group as both fell under federal jurisdiction.

As a result of the *Daniels* decision, several key issues have emerged. Did the court broaden the definition of "Métis," in effect moving away from previous

definitions that emphasized distinct Métis culture and communities? Did
the court decide that community acceptance was no longer required to be
legally recognized as Métis and assert the associated rights? Did the court
decide that both definitions of "Métis" (as a distinct people, and as a person
with any mixed ancestry) are equally valid legal definitions? A final, related
question is did the *Daniels* case succeed in achieving the goal of getting the
land back? The remainder of this chapter considers international human
rights norms and principles, including the UN Declaration on the Rights of
Indigenous Peoples, to shed light on these outstanding issues.[38]

Daniels through an International Law Lens

As noted above, as a result of the *Daniels* decision, some people have begun to assert an Indigenous (Métis) identity based on a single Indigenous
ancestor (no matter how distant). This assertion points to the concern that
the *Daniels* decision confused or expanded the definition of Métis from being limited to the distinct people recognized in *Powley* to include any individual of mixed European and Indian ancestry. Despite my belief that the
court did not change the legal definition of Métis in *Daniels* and that *Powley* still sets the legal standard, I will now consider what international law
offers to address these potential new issues, including the one concerning
definitions of who is Indigenous and the subsequent rights that flow from
this recognition.

Defining Indigenous Peoples
There is no universal definition of "Indigenous peoples" in international
law. It is widely accepted that a set definition is not required in order to protect Indigenous peoples' human rights.[39] Because of the diversity of Indigenous peoples around the world, a strict definition may be either under- or
over-inclusive.[40] Nevertheless, numerous international law instruments provide criteria that can determine whether a particular group is encompassed
within the term "Indigenous peoples."[41] Looking through these criteria, it is
clear that under international human rights law, the only people that meet
the criteria are the distinct Métis Nation as recognized in *Powley*, not those
who newly claim to be Métis based on a single ancestor.[42]

A starting point for international law's understanding of who is Indigenous is the Working Group on Indigenous Populations (WGIP).[43] The WGIP began its work in the early 1980s and was the first body to formally articulate the rights of Indigenous peoples, eventually leading to the draft Declaration on the Rights of Indigenous Peoples. A study of the WGIP summarized four factors relevant to understanding the concept of "Indigenous": (1) Indigenous peoples characteristically have prior occupation of a specific territory, (2) as well as a distinctive culture, including language, social organization, religion and spiritual values, modes of production, and laws and institutions;[44] (3) Indigenous groups self-identify as Indigenous, and are recognized by others or state authorities as a distinctive collective;[45] (4) Indigenous peoples have also typically experienced subjugation, marginalization, dispossession, exclusion, or discrimination irrespective of whether those conditions persisted.[46] The WGIP is clear that these criteria do not constitute a comprehensive definition but rather are present in different degrees in Indigenous collectives and provide guidelines on how decision makers decide whether a group is Indigenous.[47] Over the past twenty years, these criteria have become broadly accepted as reflecting an understanding of Indigenous peoples.

Applying these criteria to the various groups who claim to be Métis leads to the conclusion that only the distinct Métis Nation would meet this definition. The Métis people who are part of the historic and distinct Métis people have a clearly defined traditional territory consisting of the historic northwest of Canada, ranging from northwestern Ontario through to eastern British Columbia. The people of the Métis Nation have a distinct culture (including the sash and jigging), specific languages (Michif and Bungi), and a specific set of religious practices and values (a combination of Indigenous spirituality and Christianity). The Métis Nation had a specific form of governance, including the Buffalo Hunt organization as well as the Provisional Government. There are records of Métis-specific laws dating back to the 1800s. The Métis Nation has identified as a distinct people since at least the Battle of Seven Oaks and the Sayer Trial, culminating with the recognition of the Canadian state in the Manitoba Act, 1870. There is a long history of Métis people experiencing subjugation in Canada, which led to dispossession from their lands and discrimination (and violence), especially in the aftermath of the Riel Resistance and the Battle of Batoche. Upon reflection on the criteria for Indigenous peoples in international law, it is clear that Métis people of the Métis Nation easily meet the international standard. It should also be noted that the Métis people have long participated in the international Indigenous movement, including in the negotiations of the UN Declaration on the Rights of Indigenous Peoples, and have been accepted by the international community as an Indigenous people.

In contrast, newly asserted Indigenous groups such as the Mikinaks or those relying on a "Métis-as-mixed" definition would likely fail to meet these standards. These groups do not come from a specific or defined territory. For example, the Eastern Woodland Métis Nation of Nova Scotia (EWMNNS) membership criteria[48] simply requires someone to be "of mixed Native and non-Native heritage," self-identify as Métis, and be accepted by the Métis community (i.e., the EWMNNS). In describing itself, the EWMNNS states: "Our members come from all walks of life and heritage—Mi'kmaq, Cree, Ojibwa, Blackfoot, Sioux or any other Native peoples. What joins our Métis people together is our commonalities, our inability to walk in either Indian or White worlds comfortably, our non-acceptance within either world and our wish to simply be who we are."[49] This newly associated group fails to have a common territory (its members' ancestry is from all across Canada, with only more recent connections to Nova Scotia). This group does not have any common culture, social organization, religion or spiritual beliefs, or laws or institutions. While members of the group may have recently identified as Métis, they are not recognized or accepted by the Métis Nation. Nor do group members have a common history of subjugation or dispossession.

Further, in an expanded definition of Métis that includes "Métis as mixed," the simple blending of European and Indigenous (First Nations) ancestry would also fail to meet the criteria discussed above.[50] The question that is not answered here is whether individually, these people with Indigenous (First Nations) ancestry may be Indigenous and have a right to belong to an Indigenous people (an already existing Indigenous peoples with whom their families may have lost connection).[51] That is a very fact-specific question for each individual to demonstrate their ancestry and connection to Indigenous peoples and how they lost the connection to the community, an analysis of which is beyond the scope of this chapter.

The indicia set out by the WGIP are not the only internationally defined criteria that exist. The Inter-American Commission on Human Rights (IACHR) recognizes that self-identification is a fundamental criterion for determining who is Indigenous.[52] The IACHR recognizes that it is critical that the community in question has the power to determine its own name, composition, and ethnic affiliation, without having the state or other external entities challenge it.[53] However, self-identification is not the only requirement. A key element in determining whether a group is an Indigenous people is the historical continuity of its presence in a given territory, and an ancestral relationship with the societies that pre-existed a period of colonization or conquest.[54] At the same time, the IACHR does recognize that Indigenous peoples have their own social trajectories and evolve over time to adapt to changing times, and will maintain in whole or in part the cultural legacies of their ancestors.[55] According to their criteria, the cultural identity of an Indigenous people is shared by its members, and while some members will live with less attachment to the cultural traditions than others, this alone does not mean that Indigenous people lose their identity or the rights conferred upon them by international law.[56]

Yet even according to the IACHR definition, the newly asserted Métis groups or Métis definitions of "Métis as mixed" would fail to meet the criteria set out by the IACHR, for similar reasons to those identified above: they lack historical social and political cohesion as a group and connection to a particular territory. As the IACHR elaborates, "For indigenous communities, relations to the land are not merely a matter of possession and production but a material and spiritual element which they must fully enjoy, even to preserve their cultural legacy and transmit it to future generations"; that "the culture of the members of the indigenous communities directly relates to a specific way of being, seeing, and acting in the world, developed on the basis of their close relationship with their traditional territories and the resources therein, not only because they are their main means of subsistence, but also because they are part of their worldview, their [religiousness], and therefore, of their cultural identity."[57] As recognized by the IACHR and the Inter-American Court of Human Rights, Indigenous peoples' identity comes from connection to a particular place. New groups that assert a Métis identity or those that would try to use a "Métis-as-mixed" definition fail to meet this criterion of having a collective identity coming from a particular place. Many have never claimed their identity stems from connection to a particular territory or made a link between a particular territory as critical to their cultural identity survival.

A final consideration on the definition of Indigenous peoples relates to the definition of "people" in international law. Again, there is no set internationally agreed-on definition of a people. However, an oft-cited definition is from the UNESCO Expert Meeting final report, which concluded that while the definition of "people" is uncertain, individuals who share "a common historical tradition; racial or ethnic identity; cultural homogeneity; linguistic unity; religious or ideological affinity; territorial connection; and a common economic life" may constitute a "people."[58] Under this broader definition, the groups identified above again fail to meet most of the indicia of a "people." At this point, there is a strong argument that newly identified Métis groups who claim Métis identity based on the idea of a single Indigenous ancestor from anywhere in Canada and the idea of "Métis as mixed" fail to meet the international standards of a "people," and certainly not those of an Indigenous people. Therefore, the people of the Métis Nation are likely the only ones who can successfully assert an Indigenous identity under international law. The next section considers the right to self-define and the right to be Indigenous to address some of the remaining issues in *Daniels*, including the role of the court and Canadian state in determining who is Métis.

Right to Self-Definition and to Be Indigenous

Once a people are recognized as an Indigenous people, there are several rights recognized in international law, including in the UN Declaration. While in Canada there has been some political resistance to recognizing and implementing the rights in the UN Declaration, Canadian courts have clearly held that international human rights law, including declarations, do inform Canadian law.[59] Thus the following discussion on the rights of Métis people proceeds on the basis that even where the Canadian body politic is slow to recognize the rights of Métis people, these rights are inherent and exist in Canadian law today. The task ahead is moving forward with explicitly acknowledging these rights and implementing them; however, a discussion on how to proceed with implementation is beyond the scope of this chapter.

The next consideration for the implications of the *Daniels* decision on the definition of Métis is that Indigenous peoples have the right to be Indigenous and to self-define. This right is found throughout international law, including the UN Declaration.[60] It includes Métis peoples' right to determine their own identity and membership in accordance with their customs and traditions without impairing their right to be citizens of the states in which they live.[61] Métis peoples can determine the responsibilities of individuals to their communities.[62] The UN Declaration recognizes that Métis people have the right to belong to the Métis Nation in accordance with their traditions and customs.[63]

It is important to remember that post-*Daniels*, Métis people have the right to define who is Métis, and the rights and responsibilities that flow from being Métis. Andersen and Gaudry criticize the Supreme Court in *Daniels* for reinforcing its power to determine who is Indigenous—or Métis—in this instance.[64] They argue the court missed an opportunity to support Indigenous legal orders instead of undermining them.[65] The court's defining who is Métis is also problematic under international law because Métis people have a right to define themselves.

The Métis National Council defines a Métis as "a person who self-identifies as Métis, is distinct from other Aboriginal peoples, is of historic Métis Nation Ancestry and who is accepted by the Métis Nation."[66] As the Métis National Council is recognized as representing Métis people in Canada, it is critical that legal definitions respect this self-definition. It is also important to note that the Métis National Council and its provincial affiliates accept the definition of Métis people as articulated by the court in *Powley*. Thus, those who claim to be Métis based on a single ancestor or a "Métis-as-mixed" definitions cannot stand. The Métis Nation is a distinct Indigenous people.

Self-Determination

Based on international law criteria for defining Indigenous peoples, the Métis Nation is an Indigenous people who have the right to define themselves. The next right to consider based on this recognition is that of self-determination. Self-determination is a foundational right that is required to fully realize Indigenous peoples' rights, as all other rights flow from the right to self-determination.[67] The right to self-determination can be found extensively in international law and has been affirmed by the Charter of the United Nations, the International Covenant on Economic, Social and Cultural Rights (ICESCR), the International Covenant on Civil and Political Rights (ICCPR), and the Vienna Declaration and Programme of Action.[68] Additionally, the UN treaty bodies that monitor the ICCPR and the ICESCR have also confirmed that Indigenous peoples have the right to self-determination.[69]

S. James Anaya defines self-determination as "a human right" where "human beings, individually and as groups, are equally entitled to be in control of their own destinies, and to live within governing institutional orders that are devised accordingly."[70] The right to self-determination contains internal and external aspects, both of which are incorporated by the UN Declaration. The concept of self-determination has historically been associated with the process of decolonization and the secession of peoples from states.[71] Contemporarily, the right to self-determination means that Indigenous peoples "are entitled to participate equally in the constitution and development of the governing institutional order under which they live and, further, to have that governing order be one in which they may live and develop freely on a continuous basis."[72] Therefore, the right of self-determination for the Métis people means determining their relationship with the Canadian state.

Part of a people's right to self-determination is the right to pursue their cultural development. This has also been recognized in article 27 of the ICCPR, as follows: "In those States in which ethnic, religious or linguistic minorities exist, persons belonging to such minorities shall not be denied the right, in community with the other members of their group, to enjoy their own culture, to profess and practise their own religion, or to use their own language." Indigenous peoples have the right to practise their distinctive customs and culture in accordance with international human right standards, and these traditions, histories, and aspirations must be appropriately reflected in education and public information.[73] The preamble of the UN Declaration recognizes Indigenous peoples' right to be different, and to be respected and treated equally because of this.[74] This right reiterates both the importance of a definition of "Métis" that emphasizes a common cultural tradition and the importance of protecting the communal rights to perpetuate this distinct culture.

Another aspect of self-determination is the right to self-government. Indigenous peoples have the right to be autonomous and self-govern their internal and local affairs. This includes the right to maintain and develop their own political, economic, and social systems and institutions.[75] One of the motivators for *Daniels* was to prompt the federal government to engage in self-government negotiations with the Métis people and to "get the land back," and international human rights law, including the UN Declaration, confirms the importance of self-government toward fulfilling Métis peoples' right to self-determination.

Rights to Lands, Territory, and Natural Resources
As noted above, a key consideration in the definition of Indigenous peoples is their connection to traditional lands, territories, and resources. Indigenous peoples have a sacred relationship with the land that permeates their beliefs, customs, culture, and traditions.[76] It is for these reasons that the UN Declaration extensively protects Indigenous peoples' rights to own, use, develop, and control their lands, territories, and resources.[77] Thus, stemming from *Daniels* as well as other court decisions that recognize the rights of Métis people, Canada must give legal recognition and protection to Métis peoples' lands through demarcation and titling of lands. Further, Canada must obtain the Métis people's free, prior, and informed consent before approving any project that may affect these lands, which is discussed in further detail below.[78] The Métis people have the right to set priorities for their traditional lands and to environmentally conserve the lands.[79] These rights extend to the lands Métis people currently own or occupy as well as to their traditional territories.[80] If Indigenous peoples' rights to land are violated they are entitled to redress, including restitution and compensation.[81] At this point it is worth noting that the Manitoba Metis Federation confirmed the promise of a land base for Métis people, which has never materialized. The redress for the failure to protect Métis people's land rights ought to be part of any negotiations moving forward, including the impetus for negotiations created through the *Daniels* decision.

Right to Participate in Decision Making

Indigenous peoples have a well-recognized right to participate in decision making that may impact their rights, including their free, prior, and informed consent.[82] The right to participate in decision making is found extensively in international law, including in various human rights treaties and international jurisprudence.[83] For example, UN treaty monitoring bodies, such as the Committee on the Elimination of Racial Discrimination, have recognized the duty to consult, and in some cases seek consent, when states make decisions that impact Indigenous peoples' rights.[84] The UN Declaration has more than twenty provisions relating to Indigenous peoples' right to participate in decision making, ranging from rights to self-determination and self-government to specified duties upon states to obtain free, prior, and informed consent when approving projects that will impact Indigenous peoples' lands.[85] Métis people, as recognized in international law, have this right to participate in decision making.

Free, prior, and informed consent is required when the rights and resources of Indigenous people are impacted[86] "in ways not felt by others in society . . . because of their traditional land tenure or related cultural patterns."[87] The UN Permanent Forum on Indigenous Issues describes "free" as meaning no coercion, intimidation, or manipulation was involved.[88] "Prior" implies that consent is sought with sufficient time for the Indigenous group's consultation/consensus process, before the activity in question has been authorized or commenced.[89] "Informed" requires that pertinent information was provided to the affected Indigenous peoples in a form that is accessible, understandable, and in a language that the Indigenous peoples fully understand.[90] "Consent" indicates a process of consultation and participation undertaken in good faith, where the parties establish a dialogue allowing them to find appropriate solutions in an atmosphere of mutual respect, and where there is full and equitable participation.[91] As clearly stated by the UN Expert Mechanism on the Rights of Indigenous Peoples (EMRIP), consent also means Indigenous peoples "are entitled to give or withhold consent to proposals that affect them . . . Indigenous peoples' decision to give or withhold consent is a result of their assessment of their best interests and that of future generations with regard to a proposal."[92] The EMRIP also explains how consent relates to the idea of a veto: "Withholding consent is expected to convince the other party not to take the risk of proceeding with the proposal. Arguments of whether indigenous peoples have a 'veto' in this regard appear to largely detract from and undermine the legitimacy of the free, prior and informed consent concept."[93]

Indigenous peoples' right to participate in decision making stems from their position as the "most excluded, marginalized and disadvantaged sectors of society," which has impacted their ability to determine the direction of their societies, including making decisions on matters that affect their rights and interests.[94] Decision-making power would allow Indigenous peoples to protect their culture, language, and their lands, territories, and resources, and prevent top-down state decisions that take little or no account of their rights and circumstances.[95] This right to participate in decision making and the reasons underlying its recognition in international law reiterate the importance of a definition of Métis limited to the historic Métis Nation, and not simply to those with a single Indigenous ancestor or those who have mixed Indigenous-European ancestry. It is the collective history and experience of marginalization and dispossession that in part underlies the right to participate in decision making, such as where Métis people have been excluded from their territories and their rights ignored by the Canadian state. This right to participate in decision making further protects the importance of the Indigenous peoples' connection to their traditional lands and their collective identity. Individuals with an ancestor from any region across Canada who come together to form a modern group lack this place-specific connected identity that warrants protection under international law as an Indigenous people.

Conclusion

While the practical impacts of *Daniels* may be an increase in claims to be Métis and the assertion of various rights stemming from such claims, under international human rights law, most of these new groups fail to meet the standard of being an Indigenous people, and therefore cannot claim the accompanying international human rights of Indigenous peoples. However, *Daniels* addresses the jurisdictional wasteland and confirms an obligation of the government to enter into negotiations to ensure that Métis peoples' rights are realized. *Daniels* should also be read in light of international law and Canada's obligations thereunder. Perhaps it should be underscored that international human rights are inherent and exist regardless of a state's efforts to implement the rights. The inherent nature of human rights means that members of the Métis Nation in Canada are entitled to have their fundamental human rights, including those articulated in the UN Declaration, respected. Canada is further obligated to recognize and protect the human rights of the Métis Nation.

International law confirms that Métis people (of the historic Métis Nation) have the right to define themselves and determine the consequences of membership in the Métis Nation. International law further includes the right to self-determination, including the right to self-govern; the right to traditional lands, territories, and natural resources; the right to participate in decisions that impact specific rights; and the right to pass along Métis culture to future generations. These rights are all interconnected in that a person's Métis identity comes from the connection to particular land and a particular place. It should be noted that these rights are equally guaranteed to Métis men and women.

One final comment on looking at *Daniels* through an international law lens is that if Métis people finally succeed at gaining their right to self-government and having their traditional lands recognized, the Métis governments will also be obligated to uphold the rights set out in international law, including the standards in the U N Declaration on the Rights of Indigenous Peoples. This includes ensuring that membership (or citizenship) criteria are non-discriminatory; however, these considerations are beyond the scope of this chapter.

NOTES

1   *Daniels v. Canada* (Indian Affairs and Northern Development), 2016 SCC 12.

2   Ibid., at paras. 17, 14.

3   Ibid.

4   Chris Andersen and Adam Gaudry, "*Daniels v. Canada*: Racialized Legacies, Settler Self-Indigenization and the Denial of Indigenous Peoplehood," *TOPIA* 36 (2016): 22.

5   See note 1, at para. 2.

6   Ibid.

7   See Jennifer Adese, "A Tale of Two Constitutions: Métis Nationhood and Section 35(2)'s Impact on Interpretations of *Daniels*," *TOPIA* 36 (2016): 7–19; Andersen and Gaudry, "*Daniels v. Canada*"; Chelsea Vowel and Darryl Leroux, "White Settler Antipathy and the *Daniels* Decision," *TOPIA* 36 (2016): 30–42; and Zoe Todd, "From a Fishy Place: Examining Canadian State Law Applied in the *Daniels* Decision from the Perspective of Métis Legal Orders," *TOPIA* 36 (2016): 43–57.

8   See note 1, at para. 16.

9   Andersen and Gaudry, "*Daniels v. Canada*," 27–28.

10   Ibid., 28.

11   Claire Charters and Rodolfo Stavenhagen, "The UN Declaration on the Rights of Indigenous Peoples: How It Came to Be and What It Heralds," in *Making the Declaration Work: The United Nations Declaration on the Rights of Indigenous Peoples*, ed. Clare Charters and Rodolfo Stavenhagen (Copenhagen: IWGIA, 2009), 10–13.

12   Ibid., 13.

13   United Nations General Assembly, Declaration on the Rights of Indigenous Peoples (UNDRIP).

14   Charters and Stavenhagen, "The UN Declaration on The Rights of Indigenous Peoples," 10.

15   Indigenous and Northern Affairs, Canada's Statement of Support on the United Nations Declaration on the Rights of Indigenous Peoples, Government of Canada, 30 July 2012, https://www.aadnc-aandc.gc.ca/eng/1309374239861/1309374546142.

16   Prime Minister Justin Trudeau, Mandate letter to Dr. Carolyn Bennett, Minister of Indigenous and Northern Affairs, 2015, last modified 12 November 2015, https://pm.gc.ca/eng/minister-indigenous-and-northern-affairs-mandate-letter_2015.

17   Carolyn Bennett, Speech for the Honourable Carolyn Bennett, Minister of Indigenous and Northern Affairs at the United Nations Permanent Forum on Indigenous Issues 16th Session, 16 May 2017, Government of Canada, last modified 16 May 2017, https://www.canada.ca/en/indigenous–northern–affairs/news/2017/05/speaking_notes_forthehonourablecarolynbennett-ministerofindigenou.html.

18   Andersen and Gaudry, "*Daniels v. Canada*," 19.

19   Ibid., 17.

20   Ibid., 25. See also Darryl Leroux, Chapter 9 in this volume.

21   Andersen and Gaudry, "*Daniels v. Canada*," 26.

22   Ibid.

23   Ibid.

24   Ibid.

25   Ibid.

26   Ibid., 27.

27   Vowel and Leroux, "White Settler Antipathy," 32.

28   Ibid.

29   See note 1, at para. 49; *R. v. Powley*, 2003 SCC 43 at para. 43.

30   See note 1, at para. 17.

31   Andersen and Gaudry, "*Daniels v. Canada*," 23.

32   *Powley*, note 29, at para. 10.

33   See note 1, at para. 48.

34   Ibid., at para. 49.

35   Ibid., at para. 46.

36   Ibid., at para. 49.

37   Ibid., at para. 46.

38   UNDRIP.

39   OAS (Organization of American States), "Inter-American Commission on Human Rights, Indigenous and Tribal Peoples' Rights Over Their Ancestral Lands and Natural Resources: Norms and Jurisprudence of the Inter-American Human Rights System" (OEA/Ser.L/V/II. Doc. 56/09. 2009), 25.

40   Ibid.

41   Ibid.

42   It should be noted that this chapter only considers the ramifications of *Daniels* and international law for the definition of Indigenous peoples in relation to Métis people. It makes no comment on the scope of non–Status Indian rights or on the rights of non–Status Indians to belong to an Indigenous peoples.

43   Erica-Irene A. Daes, "Prevention of Discrimination and Protection of Indigenous Peoples: Indigenous Peoples' Permanent Sovereignty Over Natural Resources: Final Report of the Special Rapporteur," 2004, United Nations, UN Doc. E/CN.4/2004/30.

44   Ibid., 69 (a–b).

45   Ibid., 69 (c).

46   Ibid., 69 (d).

47   Ibid., 70.

48   See Darryl Leroux, Chapter 9 in this volume

49   Eastern Woodland Métis Nation Nova Scotia, Manitou Dawn, "Membership Application Information," http://easternwoodlandmetisnation.ca/main.htm (accessed 3 March 2019).

50   See the Supreme Court of Canada's discussion in *Powley*.

51   For a good overview of the development and successive amendments to the Indian Act and the differential impacts on women, see Kathleen Jamieson, *Indian Women and the Law in Canada: Citizens Minus* (Ottawa: Minister of Supply and Services Canada, 1978); and Cheryl Simon and Judy Clark, "Exploring Inequities under the Indian Act," *University of New Brunswick Law Journal* 64 (2013): 107.

52   OAS, "Inter-American Commission."

53   Ibid., 31.

54   Ibid., 35.

55   Ibid.

56   Ibid., 37.

57   Ibid., 21.

58   UNESCO, "Final Report and Recommendations of an International Meeting of Experts on the Further Study of the Concept of the Right of People for UNESCO," February 1990, UN Doc. SHS-89/Conf 602/7.

59   *Canadian Foundation for Children, Youth and the Law v. Canada* (AG), 2004 SCC 4, [2004] 1 SCR 76, 234 DLR (4th) 257 at para. 31, citing *Ordon Estate v. Grail*, [1998] 3 SCR 437 at para. 137. The presumption of conformity includes conventions not yet translated into Canadian law and non-binding obligations: *Baker v. Canada* [1999] 2 SCR 817 at 861. See *114957 Canada Ltee (Spraytech, Societe d'arrosage) v. Hudson* (Town), [2001] 2 SCR 241 at para. 30, where Justice L'Heureux-Dubé held that the municipal bylaw regulating the use of lawn chemicals was consistent with principles of international law and policy; and Paul Joffe, "Canada's Opposition to the UN Declaration: Legitimate Concern or Ideological Bias?," in *Realizing the UN Declaration of the Rights of Indigenous Peoples: Triumph, Hope, and Action*, ed. Jackie Hartley, Paul Joffe, and Jennifer Preston (Saskatoon: Purich Publishing, 2010), 201.

60   UNDRIP, art. 27.

61   Ibid., art. 33.1.

62   Ibid., arts. 33.2, 35.

63 Ibid., arts. 6, 9.

64 Andersen and Gaudry, "*Daniels v. Canada*," 28.

65 Ibid., 28.

66 Métis Nation, "Métis Nation Citizenship," http://www.metisnation.ca/index.php/who-are-the-metis/citizenship (accessed 14 March 2018).

67 S. James Anaya, "The Right of Indigenous Peoples to Self-Determination in the Post–Declaration Era," in *Making the Declaration Work*, ed. C. Charters and R. Stavenhagen (Copenhagen: IWGIA, 2009), 41; Brenda Gunn, *Understanding and Implementing the UN Declaration on the Rights of Indigenous Peoples: An Introductory Handbook* (Winnipeg: Indigenous Bar Association, 2011), 10; and Antonio Cassese, *Self-Determination of Peoples: A Legal Reappraisal* (New York: Cambridge University Press, 1995), 53.

68 ICCPR, International Covenant on Civil and Political Rights, 19 December 1966 (999 UNTS 171), art. 1; ICESCR, International Covenant on Economic, Social and Cultural Rights, 16 December 1966 (993 UNTS 3), art. 1; Gunn, *Understanding and Implementing the UN Declaration on the Rights of Indigenous Peoples*, 11.

69 UN Human Rights Committee, *Concluding Observations of the Human Rights Committee: Canada,* 20 April 2006, UN Doc. CCPR/C/CAN/CO/5, 8–9; UN Committee on Economic, Social and Cultural Rights, "Concluding Observations of the Committee on Economic, Social and Cultural Rights," 35; Gunn, *Understanding and Implementing the UN Declaration on the Rights of Indigenous Peoples*, 11.

70 Anaya, "The Right of Indigenous Peoples," 187.

71 Megan Jane Davis, "Indigenous Struggles in Standard-Setting: The United Nations Declaration on the Rights of Indigenous Peoples," *Melbourne Journal of International Law* 9 (2008): 439–71; T. Ward, "The Right to Free, Prior, and Informed Consent: Indigenous Peoples' Participation Rights within International Law," *Northwest Journal of International Human Rights* 10, no. 2 (2011): 54–84; and Daes, "Prevention of Discrimination and Protection of Indigenous Peoples," 17.

72 S. James Anaya, *Indigenous Peoples in International Law*, 2nd ed. (New York: Oxford University Press, 2004), 189.

73 UNDRIP, arts. 34, 15.1.

74 Ibid., preamble.

75 Ibid., arts. 4–5, 20.1.

76 José R. Cobo, *Study of the Problem of Discrimination against Indigenous Populations*, vol. 5, *Conclusions, Proposals and Recommendations*, 1987 (United Nations, UN Doc. E/CN.4/Sub.2/1986/7/Add.4).

77 UNDRIP, art. 26.1; L. Miranda, "Uploading the Local: Assessing the Contemporary Relationship between Indigenous Peoples' Land Tenure Systems and International Human Rights Law Regarding the Allocation of Traditional Lands and Resources in Latin America," *Oregon Review of International Law* 10, no. 2 (2008): 419.

78 UNDRIP, arts. 26.1, 32.2; Miranda, "Uploading the Local," 430.

79 UNDRIP, arts. 29.1, 32.1.

80 Ibid., art. 26.1.

81 Ibid., art. 28.1.

82   Food and Agriculture Organization of the United Nations (FAO) , "Free, Prior and
     Informed Consent," http://www.fao.org/indigenous-peoples/our-pillars/fpic/en/ (accessed 9
     September 2018).

83   Human Rights Council, "UN Expert Mechanism on the Rights of Indigenous Peoples," *Indigenous
     Peoples and the Right to Participate in Decision-Making*, Advice No. 2 (2011), http://www.ohchr.
     org/Documents/Issues/IPeoples/EMRIP/Advice2_Oct2011.pdf, 2.

84   Ibid., 7.

85   UNDRIP, arts. 3–5, 10–12, 14, 15, 17–19, 22, 23, 26–28, 30–32, 36, 37, 38, 40–41; Human
     Rights Council, "UN Expert Mechanism on the Rights of Indigenous Peoples," 2.

86   UNDRIP, art. 18; International Labour Organization, Indigenous and Tribal Peoples
     Convention, 1989 (ILO 169), art. 6 .https://www.ilo.org/dyn/normlex/en/f?p=
     NORMLEXPUB:12100:0::NO:12100:P12100_INSTRUMENT_ID:312314:NO.

87   Anaya, "The Right of Indigenous Peoples," 43.

88   UN Permanent Forum on Indigenous Issues, Report of the International Workshop on
     "Methodologies Regarding Free, Prior and Informed Consent and Indigenous Peoples,"
     UNESCOR, 4th Sess., 2005 (UN Doc. E/C.19/2005/1), 46(i); Mauro Barelli, "Free, Prior and
     Informed Consent in the Aftermath of the UN Declaration on the Rights of Indigenous Peoples:
     Developments and Challenges Ahead," *International Journal of Human Rights* 16, no. 1 (2012): 2.

89   UN Permanent Forum, "Methodologies," 46(i).

90   Ibid.

91   Ibid.

92   Human Rights Council, "UN Expert Mechanism," paras. 25–26.

93   Ibid., paras. 26–26(a).

94   Ibid., 1.

95   Ibid., 1, 15.

CHAPTER 8

Daniels v. Canada beyond Jurisprudential Interpretation: What to Do Once the Horse Has Left the Barn

CHRIS ANDERSEN

When I read the first lower court *Daniels* decision, I was sure that the issues it addressed would not be considered at the level of the Supreme Court of Canada (SCC), or in the unlikely event that they were, that the SCC would not produce a decision favourable to Métis and non–Status Indian litigants. As it turned out (and as jurisprudential scholars have discussed),[1] not only was I wrong, but spectacularly so. Part of the reason for this is, no doubt, a combination of my own arrogance and naïveté about what I thought I knew about the conservative character of Canada's courts. But from the perspective of my socio-legal training, it was also probably because I lacked an adequately sophisticated understanding of the delicate play between judicial sensibilities, current social contexts, and the political realities of the effects of SCC decisions and their logics. Indeed, socio-legal scholars often incorrectly assume that because we can diagnose and analyze the concepts upon which juridical reasoning is often based, it follows that we are equipped to understand that reasoning.

What is the relevance of my being not just wrong, but spectacularly wrong? By way of answering this question, I will relay a story—the genders may or may not have been changed to protect the innocent—about an ongoing conversation with a friend and colleague who is trained as a jurisprudential scholar. In addition to the numerous media interviews I undertook, I wrote an op-ed for the *Globe and Mail* on what I saw as the *Daniels* decision's shortcomings and how various interested groups would attempt to "run" with the various logics (they saw as) contained in it.[2] My colleague was frustrated by what she termed "incorrect" interpretations of the decision because in her mind, the decision was a relatively simple one about section 91(24) jurisdictional issues that was being "blown out of proportion" by various people who did not "know what they were talking about." I wasn't entirely certain she wasn't referring to me, so in the interests of my already-battered ego, I did not press for specifics.

I tell this story, nonetheless, to help us think about the often-vast gulf between jurisprudential thinking about the merits of any given Canadian court decision, how legal representatives for the provinces or federal governments interpret and act on it, and how social actors in a wide array of less direct contexts think about and try an act upon the various logics and possibilities (they think are) contained in the decision. In fact, this chapter was originally tentatively titled "Why the Law Is Much Too Important to Be Left Up to Lawyers." Aside from lacking originality (having been used as a rallying cry by critical legal theorists since at least the 1960s), this title is not particularly accurate. The problem is not that the law is too important to be left up to lawyers, but rather that "it" is much too diverse—too diffuse, with refractions into and out of too many contexts—to be adequately captured by jurisprudential interpretations. Indeed, there is no single thing called "law,"[3] and our tendency to write as though there is forecloses important analytical possibilities (more on this below).

Thus, I replied to my colleague that the fact that the interpretations being generated by non-legal actors were jurisprudentially "wrong" was hardly relevant from the context of understanding the broader cultural power of how we define the meanings or even the "truth" of a given court decision, or how non-juridical actors can and will interpret and act on court decisions in ways that do not always comport with juridical sensibilities. In the case of the *Daniels* SCC decision, for example, by the time jurisprudential scholars began to comment on its jurisdictional clarity, the horse was not only "out of the barn," it was arguably far from jurisprudential sightlines. So, noting that the decision's ramifications were being blown out of proportion and that the decision itself was not necessarily the "sea change" that many claimed it to be was already too late: legal and policy actors of all stripes had already declared *Daniels* a great victory for whatever issue they were most interested in and for the interpretations they drew from the decision.

As discussed in the previous chapters of this book, the scc handed down a long-anticipated decision in *Daniels v. Canada* on 14 April 2016 that was the culmination of decades-long efforts, launched by a former national Aboriginal organization leader Harry Daniels, ostensibly about whether Métis should be included in a section of the Canadian constitution that previously included only Status Indians and Inuit. In its decision, the scc found that Métis were "Indians" under section 91(24) of the British North America Act, but what is of particular relevance to this chapter is that in doing so, the court "found" two different kinds of Métis for jurisdictional purposes: the buffalo-hunting Métis people of the northern plains (the Métis Nation), and a second category of those who claimed Métis status by virtue of their mixed Aboriginal and non-Aboriginal ancestry (a more racialized understanding). What I want to tease out in this chapter are the various manners in which the range of logics contained in most of the jurisprudence on Métis and non–Status jurisdictional issues have played themselves out since the *Daniels* decision was rendered.

For purposes of this explication, the chapter is laid out in three parts. Part I positions the Canadian courts as a nationally specific example of what French sociologist Pierre Bourdieu has termed a social field, and more precisely, a juridical field.[4] Drawing on this more expansive, less instrumentalist approach to understanding "Canadian law" and tying into my own research interests, Part II lays out the growing body of discussion about Métis identity to demonstrate how the power of law often manifests itself and how *Daniels* draws from a set of dominant discourses about "Métis" already circulating in broader society. Part III then demonstrates how various social actors have interpreted the many interpretations of "Métis" (and the "to- and fro-ing" of its relationship to the administrative category of "Indian") contained in the decision to position themselves vis-à-vis the Canadian state. We will begin, however, by expanding our understanding of the role and power of Canadian courts in contemporary Canadian society.

Part I: Understanding Law as a Juridical Field

From a Bourdieuvian social field perspective, an important thing to keep in mind about scc decisions—far more so than with lower court decisions— is that they're not roadmaps for policy makers in the linear sense that commentators often make them out to be. Judges rarely issue decrees that are then taken up by policy actors to follow blindly, as though only one interpretation of any given court decision were possible. Instead, judges write decisions that, though they can and do shape public policy, rarely do so in unitary or directly linear ways. This is because court decisions are important in Canadian society—as in the societies of most liberal nation-states—not so much for what they say as for what people think they say, what they wish them to say, what actions they take based on what they draw from any given scc decision's logics, and a given organization's power, relative to other policy actors, to enact those choices, actions, or decisions. All of this is to say that higher level court decisions act as powerful *hubs* through which numerous policy actors orient themselves in terms of their desires, aspirations, and ultimately, future policy behaviours.

Understanding the courts in this manner, particularly in the context of Aboriginal rights scholarship and commentary, is a marked departure from conventional understandings. Courts and their decisions are overwhelmingly interpreted by jurisprudential scholars—usually positioned within law schools or faculties—in terms of their jurisprudential "correctness," or conversely, by socio-legal scholars (usually located in social sciences and sometimes humanities departments) in terms of the social logics that undergird and thus shape their jurisprudential decision making. In both cases, the courts are positioned as reflections, either—in the jurisprudential scholarship—in terms of their jurisprudential "correctness," or as the result of broader or more fundamental sets of forces (patriarchy, racism, heteronormativity, etc.) that shape the decisions that are produced.[5]

Instead of these two approaches, positioning our understanding of how courts operate in Pierre Bourdieu's notion of a social field[6] allows us to get beyond the kinds of "reflective" ontologies that jurisprudential and socio-legal scholarship tends to foreground and move toward a more complex and thus arguably more sophisticated understanding of the power of Canadian courts, based on a logic of "refraction."[7] Refractive logics allow for the analysis of juridical power in ways that attend both to the internal logics of jurisprudence and to the external social and cultural effects of these logics as they are taken up in myriad ways by the various social, political, and legal actors who deem any particular court decision relevant to their desires or aspirations.

Juridical fields[8] are a specific instance of Bourdieu's larger concept of social fields,[9] which he positions as analytical spaces of hierarchically organized and internally rule-bound struggle between agents who believe in the legitimacy of the field's struggle, the form it takes, as well as what is actually being struggled over. In his single concerted foray of field analysis into juridical power, Bourdieu positioned the juridical field as a site of competition to determine the very substance of law.[10] The ordered and rule-bound confrontation between authorized legal actors—who possess the technical training and competence to interpret the corpus of texts that come before them—sanctifies a correct or legitimized vision of the social world. In this site of struggle between competing actors (in an Aboriginal rights context, for example, this might take the form of lawyers, expert witnesses, interveners, and of course, judges), "a hierarchized body of professionals who employ a set of established procedures for the resolution of any conflicts between those whose profession is to resolve conflicts."[11]

Importantly, part of the juridical field's power arises from the ability and willingness of its agents to take otherwise ordinary language and imbue it with meanings specific to the internal dynamics and training of the field—in short, they are trained to undertake the crucial work of translation. This not only produces a delimited "juridical space" but sets out elaborate procedures for establishing a firm (if still ultimately permeable) borderline between actors who have the technical competency to speak, and those who do not. In short, the focus on "legalese" requires the "establishment of properly professional competence [and] the technical mastery of a sophisticated knowledge that often runs contrary to the simple counsels of common sense."[12]

Likewise, as part of their willingness to adhere to specialized language, competence within the juridical field requires a deep commitment to the field itself, even if not the field in its present form. Sanctioned legal actors nearly always work to fulfill a mutual function, since they agree in the effectiveness of law and simply work to improve their position within it. This means, Bourdieu suggests, that legal actors are highly unlikely to assume prophetic poses and postures that would bring the field into disrepute, and indeed, professional associations stand at the ready to discipline and sanction those who are deemed to have operated outside of established professional norms.[13]

Key to Bourdieu's positioning of juridical power is his emphasis that our need for and reliance upon "law" is wholly unnecessary—that is, communities had their own forms of dispute solution prior to the arrival of British and then Canadian law. That we largely take the value and legitimacy of Canadian juridical power for granted is, he suggests, due to the intense and protracted labour of legal agents who work—with various levels of pre-reflectivity—to make it appear so. He argues that of all the powers possessed by legal agents, among their most acute is "the power . . . to manipulate legal aspirations—to create them in certain cases, to amplify them or discourage them in others."[14] In this context, law operates as a form of "world making"—a forum (crucially, rather than merely a form) of struggle that monopolizes the power to impose nearly universally recognized principles of knowledge about the social world: "law is the quintessential form of the symbolic power of naming that creates the things named, and creates social groups in particular."[15]

Here, though, is where things get tricky—and if possible, even more complex: Bourdieu's positioning of juridical power means that the actual substance of law is rarely created "out of thin air," as it were. Instead, he suggests, it can only operate according to discourses and practices that already exist (to a greater or lesser extent) in society more broadly. However, because of its immense power and legitimacy, the juridical field holds the ability—again, to a greater or lesser extent, depending on each instance—to refract its own logics into other, non-juridical fields, and in that context, it possesses an indirectly generative (as opposed to directly constitutive) power to shape social relations otherwise outside of its formal purview.[16] But this is an empirical question as much as an ontological one, since the juridical field's legitimacy stems neither from its objectivity or impartiality (as jurisprudential formalists would posit) nor from the fact that dominant groups believe in it and make use of it (as socio-legal scholars might posit). Instead, juridical legitimacy is produced through and only through the struggle of its agents and the translation of rationalities of logics into—and out of—the juridical field.[17]

Admittedly, Bourdieu's juridical field methodology is both complex and highly technical. However, two of his points in particular are relevant to this chapter. First, the juridical field has firm but semi-permeable boundaries that require the translation of sometimes diffuse or abstract social aspirations (e.g., "We want justice!") into juridical discourse (it is not enough to "want" something—it has to be translated into discourses that juridical actors will understand and be able to act on). This is normally accomplished by employing a legal professional. Second is Bourdieu's insight that although "law" can be "world making," it rarely does so from scratch. Instead, it incorporates and translates discourses and practices already in wider currency and circulation. The next part of this chapter will document several of the discourses about the meaning and contours of Métis identity in particular that were available both to legal actors and to court justices in attempting to make sense of the issues at play in *Daniels v. Canada*.

Part II: "Métis" in Its Nationalist and Racialized Variants

When *Daniels v. Canada* came before the SCC, its justices heard a number of different depictions and definitions of the terms "First Nations" and "Métis." (See Chapter 4 by Arend Hoekstra and Thomas Isaac, and Chapter 6 by D'Arcy Vermette, and Chapter 7 by Brenda Gunn for additional discussion on the definition of these terms.) The debates sat along a continuum between two ideological poles: a nationalist understanding at one end ("Métis nation"), and a heavily racialized positioning at the other ("Métis as mixed"). The space between these poles formed the raw materials used by the Supreme Court justices as they built their arguments into decisions and the social contexts to which the identity claims of the various legal actors before the court, were fused. This section will lay out these variants to explain the discursive or conceptual options before the SCC when it fashioned its decision.

In *Daniels v. Canada*, the SCC defined "Métis" administratively in the following terms, notably encompassing the two poles identified above: "There is no consensus on who is considered Métis or a non-status Indian, nor need there be. Cultural and ethnic labels do not lend themselves to neat boundaries. 'Métis' can refer to the historic Métis community in Manitoba's Red River Settlement or it can be used as a general term for anyone with mixed European and Aboriginal heritage."[18] In terms of describing an identity, this is a contradictory definition, positioning "Métis" in terms of nationhood and peoplehood on the one hand, and in racialized terms of mixed ancestry on the other. However, the SCC is correct insofar as the term "Métis" as an official administrative category can and has assumed a number of different meanings over the past century and a half, two of which have been encapsulated in their definition.

These various uses boil down to a tale of three creation stories. In its most racialized variant, "Métis" is understood and positioned as an offshoot of older, pre-contact Aboriginal groups: First Nations and/or (sometimes) Inuit. In this case, Métis as a *category* is thus understood as signifying "mixedness"—usually positioned in terms of mixed Aboriginal and non-Aboriginal ancestry—in ways that First Nations and Inuit categories do not and cannot contain. Indeed, there is no fact about the Métis more taken for granted than that the name signifies "mixedness": academia, popular media, and other kinds of media are all rife with this understanding of "Métis."

Creation Story #1: "Mixed Aboriginal and Non-Aboriginal Ancestry = Métis"
The first story, some of whose representatives appeared before the SCC in *Daniels v. Canada*, is what I will term the "Maritimes creation story" of the Métis. This story is best illustrated by the numerous "Métis" organizations that have sprung up in the last half decade along the southeast corner of Quebec and the various Maritime regions, and is perhaps best summarized by a comment of the Bras D'Or Lakes Métis Nation, which explains that "the first Métis in Canada is said to be born in the 'New France' known today as Nova Scotia, approximately in and around 1628."[19] As Gaudry and Leroux note, this narrative is a theme that occurs with some regularity in settler consciousness of "the evocation of Indigenous-settler societal unification through intermarriage" rather than the self-conscious historical development of a peoplehood.[20]

Creation Story #2: Mixed Ancestry + Separate Communities = Métis
The second variant of this racialized understanding of Métis stems from the Métis Nation of Ontario, which, perhaps ironically, is also a Métis National Council provincial member. This "Great Lakes" creation story relies on tropes of the Upper Great Lakes fur trade and the manner in which French fur traders carried out their commerce. Unlike the British trading system, which (in the beginning at least) consisted of building "salt-water" fur trade forts, French traders traded inland, marrying into the Indigenous communities they traded with. Over time, as these intermarriages began to produce

their own offspring and those offspring began to marry each other, separate fur trade communities formed.[21] In this story, "Métis" is synonymous with the growth of the fur trade and the creation of those new—and separate from First Nations—fur trade communities.

Creation Story #3: Métis as a Post-Contact Indigenous People
Both of the creation stories touched on thus far rely heavily on an apparently logical connection between Métis and "mixedness." However, what happens, analytically, if Métis are not (just) the result of mixedness between First Nations women and non-Indigenous fur traders? What if their origins were not in the Maritimes or the Upper Great Lakes? Where would we look instead? An additional way to think about the term Métis is in the context of Métis nationhood, though this positioning is, with few exceptions, not one that the Canadian courts have seriously considered. This is probably not least because with very few exceptions, Aboriginal rights jurisprudence has tended to view Métis constitutional claims in the context of "community," and although a nation is a particular sort of community[22] it contains features that do not lend themselves well to jurisprudential analysis.

According to this story, the Métis, with roots going back to the end of the eighteenth century, rose to prominence as an economic force on the northern plains, centred in Red River, by the middle part of the nineteenth century. Following this rise to prominence, they led two armed resistances against the Canadian state: the first, in 1869–70, led to negotiations that created the province of Manitoba; the second, centred in what is now Saskatchewan, took place in 1885 and ended in Batoche, Saskatchewan, with the military and political defeat of the Métis at the hands of the Canadian state and its military forces. The term "Métis" as defined in this context is thus associated with specific events, leaders, geographical territories, economy, land tenure, artistic styles, language, and kinship connections[23] that emphasize its growing "nation-ness" as well as its peoplehood. Noted Métis legal scholar Paul Chartrand and colleague John Giokas write that the Métis Nation was

> the only group that was able to organize a civil government, to defend itself against Canadian intrusion, to make its place in the economic niches of the West along with Indian nations, and to insist that Canada not annex the West without dealing with it. The

Métis nation has symbols associated with this history, including "Falcon's Song," the "national anthem" proclaiming military victory against the settlers in 1816, a distinctive flag, unique languages, music, and art, and the well-known symbol of its economic independence, the Red River cart. It is the Métis nation which is mentioned in the Constitution, in the terms of the Manitoba Act, 1870, and whose rights were recognized in statutes and orders-in-council from the early 1870s until well into the twentieth century.[24]

This third creation story links the Métis to particular cultural codes and downplays notions of pre-contact "purity" in favour of the idea that Red River served as a hub or a "heart" that anchored the movement of people(s), goods, and meanings across broad geographical expanses of the growing sub-Arctic fur trade from the early nineteenth century onward. In this sense, the Métis were not just a nation but also a "people"—that is, they not only understood themselves in terms of their common roots but were recognized by other Indigenous peoples as well. Indeed, like all Indigenous peoples on the nineteenth-century northern plains, the Métis were part of the Neyihaw Pwat ("the Iron Alliance") in partnership with Plains Ojibway, Cree, and the Assiniboine.[25] In this important sense, they possessed the ability to produce and maintain respected broad intersocietal norms with other peoples.[26]

In a contemporary context, the descendants of the Métis Nation are represented through the combined efforts of the Métis National Council and its provincially based affiliates in British Columbia (the Métis Nation of British Columbia), Alberta (the Métis Nation of Alberta), Saskatchewan (Métis Nation-Saskatchewan), Manitoba (Manitoba Metis Federation), and Ontario (Métis Nation of Ontario), who have engaged in various government-to-government/nation-to-nation policy relationships with various levels of government (in particular with the federal and provincial governments). The Métis National Council intervened, for example, in the SCC level of *Daniels v. Canada*.[27]

Given the range of Métis creation stories in broader circulation among the Canadian public, the SCC had a number of options for how to interpret the issues that came before it. As it turns out, the court "split the difference," choosing to follow an administrative logic through which they could recognize both nationalist and racialized understandings, despite the fact that these directly contradict one another. Indeed, the SCC's lack of care in their understanding of the term "Métis" immediately produced several odd outcomes, not the least of which is that various organizations claiming Métis constituency claimed victory, despite the fact that they held definitions of the term nearly wholly at odds with one another. In the third and final part of this chapter, we will explore some of these reactions to demonstrate the limited extent to which the SCC, as with all courts, controls the conceptual contours of the decisions it renders.

Part III: *Daniels v. Canada*, (Possibly) beyond the Jurisprudential Imagination

As noted earlier in this chapter, *Daniels v. Canada* was the decades-long culmination of resistance to dynamics relating to the relationship between Canada's federal government system and the manner in which Métis and non–Status Indians fit (or did not fit) into that system. As the eventual SCC justices phrased it, the case boiled down to three major issues:

> Do Métis and non–Status Indians count as "Indians" under s. 91(24) of the Constitution Act, 1867?

> Does the federal Crown owe a fiduciary duty to Métis and non–Status Indians? and

> Do "Métis and non-status Indians have the right to be consulted and negotiated with, in good faith, by the federal government on a collective basis through representatives of their choice, respecting all their rights, interests and needs as Aboriginal peoples"?[28]

After summarizing the findings of lower appellate courts, Justice Abella (who wrote the actual decision) undertook a legislative analysis of the uses of "Indian" in previous Canadian jurisprudence, legislation, and policy, concluding that Métis were often thought of and treated as "Indians." As such, the SCC found that Métis should be included in s. 91(24).

Interestingly, the court spent some time explaining what they meant by and how they were employing the term "Métis." Noting the logics crafted in a 2003 SCC Métis hunting rights case, *R. v. Powley*, the SCC positioned Métis in terms of the test found in that case;[29] namely, self-identification as Métis; attachment to a contemporary Métis community; and attachment to a historical (more specifically, pre–"effective control") Métis community.[30] While not necessarily a nationalist definition, *Powley*'s logic has been taken up in useful ways by the Métis National Council and its affiliates since it was handed down more than fifteen years ago.

Following this discussion, however, Justice Abella went on to distinguish between the s. 35 rights-based context of *R. v. Powley*[31] and the s. 91(24) legislative jurisdictional context of *Daniels v. Canada*,[32] noting that this case was "about the federal government's relationship with Canada's Aboriginal peoples. This includes people who may no longer be accepted by their communities because they were separated from them." The SCC's confusion of "people" with "peoples" (individuals versus political collectivities) notwithstanding, it pronounced that "no principled reason [exists] for presumptively and arbitrarily excluding them from Parliament's protective authority on the basis of a 'community acceptance' test."[33] In short, the Daniels court removed a central pillar—community connection—and in doing so, rhetorically elevated the importance of self-declarations and identifications, as opposed to the importance of contemporary community connections, in non-juridical conversations about these issues.

What are we to make of the logics contained in *Daniels v. Canada*?[34] Perhaps equally relevant, which "we" should we be referring to? As noted earlier (and is often the case in Canadian jurisprudence), numerous organizations intervened at the SCC level, including the Attorney General for Saskatchewan, the Attorney General of Alberta, the Native Council of Nova Scotia, the New Brunswick Aboriginal Peoples Council, the Native Council of Prince Edward Island, the Metis Settlements General Council, the Te'mexw Treaty Association, the Métis Federation of Canada, the Aseniwuche Winewak Nation of Canada, the Chiefs of Ontario, the Gift Lake Métis Settlement, the Native Alliance of Quebec, the Assembly of First Nations, and the Métis National Council—fourteen in total. Each (according to jurisprudential rules) provided distinctive opinions on the issues they brought before the *Daniels* court and as such likely held distinctive opinions on the decision itself. And this does not even account for academic commentary on the issue.

Evaluating these responses along the nationalism-to-racialization spectrum laid out in this chapter's second part is instructive, though as I will make clear, most interveners at the SCC offered little public comment in the wake of the *Daniels* decision itself, and when they did, they did not often speak specifically to the meaning of "Métis." For example, immediately following the SCC decision the Native Council of Nova Scotia's chief and president, Grace Conrad, declared that "it's finally a good day to be an Indian," and that the Nova Scotia premier owed them a phone call.[35] Similarly, the president and chief of the Native Council of Prince Edward Island stated, "It was a victory for us. No more making our people feel like they're less, because non-status essentially you're saying non-person. You're a non-status, you're a non-Indian, you're a non-person, and that doesn't give our community much power feeling their merit, their worth, anything."[36]

Indigenous and Northern Affairs Minister Carolyn Bennett issued a statement immediately following the decision's delivery: "There is much work to be done. We are committed to working in partnership with Métis and non–Status Indians on a nation-to-nation basis, along with other partners, to ensure we are following the court's direction in implementing this decision."[37] This comment, seemingly supportive of the Métis Nation, is perhaps not as reassuring as it might be given that non–Status Indians do not comprise a nation, likely leaving many to wonder how deeply the federal government has thought about what a "nation-to-nation" (or perhaps more specifically, a "government-to-government") relationship would look like in practice in the post-*Daniels* era. More recently, Indian and Northern Affairs representatives have met with various organizations that sit much further along on the racialization line.

In partial juxtaposition to the lingering racialization in the *Daniels* decision, Métis National Council (MNC) president Clement Chartier responded positively to the decision, stating: "Make no mistake . . . this decision confirms what the Métis Nation has been saying for decades—Canada has a constitutional and jurisdictional responsibility to the Métis Nation. My Board of Governors and I are prepared to continue on this path of reconciliation with Canada toward a mutually respectful nation-to-nation relationship."[38] Later that year, when interviewed by *Windspeaker*, President Chartier commented further in relation to possible tensions with the Congress of Aboriginal People (one of the longer-standing national Indigenous organizations): suggesting that "we've made this point, and I believe we've won this point, with the provincial and federal governments that we're not an NAO, national Aboriginal organization, we're a government, and so on that basis we will be moving forward."[39] Following the SCC decision, the MNC went on to sign a Memorandum of Understanding with the Government of Canada, as did the Metis Settlements General Council (MSGC) and the Métis Nation of Alberta. The MSGC linked their renewed relationship with the Government of Canada directly to the *Daniels* decision, noting that they had engaged with the federal government to begin a dialogue on Metis Reconciliation in the form of a "Memorandum of Understanding for Advancing an Effective and Culturally Appropriate Structure for Metis Settlements' Self-Governance and Reconciliation."[40]

One immediately noteworthy effect of the SCC *Daniels* decision was that various organizations that had claimed "Métis and non–Status Indians" as their represented constituents declared victory, despite possessing deeply conflicting understandings of the term "Métis." To offer a couple of examples from the racialization end of the spectrum, the Métis Federation of Canada (MFC)—a recent organization that received intervener status at the SCC level—uploaded an official press release from their law firm providing their interpretation of the court's decision. In it, the authors focused on paragraph 17 from the decision, in which the court argued that the term Métis could be understood both in a national sense (i.e., "Red River Métis") and in a racial-ized sense ("mixed ancestry communities" that self-identified as Métis).[41]

Their interpretation of this judicial language is telling, suggesting that "it represents a clear judicial critique of the 'one Métis Nation' theory advanced by the Métis National Council and its members."[42] Practically speaking, the law firm suggests, until the federal government introduces a "Métis status card," any individual seeking federal programs or services must do so on the basis of their connection to a "credible organization" like that of the MFC. Following this logic to its conclusion, the firm suggests that "Canada will now be required to include Métis associations like the Métis Federation of Canada in the same programs and policy work it provides to Inuit and First Nations."[43]

Likewise, in a discussion on their official Facebook page (a major venue through which they interact with the public), the MFC stated, "Our culture, language, traditions can be diverse . . . we were here ever since the first European married an aboriginal woman . . . that hasn't changed. The only thing the new law changed is that it recognized we are diverse and are not tied to the red river . . . what we need to negotiate is what fiduciary rights do we have now . . . they say we have it but what does that look like for us . . . and we need to do this united not divided."[44] Like the MFC, the Nova Scotia–based

Unama'ki Voyageurs Métis Nation (which recently changed its organizational name to Bras d'Or Lakes Métis Nation, which I quoted earlier) stated, "After years of a gruelling battle for our rights and recognition finally came to an end today in the Supreme Court ruling which clearly decided there are no longer one distinct Metis in Canada. We exist from coast to coast to coast. [The SCC] went as far to say that the Metis in Nova Scotia first established a community in LeHeve Nova Scotia in 1650 distinct from the Acadian and the Micmac self-identifying as Metis. The Powley test is extinguished."[45] Also tellingly, in the discussion following this announcement, one of the responders raised the importance of the *Powley* decision in terms of a historical "cut-off date," to which a responder immediately replied, in apparent response to the SCC distinguishing between s. 35 and s. 91(24) issues: "The courts dropped Powley so that is no longer relevant :)" [*sic*].

Conclusion: Wrangling *Daniels* v. the Queen

To reiterate the point I made in the introduction, the small sampling of reactions to the decision—at the organizational level but also at the everyday mundane level of comments on the internet—demonstrates that the power and the meaning of an SCC decision is not, and indeed cannot be, fully captured by the logics and analysis of jurisprudential scholars. Its meanings and thus its social impacts far outstrip the limited confines of those interpretations. This is not to suggest that jurisprudential commentary does not attempt to "capture" the meanings and intents of the decision. Far from it, in fact: if Pierre Bourdieu is correct and if juridical struggle is at its base a coordinated struggle to determine the meaning and substance of law,[46] then we could expect no less from a privileged set of positions like legal experts—it is what they are trained to do and what feels "right" or "natural" to do. Therefore, there is nothing untoward or Machiavellian about these efforts—in effect, such interpretative struggles represent the most ethical way to "play the juridical game."

Nonetheless, failure to heed what I will term the entrepreneurial efforts of various organizations and individuals to derive their own meanings from the *Daniels* decision and its logics both effectively overstates the interpretative "unity" of the decision (i.e., that the decision's logics will mean the same or even similar things to everyone) and understates the level of struggle that characterizes most court decisions, even high level ones like those that appear before the scc. The legal community will concentrate its efforts on achieving a monopoly on "correct" legal interpretation, but since most social, cultural, and political actors not legally trained still possess their own forms of power and agency in Canadian society more broadly, they will read into this court decision—as all the various stripes of actors do for all high level court decisions—and emphasize the statements, passages, and paragraphs that they believe assist their cause (while downplaying—if not completely disregarding—those that do not). Since these are actors who engage with federal and provincial governments and with each other on a regular basis, we ignore the desires, aspirations, and the efforts they produce at our analytical peril.

Methodologically, the implications of these insights are both obvious and nearly completely dismissed by conventional legal scholarship: as stated earlier, scc justices and other power legal actors do not, despite their best professional attempts, control the meanings and interpretations of a decision as important, as long-awaited (and as logically confusing) as *Daniels v. Canada*.[47] With this in mind, I will conclude by moving us back to a methodological discussion of how we can and should be encouraged to understand and position the *Daniels* decision, and what this might mean for scholarly practice going forward.

What this chapter has suggested, in essence, is that Canadian courts—and particularly those as powerfully situated as the Supreme Court—are neither reflective of broader structures and discourses (such as, in this case, racism and racialization), nor are they directly constitutive, if by that term we are referring to the ability of court decisions to directly constitute social relations, as though a direct line exists between judicial decrees and the policy decisions that social and political actors make.[48] Instead, scc decisions like *Daniels* should be understood as refractive and generative: refractive in the sense that broader structures like race and racialization undergo a complex translation process to render them juridically legible; and generative in the sense that since the scc is a powerful actor in Canadian society broadly, the decisions it renders and the possibilities they contain ripple out of the courts and into a broad range of social fields, where they are taken up upon their refraction into those fields.[49]

Hence, as a matter of both methodology and theory, a useful strategy going forward would include fashioning an analytical framework that pays attention to the "before" and the "after" of the decision as well as to the decision itself, such that it is positioned methodologically as just one component in a broader chain of documents, interpretative decisions, and actors that together produce a more productively complicated understanding not just of the court decision but the manner in which Canadian courts actually function in their role as a privileged political actor in Canadian society. Understanding powerful court decisions as hubs means that although we should of course include analysis of the decision itself, we should take additional note of the interveners as well: Who made the effort to intervene, what were their arguments, and how were those translated into juridical relevancy? Who did not intervene, and why not? Likewise, following the decision—and against the proclamations of all manner of social, cultural, and political actors—we must also trace the often indirect and serendipitous effects of court decisions as they refract back into a wide array of social contexts and play themselves out within those contexts. Failure to do so leaves us with an oversimplified understanding of what court cases like the *Daniels* case are and what they do.

NOTES

1   See Joseph Magnet, "*Daniels v. Canada*: Origins, Intentions, Futures," *Aboriginal Policy Studies* 6, no. 2 (2017): 26–47.

2   See Chris Andersen, "The Supreme Court Ruling on Métis: A Roadmap to Nowhere," *Globe and Mail*, 14 April 2016, https://www.theglobeandmail.com/opinion/the-supreme-court-ruling-on-metis-a-roadmap-to-nowhere/article29636204/.

3   See Chris Andersen, "*Métis*": *Race, Recognition, and the Struggle for Indigenous Peoplehood* (Vancouver: UBC Press, 2014); Alan Hunt, "Encounters with Juridical Assemblages: Reflections on Foucault, Law, and the Juridical," in *Re-reading Foucault: On Law, Power and Rights*, ed. Ben Golder (London: Routledge, 2012), 64–84; and Nikolas Rose and Marianna Valverde, "Governed by Law?," *Social and Legal Studies* 7, no. 4 (1998): 541–51.

4   See Pierre Bourdieu, "The Force of Law: Toward a Sociology of the Juridical Field," *Hastings Law Journal* 38 (1987): 805–49.

5   Ibid.

6   Ibid.; Pierre Bourdieu and Loïc Wacquant, *Invitation to a Reflexive Sociology* (Chicago: University of Chicago Press, 1992), chap. 7.

7   See Andersen, "*Métis*."

8   Bourdieu, "The Force of Law."

9   See Bourdieu and Wacquant, *Invitation to a Reflexive Sociology,* chap. 7.

10 Bourdieu, "The Force of Law."

11 Ibid., 819.

12 Ibid., 828.

13 Ibid., 823.

14 Ibid., 833–34.

15 Ibid., 838.

16 See Andersen, *"Métis,"* 63.

17 Ibid.; Bourdieu, "The Force of Law."

18 *Daniels v. Canada (Indian Affairs and Northern Development)*, 2016 SCC 12 at para. 17.

19 Unama'ki Voyageur Métis Nation, Home Page. The webpage is no longer valid.

20 Adam Gaudry and Darryl Leroux, "White Settler Revisionism and Making Métis Everywhere: The Evocation of Métissage in Quebec and Nova Scotia," *Critical Ethnic Studies* 3, no. 1 (2017): 116.

21 See Jacqueline Peterson and Jennifer S.H. Brown, eds., *The New Peoples: Being and Becoming Métis in North America* (Winnipeg: University of Manitoba Press, 1985).

22 See Benedict Anderson, *Imagined Communities: Reflections on the Origin and Spread of Nationalism*, rev. ed. (London and New York: Verso, 2006).

23 See Peterson and Brown, eds., *The New Peoples*; Jacqueline Peterson, "Gathering at the River: The Métis Peopling of the Northern Plains," in *The Fur Trade in North Dakota*, ed. Virginia Heidenreich (Bismark: State Historical Society of North Dakota, 1990), 47–70; Douglas Sprague, *Canada and the Métis, 1869–1885* (Waterloo, ON: Wilfrid Laurier University Press, 1988); and Nicole St-Onge, Carolyn Podruchny, and Brenda Macdougall, eds., *Contours of a People: Metis Family, Mobility, and History* (Norman: University of Oklahoma, 2012), for discussions of this history.

24 Paul L.A.H. Chartrand and John Giokas, "Defining 'The Métis People': The Hard Case of Canadian Aboriginal Law," in *Who Are Canada's Aboriginal Peoples? Recognition, Definition, and Jurisdiction*, ed. Paul Chartrand (Saskatoon: Purich Publishing, 2002), 279.

25 Robert A. Innes, *Elder Brother and the Law of the People: Contemporary Kinship and Cowessess First Nation* (Winnipeg: University of Manitoba Press, 2013).

26 See Andersen, *"Métis"*; Jeremy Webber, "Relations of Force and Relations of Justice: The Emergence of Normative Community between Colonists and Aboriginal Peoples," *Osgoode Hall Law Journal* 33 (1995): 623–60.

27 See note 18.

28 Ibid., para. 1.

29 *R. v. Powley*, 2003 SCC 43.

30 See note 18, para. 48.

31 See note 29.

32 See note 18, para. 12.

33 Ibid., para. 49.

34 Ibid.

35 Rachel Ward, "Nova Scotia Indigenous Groups Welcome 'Landmark' Supreme Court Ruling," *CBC News*, 14 April 2016, https://www.cbc.ca/news/canada/nova-scotia/nova-scotia-metis-non-status-supreme-court-1.3536001.

36 Shane Ross, "Native Council of P.E.I. Applauds Supreme Court Ruling," *CBC News*, 14 April 2016, https://www.cbc.ca/news/canada/prince-edward-island/pei-native-council-indian-status-court-ruling-1.3535674.

37 Government of Canada, "Update—Statement—Minister Bennett Welcomes the Supreme Court of Canada Decision on CAP/Daniels Case," 14 April 2016, https://www.newswire.ca/news-releases/statement---minister-bennett-welcomes-the-supreme-court-of-canada-decision-on-capdaniels-case-575740761.html.

38 Métis Nation, "Supreme Court of Canada Affirms Canada Has a Constitutional and Jurisdictional Responsibility to Deal with the Métis Nation," 14 April 2016, https://www.metisnation.ca/index.php/news/supreme-court-of-canada-affirms-canada-has-a-constitutional-and-jurisdictional-responsibility-to-deal-with-the-metis-nation.

39 Shari Narine, "Métis Council, CAP May Tussle on Daniels," *Windspeaker* 34, no. 3 (2016), https://ammsa.com/publications/windspeaker/m%C3%A9tis-council-cap-may-tussle-daniels.

40 Metis Settlements of Alberta, "Engaging with Canada."

41 See Chapters 8 and 9 in this book.

42 Letter from Devlin, Gailus and Westaway, Barristers and Solicitors to Pilon, Métis Federation of Canada, 14 April 2016.

43 Ibid.

44 Métis Federation of Canada, Facebook page, 3 May 2016, https://www.facebook.com/Metisfederationofcanada/.

45 Bras d'Or Lake Métis Nation, Facebook page, 14 April 2016.

46 Bourdieu, "The Force of Law."

47 See note 18.

48 See Chapter 6 in this book.

49 For example, the impact of the *Daniels* decision might be felt differently in the social services field, the medical field, the educational field, and the crime and corrections field, to give several examples; Andersen, *"Métis,"* 63.

CHAPTER 9

Outlining the Origins of "Eastern Métis" Studies

DARRYL LEROUX[1]

Over the past decade and a half, claims to Métis identity have flourished among white French descendants in Quebec, Nova Scotia, and New Brunswick, including through over forty separate "métis" organizations that have been formed in the post-*Powley* period alone.[2] In fact, tens of thousands of people—descendants of the earliest French settlers in the Americas—have emerged in the past half-generation to claim an Indigenous identity as Métis in the region. Whereas some evidence of claims by individuals self-identifying as "métis" can be found prior to the 2003 *Powley* decision—such as in the three organizations representing Métis and non-Status or off-reserve "Indians" in the 1970s and '80s—for the most part these did not involve claims to a distinct Métis people but claims about mixed-race (*métis* in French) identity.[3] The remarkable growth in Métis self-identification picked up again following the *Daniels* decision:[4] reports in late 2016 suggest that a self-identified "métis" group in Gaspésie more than doubled its adult membership to nearly 20,000 members in the six months after *Daniels*[5] and a number of new "Eastern métis" organizations were formed in the decision's immediate aftermath.[6]

The well-documented spike in post-*Powley* claims to a distinct Métis people in Quebec has led to the development of a new, primarily French-language scholarly literature advocating for the existence of rights-bearing "Eastern métis" peoples. Though a part of what I am calling "Eastern métis" studies actively disproves the existence of distinct "Québec Métis" people(s),[7] the majority of scholarly material published in this subfield since the *Powley* decision significantly revises existing historiography on the matter.[8] Anthropologist Émmanuel Michaux succinctly encapsulates the importance of the *Powley* decision to the development of "Eastern métis" studies: "[The *Powley* decision] led to a strong surge in the number of people self-identifying as Métis . . . and at the same time fostered the development of Métis studies in Canada, especially in the East. It raised hopes and awareness about the legitimacy of affirming a certain cultural autonomy as Métis, and also the curiosity and interest of researchers."[9] As is consistent with this subfield, Michaux all but erases decades of research by and about Métis people that preceded Eastern métis claims.[10]

In order to understand the intellectual arguments in favour of the so-called Eastern métis, I survey a series of journal articles, book chapters, and PhD theses on the topic, all of which appeared post-*Powley*. Throughout the chapter, I put this material in conversation with a number of Métis scholars to illustrate some of the shortcomings of this emerging academic subfield. I have organized the chapter into two broad themes that I identified in the literature: Métis ethnogenesis reimagined and Euro-settler preoccupations.

The New "Métis": Creating a People

Métis Ethnogenesis Reimagined

Upon first reviewing this body of literature, I was struck by its self-conscious effort to rewrite history. Naturally, if one is to argue for the existence of so-called Eastern métis people and there exists little to no documented history of such a *community*, as the scholarly consensus affirms,[11] then one must work to create something new.[12] In this case, that has meant creating an origin story that finds room for Métis people on the northern plains of the West while imaginatively giving primacy to the "Eastern métis." According to the accounts in this subfield, the ethnogenesis[13] of the Métis does not lie in the vicinity of the Red River Valley in the early nineteenth century, but instead in seventeenth-century New France.

As far as I can tell, geographer Étienne Rivard is the first scholar to discuss this idea in any depth post-*Powley*. Rivard's 2004 PhD thesis cites the following passage from the Nation Métis du Québec (NMQ) website in order to support the notion of an Eastern métis ethnogenesis:

> We should never forget that the history of Métis claims in Lower
> Canada (Quebec, New Brunswick, Nova Scotia, Labrador and
> Prince Edward Island) established Métis forms of knowledge and
> political philosophy in the Prairie Provinces. Métis families in
> Québec, such as the Riel family, the Dumont family, the Morin
> family, the Bohnet family, the Desmeules family, the Rivard family
> and many others, already belonged as Métis. Their departure from
> Lower Canada, imbued as they were with their Métis identity, for
> the Promised Land of Louis Riel's Métis Nation, secured a territory
> accessible to the Métis, far from the grip and political constraints
> that the Métis lived under in Lower Canada.[14]

This passage has all the hallmarks of the Eastern ethnogenesis narrative: first, it suggests that a Métis community existed in the East ("forms of knowledge and political philosophy") prior to events in the Prairies; second, it argues that families migrated to the Prairies *already as Métis*; and third, it makes symbolic links between some of these families and key western Métis leaders (e.g., Louis Riel, Gabriel Dumont). While Rivard carefully navigates the NMQ's claims, there is nonetheless a common reliance on declarative statements by organizational leaders as "evidence" for the existence of "Eastern métis" communities in this subfield. For instance, in their respective PhD work, both Émmanuel Michaux and Anne Pelta interpret their informants' statements about their newfound Indigenous identities as factual, despite their own acknowledgements that many informants had little to no knowledge of their Indigenous origins. "A few years ago," Michaux explains, "several of the Eastern Métis that I met during my ethnographic fieldwork told me that they were not sure about their Aboriginal origins or simply didn't know at all. Their genealogical search for their Aboriginal ancestors is a recent interest."[15] Nevertheless, what stands in for evidence is assertion by politically motivated organizational leaders. In many ways, the existence of the Eastern métis is a matter of faith, as it relies on a mixture of trust and conviction. Notably, Rivard's much more recent work reiterates the same NMQ statement as actual evidence for the existence of the Eastern métis.[16]

The NMQ was created in 1993 (incorporated in 1997) and was the first organization in Quebec to argue for the existence of a distinct "Québec Métis" people. In that sense, it predates the much more recent glut of *Powley* organizations that Michaux[17] and Rivard[18] identify. The NMQ had about 2,000 members in April 2016 and considers itself the twelfth Indigenous nation in Quebec.[19] Notably, it strongly opposes the recent and widespread turn to "métis" identity in Quebec. Claude Aubin, a founding member and former "senator" for the organization, explains the NMQ's critique: "[Indigenous peoples] in Québec, those who have always maintained and asserted their distinct Indigenous identity, are being pushed aside, trampled by Québécois or French Canadian people who have self-identified as Aboriginal and who have joined a range of virtual organizations and communities that claim to be Métis . . . [They] claim that 3/4 of the Québec population [nearly 6 million people] has the right to self-identify as Métis simply because of a blood relation with an Indigenous person."[20] The NMQ's inimical relationship with post-*Powley* organizations is particularly noteworthy, because it is the only so-called Métis organization in Quebec that openly opposes these more recent *Powley* claims. "It is also necessary to understand how these French-Canadian or Québécois Métis quickly adopted such a broad definition of Indigeneity," Aubin continues, "that it allowed them to self-identify as Indigenous without being recognized as such by existing Indigenous peoples. . . . The Métis movement in Québec has become a true cultural and spiritual zoo and the laughing stock of Indigenous peoples."[21] Notwithstanding Aubin's colourful language, the NMQ's critique places the erasure of existing Indigenous peoples front and centre in the debates about the "Eastern métis." Still, the NMQ has been promoting the Eastern ethnogenesis thesis for a couple of decades now, and thus has provided the intellectual basis for the development of the post-*Powley* environment that it decries.

In the years immediately following Rivard's early work, the most prominent scholar arguing for Eastern ethnogenesis was anthropologist Denis Gagnon. In addition to a few articles that he has published on the topic in the past decade, the majority of scholarly material supporting this thesis is now being published by several of his former graduate students. Gagnon is therefore most often cited as the definitive scholarly source for the Eastern ethnogenesis narrative. Since scant empirical material is produced in history or anthropology that supports the Eastern ethnogenesis narrative, its proponents rely largely on self-citational practices that almost universally exclude Indigenous scholars.[22] The following statement by Gagnon is typical in this body of literature and follows two of the narrative elements that I identify above, notably that the Métis first existed in the East and then migrated to the West, where they founded the Métis Nation:

> Métissage between European settlers and First Nation and
> Inuit women in the Eastern part of the continent began in the
> seventeenth century, and probably before then. Some of these
> mixed-race individuals identified themselves as Métis and populate
> regions on the margins of the official state (Gaspésie, Abitibi,
> Saguenay, Labrador, Maritimes). Some assimilated into French or
> English Canadian society, and others still among First Nations or
> Inuit. The development of the fur trade encouraged the migration
> of several individuals, some of whom were already Métis, to the
> Great Lakes and out west, where they formed a distinct nation in
> what was then called Rupert's Land.[23]

Despite the fact that at no point in his existing body of work on the topic does he provide empirical evidence for his claims, Gagnon asserts that the "Eastern métis" existed as early as in the 1600s ("and probably before"). Eastern ethnogenesis has become perhaps the primary narrative structure to speak back to and oppose the specificity of Métis claims—in this case, Métis kinship relations and political alliances with Cree, Saulteaux, Assiniboine, and Dene peoples.

Gagnon's work mirrors the discourse expressed by various "Eastern métis" leaders. For example, in the 2013 Senate Report on the Recognition of Métis Identity in Canada, Claude Riel Lachapelle, a spokesperson for the NMQ, explained: "The Metis in western Canada are all from Lanaudière, Quebec, from places like Terrebonne and Saint-Gabriel-de-Brandon. It's all closely tied to the fur industry with the North West Company. That's an undeniable fact, and we can't change it."[24] Here, Lachapelle narrows down the common claim that Métis Nation origins can be traced to individuals from Quebec. In fact, he pinpoints not just a region northeast of Montreal but specific small towns that produced these men. He then forecloses the possibility that the Métis might have their own, quite distinct ontologies and histories, a common rhetorical device among Eastern métis proponents. While Lachapelle seems convinced of the truth of his specific geographical claims, Gagnon broadens the basis of "Eastern métis" origins from Labrador to east of Montreal, through Nova Scotia, New Brunswick, and Gaspésie. Whatever the details about the geographical origins of the Métis in the Eastern ethnogenesis narrative, one constant is that mixed-race people born as a result of Indigenous-French unions formed "métis" communities that travelled westwards, *already as Métis*. In these versions of history, there is little room for Plains Cree, Saulteaux, Assiniboine, or even Dene contributions to Métis peoplehood, including the contributions of women, which is counter to academic scholarship on the Métis[25] and, more importantly, to Métis claims based in their self-determination as an Indigenous people. Notably, the Plains Cree, Saulteaux, Assiniboine, and Dene women who are the basis of Métis Indigeneity must be erased to sustain the Eastern ethnogenesis thesis.

In a parallel effort to territorialize the "Eastern métis," political scientist Sébastien Malette—who has been both an academic and a lobbyist for a variety of "Eastern métis" bodies (e.g., Voyageur Métis Nation, and Métis Federation of Canada)—has gone so far as to reimagine the whole of present-day Quebec as Métis territory. I provide a long excerpt that highlights many of his key arguments:

> All of these concerns about métis-ness in Québec may surprise many. How did we come to dislocate Métis and Québécois identities to the point that some now see them as mutually exclusive? Why can't a Québécois be seen as Métis and Québécois, even though he bathes in a historically mixed society and carries a distinct culture from this fact? . . . According to the [Paquette] judgement, an individual can claim aboriginal rights if there is a continuous and strictly territorialized relationship between a "Métis community" that existed before the "effective control" of the colonial powers, and an individual still living in this same community. So, couldn't the entirety of Québec be one of these

territories, since the Métis have historically roamed through and inhabited it, just like several other places in North America? Is it not time to break down these barriers around Métis identity?[26]

Malette's claims have been among the boldest to date. Let us carefully consider the territorial aspect of his argument. He relies on the mythical narrative of métissage, one that has largely been debunked by historical and demographic research.[27] In fact, even though historians and demographers in Quebec have largely discredited the extent of *biological* mixedness among French settlers for several decades now,[28] Malette nonetheless insists that their mixed-racedness is somehow common sense: "Recognizing the Franco-Aboriginal métis-ness of [the] Québécois in strictly biological terms is now a subject that no longer offends."[29] The actual ancestral basis for his claim is an average of less than 1 percent overall ancestry over a period of nearly four centuries among today's French Québécois, meaning that most French Québécois/Canadians can trace their ancestry to one of a handful of Indigenous women in the seventeenth century.[30] Importantly, the same research has demonstrated that the average English ancestry of the French Québécois added to other European (i.e., German, Swiss, Belgian, Irish, Portuguese) ancestries is between three and five times the average Indigenous ancestry.[31] Following his bio-geographical logic and the available historical demographic research, Malette could reasonably claim that Quebec be imagined as an English-Canadian territory—though the unthinkability of that claim lays bare the specifically nationalist tinge of his argument. The small genealogical and genetic imprint of Indigenous peoples on the French Québécois and the very real possibility that other ethnicities factor into Québécois identity at a much higher rate openly complicate the Eastern métis storyline.

Michaux also participates in the re-territorialization of the Métis through amplifying the claims of his research participants: "According to another informant, the idea behind the East-West Métis dynamic could make the Métis not only a minority of the Aboriginal population, but a majority of the Canadian population; they would form 'the strongest people' and could transform Canada into more than a Métis country,[32] but a country of Métis people."[33] In following the dominant methodology in this academic subfield, participant narratives are re-packaged as oral history and truth claims go unchallenged. Both Malette—in his speculative musings—and Michaux—in his unreflexive ethnography—actively participate in the evocative re-territorialization of the entirety of Quebec and/or the rest of Canada as Métis, contributing to the Eastern ethnogenesis narrative in the same breath.

Another common, interrelated version of the Eastern ethnogenesis thesis has the Red River Métis originating in early seventeenth-century Acadia, specifically in its southwest region, along the coast between present-day Lunenberg and Yarmouth. Four "métis" organizations have been active since the *Powley* decision in this rural region of present-day Nova Scotia—each has its own political structure, though they share a belief in their historical role in founding the Métis Nation. Émmanuel Michaux explains their position: "[A prominent leader] of the Métis cause in the East contends that before reaching the Prairies, the population that would form the Métis Nation in the second half of the nineteenth century was already composed of Métis (from Acadia and Quebec)."[34] The so-called Acadian-métis leaders, in his research, tell a version of history where Acadians migrate to Quebec (usually to Trois-Rivières and at other times to Gaspésie), and after a generation or two continue their journey west as Métis and help to found the Red River settlement. Another of Michaux's "Acadian-métis" informants expressed a similar claim as Malette's, rhetorically suggesting that all of Canada may be open to a Métis title, since in his view "the Métis hunter was everywhere, he could not be contained."[35]

Whether territorially based in present-day New Brunswick and Nova Scotia or in Quebec, the "Eastern métis" ethnogenesis stories that emerged post-*Powley* imagine white French-descendant populations with long-ago Indigenous ancestry as owners of the land, repeating a centuries-old white settler preoccupation with territorial dominance. An essential component of these stories is the erasure of both past and present Indigenous presence, which exposes these emerging "métis" claims as counter to the interests of Indigenous peoples.[36] The Eastern ethnogenesis narrative has become quite common in the scholarly literature that I reviewed, despite the absence of empirical evidence supporting its claims.

Normative Euro-settler Nationalism: Language and Ethnicity
A second common narrative thread in this material is a focus on the politics of language and/or a concern with the French-English political divide

in Canada. For instance, in much of Gagnon's work, he argues that the French-speaking Métis in the West are being oppressed by the English-speaking, "assimilated" Métis. Here we see a typical battle between French and English, where the English-speaking Métis deny their French origins and side with the dominant society against all matters French. Gagnon expresses this argument when he states that "the official Métis associations of the West, who consider themselves to be the only 'true Métis' on the planet, have ignored me because of my interest in French-Canadian Métis communities, who they consider to be assimilated, and unrecognized Métis communities in Eastern Canada, who they see as opportunists."[37] Setting aside the fact that Gagnon conflates language with ethnicity here, it is clear that his concern lies with the mistreatment of French-speaking people by the Métis, which at once erases Métis Indigeneity and supports the Indigenization of French descendants in the East. Étienne Rivard's more recent work also builds on a narrative in which the French-speaking population of Quebec, and, in this case, the French-speaking "Québec Métis" are marginalized vis-à-vis the Métis: "Despite the fact that the only Francophone province in Canada is one of the regions of North America where the *métissage* of the French and Aboriginal populations goes back furthest, the Quebec Métis, unlike those of Western Canada, have never had the right to a chapter in the national historic grand narrative" (emphasis in original).[38] Playing on the victimhood of the French-speaking, white settler population of Quebec, Rivard nonetheless is calling for a place in the *Canadian* national narrative, betraying his own Quebec settler framework.

Michaux also illustrates this narrative when he quotes an "Eastern métis" activist from New Brunswick who frames potential conflict along the normative French-English language divide: "The Western Métis call themselves anglophones. So why would they accept someone who wants to change their language? Because if you become a member [of the Métis Nation] and you're French, you will ask to have your French[-language] rights."[39] Michaux relies heavily on his informants, who readily oppose the figure of the French and the English in useful political ways, to conclude the following: "Stigmatized by the English-speaking Métis who barely recognize their French-Canadian Métis cultural heritage in Manitoba, French-speaking Métis people have sought support from various Métis communities with French-Canadian origins elsewhere in Canada and the United States."[40] Michaux does not actually provide any evidence of these efforts, though Rivard includes a brief discussion of the short-lived Union Est-Ouest founded in 2005 by the Communauté métisse de l'Estrie and the Union nationale métisse Saint-Joseph du Manitoba.[41]

Michaux, Gagnon, and Rivard all build an argument that French ancestry, French culture, and/or the French language are devalued by the Métis, gesturing to how "Eastern métis" studies is trapped inside the normative French-English binary, which makes no space for the possibility that Métis individuals and communities may speak or desire to speak Indigenous languages (e.g., Plains Cree, Michif, Dene, Anishinaabemowin) and maintain practices of kinship relations that do not revolve primarily around blood. Where they see exclusion of (another) set of Euro-settler cultural practices (French language and/or culture), the Métis may see forms of Indigenous resurgence.[42] Whatever the case, their efforts to delegitimize the Métis are in keeping with their work of *Indigenizing* the so-called Eastern métis.

Connected to these wider efforts at centring the French-English binary at the heart of colonial Canada/Quebec, we see in the creative arguments brought forward by Malette that the "Western" Métis are oppressing the "Eastern métis" by refusing to recognize them as Métis (and Indigenous). As reported by an Aboriginal Peoples Television Network in November 2016, Malette has made a number of distasteful social media posts arguing that Red River Métis forms of self-determination are Nazi-like.[43] While such overheated rhetoric might seem extreme, these types of statements about Indigenous peoples, notably of the Innu, are common in popular histories of the "Eastern métis." For example, Russel-Aurore Bouchard, the most well-known historian of the "Québec métis" and a self-identified "métis," regularly speaks against Indigenous peoples.[44] In language similar to Malette's, Bouchard has compared trilateral comprehensive treaty negotiations in the Saguenay-Lac-Saint-Jean region of Quebec to a type of "apartheid" that "benefits only a tiny [Innu] minority"[45] at the expense of the majority. To be clear, Bouchard is suggesting that the Innu, who number about 14,000 people in Nitassinan[46] out of a population of nearly 400,000 in the region, or no more than 4 percent,[47] could one day politically dominate the overwhelming French Québécois majority much as Afrikaners dominated Africans in South Africa.

Even Gagnon, a former Canada Research Chair in Métis Identity, has used similarly overloaded language, this time in his oral testimony at the Senate Report on Métis Identity:

Applying the Red River Metis model to other Metis communities
sets the bar so high that nothing else can be accepted, given the
absence of archival documents. . . . The experts are failing on
every level and they arrogantly put up a wall of resistance, as if
they were the truth bearers, without showing the slightest duty to
validate their findings or an understanding towards the peoples in
question. . . . This discourse is xenophobic, this fear of the other.
We should identify why they are so afraid that there are other Métis
in Canada. What would this take away from them?

Here, Gagnon dismisses Métis efforts to determine the boundaries of their
own nation/people as xenophobic, showing a complete disregard for the
well-articulated principles at the heart of Indigenous self-determination
and sovereignty.[48] Gagnon's former PhD student, Émmanuel Michaux,
echoes these strong sentiments when he states, "[Scholars] do not seem to
realize the particularly twisted character of their approach [in denying the
historical existence of the Eastern métis], which makes it more insidious,
profoundly damaging to research and ethically indefensible."[49] Accordingly,
Métis efforts at self-determination, and in some cases, those of other Indigenous peoples such as the Innu, are constructed as Nazi-like, apartheid-like,
xenophobic, and ethically unsound by several of the leading scholars in
this subfield.

When the Métis advocate for themselves as an Indigenous people, scholars
in this subfield interpret those efforts as excluding Frenchness, and then locate
that supposed exclusion in a continuum of oppression experienced by French-
Canadian/French speakers at the hands of the English. This discursive move
is only possible if one rejects Métis understandings of their own Indigeneity.
Without irony, then, the same people who are advocating for and/or identifying the "Eastern métis" as Indigenous post-*Powley* (and post-*Daniels*) strip the
actual Métis of their Indigeneity. Métis historian Brenda Macdougall warned
against such scholarly intrusions into Métis life over a decade ago: "We need
to move past this conceptual framework of the 'people-in-between' to evaluate how the Metis, as a distinct Aboriginal people, shaped not only their own
communities and social identities in ways that sustained their political and
economic concerns, but how their notions of family or relatedness shaped
the fur trade, interaction with religious institutions, and their relations with

outsiders—Indian or white, Cree or French, Scottish or Dene."[50] By focusing intently on questions of Frenchness, scholars in this subfield participate in supporting a normative, French settler form of nationalism that has worked against Indigenous self-determination for centuries. The general dominance of the "people-in-between" framework has also facilitated the marginalization and at times erasure of Indigenous women's critical contributions to Métis life.

Again, Macdougall's work has paved the way for reconstructing the women-centred family networks at the core of Métis culture. In her work on Métis communities in northwestern Saskatchewan, she has demonstrated how "women indigenous to the region became the centripetal and centrifugal force that incorporated successive waves of outside males."[51] A singular focus on French culture, language, and/or ancestry when it comes to the Métis inevitably downplays not only Métis Indigeneity but the specific contribution of Indigenous women to Métis life. As Robert Innes, professor of Indigenous Studies and member of the Cowessess First Nation, sums up, "By highlighting the role of Aboriginal women, Macdougall not only challenges the emphasis placed on the French freemen, but also sheds light onto the importance that First Nations cultural practices had in Métis cultural development. The weight given to Métis Europeanness has unfairly overshadowed First Nations culture in the emerging Métis culture."[52] In a recent interview on the topic of Métis identity, Jennifer Adese rebukes the specific tendency in "Eastern métis" studies to centre patrilineal relations: "As a Métis woman, I find that claims made regarding Métis as 'originating in the East' or from the 'paternal homeland of Québec' are unforgivably sexist. . . . [This] elides the rootedness of Métis in their maternal homeland—and thus in the language, kinship networks, and knowledge systems of maternal relations."[53] Scholars in Eastern métis studies almost universally avoid the great deal of academic literature produced primarily by Indigenous scholars about the Métis—including that which specifically critiques the sexist and patriarchal focus on French men—ensuring that their focus remains on the French settler men at the centre of their mythical story of adventure and intrigue.[54]

Denis Gagnon illustrates these tendencies when he focuses intently on the purported Métis denial of their French-Canadian ancestry: "It should be noted that a process that has been going on for a few years now is for the Western Métis to highlight their Indigenous heritage and to pass over in silence, perhaps in an involuntary way (but one may doubt it),

their French-Canadian heritage. It is a process that could be called the
Indigenization of the Western Métis" (emphasis in original).[55] Gagnon
mistakes Indigenous resurgence, a process that, as Nathalie Kermoal argues
in Chapter 2 of this volume, has been ongoing since the end of the Second
World War and especially since the 1960s, and that is well documented by
Indigenous and non-Indigenous scholars alike, as evidence of a "xenophobic," anti-French bias of the Métis. Yet Métis resurgence is occurring in ways
that parallel other forms of Indigenous resurgence precisely because the Métis
understand themselves and are understood as Indigenous.[56] Instead of cele-
brating the fact that, for instance, English-speaking (and French-speaking)
Métis may already speak or elect to learn Plains Cree, Michif, or Dene as a
(second) language instead of another European colonial language, Gagnon
simply delegitimizes the Métis for speaking English, a language that is part
and parcel of the colonial landscape. Again, Macdougall and Innes document the rich linguistic and cultural tapestry of Métis communities in two
quite different regions of Saskatchewan—northwestern and southeastern,
respectively—that certainly goes beyond the French-English preoccupations
on display in the scholarly literature advocating for the "Eastern métis."[57] In
particular, Macdougall outlines the Cree-speaking, Dene-influenced Métis
of northwestern Saskatchewan, whose primary connection to French was
through the missionaries in the region,[58] while Innes focuses on the multicultural and multilingual Métis of southeastern Saskatchewan, who spoke
Michif, Saulteaux, and/or Plains Cree.[59] In addition, despite the French-
language domination of many of the colonial institutions at the heart of
Métis life (church, school), there is remarkably little discussion of the French
language or French settler people as forces of colonialism in this subfield.
To his credit, Rivard briefly acknowledges that French-Canadian settlers to
Manitoba in the latter half of the nineteenth century arrogantly looked down
upon those Métis who spoke Michif, ensuring that "the Métis were forcibly
exiled from the larger francophone family."[60]

In fact, archives recently unearthed by historian Émilie Pigeon illustrate
that Catholic missionaries and priests often acted as colonial agents among
the Métis, pushing French-language initiatives that displaced Indigenous
languages and Indigeneity.[61] The assumption motivating scholars in this
subfield—that the French language/culture is innocent of colonial violence—
reproduces insidious forms of colonial erasure. Besides, the idea that Métis

scholars (and the Métis more broadly) are denying their Frenchness is a red herring. As Chris Andersen has explained previously, the issue is not about whether the Métis have European ancestors, but that all Indigenous peoples are mixed according to the specific forms of colonialism that they have faced.[62] In this sense, the Métis are Indigenous due in part to the ongoing strength of their reciprocal kinship relations with other Indigenous peoples on the Prairies, and not due to their mixedness. Conversely, the so-called Eastern métis are for the most part not Indigenous because they lack these same relations with Indigenous peoples. In fact, as Adam Gaudry and I have demonstrated, many "Eastern métis" organizations are openly hostile to Indigenous peoples.[63]

We can see how Métis resurgence is problematized *at the same time* as the much more recent efforts at Indigenization of the "Eastern métis" are lauded in this subfield. We are faced with a strange paradox: an Indigenous people (Métis) who have been more or less universally recognized as such for the past two centuries is diminished for supposedly not embracing its European-ness (i.e., Frenchness, French-language), while another group of people who have been more or less universally recognized as non-Indigenous (French-Canadian/Québécois) for up to three centuries is celebrated for its courage for coming out as "Indigenous." Given the preponderance of the notion of two European founding nations, and the fact that the language politics attached to the English-French binary do not factor much into Indigenous scholarly pursuits, it is no surprise that research in Indigenous studies is pretty much ignored in "Eastern métis" studies, even though some key texts have been translated into French. Any sustained engagement with the substantial body of literature exploring Indigenous concepts of citizenship, belonging, and kinship relations would certainly trouble the efforts of "Eastern métis" schol-ars to undermine Métis forms of governance.

Further, Malette's statement that the Western Métis are oppressing the "Eastern métis" plays on a recurring trope in "Eastern métis" studies, one that all but erases the presence of *actual* Indigenous peoples in present-day Quebec. For one thing, under the existing Indian Act regime the large major-ity of Indigenous peoples were not able to hide their Indigeneity. Instead, Indigenous peoples such as the Mohawk at Kanesata:ke/Oka, the Algonquins at Barrière Lake and Kipawa, the Mi'kmaq at Listiguj/Restigouche, and the Huron-Wendat at Parc Jacques Cartier have mounted several high-profile

campaigns against Canadian and Québécois settler governments in the past
few decades. These movements, as well as literally thousands of other everyday practices and events, form the basis of vigorous and dynamic Indigenous
nations in what is generally called Quebec today. Yet instead of engaging
with Indigenous peoples, and specifically, with Indigenous forms of self-determination, scholars in "Eastern métis" studies support the notion that a
generations-old ancestral tie to an Indigenous individual—*despite the fact
that there has been no maintenance of kinship relations with Indigenous peoples
for more than three centuries*—is all it takes to be Indigenous today, which is
counter to virtually all Indigenous efforts at self-determination.[64]

For those familiar with the politics of nationalism in Quebec, Malette's
claims depend on a historical memory that situates French-Canadians as
perpetually subjugated by the British. He builds on this symbolic reper-
toire when he states: "The Québécois must overcome the suppression of
their collective identity, which has been motivated in part by the need to
appear 'purely European' in the eyes of the English master in order not to
suffer the same fate as the 'savage' Acadians after the Conquest of 1763."[65]
Accordingly, the Québécois *become* "métis" as a way to reclaim a collective
identity suppressed for several centuries by Anglo-British subjugation. It is
telling how the "Eastern métis" are commonly used as a trope that resolves
conflict between French and British settlers in a manner that centres white
settler politics.

In our previous research on "Eastern métis" organizations in both Quebec
and Nova Scotia, Adam Gaudry and I identified the instrumentalization
of the Acadian Deportation as a common way to "locate a kind of historical suffering that is either on par with or greater than 'other' Indigenous
peoples."[66] In Malette's conception, as in the case of the two organizations
in our research, French subjugation by the British led to ("métis") invisibility
as a form of historical suffering, which "explain[s] [Eastern métis] political
and social absence from public space since the eighteenth century. Thus, their
authenticity as an Indigenous people is intact."[67] According to this creative
resignification, the Québécois reclamation of their long-distant Indigenous
heritage is in fact an *anti-colonial* act, since it undermines Anglo-British power.
Becoming Métis then is a *return* to Quebec's Indigenous roots, which have
been elided for centuries in order to avoid what would become the desperate
fate of Acadians, who were ethnically cleansed from present-day Nova Scotia

and largely became assimilated into American society. In fact, Gaudry and I argue, according to these types of claims, the Eastern métis are imagined as more Indigenous than Indigenous peoples: "It follows that self-identified Métis generally understand themselves as *more Métis than Métis,* and *more Indigenous than Indigenous peoples.* In the rediscovery of their Indigenous ancestors and their authentic 'Métis' selves along with it, the self-identified Métis are likely to locate authenticity in the past rather than in the present by repeatedly evoking métissage in the early contact period. Further, not only do they denigrate nearby First Nations, but they deny Métis nationhood by claiming a new origin story for the Métis Nation itself" (emphasis in original).[68] The new origin story we refer to here is the Eastern ethnogenesis narrative, in which the French Québécois *become* "Indigenous" in a manner that buttresses Quebec nationalist opposition to Anglo-British dominance.

Notwithstanding the confident assertions in "Eastern métis" studies about the historical suffering of French settlers with limited to no Indigenous ancestry,[69] these stories do not hold up well under scholarly scrutiny. As historians have demonstrated previously, France's imperial policy in New France quickly turned against its early assimilationist logic to one that frowned upon miscegenation and politically and socially prohibited mixed unions.[70] The new approach, grounded more clearly in the exploitation of Indigenous peoples, predated the British Conquest by nearly a century. It is clear through research in history and demography that Quebec's population at the time of the Conquest was relatively homogenous, no doubt reflective of the Crown's desire to maintain a unified French presence in the Americas.

Conclusion

In this chapter, I have sought to outline two of the main narrative elements used to advocate for the existence of the so-called Eastern métis in academic literature. First, I presented the Eastern ethnogenesis narrative as a novel, post-*Powley* creation that attracts a significant amount of scholarly support in this subfield. Asserting—contra empirical evidence—that "métis" people from Acadia and Quebec ultimately founded the Métis Nation, the Eastern ethnogenesis story openly opposes Métis origin stories in Cree, Saulteaux, Assiniboine (and at times, Dene) kinship relations and political alliances.

As I explained, scholars in this subfield imaginatively revise history to suit their settler colonial ambitions.

Second, I presented the narrow French-English nationalist impulse at the basis for most of the arguments brought forward by scholars in this subfield. Whether through mobilizing the importance of French ancestry, the French language, and/or other cultural aspects linked to Frenchness, these scholars consistently represent the Métis as oppressing French-speaking people. Yet by centring Frenchness, the patriarchal basis for their arguments are laid bare, since the crucial roles of Indigenous women in constructing the Métis Nation all but disappear. The near-complete lack of engagement with Indigenous scholars by proponents of the "Eastern métis," especially with the substantial body of literature produced by Métis scholars on Métis identity, ensures that this subfield remains primarily geared toward a settler colonial readership.

NOTES

1   I would like to thank the Rupertsland Centre for Métis Research for the invitation to present an early version of this chapter at the "*Daniels*: In and Beyond the Law" conference held at the Rupertsland Centre for Métis Research in Edmonton 26–28 January 2017, where Adam Gaudry, Daniel Voth, Chelsea Vowel, David Parent, Marilyn Dumont, and the two editors of this volume all provided generative feedback. In addition, Délice Mugabo, Trycia Bazinet, Pierrot Ross-Tremblay, Edward Lee, and Leila Benhadjoudja provided me with further feedback at a workshop later in 2017.

2   Data from the 2016 Census released in October 2017 further confirmed that the largest increases in Métis self-identification between 2006 and 2016 were in Quebec (149%) and Nova Scotia (124%). Statistics Canada, "Aboriginal Peoples in Canada: Key Results from the 2016 Census," *The Daily*, 25 October 2017. The post-*Daniels* bump in self-identification in the region would have occurred mostly after the census, which took place only a few weeks after the decision in April 2016.

3   Organizations such as the Alliance laurentienne des Métis et Indiens (sans statut), founded in 1971, used the terms "métis" and "non–Status Indians" in a nearly synonymous manner. In 1975, concerns about the non-Indigeneity of some of its members saw the Alliance adopt a fourth-generation cut-off (not a strictly blood quantum measurement). Today's Alliance autochtone du Québec (AAQ), the offshoot of the original Alliance laurentienne, accepts anybody as a member. The AAQ ran into some media trouble in September 2017, when a former long-time president could not identify his Indigenous ancestry. See Jorge Barrera, "Congress National Chief 'Can't Remember' Roots of Own Indigeneity," APTN News, 27 September 2017, http://aptnnews.ca/2017/09/27/congress–national–chief–cant–remember–roots–of–own–indigenous–ancestry/.

4   See the following for analyses of the *Daniels* decision: Adam Gaudry and Chris Andersen, "*Daniels v. Canada*: Racialized Legacies, Settler Self-Indigenization and the Denial of Indigenous Peoplehood," *TOPIA* 36 (2016): 19–30; Brenda Macdougall, "The Power of Legal and Historical Fiction(s): The *Daniels* Decision and the Enduring Influence of Colonial Ideology," *International*

Indigenous Policy Journal 7, no. 3 (2016): 1–6; and Chelsea Vowel and Darryl Leroux, "White Settler Antipathy and the *Daniels* Decision," *TOPIA* 36 (2016): 30–42.

5   Alexandre Courtemanche, "Le nombre de métis gaspésiens double en six mois," *TVA*, 5 October 2016, http://chau.teleinterrives.com/nouvelle-alaune_Le_nombre_de_metis_gaspesiens_double_en_six_mois-29700 (accessed 8 October 2016).

6   For example, the Communauté Autochtone Chibougamau-Chapais Eeyou Istchee was founded in July 2016 to represent "métis" people in the northern reaches of Quebec. Guy Tremblay, "Création d'une première communauté métisse dans le Nord du Québec," *La Sentinelle*, 31 January 2017, http://www.lasentinelle.ca/creation-dune-premiere-communaute-metisse-nord-quebec/. Its chief explained, "We took the decision [to create a Métis organization] following the Supreme Court of Canada's *Daniels* decision."

7   Paul Charest, "Qui a peur des Innus? Réflexions sur les débats au sujet du projet d'entente de principe entre les Innus de Mashteuiatsh, Essipit, Betsiamites et Nutashkuan et les Gouvernements du Québec et du Canada," *Anthropologies et sociétés* 27, no. 2 (2003): 185–206; Paul Charest, "La disparition des Montagnais et la négation des droits aborigènes: Commentaires critiques sur le livre de Nelson-Martin Dawson, *Feu, fourrures, fléaux et foi foudroyèrent les Montagnais* (2005)," *Recherches amérindiennes au Québec* 39, no. 3 (2009): 81–95; Mathieu Cook, "Les droits ancestraux des Innus: Reconnaissance et contestation, Analyse des discours sur l'altérité déployés lors d'une controverse à propos de négociations territoriales" (PhD diss., Université Laval, 2016); Claude Gélinas, *Indiens et Eurocanadiens et le cadre social du métissage au Saguenay-Lac-Saint-Jean, XVIIe–XXe siècles* (Québec: Septentrion, 2011); Leila Inksetter, *Initiatives et adaptations algonquines au XIXe siècle* (Québec: Septentrion, 2017); Louis-Philippe Rousseau, "Ni tout l'un, ni tout l'autre" (PhD diss., Université Laval, 2012); and Darren O'Toole, "Y a-t-il des communautés métisses au Québec?: Une perspective juridique," *Nouveaux cahiers du socialisme* 18 (2017): 29–36.

8   Denis Gagnon, "La nation métisse, les autres Métis et le métissage: Les paradoxes de la contingence identitaire," *Anthropologie et sociétés* 30, no. 1 (2006): 180–86; Denis Gagnon, "La création des 'vrais Métis': Définition identitaire, assujettissement et résistances," *Port Acadie: Revue interdisciplinaire en études acadiennes/Port Acadie: An Interdisciplinary Review in Acadian Studies* 13/14/15 (2008/2009): 295–306; Denis Gagnon, "Identité trouble et agent double: L'ontologie à l'épreuve du terrain," *Anthropologie et sociétés* 35, no. 3 (2011): 147–65; Pascal Huot, "Les Métis de la Boréalie: Une présence autochtone au Québec," *Rabaska: Revue d'ethnologie de l'Amérique française* 8 (2010): 77–92; Pascal Huot, "La question métisse au Québec," *Histoire Québec* 21, no. 2 (2015): 10–13; Sébastien Malette, "L'identité métisse au Québec: Le fil du fléché retrouvé," *Policy options politiques*, 2 November 2014; Guillaume Marcotte, "Un 'tracé d'une grande valeur': La carte indienne de Cameron et son potentiel ethnohistorique associé à l'Outaouais supérieur, 1760–1870," *Recherches amérindiennes au Québec* 45, no. 2–3 (2015): 77–91; Émmanuel Michaux, "Ni Amérindiens ni Eurocanadiens: Une approche néomoderne du culturalisme métis au Canada" (PhD diss., Université Laval, 2014); Anne Pelta, "La judiciarisation de l'identité métisse ou l'éveil des Métis au Québec" (PhD diss., Université Laval, 2015); Étienne Rivard, "Prairie and Quebec Metis Territoriality: 'Interstices territoriales' and the Cartography of In-Between Identity" (PhD diss., University of British Columbia, 2004); Étienne Rivard, "The Indefensible In-Betweenness or the Spatio-Legal Arbitrariness of the Métis Fact in Quebec," *Justice sociale /Spatial Justice* 11 (2017): 1–16; and Étienne Rivard, "Trajectoires cartographiques et métisses de la Franco-Amérique," in *Franco-Amérique*, ed. Dean Louder and Éric Waddell (Québec: Septentrion, 2017), 313–34.

9   Michaux, "Ni Amérindiens ni Eurocanadiens," 44. All translations from French to English
     are by the author. See also Rousseau, "Ni tout l'un, ni tout l'autre," 25, and Gélinas, *Indiens et
     Eurocanadiens*, 9, on the post-*Powley* social movement.

10   See also Denis Gagnon, "Les études métisses subventionnées et les travaux de la Chaire de recher-
     che du Canada sur l'identité métisse," in *L'identité métisse en question: Stratégies identitaires et
     dynamismes culturels*, ed. Denis Gagnon and Hélène Giguère (Québec: Presses de l'Université
     Laval, 2012), 315–40.

11   Chris Andersen, *"Métis": Race, Recognition, and the Struggle for Indigenous Peoplehood* (Vancouver:
     UBC Press, 2014); Chris Andersen, "From Nation to Population: The Racialisation of 'Métis'
     in the Canadian Census," *Nations and Nationalism* 14, no. 2 (2008): 347–68; Jacqueline
     Peterson, "Red River Redux: Métis Ethnogenesis and the Great Lakes Region," in *Contours
     of a People: Metis Family, Mobility, and History*, ed. Nicole St-Onge, Carolyn Podruchny, and
     Brenda Macdougall (Norman: University of Oklahoma Press, 2012), 22–58; Adam Gaudry,
     "Respecting Métis Nationhood in Matters of Métis Identity," in *Aboriginal History: A Reader*,
     ed. Kristin Burnett and Geoff Read (Toronto: Oxford University Press, 2016), 152–63; Adam
     Gaudry, "Communing with the Dead: The 'New Métis,' Métis Identity Appropriation, and the
     Displacement of Living Métis Culture," *American Indian Quarterly* 42, no. 2 (2018): 162–90;
     Brenda Macdougall, "Wahkootowin: Family and Cultural Identity in Northwestern Saskatchewan
     Metis Communities," *Canadian Historical Review* 86, no. 3 (2006): 431–62; and Heather Devine,
     The People Who Own Themselves: Aboriginal Ethnogenesis in a Canadian Family, 1660–1900
     (Calgary: University of Calgary Press, 2004).

12   See also the work of Daniels himself on the topic: Harry Daniels and Paul L.A.H. Chartrand,
     "Unravelling the Riddles of Metis Definition" (unpublished policy paper, 2001), 60.

13   Brenda MacDougall explains that the term "ethnogenesis" was coined by historian Jacqueline
     Peterson in her PhD dissertation of the late 1970s, in reference to the Métis. Peterson argued that
     "the birth of the Métis as a separate people with a national consciousness did not occur until the
     end of the Pemmican Wars and the Battle of Seven Oaks in 1815 at Red River." Peterson, cited in
     Macdougall, "Wahkootowin," 436.

14   Rivard, "Prairie and Quebec Metis Territoriality," 205.

15   Michaux, "Ni Amérindiens ni Eurocanadiens," 138.

16   Rivard, "Trajectoires cartographiques et métisses de la Franco-Amérique," 330.

17   Michaux, "Ni Amérindiens ni Eurocanadiens," 155.

18   Rivard, "Trajectoires cartographiques et métisses," 1.

19   For example, Guillaume Bourgault-Côté and Marie Vastel, "Des 'Indiens' à part entière," *Le
     Devoir*, 15 April 2016, http://www.ledevoir.com/societe/actualites-en-societe/468283/des-indie
     ns-a-part-entiere.

20   Claude Aubin, "Nation Métis du Québec, un autre point de vue de reconnaissance," 4 November
     2010, http://claudeaubinmetis.com/viewtopic.php?f=36&t=20 (accessed 15 December 2016).

21   Ibid.

22   While it would be fair to assume that the lack of engagement with English-language literature on
     the Métis is due to a language barrier, all of the authors in question readily engage with *other* mate-
     rial in English.

23   Gagnon, "La création des 'vrais Métis,'" 300.

24 Senate of Canada, "'The People Who Own Themselves': Recognition of Métis Identity in Canada" (Ottawa: Government of Canada, 2013), 19.

25 Robert A. Innes, *Elder Brother and the Law of the People: Contemporary Kinship and Cowessess First Nation* (Winnipeg: University of Manitoba Press, 2013).

26 Malette, "L'identité métisse au Québec," para. 6.

27 For a review of what we call the "evocation of métissage," see Adam Gaudry and Darryl Leroux, "White Settler Revisionism and Making Métis Everywhere: The Evocation of Métissage in Quebec and Nova Scotia," *Critical Ethnic Studies* 3, no. 1 (2017): 116–42.

28 Yves Beauregard, "Mythe ou réalité: Les origines amérindiennes des Québécois: Entrevue avec Hubert Charbonneau," *Cap-aux-Diamants: La revue d'histoire du Québec*, no. 34 (1993): 38–42.

29 Malette, "L'identité métisse au Québec," para. 12.

30 I unpack the effects of distant consanguinity on French descendants, especially as it relates to the use of DNA ancestry testing, in Darryl Leroux, "'We've Been Here for 2,000 Years': White Settlers, Native American DNA and the Politics of Indigeneity," *Social Studies of Science* 48, no. 1 (2018): 80–100.

31 Bertrand Desjardins, "Homogénéité ethnique de la population québécoise sous le Régime français," *Cahiers québécois de démographie* 19, no. 1 (1990): 63–76.

32 John Ralston Saul, *A Fair Country: Telling Truths about Canada* (Toronto: Viking Canada, 2008).

33 Michaux, "Ni Amérindiens ni Eurocanadiens," 224.

34 Ibid., 221.

35 Ibid., 178.

36 Darryl Leroux, *Distorted Descent: White Claims to Indigenous Identity* (Winnipeg: University of Manitoba Press, 2019).

37 Gagnon, "Identité trouble et agent double," 155.

38 Rivard, "The Indefensible In-Betweenness," 2.

39 Michaux, "Ni Amérindiens ni Eurocanadiens," 226.

40 Ibid.

41 Rivard, "Trajectoires cartographiques et métisses," 330.

42 Gaudry, "Communing with the Dead."

43 Aboriginal Peoples Television Network, APTN News, "Identity Crisis: APTN Investigates," 18 April 2017, https://www.youtube.com/watch?v=lzNYGW0OimY.

44 See, for instance, Charest, "Qui a peur des Innus?"

45 Bouchard, as cited in Charest, "La disparition des Montagnais et la négation des droits aborigènes," 91.

46 Innu territory to the north of the St. Lawrence River and east of Québec City.

47 Institut de la Statistique du Québec, "Estimation de la population des régions administratives, 1er Juillet des Années 1986, 1991, 1996, 2001, 2006 et 2011 à 2016," 8 March 2017, http://www.stat.gouv.qc.ca/statistiques/population-demographie/structure/ra_total.htm.

48 Joanne Barker, *Native Acts: Law, Recognition, and Cultural Authenticity* (Durham, NC: Duke University Press, 2011); Jill Doerfler, *Those Who Belong: Identity, Family, Blood, and Citizenship among the White Earth Anishinaabeg* (Winnipeg: University of Manitoba Press, 2015); Eve

Garroutte, *Real Indians: Identity and the Survival of Native America* (Oakland: University of California Press, 2003); J. Kēhaulani Kauanui, *Hawaiian Blood: Colonialism and the Politics of Sovereignty and Indigeneity* (Durham, NC: Duke University Press, 2008); and Aileen Moreton-Robinson, *The White Possessive: Property, Power, and Indigenous Sovereignty* (Minneapolis: University of Minnesota Press, 2015).

49 Michaux, "Ni Amérindiens ni Eurocanadiens," 56.

50 Macdougall, "Wahkootowin," 439.

51 Brenda Macdougall, *One of the Family: Metis Culture in Nineteenth-Century Northwestern Saskatchewan* (Vancouver: University of British of Columbia Press, 2011), 17.

52 Innes, *Elder Brother*, 85.

53 Jennifer Adese, Zoe Todd, and Shaun Stevenson, "Mediating Identity: An Interview with Jennifer Adese and Zoe Todd," *MediaTropes* 7, no. 1 (2017): 10.

54 See Gaudry and Leroux, "White Settler Revisionism," 130–32.

55 Gagnon, "La création des 'vrais Métis,'" 305.

56 For example, John Borrows, *Recovering Canada: The Resurgence of Indigenous Law* (Toronto: University of Toronto Press, 2002); Glen Coulthard, *Red Skin, White Masks: Rejecting the Colonial Politics of Recognition* (Minneapolis: University of Minnesota Press, 2014); and Leanne Betasamosake Simpson, ed., *Lighting the Eighth Fire: The Liberation, Resurgence, and Protection of Indigenous Nations* (Winnipeg: Arbeiter Ring Publishing, 2008).

57 Macdougall, "Wahkootowin"; Macdougall, *One of the Family*; and Innes, *Elder Brother*.

58 Macdougall, "Wahkootowin," 432.

59 Innes, *Elder Brother*.

60 Rivard, "Trajectoires cartographiques et métisses," 332.

61 Émilie Pigeon, "Lost in Translation: The Michif French Diaries of William Davis," *Champlain Society*, 2017, http://champlainsociety.utpjournals.press/findings-trouvailles/the-michif-french-diaries-of-william-davis (accessed 26 November 2017).

62 Andersen, *"Métis."*

63 Gaudry and Leroux, "White Settler Revisionism"; Darryl Leroux, "Self-Made Métis," *Maisonneuve Magazine*, 1 November 2018; Leroux, *Distorted Descent*; Vowel and Leroux, "White Settler Antipathy."

64 See, for example, Damien Lee, "Adoption Is (Not) a Dirty Word: Towards an Adoption-Centric Theory of Anishinaabeg Citizenship," *First Peoples Child and Family Review: An Interdisciplinary Journal* 10, no. 1 (2015): 86–98; and Kim TallBear, *Native American DNA: Tribal Belonging and the False Promise of Genetic Science* (Minneapolis: University of Minnesota Press, 2013).

65 Malette, "L'identité métisse au Québec," para. 12.

66 Gaudry and Leroux, "White Settler Revisionism," 127.

67 Ibid., 129.

68 Ibid., 134.

69 I outline how about 30 percent of those claiming an "Indigenous" identity as part of the "Eastern métis" movement have no Indigenous ancestry, since they turn a handful of French women ancestors born prior to 1650 into "Indigenous" women. Leroux, *Distorted Descent*, 73–102.

70 Guillaume Aubert, "'The Blood of France': Race and Purity of Blood in the French Atlantic World," *William and Mary Quarterly* 61, no. 3 (2004): 439–78; Saliha Belmessous, "Assimilation and Racialism in Seventeenth and Eighteenth-Century French Colonial Policy," *American Historical Review* 110, no. 2 (2005): 322–49; Peter Cook, "Onontio Gives Birth: How the French in Canada Became Fathers to Their Indigenous Allies, 1645–73," *Canadian Historical Review* 96, no. 2 (2015): 165–69; Mairi Cowan, "Education, Francisation, and Shifting Colonial Priorities at the Ursuline Convent in Seventeenth-Century Québec," *Canadian Historical Review* 99, no. 1 (2018): 1–29; Dominique Deslandres, "'. . . alors nos garçons se marieront à vos filles, & nous ne ferons plus qu'un seul people': Religion, genre et déploiement de la souveraineté française en Amérique aux XVIe–XVIIIe siècles—une problématique," *Revue d'histoire de l'Amérique française* 66, no. 1 (2012): 5–35; and Gilles Havard, "'Nous ne ferons plus qu'un peuple': Le métissage en Nouvelle-France à l'époque de Champlain," in *Le nouveau monde et Champlain*, ed. Guy Martinière and Didier Poton (Paris: Les Indes savantes, 2008), 85–107.

CHAPTER 10

Making Kin in a Postgenomic World: Indigenous Belonging after the Genome

RICK W.A. SMITH, LAUREN SPRINGS,
AUSTIN W. REYNOLDS, AND DEBORAH A. BOLNICK

Over the past several decades, developments in genome science have provided powerful but often controversial means for making claims about human identities and our connections with one another. Through advances in DNA sequencing technologies and the commercialization of genetic ancestry testing services, both scientists and the general public have gained unprecedented access to large amounts of genetic information, which is being used more and more to assess biological relationships and reconstruct population histories. At the same time, genetic technologies are increasingly being incorporated into shifting claims about individual identities, group belongings, and questions of ethnicity and cultural heritage. For various reasons, the legitimacy of these claims has been challenged by scholars, activists, and community members alike. For example, critics have shown how the application of genetic ancestry tests to questions of ethnic and racial belonging can revive the harmful and widely discredited idea that these social, legal, and political categories originate in our biology. With commercial genetic ancestry tests proliferating among consumers as seemingly authoritative ways to answer questions of identity, belonging, and homeland, critics have also noted that one's genetic relations may not always correspond to one's social, cultural, historical, geopolitical, and/or legal ties to particular peoples and places.[1] In other words, DNA technologies might provide one picture of who our relatives are and where we come from, while history and lived experiences within communities may provide other views. This is because DNA traces only one aspect of how people can be related, and as such, DNA alone is a poor stand-in for all of the complex ways that people can and do become relatives. In spite of these critiques, the limitations of DNA-based claims to identity and belonging remain less widely appreciated in the public sphere. Because of this, many people with access to genome technologies have continued using them as a way to claim belonging in communities with which they have little or no other connection, even when the groups they are claiming to be a part of do not recognize them or their claims of belonging.

These developments have long been a concern for many Indigenous peoples in the Americas and beyond. Both Indigenous and non-Indigenous scholars have drawn attention to the implications of genome science for Indigenous peoples—including its potential advantages and pitfalls, and the ways that it can be used to impose settler colonial definitions of kinship at the expense of Indigenous self-determinations.[2] With little or no understanding of how Indigenous peoples define belonging within their communities, European settlers and others in the Americas have increasingly turned to DNA as a way to claim Indigenous identities and cultural heritage. These claims to Indigeneity have even been incorporated into claims around Indigenous status and land rights[3] as well as disputes over resource access and management.[4] Indigenous scholars and others have shown how these uses of genome science are merely the latest development in a long history of settler colonial efforts to possess, inherit, and manage Indigenous peoples and lands.[5]

In the context of the Métis, the 2016 decision in *Daniels v. Canada* is cause for concern regarding the uses of genetic ancestry testing among Canadian settlers and how these practices can work in opposition to the self-determination of the Métis as a people. While both genealogical and genomic claims to Indigenous belonging certainly preceded *Daniels v. Canada*, aspects of the decision seem to draw upon and even reinforce the racial thinking through which non-Indigenous peoples have been making various claims to Métis belonging, including claims that have been made on the basis of genetic ancestry tests. As Nathalie Kermoal, Chris Andersen, and others have discussed in the preceding chapters of this volume, the *Daniels* decision recognized two versions of what constitutes the term "Métis": one that is based on the nationhood, shared history, and culture of a distinct people; and another based on a racialized notion of mixed Aboriginal and European ancestry. Andersen (Chapter 8) has noted how these definitions drew upon pre-existing ideas about Métis as a mixed-race category that had long circulated within broader Canadian society. This mischaracterization has been "deeply troubling for Métis people who see themselves not as a mixture of races, but as distinctive political and cultural communities" (Introduction). Andersen goes on to warn that the bipartite definition of Métis in the *Daniels* decision is important not only in juridical spheres but also for the ways in which a wider array of social actors interpret and act upon the contents of the decision in the service of their own self-interests and desires. Of particular concern in this chapter are the colloquial and legal definitions of Métis people as a mixed-race group, the role of genetic ancestry testing in providing some connection (however distant) to an Indigenous ancestor, and the ways in which non-Indigenous peoples might draw upon these tests as evidence of their mixed ancestry in attempts to support their claims to the Métis.

What is so often left out in such claims, be they genomic or genealogical, is the role of community recognition. That is, these claims to Métis belonging are frequently disengaged from Métis people and therefore lack recognition from the very communities to which consumers of genetic ancestry tests seek entry. In this regard, the limitations of DNA technologies are similar to those of genealogical research that Darryl Leroux (Chapter 9) and Brenda Macdougall (Chapter 11) discuss, where European settlers and others have increasingly claimed Indigenous identities by virtue of descent from a distant Indigenous ancestor, even when meaningful relationships with Indigenous communities have ceased to exist for many centuries. Akin to the distinction that Macdougall draws between biography (which emphasizes the life of a single person) and prosopography (which emphasizes networks of relationships within a group), uses of genetic ancestry testing often make the error of constructing *individual* identity narratives for particular ways of being that can only be realized and lived in *relation* to community.

In lieu of such connections, the phenomenon of self-Indigenization through both genealogical research and genetic ancestry testing has intensified in the post-*Daniels* era (Leroux, Chapter 9). In the context of genetic ancestry testing, claims to Métis belonging hinge on the broader logic circulating within Canadian society and codified within the *Daniels* decision—that "Métis" is a mixed-race category that anyone with European and Indigenous ancestors can claim.[6] This notion has been contested by Métis scholars and others, who have rejected characterizations of Métis as a "mixed race" category and insisted upon their recognition as a historically, geographically, and culturally constituted nation that alone has the power to define its own members.[7] These issues are discussed more thoroughly by Arend Hoekstra and Thomas Isaac (Chapter 4), Brenda Gunn (Chapter 7), and D'Arcy Vermette (Chapter 6).

Given the growing role of genetic technologies in non-Indigenous claims to Métis belonging in the post-*Daniels* era and the growing implications of genome science for many Indigenous peoples in general, our goals in this chapter are to consider how genetic ancestry testing actually works, how it contrasts with the sovereignty and self-definitions of Indigenous peoples, and how it therefore provides no meaningful basis for determining Indigenous belonging. Here, our focus is on the broader context of commercial genetic ancestry testing in the public sphere rather than on the ways that genetic techniques can and have been used by Indigenous peoples to address specific questions of parentage.

We begin with a brief review of DNA and how it is used in both academic and commercial genetic ancestry research, which has provided much of the foundation for settler claims to Indigenous belonging that have proliferated in recent years. Next, we draw on publicly available genome data from the Americas to get a sense of what genetic variation exists within Indigenous communities today and whether that variation even provides a meaningful basis for making genetic claims to Indigenous belonging in the first place. Finally, we conclude with brief ethnographic vignettes from two people, both of whom have some Indigenous ancestors but whose differing relations and levels of connection with Indigenous communities have put them on different sides of history. We use these vignettes as a means to think through and complicate what it means to belong in the era of the genome.

Genetic Ancestry Testing: Past and Present

Direct-to-consumer genetic ancestry tests, such as those provided by companies like 23andMe, AncestryDNA, and National Geographic Society's Genographic Project, have rapidly proliferated over the last few decades.

Many millions of consumers have already participated in some form of direct-to-consumer genomics, and this number continues to grow. During Black Friday weekend in 2017, AncestryDNA alone sold more than 1.5 million tests, and a recent independent business report has suggested that the direct-to-consumer genomics market will more than triple by the year 2022, growing from $99 million to more than $300 million in annual revenue.[8] In the two decades since this DNA marketplace was established, various genetic ancestry companies have made a number of claims that explicitly connect questions of identity and belonging to the capabilities of emerging genome technologies, promising to help people to "reconstruct family roots," locate their "geographic origins" or "ancestral village," or identify their ethnicity or even tribal affiliation.[9]

Historically, three main types of genetic tests have been commercially available—matrilineal, patrilineal, and biparental (autosomal) ancestry tests. Matrilineal tests analyze what is known as mitochondrial DNA, or mtDNA, which is a small, circular piece of DNA that people inherit almost exclusively from their mother,[10] who inherited it from her mother, and so on into the past.[11] Unlike other portions of the human genome that are passed down from both parents, mtDNA has a simpler mode of inheritance because it never recombines[12] (or exchanges genetic material) with the father's DNA, and thus is almost always representative of a person's matrilineal descent (Figure 10.1). Because of its simple mode of inheritance and small size, mtDNA was historically the most widely used portion of the genome for genetic ancestry testing and population history analysis. However, since mtDNA is maternally inherited and makes up less than 1 percent of the human genome, it only reveals one out of many thousands of possible ancestors at any given point in history.

The second common type of genetic ancestry test looks at a small portion of the Y chromosome (NRY), which is passed from fathers to sons in most cases.[13] For individuals carrying a Y chromosome—most commonly but not exclusively males—this genetic test can be used to assess one's patrilineal descent (Figure 10.1). Similar to the mtDNA, the commonly analyzed portion of the Y chromosome makes up less than 1 percent of the genome, and again reflects only one out of many thousands of possible ancestors at any point in history.

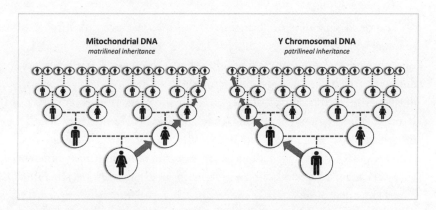

FIGURE 10.1. The Inheritance of Mitochondrial and Y Chromosomal DNA

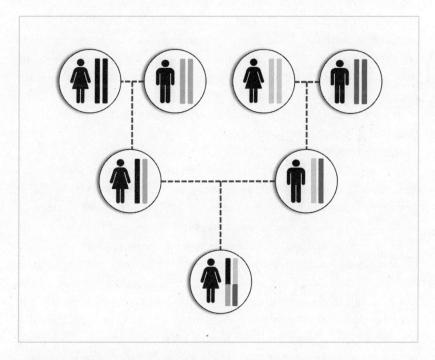

FIGURE 10.2. The Inheritance of Autosomal DNA.

The third type of genetic ancestry test looks at a person's autosomal genome, which includes DNA inherited from both the father and mother.[14] Because each set of autosomal chromosomes recombines every generation during the formation of eggs and sperm, the combination of genes present in any person is a random assortment of their ancestors' DNA (Figure 10.2). In other words, you might get one stretch of DNA from one ancestor and a neighbouring section from a completely different ancestor. This means that the autosomal genome may contain genetic contributions from many different ancestors at any given point in the past. Autosomal chromosomes therefore have a more complex pattern of inheritance than either mtDNA or the NRY, and as a result it has historically been more difficult to study them. However, as technology has improved over recent decades, tests analyzing parts of the autosomal genome have greatly increased in availability and are now the most common approach to ancestry testing among the leading commercial providers. Because these tests focus on a much larger portion of the genome than either mtDNA or NRY tests, they provide a much more detailed, though increasingly complicated, picture of a person's genetic history that is more open to multiple interpretations.

DNA is a long polymer (or chain) made up of combinations of four basic nucleotides, each represented by a letter: Adenine (A), Cytosine (C), Guanine (G), and Thymine (T). Most autosomal DNA ancestry tests work by looking at nucleotide differences that can vary in frequency and distribution across human populations, allowing for the estimation of biological relationships. For example, at any given position in the genome along the nucleotide sequence, some people might have an A, while others might have a C, G, or T. These genetic differences between people are known as single nucleotide differences, also called single nucleotide polymorphisms, or SNPs (Figure 10.3). Genetic ancestry tests based on autosomal DNA may examine several hundred thousand to a million or more of these differences. Because DNA is passed down from biological parents to their offspring and biological relatives have similar DNA, people who share more of the same nucleotides across many different positions tend to be more closely related than those who share fewer.

After a company has determined which nucleotides a person has across all of the SNPs being studied, they compare the results with many other previously studied people and search for those who share matching nucleotides (Figure 10.4). Because some SNPs are more common in some groups than

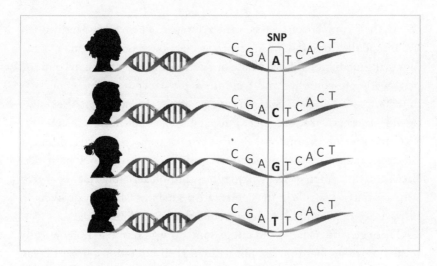

FIGURE 10.3. Single Nucleotide Differences (SNPs).

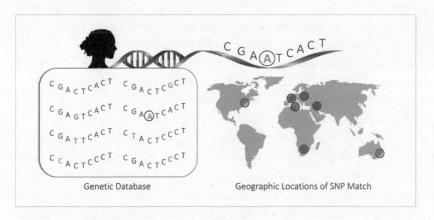

FIGURE 10.4. Predicting Genetic Ancestry Using Genetic Databases and Geographic Distributions.

This figure represents the analysis of a single SNP in a person's DNA. After determining the nucleotide that is present at a given position, the result is compared with corresponding SNPs in a reference database containing DNA sequences from many other people. When a match in the database is found, the known geographic distributions of that match are used to predict which groups a person shares relatives with. Matches in the database are indicated above with circles. The frequency of the SNP, or how common it is among different groups in the database, is indicated by the degree of shading, where darker shading indicates higher frequencies and lighter shading indicates lower frequencies. This process is repeated for many different SNPs.

others, these comparisons can be used to estimate where related individuals live around the world today. Using this information, genetic ancestry companies make predictions about where one's ancestor(s) may have lived in the past. With mitochondrial and Y chromosome DNA, the entire sequence is inherited from a single ancestor in each generation in the past, so the results provide information about a very limited number of ancestors. In contrast, SNPs in different sections of the autosomal DNA may come from different ancestors, and therefore they each can have different histories of inheritance. Because of this, different SNPs in a person's autosomal genome may be shared with a variety of people in the comparative database, who may be living in many different geographic regions around the world (Figure 10.4).

These genetic matches can tell us something about who is genetically related to whom, but they are not without their limitations. In particular, because the comparative genetic data are primarily drawn from living people, not necessarily ancestors who were living in the past, the relationships that these matches uncover are mainly with present-day peoples. Information about a person's ancestors are often *inferred* from present-day patterns, and thus estimates of the geographic source of a particular SNP, and inferences about a person's ancestry, are not necessarily absolute. Rather, the genetic ancestries reported by DNA testing companies are *estimates*—approximations of a person's most likely ancestry based on where their particular SNPs are shared with the most people. For example, when we look at the global distribution of the SNP shown in Figure 10.4, we find that it is shared with a lot of different people living in multiple places around the world. Typically, these analyses assign a geographic source based on where the SNP is found among the most people. If, for example, the SNP in Figure 10.4 were found at higher frequencies in the Middle East but at lower frequencies in northern and southern Africa, Europe, and the eastern portions of the United States and Australia, then a genetic ancestry test would identify the Middle East as the most likely ancestral source for a person with this particular SNP. When many different SNPs are considered together, their differing distributions across the world can be used to predict the overall proportions of a person's genome shared with different groups.

However, it is important to remember that while genetic ancestry analyses assume that SNPs are inherited from the region where they are present at the highest frequency today, it is possible that they could have been inherited from any of the geographic regions in the world where they are found, even if they are present there at only low frequencies. It is also possible that SNPs might have been inherited from geographic regions where they are no longer found today but where they were present in the past (when one's ancestors might have lived there), or from geographic regions that are not present in the database being used. Biases in who is represented in genetic databases can significantly affect ancestry predictions and are shaped by a variety of factors, including class, racial, ethnic, and other geopolitical disparities in who has access to DNA testing technologies as well as in the choices that scientists make about who to include in the comparative databases. In addition, because people have always moved around and exchanged their DNA throughout history, SNPs are almost always shared by a number of different groups, and which of these groups share any particular SNP changes through time. SNPs are rarely, if ever, diagnostic of only one specific place or group of people.[15] Thus, with the exception of certain very rare variants, it can be difficult or impossible to use DNA as a way to locate a person's ancestral home with full precision.

In the case of DNA sequences common in the Americas prior to European colonization, we find that many matrilineal, patrilineal, and autosomal DNA sequences are shared across many groups and geographic locations. For example, prior to the arrival of non-Indigenous peoples in the Americas, there were at least ten pan-American mtDNA lineages present among Indigenous peoples, found in groups ranging from the Arctic Circle to southern Chile.[16] Similarly, autosomal DNA sequences like the one known as D9S1120 are shared by many people throughout the Americas.[17] Given these kinds of distributions, we can see that many DNA sequences are shared across geopolitical boundaries as well as across all manner of tribal, First Nations, Aboriginal, and other Indigenous and non-Indigenous peoples. Because of this, widely distributed DNA sequences like these could never be used to reliably assign someone to a specific Indigenous community. Although more sophisticated genetic tests are being developed that could substantially improve predictions of individual and group relations, including tests that look at longer sequences of DNA rather than just SNPs, there will never be a genetic test that can predict or assign specific affiliations to Indigenous communities with complete accuracy, because there is no DNA that is specific to any single group. Ultimately, the question of who counts as a member of an Indigenous community does not centre on issues of genetic ancestry. Whether or not a person shares DNA in common with these groups, Indigenous peoples alone hold the power to decide who their people are.[18]

Another limitation of these tests stems from the fact that different labs analyze different parts of the genome and use different genetic databases. This means that taking tests provided by different labs or taking the same test at different times may yield varying results. The fact that DNA databases change over time and differ between labs means that a person may never get the same exact ancestry estimation twice. For example, we can illustrate how estimates of a person's genetic ancestry can change when we use different genetic databases for comparison. In Figure 10.5, each shaded block represents a different group that was chosen beforehand as a baseline for comparison. Any number of different groups could be chosen for the analysis, and they could be predefined in different ways by researchers. Some researchers may define groups based on geographic location, while others may define them based on language, lifestyle, culture, religion, or any number of other factors. However, the ultimate prediction of genetic ancestry resulting from the analysis depends on the baseline set of people that researchers choose to include for comparison, and these groups are therefore known as reference groups. An analysis that uses reference groups defined as African and European would yield predictions of genetic relatedness to those two groups, but such a test would not be able to say anything about DNA shared with Indigenous peoples, because they were not included in the analysis.

For the purposes of our analysis in this chapter, we selected four different reference groups (Figure 10.5) from publicly available genetic data.[19] These groups were predefined according to continental geography and include people located in sub-Saharan Africa, East Asia, Western Europe, and the Americas. Each of these groups was selected to represent people present in the Americas during the early colonial period. Thin vertical lines within each shaded block represent individuals sampled from that group, and the different shades in each of those lines represent the fraction of that person's DNA that they share in common with the pre-selected reference groups. Note that some members of a reference group may share some DNA with members of other reference groups. Here we caution that while the term Native American is widely used in the context of genetic ancestry estimation, it is not a term that all Indigenous peoples in the Americas use. On the far right of Figure 10.5,

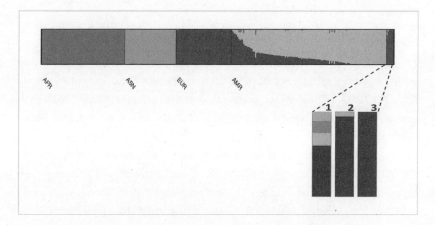

FIGURE 10.5. Genetic Ancestry Prediction Using Four Reference Groups.

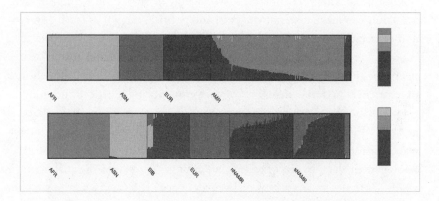

FIGURE 10.6. Genetic Ancestry Prediction Using Different Reference Groups.

This figure demonstrates how the prediction of genetic ancestry can substantially change from test to test based on the reference groups researchers choose for the analysis. Here we re-analyzed genetic ancestry for individual one. The upper graph shows the original prediction of individual one's genetic ancestry when reference groups (upper left) included the continentally defined categories of sub-Saharan Africa, East Asia, Western Europe, and the Americas. The resulting genetic ancestry prediction for individual one (upper right) showed that SNPs were shared in common with "Native Americans," sub-Saharan Africans, and East Asians. However, when we changed the reference groups to include genetic data from Siberia as well as a greater number of individuals from North and South America (bottom left), we get a different prediction of individual one's genetic ancestry. Specifically, in the second analysis we see that no SNPs are predicted to be shared in common with the "Native American" reference group, and a greater proportion of SNPs are predicted to be shared in common with East Asia (bottom right).

we show three individuals for whom we can predict genetic ancestry using the reference groups we have selected. The analysis works by looking at more than 629,000 individual SNPs in the DNA of each person and estimating which reference group each of those SNPs is shared with, as described above. It then visually represents the proportion of SNPs that are shared with each group as different shades of grey. For this analysis, we can see that individual three shares all of their SNPs in common with the Western European reference group. The other two individuals share most of their SNPs with Western Europeans, but also have some SNPs in common with other reference groups in the database. Individual one shares some SNPs with Native Americans, sub-Saharan Africans, and East Asians, while individual two shares some SNPs with Native Americans.

These kinds of genetic ancestry tests have previously been the subject of critique for their dependence upon racially defined groups and for the ways they can make it seem that social and political categories (such as race and ethnicity) originate in or align with biology.[20] Our analysis serves to substantiate prior critiques. As we have discussed, the reference groups used in genetic ancestry analyses can be named in a variety of ways at the discretion of researchers. So rather than the reference groups being genetically meaningful populations, the arbitrary naming of these reference groups beforehand and the selection of groups that fit preconceived notions about what groups actually exist underscores the ways in which racial categories can be imposed upon genetic data. In lieu of reiterating prior critiques here, the goal of our analysis is to demonstrate how differences in genetic ancestry results can be shaped by subjective differences in the reference databases used for comparison. This example shows that genetic ancestry results are not written in stone, but can change from test to test. In this analysis, we chose to define groups according to continental geography, not because these groups are genetically discrete categories but because they are similar to the categories most commonly used by genetic ancestry companies.

With these caveats in mind, we can say that genetic ancestry estimates represent the likelihood of a biological relation *based on the conditions of the particular test*, not a definitive connection to any specific group. Thus the idea that we can use DNA to conclusively link people to discrete groups or places is problematic. And while these kinds of analyses may be able to infer that an individual has some Indigenous ancestors to some degree of certainty, there

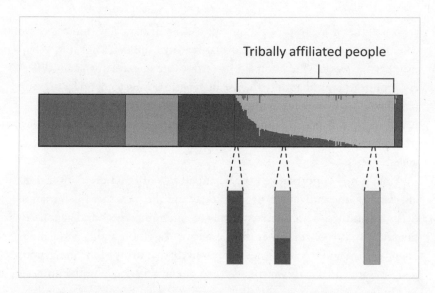

FIGURE 10.7. Genetic Variation among Indigenous People in the Americas.

There is genetic variation among Indigenous people in the Americas. In this genetic ancestry analysis of four different groups, the darker grey represents the fraction of DNA shared in common with Europeans, and the lighter grey represents the fraction of DNA shared in common with Indigenous peoples prior to the colonial period. Each of the three Indigenous people highlighted here shares varying proportions of their DNA with both European and Indigenous peoples.

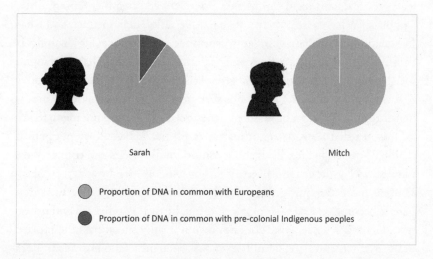

FIGURE 10.8. Genetic Ancestry Results for Sarah and Mitch.

is no way that these tests could provide a clear affiliation within a specific community—because that's not how DNA works and that's not how group membership works. The vast majority of SNPs are shared across many different groups in ways that defy the use of genetic testing to define a person's membership within any particular group. Even if this were not the case, it is still up to Indigenous people alone to decide who their people are, and membership within Indigenous communities is not the purview of genetic ancestry tests.

Finally, it is important to note what patterns of genetic variation actually exist among Indigenous peoples today and the ways that this variation defies the use of genetic ancestry testing to determine who is Indigenous. In our analysis, it is obvious that there is a lot of variation within Indigenous communities, and to varying degrees it is likely that many of the Indigenous people represented in this analysis have some combination of both European and Indigenous ancestors, as well as ancestors from other groups around the world (Figure 10.7). In fact, we can see individuals who are inferred to have solely Indigenous ancestors, others who appear have both Indigenous and non-Indigenous ancestors, and still others who show no measurable trace of DNA from Indigenous peoples as scientists have conventionally defined them. Nonetheless, these people belong to each other, having become a community not solely through biological claims but through reciprocal social, historical, political, and legal claims that flow between member, community, and place. What these patterns of genetic variation demonstrate, and what Indigenous scholars and community members have been saying all along, is that Indigenous peoples are not genetically defined groups.[21] Rather they are socially, culturally, historically, and geopolitically defined peoples (as Chapters 6, 8, and 9 demonstrate). And since such peoples are not genetically meaningful groups, there can be no solely genetic claims about belonging to them.

It is not that DNA does not matter at all; DNA is one form of relation that matters because it tells us about some of our histories and connections. However, what the genetic diversity within communities shows is that inheritance is more than just genomic, and that there are many varied ways that people become relatives—biological, social, historical, political, and otherwise. Genetic science alone does not own nor fully encompass the process of inheritance, and DNA should never be viewed in isolation because it does not exist independently of social, historical, and political processes. Rather,

DNA is embedded in irreducibly political contexts and is continually being reshaped by social life.

Experiences of "Native American DNA"

In order to think through how genetic ancestry testing plays out on the ground in relation to Indigenous communities, and what it means to belong in the era of genetic ancestry testing, we conclude with two brief ethnographic vignettes. The following stories focus on two people who took part in some form of commercial genetic ancestry testing but had very different histories of connection with Indigenous and non-Indigenous communities in their lives. These vignettes relay people's own personal experiences with commercial genetic ancestry testing companies; no original genetic data were collected for the purposes of this chapter, and participants consented to share their stories as part of this volume. While both of these stories and the particular terminologies that they use come from within the context of tribal peoples in the United States, which differs in many respects from the historical, social, political, and legal landscape in Canada, these stories nonetheless offer important insights about belonging in the postgenomic era that are relevant in countering the increasingly pervasive use of genetic ancestry testing to claim Métis belonging following the *Daniels* decision.

The two people included here, whom we will refer to as Sarah and Mitch,[22] offer knowledge that exemplifies the strange borderlands and ruptures marking the relations between DNA, personhood, and the social and historical pathways through which people come to belong in communities. If we were to take the results of their genetic tests at face value, Sarah and Mitch have mostly European ancestors and share little or no DNA in common with Indigenous peoples (Figure 10.8). But one of them is a tribally affiliated Indigenous person, while the other is not. Based on the DNA evidence alone, and what we and others have demonstrated about the limitations of genetic ancestry analyses, how would anyone even begin to mark the threshold defining which of these people is counted as Indigenous and which is not? Telling the difference, it turns out, always requires more than DNA.

Sarah

Sarah's dad left home when he was young. He was an Indigenous boy from the Deep South who felt relieved to be running away from the poverty and discrimination his family faced there. He changed his name and hitchhiked to the West Coast in the hope of something different, but what he found there were only other forms of discrimination. He learned that a new name could not cover up "dark skin" and "high cheekbones," even among all those progressive people living on the coast. So he spent the rest of his childhood homeless and on the streets. When he was old enough, he joined the military, mainly for the food and shelter. After leaving the military and re-entering civilian life, he changed his name again, and by the time he met Sarah's mother he had assumed an Irish name. He was fond of Irish names. It was not until after their wedding that he told her she was his fifth wife. In truth, he had already had several families and would have still others, and each of them knew him by a different name. He left Sarah and her mother not long after she was born, and with him, nearly all knowledge of her Indigenous relations was gone. Sarah only knew that her father had been Indigenous at one time in his life but that he had chosen to sever those ties. She could not really be sure of her father's real name or whether he was even dead or alive, much less which Indigenous folks might be her kin.

Sarah grew up on the West Coast with her mother but moved east after marrying an Indigenous man. Much like Sarah's dad, her husband's grandfather had left his reservation as a child and enrolled in an Indian school. His family had also assumed an Irish name at one time, but under different circumstances. When the U.S. government had come insisting that all the Indians had to have a last name, his family had chosen the name of the closest train station, which happened to be Irish. When he arrived at Indian school, however, the white people there would not enroll him because he did not have an "Indian-sounding" surname. So he chose a more stereotypical name to convince the white people that he was an Indian and enrolled in school. It became the new family name. When Sarah married his grandson, she took this name, and her son after her.

Sarah was the daughter of a man who had once been Indigenous, and she had married into an Indigenous family. Yet in spite of these relations, both severed and adopted, she never saw herself as an Indigenous person. She had been raised by white people and she identified as white. Whatever that might mean and whatever connections it had erased, she felt the weight of her privilege in relation to the Indigenous people around her. Her identity was formed somewhere adjacent to but nonetheless outside of them. When she attended homecomings and powwows with her husband's family, she would watch the dances from the sidelines, not wanting to join all the white people there who she felt were too eager to put themselves in the centre of the action. She was not as willing as they were to raise their voices above the elders.

Sarah's marriage was a turbulent one and it did not last long, but she still takes her son to the bear dances. She makes sure he stays connected to his father's family and his Indigenous heritage. For her son's sake, she says, Sarah also kept her married name, even after her in-laws asked her to leave it behind with their son. She may not be Indigenous, but she felt that she had been their kin after all, and keeping the name was important for the sake of her son. In addition, this name felt more real to her than the one her father had made up, in part because it represented the kinships that she had chosen for herself.

While she was facing pressure to give up her married name, Sarah's sister had given her a gift certificate for a commercial genetic ancestry test. Some people thought that if she could prove that she shared DNA with Indigenous peoples, it might strengthen her case with her husband's family to keep their name. She took the test, and it told her that she shared 21 percent of her DNA with Indigenous people in the Americas (Figure 10.8). Knowing that her father was Indigenous, this result did not come entirely as a surprise, but it also did not make her feel any greater sense of belonging with the community. She shared the results with her husband and his family, and it did not change their feelings either. The DNA results showed that she had Indigenous ancestors—but she had never known them, and for her the DNA could not stand in place of a missing history. She was still her mother's daughter. In spite of her various biological and social connections to Indigenous people, she felt that she had still been constituted as white. This is not to say there is no way back for Sarah, but to her, Indigenous belonging was about more than just her father's DNA: it had to include other kinds of networks and histories with Indigenous peoples and places that she felt she may never have. She would do her best to make sure that her son would.

Mitch

Mitch has never not known that he was an Indian. He has always been an Indian. His father was an Indian and all four of his paternal great-grandparents were Indians. But when he saw his genetic ancestry results for the first time and they showed no genetic connection with Indigenous people in the Americas (Figure 10.8), it broke his heart. He wondered how it could be possible that he did not have more Indigenous ancestors than the DNA was showing him. Mitch is the youngest fluent speaker of his Indigenous language. He and his family have long been practitioners of traditional medicine and ceremony. He is a leader in his tribe who has spent much of his life working to return his people to their ancestral homelands. He knows that all of his ancestors have surrounded him and guided his life, but he suddenly found himself deeply troubled by who these ancestors could be. He was worried about his vulnerability to the voices of so many non-Indigenous ancestors, and to what extent he should let those voices in.

Mitch's father was Native, and his mother was white. By all accounts, he says, he could have easily been raised as white, and so many odds had been against his connecting to his Indigenous community. In the Jim Crow South, many of his older relatives came of age at a time when people were heavily discriminated against and there were deep fears of being outwardly Indian in public. His family was not in a position to hide, though, because they "looked the part." Even those relatives who did not "look Indian" were so socially and politically tied to Native communities that they were never considered to be pure white folks. Discrimination against Mitch's family, of course, has even deeper roots, and has existed since the day that settlers arrived on their land. As a child, he visited a ninety-six-year-old relative, and when he spoke to her in their language, she silenced him for fear that white people would be able to find them and force them off the land. The history of Indian removals, and those who had survived them, had long been a part of living memory in his family, and the threats remained all too real.

Mitch came of age as an Indigenous person in a time of Indian revitalization, when people were again pushing back against their own erasure. His father had a great deal of Indian pride, and Mitch had a strong understanding of his identity as an Indigenous person as far back as he could remember. He was always immersed in the tribal culture, the language, the ceremony, the medicine, the land, the stories, the laws, and the people. Some of his relatives were so adamant about preserving the culture that they forbade him to speak English in their homes. He has carried those traditions forward in his own family and has never uttered a word of English to his own children. Through his cultural performance and his connection to his many Indigenous relations, he feels that he becomes more Indigenous each day. Whether or not DNA connects him to the Indigenous peoples of the Americas, these people and these places are the relations through which Mitch constitutes himself as an Indigenous person.

In some ways thinking about DNA has brought Mitch grief, because the stakes of these tests can feel high and the emotional toll they can take is very real, especially when they do not match with a person's prior expectations about the connections between their own biological and cultural heritage. But in other ways, these tests have also made clear to him the places where his Indigeneity lives—in relation to people, place, and practice—not solely in DNA. At the same time, he thinks about the many non-Indigenous people who seek connections with Indigenous communities through genetic ancestry tests. This is not to diminish the problems of self-Indigenization that are actualized through genetic technologies, but Mitch nonetheless wonders about the thresholds past which one cannot become Indian again. Mitch's elders were welcoming people. They taught him to be welcoming. He often wonders, thinking beyond the problematic ways that people use DNA information to possess and manage Indigenous bodies and lands, whether there are also ways in which the ancestors are calling certain people back to them. But Mitch also warns that DNA alone is not enough to do this work. The question for him is ultimately never about what proportions of genes someone shares with his people, but rather, whether someone seeking Indigenous belonging will make themselves vulnerable enough to relearn how to live in the world as one of them. Mitch says you have to be willing to go all the way. You cannot burn sage and "be spiritual," and then leave behind the very people you say you claim. Maybe there are ways to come back to us, he says, but DNA tests and vague gestures to Indigenous culture are not nearly enough. These are simply not the kinds of relations that define someone as a member of his community.

Conclusion

In their own distinct and difficult ways, these brief stories show how people thread inferences of genetic ancestry through other aspects of their individual and group identities, as well as their more-than-human relations with place. Importantly, these perspectives refuse any simple correspondence between DNA and belonging; often, they also refuse hierarchies of knowledge that would privilege either genetic or social relations in the processes of making identity. Perhaps more importantly, these stories compel movement beyond pervasive notions of DNA as the sole arbiter of Indigenous belonging and train greater attention upon the broader spectra of biological, social, historical, and geopolitical entanglements in which our identities and belongings are made. They also urge us to remember the affective registers of DNA via the biological and social histories it is bound up in. DNA analysis holds meaning in people's lives—it can wound and it can heal, even when it does not reshape core conceptions about who they are.

It isn't that DNA is not important. We must be wary of critiques of DNA that deny any significance to material domains in at least partially shaping who we are, and the histories they are bound up within. Neither is it true that DNA is simply imposing material relations over social relations. Material relations are simultaneously social relations. Social relations are simultaneously material relations. They are inextricably tied together. Rather, the problem with DNA-based claims to Indigenous identities and cultural heritage is that it is often imposing settler forms of social relation, with all the associated investments in biological race as the foundation of belonging, over other forms of relating to which DNA is also subject. What both the critical views of genomics and ethnographic stories collectively tell is that DNA alone is a poor stand-in for all the complex material and social relations that inscribe bodies with meaning and connection. Removed from context, DNA cannot illuminate the processes that make someone Indigenous, and the full spectrum of material, social, historical, and political relations that differentially tie us to people and to place.

NOTES

1   Catherine Nash, "Genetic Kinship," *Cultural Studies* 18 (2004): 1–33; Deborah A. Bolnick et al.,
    "The Science and Business of Genetic Ancestry Testing," *Science* 80, no. 318 (2007): 399–400;
    Alondra Nelson, "Genetic Genealogy Testing and the Pursuit of African Ancestry," *Social Studies
    of Science* 38 (2008): 759–83; Sandra Soo-Jin Lee et al., "The Illusive Gold Standard in Ancestry
    Genetic Testing," *Science* 325 (2009): 38–39; Charmaine D. Royal et al., "Inferring Genetic
    Ancestry: Opportunities, Challenges, and Implications," *American Journal of Human Genetics* 86
    (2010): 661–73; Keith Wailoo, Alondra Nelson, and Catherine Lee, *Genetics and the Unsettled
    Past: The Collision of DNA, Race, and History* (New Brunswick, NJ: Rutgers University Press,
    2012); Kim TallBear, *Native American DNA: Tribal Belonging and the False Promise of Genetic
    Science* (Minneapolis: University of Minnesota Press, 2013); Jessica Kolopenuk, "Wiindigo
    Incarnate: Consuming 'Native American DNA,'" *GeneWatch* 27, no. 2 (2014): 18–20; Noah
    Tamarkin, "Genetic Diaspora: Producing Knowledge of Genes and Jews in Rural South Africa,"
    Cultural Anthropology 29 (2014): 552–74; Catherine Nash, *Genetic Geographies: The Trouble
    with Ancestry* (Minneapolis: University of Minnesota Press, 2015); Troy Duster, "A Post-Genomic
    Surprise: The Molecular Reinscription of Race in Science, Law and Medicine," *British Journal of
    Sociology* 66 (2015): 1–27; and Alexa Walker, Brian Egan, and George Nicholas, eds., *DNA and
    Indigeneity: The Changing Role of Genetics in Indigenous Rights, Tribal Belonging, and Repatriation*
    (Symposium proceedings, Simon Fraser University, 2016).

2   Debra Harry, "The Human Genome Diversity Project: Implications for Indigenous Peoples,"
    Abya Yala News 8 (1994): 13–15; Jenny Reardon and Kim TallBear, "'Your DNA Is *Our* History':
    Genomics, Anthropology, and the Construction of Whiteness as Property," *Current Anthropology*
    53 (2012): S233–45; Jessica Kolopenuk, "'Pop-Up' Métis and the Rise of Canada's Post-
    Indigenous Formation," *American Anthropologist* 120 (2018): 333–37; Kolopenuk, "Wiindigo
    Incarnate"; Joanne Barker, "The Human Genome Diversity Project: 'Peoples,' 'Populations' and
    the Cultural Politics of Identification," *Cultural Studies* 18 (2004): 571–606; Kim TallBear,
    "Genomic Articulations of Indigeneity," *Social Studies of Science* 3 (2013b): 509–33; Kim TallBear,
    "Narratives of Race and Indigeneity in the Genographic Project," *Journal of Law, Medicine, and
    Ethics* 35 (2007): 412–24; TallBear, *Native American DNA*; and Nanibaa Garrison, "Genomic
    Justice for Native Americans: Impact of the Havasupai Case on Genetic Research," *Science,
    Technology, and Human Values* 38 (2013): 201–23.

3   Tobler et al., "Ancestral Mitogenomes Reveal 50,000 Years of Regionalism in Australia," *Nature*
    544 (2017): 180–84; Darryl Leroux, "'We've Been Here for 2,000 Years': White Settlers, Native
    American DNA and the Politics of Indigeneity," *Social Studies of Science* 48, no. 1 (2018):
    80–100; Jessica Bardill et al., "Advancing the Ethics of Paleogenomics," *Nature* 360, no. 6387
    (2018): 384–85.

4   Darren O'Toole, "A Legal Look at the Métis of Chibougamau," *The Nation: First Nation
    Cree Newspaper Serving Aboriginal Canada*, 3 March 2017, http://www.nationnews.ca/
    legal-look-metis-chibougamau/.

5   TallBear, *Native American DNA*.

6   Leroux, "'We've Been Here for 2,000 Years'"; Darryl Leroux, *Distorted Descent: White Claims
    to Indigenous Identity* (Winnipeg: University of Manitoba Press, 2019); Kolopenuk, "'Pop-
    Up' Métis.'"

7   Chris Andersen, *"Métis": Race, Recognition, and the Struggle for Indigenous Peoplehood* (Vancouver:
    UBC Press, 2014).

8 Kalorama Information, Report: The Market for Direct-to-Consumer Genetic Health Testing, 2018.

9 Bolnick et al., "The Science and Business of Genetic Ancestry Testing."

10 Shiyu C. Luo et al., "Biparental Inheritance of Mitochondrial DNA in Humans," *PNAS* 115 (2018): 13039–44.

11 John H. Relethford and Deborah A. Bolnick, *Reflections of Our Past: How Human History Is Revealed in Our Genes* (Boulder, CO: Westview Press, 2017).

12 Recombination occurs during the formation of egg and sperm cells where sets of each chromosome exchange some of their genetic material with each other.

13 Relethford and Bolnick, *Reflections of Our Past.*

14 Ibid.

15 Bolnick et al., "The Science and Business of Genetic Ancestry Testing."

16 Erika Tamm et al., "Beringian Standstill and Spread of Native American Founders," *PLoS One* 2, no. 9 (2007): e829; Ugo A. Perego et al., "The Initial Peopling of the Americas: A Growing Number of Founding Mitochondrial Genomes from Beringia," *Genome Research* 20 (2010): 1174–79; Deborah Bolnick et al., "Native American Genomics and Population Histories," *Annual Review of Anthropology* 45 (2016): 319–40.

17 Schroeder et al., "A Private Allele Ubiquitous in the Americas," *Biology Letters* 3 (2007): 218–23.

18 TallBear, *Native American DNA.*

19 Publicly available genetic data used in this chapter were produced using the Affymetrix AxiomTM Genome-Wide Human Origins Array.

20 Deborah A. Bolnick, "Individual Ancestry Inference and the Reification of Race as a Biological Phenomenon," in *Revisiting Race in a Genomic Age*, ed. Barbara A. Koenig, Sandra Soo-Jin Lee, and Sarah S. Richardson (New Brunswick, NJ: Rutgers University Press, 2008), 70–88.

21 Andersen, *"Métis"*; and Kolopenuk, "Wiindigo Incarnate."

22 For the sake of anonymity, names and various aspects of personal histories have been altered.

CHAPTER 11

How We Know Who We Are: Historical Literacy, Kinscapes, and Defining a People[1]

BRENDA MACDOUGALL

Since Canada's Supreme Court handed down the *Powley* decision in 2003, there has been a slow but steady rise, particularly in Eastern Canada, in the numbers of people publicly claiming a Metis identity (see Darryl Leroux, Chapter 9).[2] Between 2006 and 2016, according to Statistics Canada, the number of people self-identifying as Metis on the Canadian census increased 51.2 percent, with the highest increases occurring in Quebec (up 150 percent, to just under 7,000 people) and Nova Scotia (up 125 percent, to approximately 23,000). This is especially remarkable since these two provinces have no history of distinctive Metis communities.[3] Referred to by some as ethnic mobility and to others as racial shifting, this phenomenon has not happened in a vacuum. There are the businesses encouraging people to go beyond family lore and submit their DNA to locate more exotic roots, and myriad online sites and web forums where users assert that they only recently learned that their great-great-great grandmothers were Indian and therefore, proof of a long-forgotten (and hidden) Indigeneity within the family.

The *Daniels* Supreme Court decision in 2016 has accelerated this trend. One has only to visit genealogical forums on a number of websites to gauge the level of interest in knowing whether there is an Indigenous forebear embedded in the family lineage, as the recent case of Catherine Pillard had demonstrated, for instance. Pillard, one of France's *filles du roi,* an unmarried young woman sent from France to marry a male colonist in New France in the mid-seventeenth century, was reinvented in 2008 as the daughter of a Huron chief. One of the thousands of Pillard's modern descendants admitted that although she believed her ancestor was from France, she was in fact disappointed because "it's kind of boring just to be European."[4] A number of scholars have explored the possible motives behind people changing their self-identification, including the kind asserted by Pillard's descendants, but none have addressed the profound lack of historical literacy possessed by non-Indigenous Canadians about Metis peoples and their traditional systems of reckoning how people were included (or excluded) from a polity based on internal categories for identifying family, friends, allies, enemies, neighbours, or strangers.[5] While there is a general knowledge about the basic "facts" of Metis history as it relates to the formation of Canada and processes of colonial expansion, there is much less understanding of how this Indigenous people defined themselves as a society.

This lack of historical literacy about the nature of Metisness played out sensationally in the winter of 2016–17, after Aboriginal People's Television Network's Jorge Barrera published his exposé on novelist Joseph Boyden's often competing and contradictory claims to a number of Indigenous ancestries.[6] The Boyden case reflects a common discourse about how people describe their newly discovered and/or understood histories, and therefore serves as a useful example of how the lack of historical literacy impacts racial shifting. As a novelist, Boyden produced narratives with Indigenous characters within Indigenous settings, and his readership accepted that the authenticity of these stories—the truth of them—was connected inextricably to his personal history as an Indigenous man. While he made a number of statements in interviews and promotional literature over the years about his Indigeneity, I am only concerned with his specific statements about being Metis. Over the years, when explaining his Metisness, he said he was "[a] member of the Woodlands Metis raised in Willowdale, [Ontario]," a "Canadian with Irish, Scottish, and Metis roots," and from a Metis family because they were "mixed blood," with Irish, Scottish, and Ojibwa heritage—"essentially English Metis."[7] In January 2017, in response to Barrera's

article and the subsequent media storm it generated, Boyden stated, "There
has been some confusion as to my Indigenous identity, and I am partly to
blame. . . . I've used the term Metis in the past when referring to myself as a
mixed blood person."[8] Although Boyden became a focal point in a long-overdue discussion in Canada about ethnic/racial shifting, in reality, there was
nothing especially remarkable or even new about the story he fashioned about
himself. Claiming Indigeneity in this manner is a phenomenon studied by
anthropologist Circe Sturm. She concludes that those who become convinced
that they have "Indian blood" often seek to claim their birthright by "rein-
scribing their autobiographies," believing that there exists a "deep personal
and collective meaning in reclaiming their Indianness" to be found.[9]

But this type of almost spiritual awakening of, or connection to,
Indigeneity is only possible if one does not understand how Indigenous
peoples define their polities. Boyden, like many other Canadians, had a vision
of Metisness as characterized by being part something (usually First Nations)
rather than a part *of* something. Attributing this confusion about who he
was to a series of errors and misunderstandings, Boyden stated that "Métis,
when I used it, it was as the Canadian federal government defines it."[10] Yet
the Canadian government has never defined the term Metis historically (or
even now) in law, policy, or practice. But popular discourse conceptualizes
the Metis as a derivative French-Canadian population—mostly francophone
and Roman Catholic—and not a distinct Indigenous nation.[11] Certainly part
of this perception is tied to the term *métis*, a French-language adjective that
simply means "mixed." Accordingly, the word could be applied to anything
that is blended, including economies, political systems, cultural attributes,
and even a nation. Certainly, John Ralston Saul thought so when he confidently declared Canada was "a métis civilization" in order to make the point
that Canada's political ideology and legal orders were informed by those of
First Nations societies and therefore were not reflective of purely European
values.[12] *Métis* in a French-language context, therefore, is not much different
from the English and Indigenous terms like half-breed and *âpihtawikosisân*
(Cree for "half-son"), all speaking to a sense of mixedness although the latter
two are not as widely used. Half Breed is certainly a term emphasizing the
notion of biological difference, while *âpihtawikosisân* frames it within the
context of families. Yet we invest a great deal of energy in establishing the

veracity of the term *Métis* to the exclusion of other terms to *prove* conclusively the authenticity of a people.

The reality today is that "Metis" is the word we are left with, no matter its flaws, to identify an historic people, regardless of its etymology. But the name Metis has evolved in usage to reflect, in Canada, a specific historical and geographical context. "Metis" in Canada is now a proper noun identifying an Indigenous nation with a history rooted in the contact experience of the fur trade that encouraged and fostered the emergence of a population of people—the offspring of traders and First Nations women—dedicated to its labour. More importantly, this society emerged in the late eighteenth and early nineteenth centuries in the western interior of Canada, between Lake Superior up to the Rocky Mountains and in the northwestern United States between Minnesota and Montana, and carved out for itself a new and distinct cultural identity. And as fur companies, driven by profit-motive logic, disinvested from them at various points in time and in different regions, this new people carved out an independent economy so that their families not only survived but flourished. In turn, this society forged a political philosophy with attendant structures of governance rooted in their collective well-being and a sense of independence from other peoples. In short, by the early nineteenth century this people—Metis, Half Breed, or Âpihtawikosisân—developed a sense of loyalty to one another that superseded their loyalties to others.[13]

Within the context of this way of life, Metis fashioned a world view emphasizing familial relationships as a system of reciprocal social obligations and material responsibilities. Metis society revolved around what historian Sami Lakomäki called kinscapes—relational constellations defining a cultural landscape that, in turn, permitted a people to maintain political and economic cohesiveness despite being dispersed across large geographic expanses.[14] Historical Metis kinscapes were represented by a series of interfamilial communities connecting people who shared and acted upon mutually supportive economic and political agendas, not just geographically but also intergenerationally. Appreciating these kinscapes is critical to developing a historical literacy about who the Metis were and still are. To persist in using the term Metis as an adjective equivalent to "mixed" in the context of this people reflects a stubborn refusal to fully accept how their culture evolved based on a coherent set of values not determined by lineage alone.

But the power of genealogy to frame a Metis story runs deep in popular imagination. This sensibility about genealogy is integral to how Boyden's story played out. Further rationalizing the manner in which he presented himself over the years, Boyden pointed to his sincere belief that historical sources were either non-existent or unreliable, and this prevented him from being able to prove integral facts about his family's Indigenous history. This belief led to the following heartfelt assertion: "My family's heritage is rooted in our stories. I've listened to them, both the European and the Indigenous ones, all my life. . . . My mother's family history is certainly not laid out neatly in the official records, or on ancestry.ca either."[15] This statement, more than any other, reflects another common discourse—that the evidence required to definitively prove any one person's Indigeneity is non-existent because of the ambiguous and elusive nature of historical records. Just as genealogies loom large in the popular imagination as the benchmark to prove Metisness, they are increasingly central to historical studies of Metis families and communities within specific geographies. If the public spectacle of Boyden's unmasking shows us anything, it is that claiming Indigeneity is one thing but locating the evidence to support such a claim is quite another. And although many would have us believe that this is an impossible task, they are, quite simply, wrong.

A great deal of primary source material specific to Metis histories has been compiled and made publicly accessible through print or online platforms by various individuals and organizations, including Gail Morin's voluminous genealogical compendiums; Douglas N. Sprague and Ronald P. Frye's work with land records and censuses; Frank Tough's Metis Archival Project, comprising transcribed scrip and census returns; Bruce McIntyre Watson's biographical dictionary of fur traders in British Columbia; Gerhard Ens and Ted Binnema's transcriptions of the Edmonton House post records; Dale Gibson's edited and annotated publication of records associated with the Council of Assiniboia's General Quarterly Court; Mike Evans's transcription of the Hudson's Bay Company records from Fort St. John and area; Lawrence Barkwell's many biographical essays and annotations of people associated with specific Metis historical events such as the 1885 Northwest Resistance; the Gabriel Dumont Institute's Virtual Museum of Métis Culture and History, representing their thirty-plus years of documenting the histories of Metis people and communities in Saskatchewan; Nicole St-Onge's online Voyageur Contracts Database, populated with thousands of transcribed voyageur contracts; and, more recently, the Digital Archives Database (DAD) project, an online archive created by St-Onge, Evans, Chris Andersen, Ramon Lawrence, and me, containing transcribed historical records such as sacramental and census records.[16] Resources such as these represent years of research in church, government, and community archives, museums, and even private collections.

Importantly, these resources represent a corpus of data that is invaluable to anyone undertaking historical scholarship or genealogical research on Metis peoples in a variety of contexts, but at the same time they speak to the availability and range of historical documents accessible to Metis people and families in a variety of regions associated with the historic Metis nation. The breadth of documentation available about the Metis is because their distinctive appearance and way of life along with their political and military campaigns throughout the nineteenth century against fur companies, other Indigenous nations, and the Canadian state captured the attention of many types of people and institutions.[17] The history of this nation is far from shrouded in mystery. While there may yet be records to be identified, to argue that they do not exist is not only misleading, it is incorrect. But locating records is only step one. Synthesizing, analyzing, and contextualizing them within a broader body of records that describe events and processes is also required. Genealogies must be triangulated against additional ethnographic sources such as oral traditions (including family histories), trade journals and correspondence, missionary accounts, newspaper and magazine articles, personal diaries and wills, and travel logs. These types of textual sources contain details that demonstrate the range of material and social relationships between Metis people, families, and communities across time and space.

Understanding the place of individuals within their families and communities is, to varying degrees, a critical methodological approach within Metis historical research, necessarily an evidence-based approach. Scholars such as Jennifer Brown, Gerhard Ens, Nicole St-Onge, Nicholas Vrooman, Heather Devine, Melinda Marie Jetté, Tanis Thorne, Diane Payment, Émilie Pigeon, Martha Harroun Foster, and me, among others, have all utilized some variation of genealogical method in order to understand the experiences of different communities across central and western North America.[18] Conducting this type of research necessitates the collection of records often spread out over multiple archival repositories across different national jurisdictions, and organizing them in a way that makes them easily searchable. In this digital age, many scholars have turned to transcribing and databasing their research, all of which requires a great deal of time and effort, along with an often self-taught knowledge about how to read, translate, and interpret historical records.

While a robust scholarship engaged with genealogical records and methods exists, a cautionary note is required. Genealogies, while informative, are inherently problematic because, by their very nature, they are about tracing a person's (or family's) biological pedigree—their recorded ancestry—to determine their lineage—direct line of descent—by demonstrating how one generation connects to the next, backwards through time. By their very definition, genealogies are theoretically endless, because they are intended to trace lineages as far back in time as possible through the recorded history. Because they can go on endlessly, creators and readers of genealogies often have a difficult time understanding that not everyone within that lineage shares the same cultural, ethnic, racial, class, or social position. Genealogies, in short, decontextualize people from the era and social construct in which they existed. Furthermore, how we understand who people are within genealogies requires careful analysis and reading of the documents. For instance, there is a perception that the term Metis is historically synonymous with *voyageur, coureur de bois*, and/or French Canadian and even mixed-blood, yet to assume an individual identified as a voyageur is also Metis is a potentially gross misreading of the records. Often, too, people tracing genealogies assume transhistorical consistency in identity markers, which is to say they believe that culture, "race," and nationality are all concepts bequeathed in an unbroken line from their ancestor to them. Genealogical reconstruction alone does not, and cannot, take into account the lived realities of those in the past (or the present) as central to their personal identity (see Chapters 9 and 10 for a detailed explanation of genealogical reconstruction through DNA). As Sturm has astutely observed, whether or not people can properly document their Indigenous forebears, the question that needs to be asked is, "How does the fact of genealogy get translated into an identity claim, and why would this sort of kinship claim be privileged as the key to [being Indigenous] over ... other self-ascription, social relationship, or even citizenship?"[19] The answer is rooted in a lack of historical literacy about the nature of what historical records can do, but also about how to read and make use of historical sources.

Only by mobilizing all types of historical sources about the Metis is it possible, in the words of historian Natalie Zemon Davis, to begin to understand a people's "hopes and feelings . . . the ways in which they experienced the constraints and possibilities in their lives."[20] To explore the relationship between genealogies and identities, then, requires us to dig deeper to locate the simple clues embedded in historical documents. These "inadvertent little gestures" reveal the nature of relationships between individuals and communities as we strive to gain insight from what microhistorian Carlo Ginzberg referred to as the "apparently insignificant experiential data" that often reveals "a complex reality that could not be experienced directly."[21] By mobilizing a variety of sources rather than relying on one type, we can begin to determine how specific families formed alliances with one another, explore whether such alliances were short term or traceable intergenerationally, and then ascertain how newcomers to a region were acculturated into trading societies, how people were granted or denied entrance into a community, and pursue a host of otherwise intangible aspects of a people's lives embedded in the values and beliefs that defined them.[22] At the same time that we explore the ways people may have felt based on how they behaved—the actions they took or the decisions they made—we can also consider investigating the common background characteristics of a group or people by engaging in a collective study of their lives through the methods of prosopography.[23] Unlike biography, prosopography is not about understanding the life of an individual but is instead centred on understanding how groups operate within networks of relationships. According to Lawrence Stone, this method requires us to first establish the universe to be studied by asking a uniform set of questions about "birth and death, marriage and family, social origins and inherited economic position, place of residence, education, amount and source of personal wealth, occupation, religion, experience of office, and so on," so that we can make sense of political action and help explain ideological, cultural, or other kinds of change over time. Prosopography requires the blending of large-scale biographic profiles of people within a collectivity so that the networks of political, economic, or social engagement can be analyzed. Accordingly, data within individual biographies are collected and exploited to understand the context in which linkages between people are best understood.[24]

If we establish a general historical literacy about the Metis through the methodologies of both microhistory and prosopography, we begin to understand that the nature and core of Metis history does not hinge on any single person or their genealogy. Instead, it rests with the collectivity how the Metis reckoned their social and material relations. More simply, who is identified in the historical record as Metis is determined not by genealogy alone, but by historical contextual social values that dictated a person's actions, decisions, and life choices. To explore this further, it is useful to consider the relationship between genealogies and way of living by using two prominent Metis historical figures about whom there is an agreed-upon foundation of historical knowledge: Louis Riel and Gabriel Dumont, the two most signif-icant Metis political and military figures of the latter half of the nineteenth century. Both of these men, in the Western tradition of biography, embody the values and spirit of *la nouvelle nation* in the late nineteenth century, but if we instead place them within the matrix of their kinscape, we can explore their actions and behaviours not according to individual, exceptional char-acter traits but within a collectivity.

The focus on Louis Riel as an individual continues to be shaped by eval-uations of his lineage, and therefore he represents one of the best, yet most frustrating, examples of Canadian historical illiteracy. Riel is still often char-acterized as more French than Indian, which is a complete misreading of what it is to be Metis. In particular, Riel is frequently described as one-eighth Indian because of his genealogy (Figure 11.1), a lineage that clearly indi-cates that both his maternal grandparents and his paternal grandfather were French Canadians born in Lower Canada. Furthermore, Riel had only one "part-Indian" ancestor—his paternal grandmother, Marguerite Boucher, was the daughter of a Dene woman from what is now north-western Saskatchewan and a French Canadian trader from Lower Canada. Marguerite, like her Dene mother, also married a French Canadian trader, and the first two of their children, including Riel's father, Jean-Louis, were born at Île à la Crosse. This French Canadian–heavy lineage led one scholar to write of Riel that "both his parents were westerners, and he [was] said to have had one-eighth Indian blood, his paternal grandmother being a Franco-Chipewyan Métisse."[25] Another biographer asserted that Riel "was a Métis because his French-Canadian grandfather had married a woman of French and Chipewyan parentage."[26] The subtext of all of this is that because Riel was *only* one-eighth Indian, then he must actually be seven-eighths French Canadian. Such scrutiny of his blood quantum delegitimizes Riel's identity as a Metis man by reducing him to a product of his lineage, an individual of mixed blood without a place in a broader Metis collectivity. Casting him in this light, however, fails to account for the array of Riel's lived experiences, including growing up at Red River (one of several regions west of Lake Superior identified as a Metis space, but notably the only one that was home to 10,000 Metis people at the time of Confederation), his role as the leader of two political and military resistances that defined Metis political realities at the end of the nineteenth century, his marriage into a well-known Metis buffalo-hunting family associated with the Montana territory, or his execution by the Canadian state for his efforts on behalf of Metis and First Nations in the North-West Territories. Instead, because he is treated historically as "mostly" French Canadian, Riel's actions, choices, decisions are attributed to his education and lived experience in Montreal between the ages of fourteen and twenty-four, rather than to his life in Red River or on the southern plains among an array of relatives and deep within a broader Metis collectivity. By considering the array of his life choices and actions, his historical narrative is reoriented.

Consider instead that Riel was a son of the Red River Valley, a community at the forks of the Red and Assiniboine Rivers, a place long understood to be central to Metis history. Here a community defined by many large extended families imbued with a worldview valuing alliances based on relatedness was formed. It was this web of social and material relations that defined Riel as Metis, not his blood quantum, genealogical lineage, or recorded ancestry. To further explore this perspective, we need to consider Riel's lateral connections to the broader Metis polity existing not just in Red River but spread out from the western edge of Lake Superior and across the southern Great Plains, reaching as far south as Montana (see Figure 11.2). For example, when we look at Riel's siblings and the families to whom they were connected, we see a pattern common across Metis communities. By establishing the genealogical biographies of individuals within a kinscape, it becomes apparent that it was relatively common within Metis kinscapes for two or three siblings from one family to marry two or three siblings from another family. In this instance, two of Riel's brothers, Alexandre and Joseph, and a sister, Henriette, married the children of Francois Poitras and Madeleine Fisher—Elise, Eleanore, and Jean Marie Poitras, respectively.[27] The connections between the Riel and Poitras families, however, were more complex when explored intergenerationally

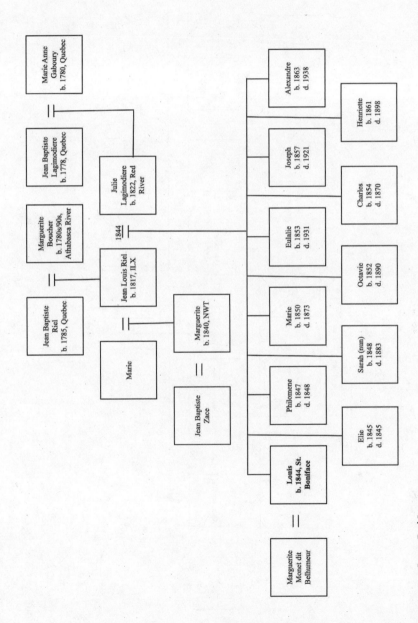

FIGURE 11.1. Louis Riel Lineage.

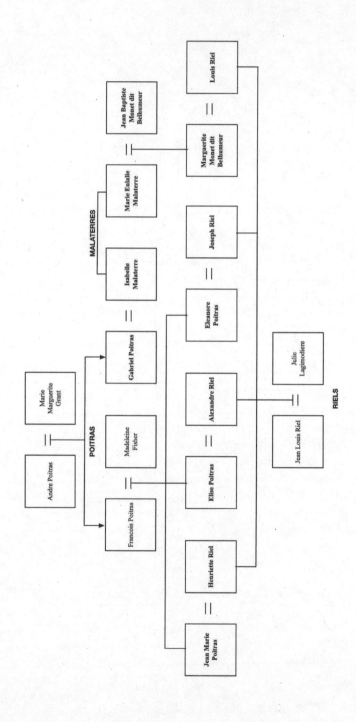

FIGURE 11.2. Riel's Extended Family.

over time, not just laterally within a single generation. An uncle of the three Poitras siblings, Gabriel Poitras, married Isabelle Malaterre, sister of Marie Eulalie, a woman who became Louis Riel's mother-in-law in the early 1880s. The Poitras and Riel families were directly connected across Riel's immediate generation, but the Poitras connection to the Monet dit Belhumeur family, which by the late nineteenth century was a part of the buffalo-hunting brigades of the Montana territories, was also important. Through intergenerational connections between the Riels and Poitras, we can consider how such family ties helped Riel integrate into the Montana territory after 1880 and become a part of the kinscapes of buffalo-hunting families such as those of the Malaterre and Monet dit Belhumeur families. The subsequent marriage of Louis Riel to Marguerite Monet dit Belhumeur appears less out of character when we begin to imagine Metis communities as a complex network of interfamilial spaces—kinscapes—across time and space.

The types of marital arrangements and intergenerational ties as represented by the Riel-Poitras-Malaterre-Monet dit Belhumeur families wove a web of relatedness around people and between communities, tightly binding Metis families to one another despite often incredible distances between communities, the passage of time, or a host of religious and/or cultural differences.[28] But the connections between families such as these are not simply about genealogies or a shared lineage. Rather, the types of family connections represent expressions of what Kim TallBear refers to as the social and material relations that societies develop to define themselves not by lineages, blood ties, or even DNA sequences, but by the manner in which people establish, maintain, and sustain their lives economically, politically, socially, and culturally according to shared values, principles, beliefs, and expectations.[29] Knowing how the Metis defined their social and material relations permits a broader exploration into how they collectively made and acted on decisions, and permits us to evaluate Riel's individual biography as a part of a social network rather than a reflection of individual exceptionalism.

Conceiving of Metis society as ordered by a series of large extended family units or kinscapes that are focused on shared economic activities (e.g., commercial hunting, freighting, agriculture, or mercantilism) and spread across the prairie region, yet connected by shared threads of relatives, is necessary if we seek to make sense of Metis political and military actions throughout the nineteenth century. When circumstances demanded

it, kinscapes such as those constructed by the Riel and Poitras families were
the mechanism by which people could unite to pursue political goals central
to their shared well-being as a people. It is only by combining genealogical reconstructions with other documentary evidence, so that we can build
appropriate profiles of the community's families as informed by Metis intel-
lectualizations of self and family, that it is possible to begin addressing how
this society mobilized collectively in a manner that has come to define their
sense of nationalism as different from Canada's historical narrative. In this
way, Riel's blood quantum is less important than descriptions by historians
and biographers would suggest. By analyzing instead the social and material relations of his family and, in turn, his own life choices, it is clear that
his Metisness existed despite his limited "Indianness" or his overly abundant
"French Canadianness."

To explore this further, we can turn to other aspects of Riel's family history.
Jean-Louis Riel, although born in Île à la Crosse, was raised in Berthier-en-
Haut, Lower Canada (now Berthierville, Quebec). By 1838, he had begun
to break away from French Canada, forging a new path independent of the
socio-cultural realities in which he was raised. In that year, Riel Sr. became a
Hudson's Bay Company (HBC) servant and was stationed at Rainy River (in
present-day Ontario) for the duration of his contract.[30] After leaving HBC's
employ, and after a brief period in Lower Canada, Riel Sr. settled at Red River
in 1843, where he obtained a river lot at St-Boniface. It was here in 1844 that
he met and married Julie Lagimodiere, a French Canadian woman born in
Western Canada.[31] Within their first year of marriage the first of their eleven
children, Louis, was born. Riel Sr. was a farmer and the owner-operator of a
grist-mill at Red River, but he also became a well-respected political activist.[32]
After his arrival in Red River, he became an ardent defender of the right of
buffalo hunters to free trade. By then, these hunters were actively challenging
the HBC's trade monopoly by transporting and selling the products of their
labour to the American Fur Company or to independent American traders.
Although not a hunter himself, Riel Sr. served as an advisor and defender of
their right to pursue an independent economy. The history of the free trade
movement and its conflict with the HBC culminated in the 1849 Sayer Trial,
when Pierre-Guillaume Sayer, a member of the well-known buffalo-hunting community at St-François-Xavier, was arrested and tried by the General

Quarterly Court of Assiniboia for trading with Americans in violation of the HBC's Royal Charter.[33]

By the 1840s, the Metis buffalo-hunting economy was a central defining feature of prairie Metis life, having emerged out of the North West Company's late eighteenth- to early nineteenth-century pemmican trade. Sayer was a member of one of many hunting families who moved between various wintering sites on the Prairies, as well as Red River and St. Paul, Minnesota, to procure and then sell hides, meat, and robes. Families like Sayer's experienced persistent harassment because of HBC efforts to control their livelihood, and so faced a precarious economic situation if the HBC succeeded in curtailing their trade and preventing them from negotiating the best prices for their products. Consequently, all buffalo hunters engaged in free trading were politically invested in the outcome of Sayer's trial. Urged on by Riel Sr., they gathered around the courthouse in anticipation of the verdict and to bear witness to events. Caught in the act of free trading, Sayer pled guilty, but the jury recommended mercy and he was freed without punishment. As this verdict was rendered, Riel Sr. announced to the waiting hunters that both Sayer and the trade were free. Word of the verdict and outcome spread rapidly among the assembled hunters, who believed the court had affirmed their rights as free people, a sensibility that was broadcast rapidly throughout the communities spread across the Prairies.[34] Through his work and political activism, Riel Sr. became well-known in the Red River community, but it was through his children and grandchildren that he became a part of a kinscape. To be clear, this is not a statement affirming Riel Sr. as Metis; although he supported Metis rights to a free economy, he also supported the protection of French language rights at Red River, a cause synonymous with francophone activism. Nevertheless, by living in Red River and engaging politically, Riel Sr. contributed to Metis society by supporting their world view (perhaps not wholly incompatible with his own), which valued and believed in its collective autonomy expressed through independent economic activity and spirited politics. This philosophy of being had a lasting impact on his children's experiences as they became integrated into Metis kinscapes through marriage, socio-cultural outlook, and livelihood.

Biographies of Louis Riel often focus heavily on his father's influence, political activism, and leadership, with some attention given to his mother's religiosity. Julie Lagimodiere, devoutly Catholic, is believed to have influenced

her eldest son's commitment to her faith, eventual adherence to a conservative ultramontane doctrine, and messianic impulses toward the end of his
life.[35] Because of Riel's religious and intellectual aptitude, the Catholic clergy
at Red River selected him (one of four boys) to attend school in Montreal
with the intent that he would eventually take priestly vows. Although he did
not become a priest, Riel was physically separated from his home and family
for a decade. Certainly, this absence likely influences the popular perception that he was more French than Metis. This type of biographical focus
on determining the source of Riel's exceptionalism is based on a fundamentally Western liberal preoccupation with the individual, where the individual
either rises above or succumbs to the group. However unconsciously, it affirms
Riel as a product of the European (i.e., French) tradition. But emphasis must
also be placed on the role that interfamilial and intercommunity relationships, as fostered by his siblings and other members of his extended family
who remained behind in Red River, had on Riel's outlook. It was the lived
experiences of these relatives that ensured Riel was easily reintegrated into a
kinscape upon his return to Red River as a young man of twenty-four. His
youngest siblings connected the Riel family intimately to the Poitras and
their extended kin, like the Malaterres, but attention must also be given to his
sister Sara Riel, who joined the Order of the Sisters of Charity (Grey Nuns)
in 1865. As a nun, Sara could not be expected to extend her family's kinscape
through marriage and children, but that did not preclude her from building
relationships that came to define her brother's story.

As a novice, Sara was sent by the order in 1871 to Île à la Crosse, her
father's birthplace, to serve in the school and hospital. Sister Sara spent little
more than a decade in Île à la Crosse before tuberculosis claimed her life, but
between her arrival and death in December 1883, she made a lasting impression on the local Metis community. Sara was selected to serve as godmother
to four babies born in the region, an unusual role for Catholic clergy in that
era (let alone now).[36] Perhaps she was asked because the people of Île à la
Crosse recognized that she had a connection to them through her father
and grandmother, and chose to extend their kinscape with her as a family
member. And perhaps it was her inclusion in the northwestern Saskatchewan
Metis kinscape that contributed to the panic felt by the Oblates during the
1885 Northwest Resistance. The close relationship that Sara had with her
elder brother Louis was well understood by the clergy, and in 1885, a year

after her death, the priests at Île à la Crosse came to believe that Riel thought they had permitted his sister to die in misery and planned to exact revenge on the missions in the north.[37] And so the Île à la Crosse mission evacuated its personnel and dependents, all of whom fled north to a small island near Patuanak where they spent the month of May in hiding, returning only after receiving word that the Metis had been defeated at Batoche and Riel was in custody. Regardless of whether the clergy's fears were valid, they believed that the closeness between Riel and his sister was powerful enough to mobilize people against them to destroy the mission.

Within this broader familial context, it is evident that Riel existed within a Metis kinscape. From this point, then, it is possible to analyze how his actions, decisions, and behaviours propelled him into a position of national leadership within the Metis collective at Red River by the age of twenty-four. During his lifetime, Riel led the 1869–70 resistance at Red River, developed a well-articulated political philosophy and system of governance, negoti- ated the creation of the Province of Manitoba and its subsequent admission to Canadian Confederation in 1870, was elected three times to Canadian Parliament, was exiled from 1875 to 1880, taught school at St. Peter's Mission in Montana, where he married and began a family, fought for Metis rights again along the South Saskatchewan River in 1885, and was tried for high treason and died on the gallows at Regina 16 November 1885. Leaders of the Canadian state were deeply concerned about the power he had amassed as leader of this militarily and economically strong Indigenous people and needed to crush their political aspirations. None of the basic facts of his life are in question, but how to understand his choices, actions, and decisions requires an interpretive framework. Yet even within sympathetic historical discourse, Riel is decontextualized from the cultural context of his commu- nity, as many of his relatives are stripped away from his story.[38] As a result, Riel appears as an individual of considerable charisma and leadership ability but not part of a collectivity with a world view that privileged familial rela- tionships as the basis for all action and reactions to external forces.

If we instead consider him as an extension of his family—his father, mother, siblings, in-laws, spouse, and cousins—we alter the lens by which we are able to see and understand Riel. Between 1875 and 1880, while exiled, Riel travelled throughout the northern United States before coming to live in the Judith Basin of Montana near St. Peter's Mission, a place already known to and frequented by Metis buffalo-hunting families such as the Bergers, Wilkies, Dumonts, and Monet dit Belhumeurs. The latter were connected to the Poitras family through Gabriel Poitras, the uncle of the three siblings who married into the Riel family about the same time that Riel was exiled (see Figure 11.2). It was in this place and among his own family's growing kinscape that Riel, no longer exiled but nevertheless alienated from his home-land due to years of state persecution, met and married Marguerite Monet dit Belhumeur, the daughter of Jean Baptiste Monet dit Belhumeur and Marie Eulalie Malaterre.[39] In marrying Marguerite, Riel became a part of a world with a very different geographic, political, and economic orientation than that of Red River. And yet even as he lived among buffalo-hunting families in Montana, he was enveloped within a familiar social and material world full of relatives. Through Marguerite, Louis was connected to other buffa-lo-hunting families of the northern Great Plains and, significantly, to the world of Gabriel Dumont, a figure to whom his name is intimately linked.

While Riel was most certainly a man of the Red River Valley, it is equally apparent that Gabriel Dumont was a part of the western and northern plains, born into and living among Metis buffalo-hunting communities. But as with Riel, if we look at Dumont's actual genealogy in isolation from a broader familial and societal context, we have to ask what about his lineage demon-strates his identity as a Metis man and not just someone of mixed ancestry. Dumont had a French-Canadian grandfather and two Indian grandmothers, and so had a higher percentage of "Indian blood" than Riel, but just as being "part French Canadian" did not make Riel Metis, being "part Indian" did not make Dumont Metis. Both these popular perceptions of Metisness hinge on a belief that people like Riel and Dumont were "part" something, rather than allowing that they were completely Metis. To get past this belief, we have to consider why we believe mixed marriages between non-Indigenous men and First Nations women necessarily define a Metis experience. If we accept that they do not, then we can ask very different questions.

To approach the issue of what defines a Metis experience, and get at the essence of, in this case, Dumont's life, we need to explore the lives of his parents and broader extended kinscape as we did with Riel. Gabriel was the son of Isadore dit Ecapow Dumont and Louise Laframboise, themselves chil-dren of families from the Fort des Prairies (Edmonton) region. Isadore's father, Jean Baptiste Dumont, was a voyageur contracted to this region in the late

1790s, and it was here, around 1794, that he met and married Josette Sarcee according to the custom of the country (see Figure 11.3).[40] The focus on Metis buffalo hunters typically centres on the role of men as hunters and traders because of the exhilarating aspects of their lives on the Prairies, running down buffalo herds, and the masculinity of this occupation. Yet we know that this economic tradition required the labour of women and children to produce pemmican, tan hides, and prepare buffalo robes for market. But because male buffalo hunters interacted with trade companies to sell their wares, the historical record is replete with narratives of their activities, what they looked like, and how they lived these wholly masculine lives. When we use genealogical reconstructions to determine who comprised those buffalo-hunting communities, the centrality of women—especially groups of related women—within hunting brigades becomes especially evident.

Women are certainly harder to track through historical records for a variety of reasons, but generally it was because it was literate men, at least in the late eighteenth and early nineteenth centuries, who were in contact with Indigenous communities, and they tended not to notice the labour (or other activities) of women except as decoration at social gatherings and as sexual partners. Thus, the narratives of women's lives went largely unrecorded.[41] As a result, while we know something about Dumont's male relatives, we know much less about his two grandmothers, Josette Sarcee and Josephte Assiniboine. Of the two, more is known about Josette. According to existing albeit fragmentary records, Josette was first married to trader Jean Baptiste Bruneau in the Fort des Prairies region. However, when his contract ended, so too did their relationship, and Josette took her next husband, Jean Baptiste Dumont, around 1794. Josette had already had a son with Bruneau, and her first child with Dumont, Gabriel (not to be confused with the famed namesake), was born in 1795 in what is now the Edmonton region. By 1801, Jean Baptiste had returned to Quebec and so Josette began living with trader Paul Durant, with whom she had another son. According to legend, Dumont returned to Fort Edmonton in 1803–4 and fought Durant to get Josette back, which he did. Dumont and Josette raised their large family, including her two sons with Bruneau and Durant, on the Prairies among the other buffalo-hunting family-based communities.

Nevertheless, we know little about Josette beyond this story. Some speculate that she was Tsuu T'ina because of her surname, while others argue

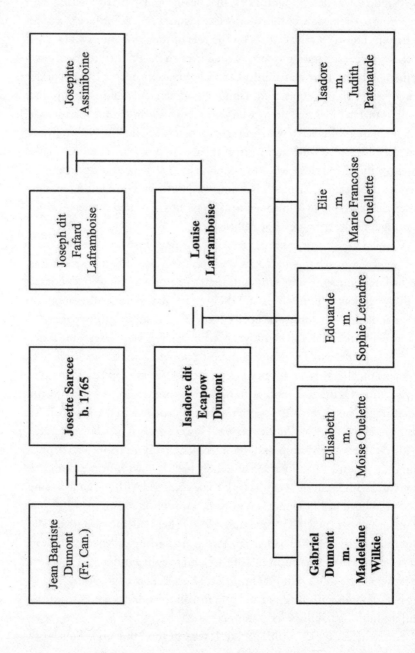

FIGURE 11.3. Gabriel Dumont's Immediate Family.

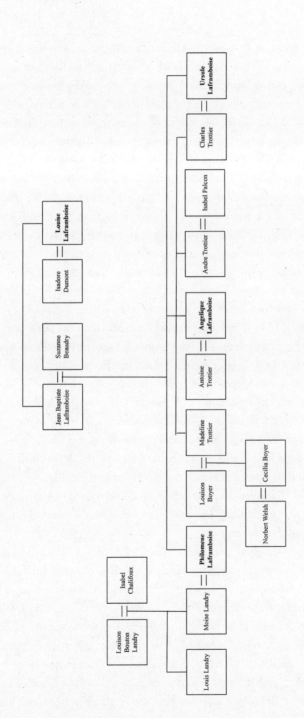

FIGURE 11.4. Trottier-Laframboise Family Connections.

she was Cree and simply spoke an Athabascan language (among others) and so acquired the nickname Sarcee.[42] Both are interesting ideas, but neither is conclusive. We can only speculate how she may have felt about these three men and the subsequent physical contest for her hand in marriage. It could be argued that she was being bought and sold by men who only understood an inherently violent, patriarchal, Eurocentric world. But we could also speculate, in the tradition of Zemon Davis, about the options and opportunities available to women in this era, in this economic environment, and in their homeland where they were surrounded by friends and family. We could also speculate about the range of power held by Indigenous women because of their ancestral connections to space, place, and people, while their non-Indigenous husbands were less powerful because they were separated from their homelands and living in unfamiliar situations.[43] All these interpretive frameworks are valid and useful to consider. They all acknowledge, notably, that Indigenous people had agency and permit us to evaluate the impact of Josette's life on the birth of Metis buffalo-hunting brigades along the north and south branches of the Saskatchewan River from a perspective where Indigenous women were not victims of European patriarchy. Because of her six children with Dumont—three sons and three daughters—along with two additional sons with her first and third husbands, Josette (and women like her) fostered a world where her Metis offspring were connected and integrated intergenerationally into a broad constituency of trading families across multiple locations throughout their homeland. What made Josette's children Metis was not the fact of their biology but rather the efforts of families like the Dumonts (and the Riels) to ensure that their children and children of similar families grew up together and married as adults, carrying on this way of life within the economy of the fur trade.

Similarly, looking at the life of Gabriel Dumont's mother, Louise Laframboise, is critical to understanding the kinscapes of buffalo-hunting communities. Louise, along with her husband, Isadore, left the Fort des Prairies region for the southern prairies by the 1860s. There they joined the Trottier Brigade, a band of Metis buffalo hunters who operated between Round Prairie (south of Saskatoon, Saskatchewan), Batoche, and Havre, Helena, and the Judith Basin in Montana in the latter half of the nineteenth century.[44] The leader of this community of hunters, Charles Trottier, worked closely with his brothers, Antoine and Andre, as well as with brothers

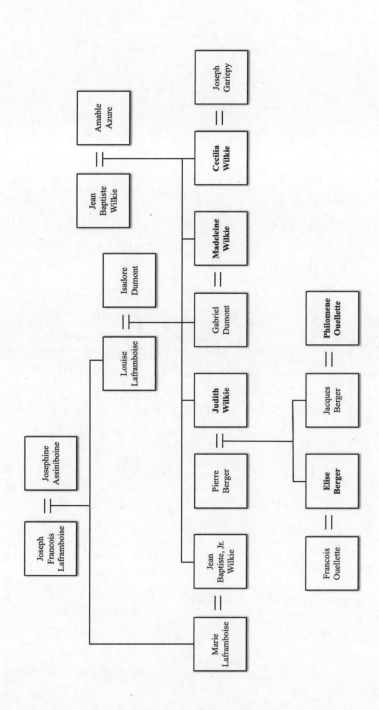

FIGURE 11.5. Intra-Brigade Connections for Dumont.

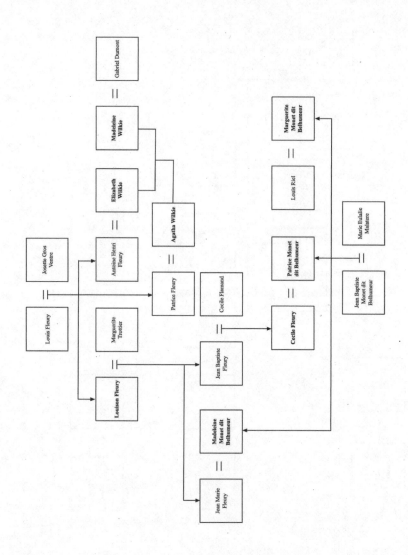

FIGURE 11.6. Riel-Dumont Familial Connections.

Moise and Louis Landry, and father and son Isadore and Gabriel Dumont. Charles, like Isadore and other men in this hunting brigade, was married to a Laframboise woman. Charles and Antoine Trottier and Moise Landry were married to sisters Ursule, Angelique, and Philomene Laframboise, respectively; these three women were all daughters of Jean Baptiste Laframboise and Susanne Beaudry, and nieces of Louise Laframboise (see Figure 11.4).[45] Being able to construct detailed biographies of women like Josette and Louise is not possible, but we can reconstruct the world that they helped to create by looking more closely at the society that emerged because of them.

Within the context of this family coalescing at Fort des Prairies and then spreading east and south through the Prairies, the narrative of Dumont's life is fairly indicative of a Plains Metis experience. He was born into a buffalo-hunting tradition and so, as he matured, he assumed more and more responsibility as a hunter within this society. There is no evidence that he was ever in Red River proper, although for a brief time Isadore and Louise had a river lot at St-François-Xavier. Dumont did interact a great deal with the Wilkie Brigade, which congregated at Pembina, a village and trade post to the south of the Forks. Brigade leader Jean Baptiste Wilkie was, by the 1840s, one of the best-known chiefs of the buffalo hunt and, like Dumont and other people from the Trottier Brigade, was at the Battle of Grand Coteau as well as a number of other significant battles waged over space and economy. As a community leader and hunter, Wilkie possessed skills in plains diplomacy and was eventually one of the leaders responsible for negotiating the lasting peace with the Dakota in the 1860s. Similarly, Dumont was recognized for his skills as a hunter and plains warrior, along with his role as a diplomat and politician, all based on the education he received from men like his father, his uncles, Wilkie, and other relatives. This plains Metis education led to his eventual selection as a hunt chief by the Metis community when he was a young man.[46] Later in his life, with a river lot near the village of Batoche on the South Saskatchewan River, Dumont was elected as president of the St. Laurent community council by the local Metis and began working in this capacity to ensure his people's interests were not overlooked in Confederation.[47] Like Riel, he had a vision for the future inspired by the society in which he lived, worked, and loved.

Equally important to the narrative of Dumont's family and public life was his 1858 marriage to Madeleine Wilkie, the daughter of hunt chief Jean

Baptiste Wilkie (see Figure 11.5). When Madeleine's family is taken into account as a part of the Dumont kinscape, we begin to understand the scope of geography that these interconnected families—Dumont-Laframboise-Trottier-Wilkie—encompassed across the Prairies. Through his wife's sisters, Dumont was connected to an additional series of brigades. Madeleine's sisters Judith and Cecilia both married buffalo hunters, Pierre Berger and Joseph Gariepy, who like Dumont became chiefs of the hunt and leaders of their own hunting brigades along the forty-ninth parallel.[48] Dumont's kinscape linked him to regions now a part of Alberta, Saskatchewan, Manitoba, and North Dakota, and to a host of families who shaped the culture of Metis buffalo-hunting society. Dumont emerged as a leader not because of his biology, genealogy, or lineage, but because of the interfamilial connections that trained him to be a hunter and that supported and nurtured his abilities to lead. The world the Metis created on the Prairies was not made up of random collections of mixed-blood hunters but was rather a place populated with friends, family, and, at times, enemies.

If we probe deeper into these familial constructs of the Prairie-based families, we can see that Dumont and Riel shared relatives largely because by 1880, they were sharing space via a common connection to the Montana territory and because of an extended family connection shared by their wives to the Fleury family. Marguerite Monet Belhumeur's brother and sister, Patrice and Madeleine, were married to siblings Cecile and Jean Marie Fleury, the children of Louison Fleury and Marguerite Trottier (the elder sister of Charles Trottier). In turn, Louison's brothers, Patrice and Antoine Henri Fleury, were married to Agathe and Elizabeth Wilkie, two more of Madeleine's sisters (see Figure 11.6). Again, as we witness these types of relationships appear over and over, it becomes difficult to regard them as coincidental rather than deliberate efforts to build alliances and keep families loyal to one another. Did Riel and Dumont meet before 1884? Given the likelihood that these families all converged in the Montana region to hunt, address their political aspirations, and make and renew the types of familial connections necessary to keep the threads of their society tightly woven together, it is possible that they met in the early 1880s. But whether or not they did is a minor point. By exploring the context of their lives on the plains, it seems clear that when Dumont travelled to Montana with the other emissaries from Batoche to ask Riel to come north and lead them as they fought to ensure that their rights as original peoples were respected by the ever-expanding Canadian state, he was able to appeal to a relative. Riel and Dumont were not close kinsmen, but they shared relational connections to many of the same buffalo-hunting families within a society that formed a cohesive kinscape that existed across the Prairies and was not centred in any one region. Furthermore, they shared a political sensibility and vision for community governance. Who people were is only important inasmuch as we know the broad range of their connections at the same time that we explore and analyze their social and material relations. How a people behaved is the best indication of how they felt, what they thought, and how they understood their responsibility to others.

These types of interfamilial connections are complex and challenging to unravel and track down. They are not clearly laid out in ancestry.com or neatly catalogued in easy-to-locate records. But the documentary evidence does exist, and working to understand it within the appropriate and relevant context is vital in order to have a full rendering of what it meant and means to be Metis. This type of analysis permits us to move beyond the notion that Metis history only exists as a vague family memory of a long-dead, temporally distant Indigenous ancestor and instead see how people were enmeshed within a system of relatives with shared values. This is not simply a matter of scholarly concern. Metis people themselves often struggle to articulate to those beyond their families and communities how their society defined and defines itself. As a result, it is not unusual to hear them declare—much like Joseph Boyden—"we know who we are," although they do so as an attempt to counteract some of the stereotypical perceptions outsiders carry about who the Metis are, particularly the emphasis on their "mixedness." As noted by Indigenous studies scholar Chris Andersen, all Indigenous people are to some degree mixed as a result of contact with European societies, and so relying on mixedness as a critical element for defining who the Metis are is unhelpful and misleading (see Chapter 8). The presumptive conclusion is that the Metis, defined by their "mixedness," are somehow less authentically Indigenous than the Cree, Mohawk, Dene, or other First Nations.[49] It is crucial, therefore, to take the definitive statement that "we know who we are," an often highly personal expression of being and belonging supported by a backstory of family and community norms but lacking substantive content, and transform it into a fuller articulation of how Metis society functioned through the ongoing effort to create and maintain families. The notion that "we know who we are" because of our stories cannot, and should not, exist independently of historical data, speaking to what being Metis means via the values forged by this people. This matters in a world where Metis are recognized as section 35 rights holders and who since 1982 have lived under constant pressure from all levels of government to establish, codify, and formalize an independently verifiable citizenship system based on a clearly articulated definition of Metis. The *Daniels* decision was not an exception to this rule.

The aspirations of the contemporary Metis nation are tied closely to the social and material relations of the historic Metis kinscape. The Metis goal of self-governance managed by community values, goals, and aspirations did not die in 1885 with the defeat at Batoche, the execution of Riel, or exile of Dumont. After 1885, Metis political organizations began reformulating. In 1887, l'Union Nationale Metis Saint-Joseph du Manitoba was started in St. Vital (now a neighbourhood in Winnipeg) by Joseph Riel and others, and around the same time, the people of St. Paul des Metis in northern Alberta organized to protect their land rights. Both these organizations carried on the traditions of older Metis governance structures by defending Metis rights. Created by local communities, these types of political bodies were eventually found in communities across the Prairies, and by the 1930s to '40s had begun uniting to establish provincial bodies, called Societies, that promoted socio-cultural activities, developed service-delivery programs, and advocated for the protection of their rights within each province.[50] The Metis nation continues to exist not because of the genealogical lineages of individuals or even communities, but because as a collectivity people continue to maintain their social and material connections to one another, politically and culturally. The ability of people to recognize one another cannot rest on lineages to long-dead ancestors but instead must be dependent on the lived relationships that continue to be forged between them. While historical literacy about who is Metis is required of non-Indigenous Canadians, it is also a fundamental teaching that Metis people themselves must become proficient in. Understanding how we know who we are is a critical responsibility of all Metis people. Only then can we safeguard against fraudulent or simply mistaken claims to our history and contemporary identity. This responsibility rests not with political representatives or with the state, but rather with the people themselves.

NOTES

1   This chapter is the product of three papers I have given since the *Daniels* decision was announced by the Supreme Court of Canada on 14 April 2016: one for the *"Daniels*: In and Beyond the Law" conference, hosted by the Rupertsland Centre for Métis Research 26–28 January 2017; a keynote address for the Western Canadian Lecture Series, hosted by the Department of History and Classics at the University of Alberta in December 2017; and finally, a FEDTalk given to federal government employees, also in December 2017. Each paper addressed distinct but complementary ideas around the role of historical research, methodology, and contemporary Metis identity and legal issues within the scope of *Daniels* and the types of popular debates within Canadian public discourse that have been developing since the 2003 *Powley* decision. The research data, theory of kinscapes, and methodological approach I will be highlighting come from my scholarly partnership with Dr. Nicole St-Onge and our multi-year research projects, along with my previous research on northwestern Saskatchewan, which was based on genealogical reconstructions of multiple generations of Metis families in the nineteenth century. The conclusions I reach here, however, are my own.

2   For a point of clarity, Eastern Canada in this context refers to the geography east of Manitoba but most especially Quebec, New Brunswick, and Nova Scotia, provinces with significant francophone populations.

3   Statistics Canada, "Aboriginal Peoples in Canada: Key Results from the 2016 Census," http://www.statcan.gc.ca/daily-quotidien/171025/dq171025a-eng.htm (accessed 8 January 2018). See also Chris Andersen, "Who Can Call Themselves Métis?," *Walrus*, 27 December 2017. Of course, both Quebec and Nova Scotia have significant francophone populations that would have an understanding of the term *métis* as simply meaning mixed and might interpret the census questions through that linguistic, rather than an Indigenous national, lens.

4   For detailed explanations and analysis of the trend of French Canadians race-shifting, see Darryl Leroux, *Distorted Descent: White Claims to Indigenous Identity* (Winnipeg: University of Manitoba Press, 2019). See also Maura Forrest, "A New World Mystery: How a 17th Century French Woman Became Indigenous, Then Became White Again," *National Post*, 30 January 2018, http://nationalpost.com/news/canada/a-new-world-mystery-how-a-17th-century-french-woman-became-indigenous-then-became-white-again.

5   See in particular Leroux, *Distorted Descent*; Andersen, "Who Can Call Themselves Métis?"; Darryl Leroux and Adam Gaudry, "Becoming Indigenous: The Rise of Eastern Métis in Canada," *The Conversation,* 25 October 2017, https://theconversation.com/becoming-indigenous-the-rise-of-eastern-metis-in-canada-80794; Kim TallBear, *Native American DNA: Tribal Belonging and the False Promise of Genetic Science* (Minneapolis: University of Minnesota Press, 2013); and Circe Sturm, *Becoming Indian: The Struggle over Cherokee Identity in the Twenty-First Century* (Santa Fe: School for Advanced Research Press, 2010).

6   See Jorge Berrera, "Author Joseph Boyden's shape-shifting Indigenous identity," *APTN National News*, 23 December 2016, https://www.aptnnews.ca/national-news/author-joseph-boydens-shape-shifting-indigenous-identity/. Boyden is not the first to have done this, and we can also point to Ward Churchill's and Thomas King's similar such assertions of Metisness to express mixedness. The notion of historical literacy is one that has concerned scholars of historical education, and between 2006 and 2013, a group of Canadian researchers explored how ordinary Canadians understand and engage with the past. They found that Canadians are interested in the past but are more invested in the histories of their families and the larger group to which they belong than they are to the histories of other peoples. That is, the majority of people surveyed in this study (2,000 of them) rely on family history to anchor themselves in time and place, and

importantly, to judge the past. While this way of experiencing the past can be profound, it also means that an imperfect understanding of your own family's history will skew how you understand/read another people's historical experience. See Margaret Conrad et al., *Canadians and Their Pasts* (Toronto: University of Toronto Press, 2013).

7   Vit Wagner, "Northern Roots Still Fuel Joseph Boyden's Fiction," *Toronto Star*, 20 September 2008, https://www.thestar.com/entertainment/books/2008/09/20/northern_roots_still_fuel_ joseph_boydens_fiction.html. One of the profiles of Boyden used most often in promotional literature associated with awards and speaking enagements is "Author Joseph Boyden Wins the 2008 Scotiabank Giller Prize," 11 November 2008, http://www.scotiabank.com/gillerprize/ files/12/10/news_111108.html (accessed 27 November 2008). While one could argue that this description is generated by the promoters of such events, such biographies are typically by speakers (in this case, Boyden) themselves. See also Thom Ernst, "Talking to Joseph Boyden," *Toro Magazine*, 13 July 2009, http://toromagazine.com/features/talking-to/20090713/joseph-boyden (accessed 28 November 2017); and Eric Friesen, "Joseph Boyden: A Spirited Voice," *Nuvo*, 28 May 2011, http://nuvomagazine.com/magazine/spring-2011/novelist-joseph-boyden.

8   Marsha Lederman, "Amid Heritage Controversy, Publishing Heavyweights Stand by Joseph Boyden," *Globe and Mail*, 6 January 2017.

9   Sturm, *Becoming Indian*, 6.

10   Mark Medley, "Boyden Admits to Mistakes, Backs Down as Indigenous Spokesperson," *Globe and Mail*, 11 January 2017.

11   This discourse also then fails to account for either the Indigenous origins—Cree, Saulteaux, Assiniboine, Dene, etc.—of Metis, as well as other European origins, particularly the large number of people who descend from Highland and Orcadian Scots. This might be a good time to note that I use "Metis" unaccented in my scholarship because when accented, people tend to believe that you are referring to the so-called French-speaking, Roman Catholic Metis descended from French traders. My decision to write the name as "Metis," therefore, is both to acknowledge the evolution of the term to denote a distinct Indigenous people and to signify that this nation is comprised of far more diversity than the use of "Métis" would imply. These are a people who came into their own to form a distinct society, although many families have ancestral roots in Scottish, French, English, and other European male forebears as well as Cree, Saulteaux, Dene, Assiniboine, Dakota, and women from other First Nations. When "Métis" appears in this chapter it signifies the proper name of an organization, how it is used in archival and contemporary government documents, or when it appears so in direct quotes from other sources, otherwise I will use Metis.

12   John Ralston Saul, *A Fair Country: Telling Truths about Canada* (Toronto: Viking Canada, 2008), 1.

13   Brenda Macdougall, *One of the Family: Metis Culture in Nineteenth-Century Northwestern Saskatchewan* (Vancouver: University of British of Columbia Press, 2011). While the entire book addresses this topic in the environment of northwestern Saskatchewan, see especially the introduction and pp. 1–22.

14   Sami Lakomäki, *Gathering Together: The Shawnee People through Diaspora and Nationhood, 1600–1870* (New Haven, CT: Yale University Press, 2014). Lakomäki's study of the Shawnee over the course of three centuries reveals how they were able to draw "from their culture, creativity, and power to shape the new geographic order" (p. 2) in which they existed as a result of American colonial expansion.

15   Statement by Joseph Boyden, @josephboyden, 11 February 2017, https://twitter.com/ josephboyden?ref_src=twsrc%5Eappleosx%7Ctwcamp%5Esafari%7Ctwgr%5Eprofile.

16 Gail Morin, *Métis Families: A Genealogical Compendium*, 11 vols. (self-published, 2016 editions);
   Douglas N. Sprague and R.P. Frye, *The Genealogy of the First Metis Nation: The Development
   and Dispersal of the Red River Settlement, 1820–1900* (Winnipeg: Pemmican Publications,
   1983); Frank J. Tough, Metis Archival Project, MNC Historical Online Database, http://metis-
   nationdatabase.ualberta.ca/MNC/about.jsp; Bruce McIntyre Watson, *Lives Lived West of the
   Divide: A Biographical Dictionary of Fur Traders Working West of the Rockies, 1793–1858*, 3
   vols. (Kelowna: Centre for Social, Spatial and Economic Justice, University of British Columbia
   Okanagan, 2010); Gerhard J. Ens and Ted Binnema, eds., *The Hudson's Bay Company Edmonton
   House Journals, Correspondence, and Reports*, vol. 1, *1806–1821*; vol. 2, *1821–1826* (Edmonton:
   Alberta Records Publication Board, 2012 and 2016); Dale Gibson, *Law, Life, and Government
   at Red River*, 2 vols. (Montreal: McGill-Queen's University Press, 2015); Mike Evans, "Frank
   Beatton and the Fort St. John Fur Trade," Digital Archives Database (DAD) Project, http://dadp.
   ok.ubc.ca/beatton; for Lawrence Barkwell, see much of his collection at the Virtual Museum of
   Métis Culture and History, Gabriel Dumont Institute, http://www.metismuseum.ca; Nicole
   St-Onge, Voyageur Contracts Database, Centre du patrimonie, http://shsb.mb.ca/en/Voyageurs_
   database; and St-Onge et al., DAD Project, http://dadp.ok.ubc.ca.

17 The type of primary, eye-witness accounts of such communities ranges from local histories such
   as Alexander Ross, *The Red River Settlement: Its Rise, Progress, and Present State; With Some
   Account of the Native Races and Its General History to the Present Da*y (London: Smith, Elder and
   Co., 1856); trade and missionary journals, such as Barry M. Gough, ed., *The Journal of Alexander
   Henry the Younger 1799–1814*, vol. 1, *Red River and the Journey to Missouri* (Toronto: Champlain
   Society, 1988); John McLean, *John McLean's Notes of a Twenty-Five Years' Service in the Hudson's
   Bay Territory* (Toronto: Champlain Society, 1932); and Father Louis Laflèche, *Saint-François-
   Xavier*. 1er juin 1847. Ann. de la Prop. de la Foi, Québec; magazine and newspaper articles such
   as "The People of the Red River," *Harper's New Monthly Magazine*, January 1859, 172; surveyor
   reports such as George M. Grant, (Rev'd.), *Ocean to Ocean: Sandford Fleming's Expedition through
   Canada in 1872; Being a Diary Kept during a Journey from the Atlantic to the Pacific* (Toronto:
   James Campbell and Son, 1873); and paintings like Peter Rindisbacher's *A Halfcast and His Two
   Wives*, 1825–26 (Library and Archives Canada, Acc. No. 1973-84-1); as well as later government
   descriptions such as those found within Alexander Morris, *The Treaties of Canada with the Indians
   of Manitoba and the North-West Territories* (Toronto: Belfords, Clarke, 1880).

18 Jennifer S.H. Brown, *Strangers in Blood: Fur Trade Company Families in Indian Country*
   (Vancouver: UBC Press, 1980); Gerhard J. Ens, *Homeland to Hinterland: The Changing Worlds
   of the Red River Metis in the Nineteenth Century* (Toronto: University of Toronto Press, 1996);
   Nicole St-Onge, *Saint-Laurent, Manitoba: Evolving Métis Identities, 1850–1914* (Regina:
   University of Regina Press, 2004); Nicholas C.P. Vrooman, *"The Whole Country Was . . . 'One
   Robe'": The Little Shell Tribe's America* (Helena, MT: Drumlummon Institute, 2012); Heather
   Devine, *The People Who Own Themselves: Aboriginal Ethnogenesis in a Canadian Family,
   1660–1900* (Calgary: University of Calgary Press, 2004); Melinda Marie Jetté, *At the Hearth
   of the Crossed Races: A French-Indian Community in Nineteenth-Century Oregon, 1812–1859*
   (Corvallis: Oregon State University Press, 2015); Tanis C. Thorne, *The Many Hands of My
   Relations: French and Indian on the Lower Missouri* (Columbia: University of Missouri Press,
   1996); Diane Payment, *"The Free People—Otipemisiwak": Batoche, Saskatchewan, 1870–1930*
   (Ottawa: Canadian Parks Service, 1990); Émilie Pigeon, "Au Nom du Bon Dieu et du Buffalo:
   Metis Lived Catholicism on the Northern Plains" (PhD diss., York University, 2017); Martha
   Haroun Foster, *We Know Who We Are: Métis Identity in a Montana Community* (Norman:
   University of Oklahoma Press, 2006); and Macdougall, *One of the Family*.

19 Sturm, *Becoming Indian*, 8.

20 Natalie Zemon Davis, *The Return of Martin Guerre* (Cambridge, MA: Harvard University Press, 1983), 1.

21 Carlo Ginzburg, *Clues, Myths, and the Historical Method: The Cosmos of a Sixteenth-Century Miller,* transl. John and Anne C. Tedeschi (New Jersey: Routledge, 1980), 98 and 103.

22 See Macdougall, *One of the Family*; and Brenda Macdougall, "Space and Place within Aboriginal Epistemological Traditions: Recent Trends in Historical Scholarship," *Canadian Historical Review* 98, no.1 (2017): 64–82.

23 Lawrence Stone, "Prosopography," *Daedalus* 100, no. 1 (1971): 46.

24 Ibid., 46–47; and Katherine S.B. Keats-Rohan, "Pursuit of the Individual in Prosopography," in *Prosopography Approaches and Applications: A Handbook*, ed. K.S.B. Keats-Rohan (Oxford: Unit for Prosopographical Research, 2007), 140.

25 Lewis H. Thomas, "Louis Riel," *Dictionary of Canadian Biography Online*, http://www.biographi. ca/en/bio/riel_louis_1844_85_11E.html (accessed 1 January 2016).

26 Sharon Stewart, *Louis Riel: Firebrand* (Montreal: XYZ Publishing, 2007), 8.

27 The basic marital information for Riel's siblings can be found in Maggie Siggins, *Riel: A Life of Revolution* (Toronto: HarperCollins, 1994) but I was able to confirm the connections between the siblings in both the Riel and Poitras families with Jean Teillet, a descendant of Joseph Riel.

28 See Macdougall, *One of the Family*; St-Onge, *Saint-Laurent, Manitoba*; Brenda Macdougall and Nicole St-Onge, "Rooted in Mobility: Metis Buffalo Hunting Brigades," *Manitoba History* 71 (2013): 21–32. See also Irene M. Spry, "The Métis and Mixed-Bloods of Rupert's Land before 1870," in *The New Peoples*, ed. Jacqueline Peterson and Jennifer S.H. Brown (Winnipeg: University of Manitoba Press, 1981), 95–118. Not all Metis people were the same, even within the rubric of the Metis nation. Some lived in the north and were descended from Dene people, others on the southern prairies were more likely to be descended from Cree, Saulteaux, or Assiniboine people (among others); some families at Red River who came in from far-flung trade regions had mothers and grandmothers from York Factory on James Bay or from one of the nations in British Columbia. Still others were descended from French, Scottish, English, and Iroquois traders. Each of these groups also brought to their families different cultural and religious traditions. Furthermore, while they all worked within the fur trade, there were significantly different jobs. The role of a buffalo hunter on the plains offered a great deal more personal freedom than that of someone holding a contract as a clerk or interpreter with a fur company, and those roles were different than operating boat brigades in the northern trade regions. Yet in Red River in particular, there's a sense that Metis history played out as Canadian history—with a cultural and political divide between English-speaking Protestants and French-speaking Roman Catholic Métis. However, Spry argues against the prevailing intellectual paradigm that posits that intermarriage between the so-called English- and French-speaking families at Red River was fairly widespread, and so the emphasis on division was less useful for assessing the community's social makeup.

29 TallBear argued during the keynote address for the *"Daniels"* conference that the social and material relations of Indigenous people were what defined them as sovereign nations rather than their biological connections as expressed through ideas of blood and biology, which are increasingly being highjacked by non-Indigenous interests in DNA and genealogical ancestry. Kim TallBear, "Molecular Death and Redface Reincarnation: Indigenous Appropriations in the U.S. and Canada," keynote address at *"Daniels*: In and Beyond the Law" conference, Rupertsland Centre for Métis Research, 26–28 January 2017. For a full rendering of her argument, see TallBear, *Native American DNA*.

30 It was while in Rainy River that Jean Louis entered a relationship with a woman known as Marie and had a daughter, Marguerite, who married Jean Baptiste Zace.

31 Julie Lagimodiere was one of the youngest children of Jean Baptiste Lagimodiere and Marie-Anne Gaboury, both of whom were from Lower Canada. Fur trader Jean Baptiste married Marie-Anne, a French-Canadian woman from Maskinongé, Lower Canada, in 1804 and that year they travelled west together. Jean Baptiste had promised his bride he would remain in Lower Canada if they married but within weeks of their marriage, he announced plans to return to the West to trade. Refusing to be abandoned by her husband, Marie-Anne insisted on going with him; neither of them ever returned to Quebec. It was unusual for non-Indigenous women to live in fur trade country in this era and equally unusual was their fully French-Canadian family. By 1816 the Lagimodieres were living in Red River after being stationed in the Edmonton region. See Maggie Siggins, *Marie-Anne: The Extraordinary Life of Louis Riel's Grandmother* (Toronto: McClelland and Stewart, 2008).

32 Thomas, "Jean-Louis Riel." Riel's parents are well documented in a number of biographies produced about their famous son, including Siggins, *Riel*; George Stanley, *Louis Riel* (Toronto: Ryerson Press, 1963); Thomas Flanagan, *Louis "David" Riel: Prophet of the New World* (Toronto: University of Toronto Press, 1996); Edmund B. Osler and Rossel Vien, *Louis Riel: Un homme à pendre* (Montréal: Éditions du Jour, 1964); Antoine Champagne, *La famille de Louis Riel: Notes généalogiques et historiques* (Quebec: A. Champagne, 1969); and Peter Charlebois, *The Life of Louis Riel* (Toronto: New Canada Publications, 1975).

33 St. François Xavier parish was located at Grantown, a community named for Cuthbert Grant Jr., a community founder. Grantown and, in turn, St. François Xavier were in the more broadly defined area of Whitehorse Plains. Grant was the leader of the Metis and NWC forces at the Battle of Seven Oaks in 1817 and in 1821, Grant was made the clerk at the HBC's Fort Garry by George Simpson, who was concerned he still had a great deal of influence over the local hunters. In 1823, to try to keep the buffalo hunters close to Red River and away from growing American influence, Simpson asked Grant to form a community and they chose the site for Grantown along the Assiniboine River. In 1828 Grantown became St. François Xavier after the church built in the community.

34 A.A. den Otter, *Civilizing the Wilderness: Culture and Nature in Pre-Confederation Canada and Rupert's Land* (Edmonton: University of Alberta Press, 2012); W.L. Morton, "Pierre-Guillaume Sayer," *Dictionary of Canadian Biography Online*, http://www.biographi.ca/en/bio/sayer_pierre_guillaume_7E.html (accessed 30 January 2018); and Nelly Laudicina, "The Rules of Red River: The Council of Assiniboia and Its Impact on the Colony, 1820–1869," *Past Imperfect* 15 (2009): 36–75.

35 See Siggins, *Marie-Anne*; Siggins, *Riel*; and Gilles Martel, *Le messianisme de Louis Riel* (Waterloo: Wilfrid Laurier University Press, 1984).

36 Godparents are sponsors, and every child baptized in the Roman Catholic Church is required to have at least one. Being a godparent came with ecclesiastical and legal responsibilities and therefore, clergy were not regarded as ideal for this role. As such, it was very unusual for them to serve as godparents. Macdougall, *One of the Family*, xx. See also Thérèse Castonguay, s.g.m., *The Grey Nun Ministries in Western and Northern Canada*, vol. 2, (Edmonton: Grey Nuns of Alberta, 2001), 17–44; and Mary Jordan, *To Louis from your sister who loves you: Sara Riel* (Toronto: Griffin House, 1974).

37 There is no direct evidence that Riel planned to head north and destroy the mission. However, the HBC post at Green Lake was looted by Cree and Metis from the region on 26 April 1885, two days after the Battle of Fish Creek.

38　Political biographies and analyses of Riel's life abound and are found in a variety of secondary literature, including Siggins, *Riel*; David Doyle, *Louis Riel: Let Justice Be Done* (Vancouver: Ronsdale Press, 2017); Flanagan, *Louis "David" Riel*; Thomas Flanagan, *Riel and the Rebellion: 1885 Reconsidered* (Toronto: University of Toronto Press, 2000); and Jennifer Reid, *Louis Riel and the Creation of Modern Canada* (Santa Fe: University of New Mexico Press, 2008).

39　Riel's marriage to Marguerite is well documented. See Siggins, *Riel*; Champagne, *La famille de Louis Riel*; and Charlebois, *The Life of Louis Riel*.

40　Like Riel, Dumont's life is encapsulated in a series of biographies. See George Woodcock, *Gabriel Dumont* (Montréal: Lidec, 1979); Gabriel Dumont, *Gabriel Dumont Speaks* (Vancouver: Talon Books, 2009); and Darren Préfontaine, *Gabriel Dumont: Li Chef Michif in Images and Words* (Saskatoon: Gabriel Dumont Institute, 2011). For genealogical information, see also Cheryl Troupe, "Métis Women: Social Structure, Urbanization, and Political Activism, 1850–1980" (MA thesis, University of Saskatchewan, 2010); and Macdougall and St-Onge, "Rooted in Mobility."

41　There are exceptions, of course. Both Sylvia Van Kirk and Jennifer Brown have done extensive and ground-breaking studies on gender and the fur trade, unearthing the lives of Indigenous women. See Sylvia Van Kirk, *Many Tender Ties: Women in Fur Trade Society in Western Canada, 1670–1870* (Winnipeg: Watson and Dwyer, 1980); Brown, *Strangers in Blood*; Sarah Carter, *The Importance of Being Monogamous: Marriage and Nation Building in Western Canada to 1915* (Edmonton: University of Athabasca Press, 2008); Susan Sleeper-Smith, *Indian Women and French Men: Rethinking Cultural Encounter in the Western Great Lakes* (Amherst: University of Massachusetts Press, 2001); Nathalie Kermoal, *Un passé metis au feminine* (Québec: Les Éditions GID, 2006); and Diane Payment, "Une femme en vaut deux—'Strong Like Two People': Marie Fisher Gaudet of Fort Good Hope, Northwest Territories," in *Contours of a People: Metis Family, Mobility, and History*, ed. Nicole St-Onge, Carolyn Podruchny, and Brenda Macdougall (Norman: University of Oklahoma Press, 2012), 265–99.

42　Joachim Fromhold, *The Western Cree Maski Pilon's Ban (Maskepetoon, Broken Arm) of the Plains Cree*, vol. 1, to 1860 (Mirror, AB: Heritage Consulting, 2012); *Joachim Fromhold, Western Canadian People in the Past, 1600–1900, R–Z* (Mirror, AB: Heritage Consulting, 2012); and Woodcock, *Gabriel Dumont*.

43　Davis, *The Return of Martin Guerre*; and Natalie Zemon Davis, "Ghosts, Kin, and Progeny: Some Features of Family Life in Early Modern France," *Daedalus* 106, no. 2 (1977): 87–114.

44　Fellow brigade member Norbert Welsh, nephew of Charles Trottier, identified his friends and relatives within the Trottier brigade, including Isadore, who was chief of a hunt one winter. See Mary Weekes, *The Last Buffalo Hunter* (Saskatoon: Fifth House Publishers, 1994).

45　See Macdougall and St-Onge, "Rooted in Mobility." Additionally, Cheryl Troupe's MA thesis on the history of urbanization of the Metis in Saskatoon details this early history of the Trottier brigade. She begins the genealogical reconstruction of the Trottier brigade at Round Prairie, and a version of the genealogy in Figure 10.2 can be found in her thesis. Troupe, "Métis Women."

46　The terms hunt chief and hunt captain are used fairly interchangeably in the literature. Norbert Welsh, for instance, often used the phrase hunt chief, while Alexander Ross called leaders of the hunts captains. Perhaps the choice of language reflected the relative difference between men like Welsh, a Metis buffalo hunter and free trader, and Ross, a Scottish-born former trade company employee settled at Red River, where he eventually became a member of the Council of Assiniboia.

47　Woodcock, *Gabriel Dumont*.

48　Macdougall and St-Onge, "Rooted in Mobility."

49 Chris Andersen, "From Nation to Population: The Racialisation of 'Métis' in the Canadian Census," *Nations and Nationalism* 14, no. 2 (2008): 353.

50 Diane Payment, *The Free People—Li Gens Libres: A History of the Metis Community of Batoche, Saskatchewan* (Calgary: University of Calgary Press, 2009), 267; and John Weinstein, *Quiet Revolution West: The Rebirth of Métis Nationalism* (Saskatoon: Fifth House, 2007), 24; Siomonn P. Pulla, "Regional Nationalisms or National Mobilization," in *Métis in Canada: History, Identity, Law, and Politics*, ed. Christopher Adams, Gregg Dahl, and Ian Peach (Edmonton: University of Alberta Press, 2013), 412; and Kelly L. Saunders, "No Other Weapon: Metis Political Organization and Governance in Canada," in *Métis in Canada: History, Identity, Law, and Politics*, 352–53.

The Multiple Lives
of the *Daniels* Case

Six blind men approach an elephant in order to learn more about it.
The first man touches the side of the elephant, and concludes that an
elephant is like a wall. The second man feels the tusk, and deduces
that the elephant is like a spear. A third man grabs the squirming
trunk, and resolves that the elephant is like a snake. The fourth
man reaches out and pats the huge leg, thereby determining that
the elephant is like a tree. The fifth man touches the ear, and thus
infers that the elephant is like a fan. Finally, the sixth man seizes the
swinging tail, and judges an elephant to be like a rope.[1]

Like the elephant of this fable, "law" tends to take on the meaning of the
context in which any given person is located and to the extent that we experience "it" specifically as, say, a lawyer, a judge, a police officer, a social justice advocate, a politician, an academic scholar, someone who has just been
given a speeding ticket, or an Indigenous youth who has just been stopped
and searched for no apparent reason. Law assumes multiple presences in
a wide variety of social contexts and as such, takes on multiple lives, so to

speak, within the lives of those who experience it. A starting position for
this edited collection was that we would invite an array of contributors who
have experienced law—and more specifically, the *Daniels* case and its various decisions—from a comprehensive range of professional contexts and in
a broad variety of ways. To that end, although we adopted the subtitle "in
and beyond the courts," we could just as easily have chosen other phrases to
highlight the extent—and the different ways—the *Daniels* case continues to
travel and to "echo" through a wide variety of social contexts.

Law is predominantly understood in non-academic circles as being the
purview of lawyers, judges, and other agents of the criminal justice appara-
tus. However, academically speaking it possesses a much broader genealogy
and has been analyzed from a number of angles outside of the jurisprudential field. Many sociology of law positionings, for example, have been based
in arguments about the increasingly intensive impact of law on our lives.
Such perspectives present "law" as a unitary institution that affects our lives
in myriad ways on a daily basis. On this basis, sociology of law scholars have
confidently articulated the role of law in the relationship between law and
society as in which, to quote a classic sociology of law text:

> Law regulates prenuptial agreements, marriage, divorce, and
> the conduct of professors in the classroom. Law sets the speed
> limit and the length of school attendance. Laws control what we
> eat and where and what we buy and when, and how we use our
> computers. Laws regulate business, raise revenue, provide for
> redress when agreements are broken, and uphold social institutions,
> such as the family. Laws protect the prevailing legal and political
> systems by defining power relationships, thus establishing who
> is superordinate and who is subordinate in any given situation.
> Laws maintain the status quo and provide the impetus for change.
> Finally, laws, in particular criminal laws, not only protect private
> and public interests but also preserve order. There is no end to the
> ways in which the law has a momentous effect on our lives.[2]

Other sociological forays into law have moved away from a study of law conceived as a formal system of rules *a la* legislative law or judicial notions of
stare decisis toward a study of legality more broadly conceived as a cultural

artifact existing outside the specific edifice of legal rules or norms and formal legal institutions, and within the cultural tapestry of society: "legal meaning is found and invented in the variety of locations and practices that comprise the domains of culture . . . those locations and practices are themselves encapsulated, though always incompletely, in legal forms, regulations and legal symbols."[3] If instrumentalist studies of law focus on the study of principles of/and legal reasoning, the sensibilities underlying cultural critiques of law are based on the assumption that we should study everything about law *but* the rules.[4]

Such so-called legal consciousness theories of law are concerned with exposing what is perceived to be its overly institutionalized, overly homogenous, and overly intrusive constructions. Law does not exist, as it were, "outside" of society—it is constituted by society and exists within it, while concomitantly, social forms are themselves embodied within and produced through legal sensibilities and expressed in legal forms. Thus, such theorists argue that the power of law and legality must be understood for the extent to which they have permeated the broad reach of society and for their places as background *norms* that shape in powerful ways how people constitute themselves, how they imagine their relationships with others, and thus how their normative sensibilities are formed. That is to say, "law" and legal consciousness serve as a mediating force between citizenry and in doing so, constitute particular for(u)ms of meaning-making activities between competing groups.[5]

The problem with both instrumental and legal consciousness accounts is that they position law as either being nowhere or everywhere, respectively. That is to say, law is either captured tightly within legal rules and reasoning, or it is a dominant force in the very makeup of our being as (for example) Canadian citizens. Rather than siding with either of these two constructions—choosing scarcity or plenitude—the contributors to this volume effectively bypass these debates altogether by "fissuring" a singular notion of law. Indeed, at least in Canada, what we normally talk about as "law" encapsulates a wide swath of social actors that derive different meanings from court cases such that its effects (or, to repeat a term used earlier, "echoes") never begin or end at the doorways of courthouses, though courthouses remain crucial bulwarks through which the meaning and power of law—manifested in cases such as *Daniels*—are reproduced.

Toward that end, the contributors to this volume include among them a retired Métis politician, law professors, lawyers, DNA specialists, anthropologists, sociologists (one of whom specializes in genealogical reconstruction), and historians. Even within such comparatively narrow professional contexts, the volume makes clear—perhaps startlingly so—the myriad ways that the *Daniels* case has travelled not just into different professional contexts but into sociologically diverse nooks and crannies of Canadian society. As we just noted, part of the power of court cases—especially those held at such a prominent level as the Supreme Court of Canada—is that they indeed reach far beyond the boundaries of the courtroom, the legal actors, and the legal documents that originally framed a case. And insofar as this is the case, part of the work undertaken in this volume (and part of the original desires of the co-editors) has been to pick apart otherwise instrumentalist understandings that present "law" as a unified, monolithic entity, and to move beyond critiquing the legal reasoning contained within the decisions—though this constitutes crucial analytical labour in its own right—to understanding its variegated material effects.

Indeed, *Daniels v. Canada* at the Supreme Court of Canada was a widely anticipated decision, not least by lawyers, policy actors, and jurisprudential scholars. In this volume's jurisprudential chapters, legal scholars position themselves in various ways with respect to the decision, for what it did and did not say, what it should have said and what its potential policy effects might be. For example, legal scholar Catherine Bell notes the ambiguity contained in the *Daniels* decisions on the contours and boundaries of fiduciary relationships and the duty to consult Indigenous communities that follow from it—as well as the complications that will potentially ensue from reading it in relation to other recent Supreme Court of Canada Indigenous rights decisions. Similarly, Brenda Gunn explores the impact of the decision on the manner in which Indigeneity is understood in international law and its implications for Canada's stated commitment to the United Nations Declaration on the Rights of Indigenous Peoples. D'Arcy Vermette echoes this discussion, pointing out the extent to which the *Daniels* decision dismisses Métis peoplehood and the racism that undergirds such a dismissal.

In their chapter, Hoekstra and Isaac discuss both the manner in which the Supreme Court of Canada attempted to dignify the terminology used to speak about First Peoples and the manner in which the *Daniels* decision offers the potential of a powerful charter for reconciliation with Indigenous peoples (though their analysis of subsequent jurisprudence's language use is less hopeful). In his helpful analysis and contextualization, lawyer Jason Madden provides some legal and political context for the litigation that led to the Daniels case, a jurisprudential overview of section 91(24), within which the Daniels decision was "appearing," and the legal and policy implications that have ensued. A key point that Madden makes is that one of the necessary but unfortunate side effects of appearing before the Canadian courts is that the eventual decisions rendered reflect Canadian jurisprudential logics rather than a Métis legal order and world view.

The issues, contexts, and motivations surveyed by Madden are reflected in different disciplinary contexts in much of the rest of the volume. For example, Kermoal provides a broader political context for why *Daniels* was necessary in relationship to the Métis people's unfolding relationship to the Canadian state—not just in the years or decades leading up to the decision to litigate, but in the *longue dureé* of the nineteenth and twentieth centuries. Harry Daniels understood well the fractured (or perhaps more strategically, the "fracturable") landscape of law and its relationship to the ongoing and —in the context of the upheaval around the 1982 patriation of the constitution—evolving political positioning for Indigenous organizations in Ottawa. This landscape is meticulously laid out by the former president of the Métis Nation of Ontario, Tony Belcourt, in his contribution to the volume. Like any experienced advocates, Belcourt and Daniels were able to expertly manoeuvre among and between the various social, cultural, and political actors that availed themselves to the gravitational pull of the *Daniels* case.

This broader metaphor of gravitational pull is crucial to understanding the full impact of *Daniels*. In his contribution to the volume, for example, Andersen notes that some of the judicial phrasing in the *Daniels* decision at the Supreme Court of Canada level, when taken out of its judicial context, has since spawned numerous (probably) unintended and even serendipitous consequences as it has been taken up by individuals and organizations attempting to define Indigenous identity in provincial contexts. In his chapter, Leroux documents the explosive growth of "Métis" organizations following the Supreme Court's 2003 *Powley* decision and more recently, the scc *Daniels* decision, fuelled by their interpretation of some of the logics contained in the latter decision. Leroux also explores the growing body of research on "Eastern métis" that arguably mimics one of the definitions of Métis contained in the *Daniels* decision.

As Andersen notes in his framing of the courts, court decisions do not appear out of thin air, as it were; instead, they tend to reflect (and importantly, to refract) broader social discourses already in existence. In the case of the Canadian courts (and the Supreme Court *Daniels* decision in particular), more often than not the logics of court decisions tend to reflect broader racialized understandings of Indigeneity in general and Métis identity more specifically. For example, Macdougall's chapter usefully reframes anthropologist Circe Sturm's exploration of white claims to Cherokee identity in the United States to discuss the manner in which historical documentation gets used and misused to define Métis identity.

The fundamental issue, according to Macdougall, is ultimately about how genealogical resources are reframed into identity claims (claims that are limited not just to genealogy but include DNA as well, as described by Rick Smith and colleagues in their contribution) and the lack of literacy about historical documents such as genealogical records and the limits of what they can be used for. While noting the importance of genealogical records, Macdougall advocates for the central importance of microhistories and prosopography (understanding how individuals operate within networks of relationships) to contextualize them.

All of the contributions to this volume demonstrate two fundamental principles for positioning the importance of court decisions, in particular powerful court decisions like those rendered by the Supreme Court of Canada. First, the meaning of *text*—all text, but perhaps especially court decisions—is necessarily circumscribed by *context* such that often, the professional contexts within which we understand the meaning and the power of a court decision like *Daniels v. Canada* are shaped by the training and its associated "lenses" brought to bear on it. Second, the contributors effectively demonstrate the extent to which high-level court decisions like *Daniels* make use of fundamental concepts—fiduciary responsibilities, consultation, race, nation, peoplehood, and so forth—that circulate in specific ways within the juridical field (mainly through other court cases) and outside the juridical field as well, taken up by non-legal scholars.

To return to the parable we used to open this Conclusion, prominent judicial discourses such as those produced in the Supreme Court of Canada operate metaphorically in broadly the same way as the elephant. Like the blind men in the fable, we are each positioned at different points around the legal elephant; unlike those men, we each have the opportunity through this volume and its contributions to move beyond the limitations of our academic and professional contexts to think in a more nuanced manner about the full power of *Daniels v. Canada*. Supreme Court of Canada court cases like *Daniels v. Canada* are complex in their meanings and their effects, and our analyses would benefit greatly from treating them like the elephants that they are and thus, accord them the analytical care and attention that they deserve. Indigenous peoples deserve no less (indeed, nearly all of the contributors have long histories of working with Indigenous communities and organizations) and neither do our analyses.

NOTES

1   Charles R. Snyder and Carol E. Ford, *Coping with Negative Life Events: Clinical and Social Psychological Perspectives* (New York: Springer Science, 2013), 12. This quote is part of an ancient parable widely known as the "The Blind Men and the Elephant." Like many venerable fables it has "travelled" in meaning and context and in doing so, has taken on a number of different meanings and conclusions. However, it is generally understood to be a story about a group of blind men who, never having encountered an elephant before, begin to "make meaning" about what the elephant is by touching it. However, each blind man touches a different part of the elephant (the ears, the tail, the tusks, the feet, etc.) and fashions a description of the elephant based on the limited context of what they have touched. The general moral of the story is that as humans, we tend to claim ultimate knowledge or truth about an object, an event, a situation—or, of more specific relevance to this volume, a court case—based on our circumscribed, subjective experience. Likewise, we tend to push away other subjective experiences when they do not accord with our own.

2   Steven Vago and Adie Nelson, *Law and Society* (Toronto: Pearson Prentice Hall, 2003), 1.

3   Austin Sarat and Thomas Kearns, "The Cultural Lives of Law," in *Law in the Domains of Culture*, ed. Austin Sarat and Thomas Kearns (Ann Arbor: University of Michigan Press, 1998), 10.

4   Richard Abel, "What Do We Talk About When We Talk About Law?" in *The Law and Society Reader*, ed. Richard Abel (New York: New York University Press, 1995), 1; see also Robert Gordon, "Critical Legal Histories," *Stanford Law Review* 36 (1984): 57–125.

5   Michael McCann, "How Does Law Matter for Social Movements?," in *How Does Law Matter?* ed. Bryant Garth and Austin Sarat (Evanston, IL: Northwestern University Press, 1998), 76–108; see also Gordon, "Critical Legal Histories."

Bibliography

Abel, Richard. "What Do We Talk About When We Talk About Law?" In *The Law and Society Reader*, edited by Richard Abel, 1–12. New York: New York University Press, 1995.

Aboriginal Peoples Television Network. APTN News. "Identity Crisis: APTN I Investigates." 18 April 2017. https://www.youtube.com/watch?v=lzNYGW0OimY.

Adams, Howard. *Prison of Grass: Canada from a Native Point of View*. Saskatoon: Fifth House Publishers, 1975, 1989.

Adese, Jennifer. "A Tale of Two Constitutions: Métis Nationhood and Section 35(2)'s Impact on Interpretations of *Daniels*." *TOPIA: Canadian Journal of Cultural Studies* 36 (2016): 7–19.

Adese, Jennifer, Zoe Todd, and Shaun Stevenson. "Mediating Identity: An Interview with Jennifer Adese and Zoe Todd." *MediaTropes* 7, no. 1 (2017): 1–25.

Anaya, S. James. *Indigenous Peoples in International Law*. 2nd edition. New York: Oxford University Press, 2004.

———. "The Right of Indigenous Peoples to Self-Determination in the Post-Declaration Era." In *Making the Declaration Work*, edited by C. Charters and R. Stavenhagen, 184–199. Copenhagen: IWGIA, 2009.

Andersen, Chris. "From Nation to Population: The Racialisation of 'Métis' in the Canadian Census." *Nations and Nationalism* 14, no. 2 (2008): 347–68.

———. *"Métis": Race, Recognition, and the Struggle for Indigenous Peoplehood*. Vancouver: UBC Press, 2014.

———. "Mixed Ancestry or Métis?" In *Indigenous Identity and Resistance: Researching the Diversity of Knowledge*, edited by Brendan Hokowhitu et al., 23–36. Dunedin, NZ: University of Otago Press, 2010.

———. "The Supreme Court Ruling on Métis: A Roadmap to Nowhere." *Globe and Mail*, Opinion. 14 April 2016. https://www.theglobeandmail. com/opinion/the-supreme-court-ruling-on-metis-a-roadmap-to-nowhere/ article29636204/.

———. "Who Can Call Themselves Métis?" *Walrus*, 27 December 2017.

Andersen, Chris, and Adam Gaudry. "*Daniels v. Canada*: Racialized Legacies, Settler Self–Indigenization and the Denial of Indigenous Peoplehood." *TOPIA: Canadian Journal of Cultural Studies* 36 (2016): 19–30.

Anderson, Benedict. *Imagined Communities: Reflections on the Origin and Spread of Nationalism*. Revised edition. London and New York: Verso Publishers, 2006.

Attorney General of Canada v. Canard, [1976] 1 SCR 170.

Aubert, Guillaume. "'The Blood of France': Race and Purity of Blood in the French Atlantic World." *William and Mary Quarterly* 61, no. 3 (2004): 439–78.

Aubin, Claude. "Nation Métis du Québec, un autre point de vue de reconnaissance." 4 November 2010. http://claudeaubinmetis.com/viewtopic. php?f=36&t=20 (accessed 15 December 2016).

Aundeck Omni Kaning v. Canada, 2014 SCTC 1.

"Author Joseph Boyden Wins the 2008 Scotiabank Giller Prize." 11 November 2008. http://www.scotiabank.com/gillerprize/files/12/10/news_111108. html (accessed 27 November 2008).

Axmann, Stephanie. "Métis and Non–Status Indians No Longer in a 'Jurisdictional Wasteland,' SCC Confirms." McCarthy Tétrault LLP, 11 May 2016. http://www.mccarthy.ca/article_detail.aspx?id=7258#utm_source= Mondaq& utm_medium=syndication&utm_campaign=inter–article–link (accessed 23 January 2018).

Backhouse, Constance. "'Race' Definition Run Amuck: 'Slaying the Dragon of Eskimo Status' before the Supreme Court of Canada, 1939." In *Law, History, Colonialism: The Reach of Empire*, edited by Dianne Kirkby and Catharine Coleborne. Manchester: Manchester University Press, 2001.

Bardill, Jessica, Alyssa C. Bader, Nanibaa A. Garrison, Deborah A. Bolnick, Jennifer A. Raff, Alexa Walker, and Ripan S. Malhi. "Advancing the Ethics of Paleogenomics." *Nature* 360, no. 6387 (2018): 384–5.

Barelli, Mauro. "Free, Prior and Informed Consent in the Aftermath of the UN Declaration on the Rights of Indigenous Peoples: Developments and Challenges Ahead." *International Journal of Human Rights* 16, no. 1 (2012): 1–24.

Barker, Joanne. "The Human Genome Diversity Project: 'Peoples,' 'Populations' and the Cultural Politics of Identification." *Cultural Studies* 18 (2004): 571–606.

———. *Native Acts: Law, Recognition, and Cultural Authenticity.* Durham, NC: Duke University Press, 2011.

Barrera, Jorge. "Congress National Chief 'Can't Remember' Roots of Own Indigeneity." APTN News. 27 September 2017. http://aptnnews. ca/2017/09/27/congress–national–chief–cant–remember–roots–of–own–indigenous–ancestry/.

Bauman, Zygmunt. *Modernity and the Holocaust.* Ithaca, NY: Cornell University Press, 1989.

Bear Nicholas, Andrea. "Linguicide." *Briarpatch Magazine*, March/April 2011.

Beauregard, Yves. "Mythe ou réalité. Les origines amérindiennes des Québécois: Entrevue avec Hubert Charbonneau." *Cap–aux–Diamants: La revue d'histoire du Québec*, no. 34 (1993): 38–42.

Beckman v. Little Salmon/Carmacks First Nation, 2010 SCC 53.

Belcourt, Tony. "For the Record ... On Métis Identity and Citizenship within the Métis Nation." *aboriginal policy studies* 2, no. 2 (2013): 128–41.

Belmessous, Saliha. "Assimilation and Racialism in Seventeenth and Eighteenth-Century French Colonial Policy." *American Historical Review* 110, no. 2 (2005): 322–49.

Bennett, Carolyn. Speech for the Honourable Carolyn Bennett, Minister of Indigenous and Northern Affairs at the United Nations Permanent Forum on Indigenous Issues 16th Session, 16 May 2017. Government of Canada. Last modified 16 May 2017. https://www.canada.ca/en/ indigenous–northern affairs/news/2017/05/speaking_notes_forthehonourablecarolynbennettministerofindigenou.html.

Bergner, Keith, Shailaz Dhalla, and John Olynyk. "The *Daniels* Decision: All Aboriginal Peoples, Including Métis and Non–Status Indians, Are "Indians" under Section 91(24) of the Constitution Act, 1867." Lawson Lundell *Project Law Blog*, 15 April 2016. https://www.lawsonlundell.com/project-law-blog/the-daniels-decision-all-aboriginal-peoples-including-metis-and-non-status-indians-are-indians-under-section-9124-of-the-constitution-act-1867 (accessed 18 May 2018).

Bolnick, Deborah A. "Individual Ancestry Inference and the Reification of Race as a Biological Phenomenon." In *Revisiting Race in a Genomic Age*, edited by Barbara A. Koenig, Sandra Soo-Jin Lee, and Sarah S. Richardson, 70–88. New Brunswick, NJ: Rutgers University Press, 2008.

Bolnick, Deborah A., Duana Fullwiley, Troy Duster, Richard S. Cooper, Joan H. Fujimura, Jonathan Kahn, Jay S. Kaufman, Jonathan Marks, Ann Morning, Alondra Nelson, Pilar Ossorio, Jenny Reardon, Susan M. Reverby, and Kimberly TallBear. "The Science and Business of Genetic Ancestry Testing." *Science* 80, no. 318 (2007): 399–400.

Bolnick, Deborah A. Jennifer A., Raff, Lauren C. Springs, Austin W. Reynolds, and Aida T. Miró-Herrans. "Native American Genomics and Population Histories." *Annual Review of Anthropology* 45 (2016): 319–40.

Borrows, John. *Canada's Indigenous Constitution*. Toronto: University of Toronto Press, 2010.

———. *Recovering Canada: The Resurgence of Indigenous Law*. Toronto: University of Toronto Press, 2002.

Bourdieu, Pierre. "The Force of Law: Toward a Sociology of the Juridical Field." *Hastings Law Journal* 38 (1987): 805–849.

Bourdieu, Pierre, and Loïc Wacquant. *Invitation to a Reflexive Sociology*. Chicago: University of Chicago Press, 1992.

Bourgault-Côté, Guillaume, and Marie Vastel. "Des 'Indiens' à part entière." *Le Devoir*, 15 April 2016. http://www.ledevoir.com/societe/actualites-en-societe/468283/des-indie ns-a-part-entiere.

Bracken, Harry M. "Essence, Accident and Race." *Hermathena*, no. 116 (1973): 81–96.

———. "Philosophy and Racism." *Philosophia: Philosophical Quarterly of Israel* 8 (1978): 241–60.

British North America Act, 1867, 30 & 31 Victoria, c. 3 (U.K.) s. 133. In *A Consolidation of the Constitution Acts 1867 to 1982*. Ottawa: Department of Justice Canada, 1999.

Brown, Jennifer S.H. *Strangers in Blood: Fur Trade Company Families in Indian Country*. Vancouver: UBC Press, 1980.

Burley, David. "Rooster Town: Winnipeg's Lost Métis Suburb, 1900–1960." *Urban History Review/Revue d'histoire urbaine* 42, no. 1 (2013): 3–25.

Cairns, Alan C. *Citizens Plus: Aboriginal Peoples and the Canadian State*. Vancouver: UBC Press, 2000.

———. "Commentaries: An Overview of the Trudeau Constitutional Proposals." *Alberta Law Review* 19, no. 3 (1981): 401–9.

Calder v. British Columbia (Attorney General), [1973] SCR 313, 34 DLR (3d) 145 (SCC).

Callaway, Ewen. "Ancient Genome Delivers 'Spirit Cave Mummy' to U.S. Tribe." *Nature* 540 (2016): 178–79.

Campbell, Maria. *Halfbreed*. Lincoln: University of Nebraska Press, 1982.

Campbell v. British Columbia (Attorney General), 2000 BCSB 1123.

Canada Mortgage and Housing Corporation. *Report of the Federal Task Force on Housing and Urban Development*. Ottawa: Task Force on Housing and Urban Development, 1969.

Canada–Métis Nation Accord between the Government of Canada and the Métis Nation as Represented by the MNC and Its Governing Members. 13 April 2017. https://pm.gc.ca/eng/canada-metis-nation-accord.

Canadian Charter of Rights and Freedoms, Part I of the Constitution Act, 1982 (UK), 1982, c 11, s 15.

Canadian Foundation for Children, Youth and the Law v. Canada (AG), 2004 SCC 4, [2004] 1 SCR 76, 234 DLR (4th) 257.

Carter, Sarah. *The Importance of Being Monogamous: Marriage and Nation Building in Western Canada to 1915*. Edmonton: University of Athabasca Press, 2008.

Cassese, Antonio. *Self-Determination of Peoples: A Legal Reappraisal*. New York: Cambridge University Press, 1995.

Castonguay, Thérèse, s.g.m. *The Grey Nun Ministries in Western and Northern Canada*.Vol. 2. Edmonton: The Grey Nuns of Alberta, 2001.

Champagne, Antoine. *La famille de Louis Riel: Notes généalogiques et historiques*. Quebec: A. Champagne, 1969.

Charest, Paul. "La disparition des Montagnais et la négation des droits aborigènes: Commentaires critiques sur le livre de Nelson-Martin Dawson, *Feu, fourrures, fléaux et foi foudroyèrent les Montagnais* (2005)." *Recherches amérindiennes au Québec* 39, no. 3 (2009): 81–95.

———. "Qui a peur des Innus? Réflexions sur les débats au sujet du projet d'entente de principe entre les Innus de Mashteuiatsh, Essipit, Betsiamites et Nutashkuan et les Gouvernements du Québec et du Canada." *Anthropologies et sociétés* 27, no. 2 (2003): 185–206.

Charlebois, Peter. *The Life of Louis Riel*. Toronto: New Canada Publications, 1975.

Charters, Claire, and Rodolfo Stavenhagen. "The UN Declaration on the Rights of Indigenous Peoples: How It Came to Be and What It Heralds." In *Making the Declaration Work: The United Nations Declaration on the Rights of Indigenous Peoples*, edited by Clare Charters and Rodolfo Stavenhagen, 10–15. Copenhagen: IWGIA, 2009.

Chartier, Clément. "'Indian': An Analysis of the Term as Used in Section 91 (24) of the British North America Act, 1867." *Saskatchewan Law Review* 43 (1978-79): 37-80.

Chartrand, Larry N. "The Failure of the *Daniels* Case: Blindly Entrenching a Colonial Legacy." *Alberta Law Review* 51, no. 1 (2013): 181–89.

———. "The Political Dimension of Aboriginal Rights." LLM Thesis, Queen's University Faculty of Law, 2001.

Chartrand, Paul L.A.H. *Manitoba's Métis Settlement Scheme of 1870*. Saskatoon: Native Law Centre, University of Saskatchewan, 1991.

Chartrand, Paul L.A.H., and John Giokas. "Defining 'The Métis People': The Hard Case of Canadian Aboriginal Law." In *Who Are Canada's Aboriginal Peoples? Recognition, Definition, and Jurisdiction*, edited by Paul Chartrand. Saskatoon: Purich Publishing, 2002.

Chemainus First Nation v. British Columbia Assets and Lands Corporation, [1999] 3 CNLR 8

Cherokee Nation v. Georgia, (1831) 30 U.S. (5 Pet.) 1.

Chippewas of the Thames First Nation v. Enbridge Pipelines Inc., 2017 SCC 41, 411 DLR (4th) 596.

Chrisjohn, Roland. Transcript of presentation, "Racism: Back to the Basics." http://www.nativestudies.org/native_pdf/Racismbacktobasics.pdf (accessed 25 July 2011).

Christie, Gordon. "Justifying Principles of Treaty Interpretation." *Queen's Law Journal* 26, no. 1 (2000): 143–224.

Clyde River (Hamlet) v. Petroleum Geo-Services Inc., 2017 SCC 40, 411 DLR (4th) 571.

Cobo, José R. Martinez. *Study of the Problem of Discrimination against Indigenous Populations*. Vol. 5, *Conclusions, Proposals and Recommendations*. 1987. United Nations, UN Doc. E/CN.4/Sub.2/1986/7/Add.4.

Conrad, Margaret, Kadriye Ercikan, Gerald Friesen, Jocelyn Létourneau, Delphin Muise, David Northrup, and Peter Seixas. *Canadians and Their Pasts*. Toronto: University of Toronto Press, 2013.

Constitution Act, 1867, (UK), 30 and 31 Vict, c 3, reprinted in RSC 1985.

Constitution Act, 1982, being Schedule B to the Canada Act 1982 (UK), 1982, c 11.

Constitution of Alberta Amendment Act, 1990, RSA 2000, c C-24.

Cook, Mathieu. "Les droits ancestraux des Innus: Reconnaissance et contestation, Analyse des discours sur l'altérité déployés lors d'une controverse à propos de négociations territoriales." PhD diss., Université Laval, 2016.

Cook, Peter. "Onontio Gives Birth: How the French in Canada Became Fathers to Their Indigenous Allies, 1645–73." *Canadian Historical Review* 96, no. 2 (2015): 165–69.

Corntassel, Jeff J. "Who Is Indigenous? 'Peoplehood' and Ethnonationalist Approaches to Rearticulating Indigenous Identity." *Nationalism and Ethnic Politics* 9, no.1 (Spring 2003): 75–100.

Coulthard, Glen. *Red Skin, White Masks: Rejecting the Colonial Politics of Recognition*. Minneapolis: University of Minnesota Press, 2014.

Courtemanche, Alexandre. "Le nombre de métis gaspésiens double en six mois." *TVA*, 5 October 2016. http://chau.teleinterrives.com/nouvelle-alaune_Le_ nombre_de_metis_gaspesiens_ double_en_six_mois-29700 (accessed 8 October 2016).

Cowan, Mairi. "Education, Francisation, and Shifting Colonial Priorities at the Ursuline Convent in Seventeenth-Century Québec." *Canadian Historical Review* 99, no. 1 (2018): 1–29.

Daes, Erica-Irene A. "Prevention of Discrimination and Protection of Indigenous Peoples: Indigenous Peoples' Permanent Sovereignty Over Natural Resources: Final Report of the Special Rapporteur." 2004. United Nations, UN Doc. E/ CN.4/2004/30.

Daniels, Harry. *Native People and the Constitution of Canada: The Report of the Métis and Non-Status Indian*. Ottawa: Mutual Press, 1981.

———. *We Are the New Nation/Nous sommes la nouvelle nation*. Ottawa, Native Council of Canada, 1979.

Daniels, Harry, and Paul L.A.H. Chartrand. "Unravelling the Riddles of Metis Definition." Unpublished Policy Paper, 2001.

Daniels, Canada Briefing Note for Constitutional Conference, 1984 (Appeal Book, Vol 35, 1431, Trial Exhibit P52 at 1435).

"*Daniels:* In and Beyond the Law." Unpublished conference notes. Hosted by the Rupertsland Centre for Métis Research, University of Alberta, Edmonton, 26–28 January 2017.

Daniels v. Canada (Minister of Indian Affairs and Northern Development), 2002 FCT 295.

Daniels v. Canada (Minister of Indian Affairs and Northern Development), 2005 FC 699, affirmed in 2005 FC 1109.

Daniels v. Canada (Minister of Indian Affairs and Northern Development), 2008 FC 823.

Daniels v. Canada (Minister of Indian Affairs and Northern Development), 2011 FC 230.

Daniels v. Canada (Minister of Indian Affairs and Northern Development), 2013 FC 6, [2013] FCJ No 4.

Daniels v. Canada (Minister of Indian Affairs and Northern Development), 2014 FCA 101, 371 DLR (4th) 725.

Daniels v. Canada (Minister of Indian Affairs and Northern Development), 2016 SCC 12, [2016] 1 SCR 99.

Daniels v. Canada (Minister of Indian Affairs and Northern Development), 2016 SCC 12, [2016] 1 SCR 99. Appellant's Factum. online (PDF): https://www. scc-csc.ca/WebDocuments-DocumentsWeb/35945/FM010_Appellants_ Harry-Daniels-et-al.pd.

"*Daniels v. Canada* (Indian Affairs and Northern Development) 2016 SCC 12 - Case Summary," Mandell Pinder LLP. 15 April 2016. http://www. mandellpinder.com/daniels-v-canada-2016-scc-12-case-summary/.

Davis, Megan Jane. "Indigenous Struggles in Standard-Setting: The United Nations Declaration on the Rights of Indigenous Peoples." *Melbourne Journal of International Law* 9 (2008): 439–71.

Davis, Natalie Zemon. "Ghosts, Kin, and Progeny: Some Features of Family Life in Early Modern France." *Daedalus* 106, no. 2 (1977): 87–114.

———. *The Return of Martin Guerre.* Cambridge, MA: Harvard University Press, 1983.

DeCoste, Frederick Charles. *On Coming to Law: An Introduction to Law in Liberal Societies.* 2nd ed. Markham, ON: LexisNexis Canada, 2007.

Delgamuukw, v. British Columbia, (1991) 79 D. L. R. (4th) 185 (B.C.S.C.)

Delgamuukw v. British Columbia, [1997] 3 SCR 1010, 153 DLR (4th) 193.

den Otter, A.A. *Civilizing the Wilderness: Culture and Nature in Pre-Confederation Canada and Rupert's Land.* Edmonton: University of Alberta Press, 2012.

Department of Justice. "Principles Respecting the Government of Canada's Relationship with Indigenous Peoples." Government of Canada. Last modified 4 October 2017. http://www.justice.gc.ca/eng/csj-sjc/principles-principes. html.

Desjardins, Bertrand. "Homogénéité ethnique de la population québécoise sous le Régime français." *Cahiers québécois de démographie* 19, no. 1 (1990): 63–76.

Deslandres, Dominique. "'. . . alors nos garçons se marieront à vos filles, & nous ne ferons plusqu'un seul peuple': Religion, genre et déploiement de la souveraineté française en Amérique aux XVIe–XVIIIe siècles – une problématique." *Revue d'histoire de l'Amérique française* 66, no. 1 (2012): 5–35.

Devine, Heather. *The People Who Own Themselves: Aboriginal Ethnogenesis in a Canadian Family, 1660–1900.* Calgary: University of Calgary Press, 2004.

Dick, Lyle. "The Seven Oaks Incident and the Construction of a Historical Tradition, 1816–1970." *Journal of the Canadian Historical Association* 2 (1991): 91–113.

Dickason, Olive P. "Metis." In *Aboriginal Peoples of Canada: A Short Introduction,* edited by Paul Robert Magocsi, 189–213. Toronto: University of Toronto Press, 2002.

Dobbin, Murray. *The One-and-a-Half Men: The Story of Jim Brady and Malcolm Norris, Metis Patriots of the Twentieth Century.* Vancouver: New Star Books, 1981.

Doerfler, Jill. *Those Who Belong: Identity, Family, Blood, and Citizenship among the White Earth Anishinaabeg.* Winnipeg: University of Manitoba Press, 2015.

Dollinger, Stefan, and Margery Fee, eds. "Road Allowance People." *DCHIP-2: The Dictionary of Canadianisms on Historical Principles,* 2nd edition. With the assistance of Baillie Ford, Alexandra Gaylie, and Gabrielle Lim. Vancouver: University of British Columbia, 2017. https://www.dchp.ca/dchp2/entries/ view/Road%252520Allowance%252520People.

Douaud, Patrick C. "Genesis." In *The Western Métis: Profile of a People,* edited by Patrick C. Douaud, 1–20. Regina: Canadian Plains Research Center, 2007.

Doyle, David. *Louis Riel: Let Justice Be Done.* Vancouver: Ronsdale Press, 2017.

Dubois, Janique. "The Emerging Policy Relationship between Canada and the Métis Nation." Institute for Research of Public Policy. https://on-irpp. org/2LJOPgf.

Dubois, Janique, and Kelly Saunders. "Explaining the Resurgence of Métis Rights: Making the Most of 'Windows of Opportunity.'" *Canadian Public Administration* 60, no. 1 (2017): 48–67.

Dumont, Gabriel. *Gabriel Dumont Speaks*. Vancouver: Talonbooks, 2009.

Duster, Troy. "A Post-Genomic Surprise: The Molecular Reinscription of Race in Science, Law and Medicine." *British Journal of Sociology* 66 (2015): 1–27.

Eastern Woodland Métis Nation Nova Scotia, Manitou Dawn. "Membership Application Information." http://easternwoodlandmetisnation.ca/main.htm (accessed 3 March 2019).

English, John. *Just Watch Me: The Life of Pierre Elliott Trudeau*. Vol. 2, *1968–2000*. Toronto: Vintage Canada, 2010.

Ens, Gerhard J. "The Battle of Seven Oaks and the Articulation of a Metis National Tradition." In *Contours of a People: Metis Family, Mobility, and History*, edited by Nicole St-Onge, Carolyn Podruchny and Brenda Macdougall, 93–119. Norman: University of Oklahoma Press, 2012.

———. *Homeland to Hinterland: The Changing Worlds of the Red River Metis in the Nineteenth Century*. Toronto: University of Toronto Press, 1996.

Ens, Gerhard J., and Ted Binnema, eds. *The Hudson's Bay Company Edmonton House Journals, Correspondence, and Reports, 1806–1821* and *1821–1826*. 2 vols. Edmonton: Alberta Records Publication Board, 2012 and 2016.

Ernst, Thom. "Talking to Joseph Boyden." *Toro Magazine*. 13 July 2009. http://toromagazine.com/features/talking-to/20090713/joseph-boyden (accessed 28 November 2017).

Evans, Mike. "Frank Beatton and the Fort St. John Fur Trade." Digital Archives Database Project, http://dadp.ok.ubc.ca/beatton.

Eyford, Douglas R. "A New Direction: Advancing Aboriginal and Treaty Rights." Indigenous and Northern Affairs Canada, April 2015, http://www.aadnc-aandc.gc.ca/eng/1426169199009/1426169236218 (accessed 23 January 2018).

Fine, Sean. "Chief Justice Says Canada Attempted "Cultural Genocide" on Aboriginals." *Globe and Mail*, 28 May 2015. https://beta.theglobeandmail.com/news/national/chief-justice-says-canada-attempted-cultural-genocide-on-aboriginals/article24688854/?ref=http://www.theglobeandmail.com&.

———. "Indigenous Peoples Can Decide Fate of Residential-School Settlement Records, Supreme Court Rules." *Globe and Mail*. 6 October 2017. https://beta.theglobeandmail.com/news/national/

records-of-residential-school-abuse-can-be-destroyed-supreme-court/
article36511037/?ref=http://www.theglobeandmail.com&.

*First Nations Child and Family Caring Society of Canada v. Attorney General of
Canada* (for the Minister of Indian and Northern Affairs Canada), 2016
CHRT 2, [2016] 2 CNLR 270.

Flanagan, Thomas. *First Nations? Second Thoughts*. Montreal: McGill-Queen's
University Press, 2008.

———. "The History of Métis Aboriginal Rights: Politics, Principle, and Policy."
Canadian Journal of Law and Society 5 (1990): 71–94.

———. *Louis "David" Riel: Prophet of the New World*. Toronto: University of
Toronto Press, 1996.

———. "New Reservations: Canadians Must Challenge the 'Aboriginal
Orthodoxy.'" *Ottawa Citizen*, 10 May 2001. http://www.tom-flanagan.ca/
uploads/articledocs/New%20reservations-%20Canadians%20must%20
challenge%20the%20aboriginal%20orthodoxy_ottawa%20citizen_may%20
2001.pdf.

———. *Riel and the Rebellion: 1885 Reconsidered*. Toronto: University of
Toronto Press, 2000.

Flood, Dawn Rae. "A Black Panther in the Great White North: Fred Hampton
Visits Saskatchewan, 1969." *Journal for the Study of Radicalism* 8, no. 2 (2014):
21–49.

Food and Agriculture Organization of the United Nations (FAO). "Free, Prior
and Informed Consent." http://www.fao.org/indigenous-peoples/our-pillars/
fpic/en/ (accessed 9 September 2018).

Forrest, Maura. "A New World Mystery: How a 17th-Century French Woman
Became Indigenous, Then Became White Again." *National Post*, 30 January
2018. http://nationalpost.com/news/canada/a-new-world-mystery-how-a-
17th-century-french-woman-became-indigenous-then-became-white-again.

Fort Chipewyan Métis Nation, Local 125 v. Alberta (Minister of Aboriginal
Relations), 2016 ABQB 713.

Foster, Martha Haroun. *We Know Who We Are: Métis Identity in a Montana
Community*. Norman: University of Oklahoma Press, 2006.

Fournier, Pierre. *Meech Lake Post-Mortem : Is Quebec Sovereignty Inevitable?*
Montreal: McGill-Queen's University Press, 2014.

Freire, Paulo. *Pedagogy of the Oppressed*. 20th anniversary edition. Translated by
Myra Bergman Ramos. New York: Continuum, 1997.

Frideres, James S. *First Nations in the Twenty-First Century*. 2nd edition. Don Mills, ON: Oxford University Press, 2016.

Friesen, Eric. "Joseph Boyden: A Spirited Voice." *Nuvo*. 28 May 2011. http://nuvomagazine.com/magazine/spring-2011/novelist-joseph-boyden.

Friesen, Gerald. *The Canadian Prairies: A History*. Toronto: University of Toronto Press. 1987.

Fromhold, Joachim. *Western Canadian People in the Past, 1600–1900 R–Z*. Mirror, AB: Heritage Consulting, 2012.

———.*The Western Cree Maski Pilon's Ban (Maskepetoon, Broken Arm) of the Plains Cree*. Vol. 1, *To 1860*. Mirror, AB: Heritage Consulting, 2012.

Gagnon, Denis. "Identité trouble et agent double: L'ontologie à l'épreuve du terrain." *Anthropologie et sociétés* 35, no. 3 (2011): 147–65.

———. "La création des 'vrais Métis': Définition identitaire, assujettissement et résistances." *Port Acadie: Revue interdisciplinaire en études acadiennes/ Port Acadie: An Interdisciplinary Review in Acadian Studies*, no. 13/14/15, (2008/2009): 295–306.

———. "La nation métisse, les autres métis et le métissage: Les paradoxes de la contingence identitaire." *Anthropologie et sociétés* 30, no. 1 (2006): 180–86.

———. "Les études métisses subventionnées et les travaux de la Chaire de recherche du Canada sur l'identité métisse." In *L'identité métisse en question: Stratégies identitaires et dynamismes culturels*, edited by Denis Gagnon and Hélène Giguère, 315–40. Québec: Presses de l'Université Laval, 2012.

Garrison, Nanibaa. "Genomic Justice for Native Americans: Impact of the Havasupai Case on Genetic Research." *Science, Technology, and Human Values* 38 (2013): 201–23.

Garroutte, Eve. *Real Indians: Identity and the Survival of Native America*. Oakland: University of California Press, 2003.

Gaudry, Adam. "Better Late Than Never? Canada's Reluctant Recognition of Métis Rights and Self- Government." *Yellowhead Institute*, Policy Brief Issue 10 (2018): 1–5.

———. "Communing with the Dead: The 'New Métis,' Métis Identity Appropriation, and the Displacement of Living Métis Culture." *American Indian Quarterly* 42, no. 2 (2018): 162–90.

———. "Kaa-tipeyimishoyaahk—'We are those who own ourselves': A Political History of Métis Self-Determination in the North-West, 1830–1870." PhD diss., University of Victoria, 2014.

———. "Respecting Métis Nationhood in Matters of Métis Identity." In *Aboriginal History: Reader,* edited by Kristin Burnett and Geoff Read, 152–63. Toronto: Oxford University Press, 2016.

Gaudry, Adam, and Chris Andersen. "*Daniels v. Canada*: Racialized Legacies, Settler Self-Indigenization and the Denial of Indigenous Peoplehood." *TOPIA: Canadian Journal of Cultural Studies* 36 (2016): 19–30.

Gaudry, Adam, and Darryl Leroux. "White Settler Revisionism and Making Métis Everywhere: The Evocation of Métissage in Quebec and Nova Scotia." *Critical Ethnic Studies* 3, no. 1 (2017): 116–42.

Gélinas, Claude. *Indiens et Eurocanadiens et le cadre social du métissage au Saguenay-Lac-Saint-Jean, XVIIe–XXe siècles.* Québec: Septentrion, 2011.

Gibson, Dale. *Law, Life, and Government at Red River.* 2 vols. Montreal: McGill-Queen's University Press, 2015.

Ginzburg, Carlo. *Clues, Myths, and the Historical Method: The Cosmos of a Sixteenth-Century Miller,* translated by John and Anne C. Tedeschi. New Jersey: Routledge, 1980.

Gordon, Robert. "Critical Legal Histories." *Stanford Law Review* 36 (1984): 57–125.

Gough, Barry M. ed. *The Journal of Alexander Henry the Younter 1799–1814.* Vol. 1, *Red River and the Journey to the Missouri.* Toronto: Champlain Society, 1988.

Government of Canada. "Update—Statement—Minister Bennett Welcomes the Supreme Court of Canada Decision on CAP/Daniels Case." 14 April 2016. https://www.newswire.ca/news-releases/statement---minister-bennett-welcomes-the-supreme-court-of-canada-decision-on-capdaniels-case-575740761.html.

Grant, George M. (Rev'd.). *Ocean to Ocean: Sandford Fleming's Expedition through Canada in 1872. Being a Diary Kept during a Journey from the Atlantic to the Pacific.* Toronto: James Campbell and Son, 1873.

Grassy Narrows First Nation v. Ontario (Natural Resources), 2014 SCC 48, [2014] SCR 447.

Gunn, Brenda. "Defining Métis People as a People: Moving beyond the Indian/Métis Dichotomy." *Dalhousie Law Journal* 38, no. 1 (2015): 413–46.

———. *Understanding and Implementing the UN Declaration on the Rights of Indigenous Peoples: An Introductory Handbook.* Winnipeg: Indigenous Bar Association, 2011.

Haida Nation v. British Columbia (Minister of Forests), 2004 SCC 73, [2004] 3 SCR 511.

Harry, Debra. "The Human Genome Diversity Project: Implications for Indigenous Peoples." *Abya Yala News* 8 (1994): 13–15.

Havard, Gilles. "'Nous ne ferons plus qu'un peuple': Le métissage en Nouvelle-France à l'époque de Champlain." In *Le nouveau monde et Champlain*, edited by Guy Martinière and Didier Poton, 85–107. Paris: Les Indes savantes, 2008.

Hellyer, Paul. *Report of the Federal Task Force on Housing and Urban Development.* Ottawa: Task Force on Housing and Urban Development, 1969.

Hopper v. R., 2008 NBCA 42, 331 NBR (2d) 177.

Hunt, Alan. "Encounters with Juridical Assemblages: Reflections on Foucault, Law and the Juridical." In *Re-reading Foucault: On Law, Power and Rights,* edited by Ben Golder, 64–84. London: Routledge, 2012.

Huot, Pascal. "La question métisse au Québec." *Histoire Québec* 21, no. 2 (2015), 10–13.

————. "Les Métis de la Boréalie: Une présence autochtone au Québec." *Rabaska: Revue d'ethnologie de l'Amérique française* 8 (2010): 77–92.

Huron-Wendat Nation of Wendake v. Canada, 2014 FC 1154.

ICCPR. International Covenant on Civil and Political Rights. 19 Dec 1966, 999 UNTS 171.

ICESCR. International Covenant on Economic, Social and Cultural Rights. 16 Dec 1966, 993 UNTS 3.

Indian Act, RSC 1985, c I–5, s 88.

Indian [also known as Aboriginal or Indigenous] and Northern Affairs Canada. Canada's Statement of Support on the United Nations Declaration on the Rights of Indigenous Peoples. Government of Canada, 30 July 2012. https://www.aadnc-aandc.gc.ca/eng/1309374239861/1309374546142.

————. Framework Agreement for Advancing Reconciliation. Last modified 31 August 2017. http://www.aadnc-aandc.gc.ca/eng/1502395273330/1502395 339312.

————. Memorandum of Understanding on Advancing Reconciliation. Government of Canada. Last modified 9 August 2017. https://www.aadnc-aandc.gc.ca/eng/1500480929912/1500480979726.

————. Statement of the Government of Canada on Indian Policy (The White Paper, 1969). Government of Canada. Updated 15 August 2010. https://www.aadnc-aandc.gc.ca/eng/1100100010189/1100100010191.

Indigenous Peoples Atlas of Canada. "Métis"; "Métis and the Constitution"; "Road Allowance People." Ottawa: The Royal Canadian Geographical Society, 2016.

Inksetter, Leila. *Initiatives et adaptations algonquines au XIXe siècle.* Québec: Septentrion, 2017.

Innes, Robert A. *Elder Brother and the Law of the People: Contemporary Kinship and Cowessess First Nation.* Winnipeg: University of Manitoba Press, 2013.

Institut de la Statistique du Québec. "Estimation de la population des régions administratives, 1er juillet des années 1986, 1991, 1996, 2001, 2006 et 2011 à 2016." 8 March 2017. http://www. stat. gouv.qc.ca/statistiques/population-demographie/structure/ra_total.htm.

International Labour Organization. *Convention Indigenous and Tribal Peoples in Independent Countries.* ILO Doc. 169. Adopted 27 June 1989, entered into force 5 September 1991. 28 ILM 1382.

Isaac, Thomas. "A Matter of National and Constitutional Import: Report of the Minister's Special Representative on Reconciliation with Métis: Section 35 Métis Rights and the Manitoba Metis Federation Decision." Indigenous and Northern Affairs Canada, June 2016. http://www.aadnc-aandc.gc.ca/eng/146 7641790303/1467641835266.

Isaac, Thomas, and Arend Hoekstra. "Identity and Federalism: Understanding the Implications of *Daniels v. Canada.*" *Supreme Court Law Review* 81 (2017): 27–51.

Jamieson, Kathleen. *Indian Women and the Law in Canada: Citizens Minus.* Ottawa: Minister of Supply and Services Canada, 1978.

"Jean-Louis Riel." *Canadian Encyclopedia.* https://www.thecanadianencyclopedia.ca/en/article/jean-louis-riel/ (accessed 1 February 2018).

Jetté, Melinda Marie. *At the Hearth of the Crossed Races: A French-Indian Community in Nineteenth-Century Oregon, 1812–1859.* Corvallis: Oregon State University Press, 2015.

Joffe, Paul. "Canada's Opposition to the UN Declaration: Legitimate Concern or Ideological Bias?" In *Realizing the UN Declaration of the Rights of Indigenous Peoples: Triumph, Hope, and Action*, edited by Jackie Hartley, Paul Joffe, and Jennifer Preston. Saskatoon: Purich Publishing, 2010.

Johnson v. M'Intosh, (1823) 21 U.S. 543.

Jordan, Mary. *To Louis from your sister who loves you: Sara Riel*. Toronto: Griffin House, 1974.

Junger, Robin M., Timothy John Murphy, and Brent Ryan. "A Thunderbolt Decision on Métis Rights: *Daniels v. Canada* (Indian Affairs and Northern Development)." McMillan LLP, April 2016, http://www.mcmillan. ca/A-Thunderbolt-Decision-on-Metis-Rights-Daniels-v-Canada-Indian-Affairs-and-Northern-Development (accessed 23 January 2018).

Kalorama Information. *Report: The Market for Direct-to-Consumer Genetic Health Testing*. 2018.

Kauanui, J. Kēhaulani. *Hawaiian Blood: Colonialism and the Politics of Sovereignty and Indigeneity*. Durham, NC: Duke University Press, 2008.

Keats-Rohan, Katherine S.B. "Pursuit of the Individual in Prosopography." In *Prosopography Approaches and Applications: A Handbook*, edited by K.S.B. Keats-Rohan. Oxford: Unit for Prosopographical Research, 2007.

Kermoal, Nathalie. "Canative, 'Un propriétaire qui fait toute la différence': Mise en place d'une société de logement métisse à Edmonton dans les années 1970." *Recherches amérindiennes au Québec* 47 no. 1, (2017): 111–19.

———. "Les rôles et les souffrances des femmes Métisses lors de la Résistance de 1870 et de la Rébellion de 1885." *Prairie Forum* 19, no. 2 (1994): 153–68.

———. "Navigating Troubled Political Waters for Better Housing: The Canative Example." In *Métis Rising*, edited by Larry Chartrand and Yvonne Boyer, UBC Press, forthcoming.

———. *Un passé métis au feminin*. Québec: Les Éditions GID, 2006.

Kimlycka, Will. "Le fédéralisme multinational au Canada: Un partenariat à repenser." In *Sortir de l'impasse: Les voies de la reconciliation*, edited by Guy Laforest and Roger Gibbins, 15–54. Montréal: IRPP, 1998.

Kolopenuk, Jessica. "'Pop-Up' Métis and the Rise of Canada's Post-Indigenous Formation." *American Anthropologist* 120 (2018): 333–37.

———. "Wiindigo Incarnate: Consuming 'Native American DNA.'" *GeneWatch* 27, no. 2 (2014): 18–20.

Kruger et al. v. The Queen, [1978] 1 SCR 104, 75 DLR (3d) 434.

"Lac Ste. Anne Pilgrimage." Wikipedia. https://en.wikipedia.org/wiki/Lac_Ste._Anne_(Alberta)#Lac_Ste._Anne_Pilgrimage (accessed 22 January 2020)

Laflèche, Father Louis. *Saint-François-Xavier*. 1er juin 1847. Ann. de la Prop. de la Foi, Québec.

Lakomäki, Sami. *Gathering Together: The Shawnee People through Diaspora and Nationhood, 1600–1870*. New Haven, CT: Yale University Press, 2014.

Laliberté, Ron. "Howard Adams, 1921–2001." *Indigenous Saskatchewan Encyclopedia*. https://teaching.usask.ca/indigenoussk/import/adams_howard_1921-2001.php (accessed 5 December 2019).

Laudicina, Nelly. "The Rules of Red River: The Council of Assiniboia and Its Impact on the Colony, 1820–1869." *Past Imperfect* 15 (2009): 36–75.

Lederman, Marsha. "Amid Heritage Controversy, Publishing Heavyweights Stand by Joseph Boyden." *Globe and Mail*, 6 January 2017.

Lee, Damien. "Adoption Is (Not) a Dirty Word: Towards an Adoption-Centric Theory of Anishinaabeg Citizenship." *First Peoples Child and Family Review: An Interdisciplinary Journal* 10, no. 1 (2015): 86–98.

Lee, Sandra Soo-Jin, Deborah A. Bolnick, Troy Duster, Pilar Ossorio, and Kimberly TallBear. "The Illusive Gold Standard in Ancestry Genetic Testing." *Science* 325 (2009): 38–39.

Leroux, Darryl. *Distorted Descent: White Claims to Indigenous Identity*. Winnipeg: University of Manitoba Press, 2019.

———. "Self-Made Métis." *Maisonneuve Magazine*, 1 November 2018, https://maisonneuve.org/article/2018/11/1/self-made-metis/ (accessed 31 August 2020).

———. "'We've Been Here for 2,000 Years:' White Settlers, Native American DNA and the Politics of Indigeneity." *Social Studies of Science* 48, no. 1 (2018): 80–100.

Leroux, Darryl, and Adam Gaudry. "Becoming Indigenous: The Rise of Eastern Métis in Canada." *The Conversation*, 25 October 2017. https://theconversation.com/becoming-indigenous-the-rise-of-eastern-metis-in-canada-80794.

"Lessons from the Ancient One." Editorial. *Nature* 533 (2016): 7.

L'Hirondelle v. Alberta [Minister of Sustainable Resource Development], 2013 ABCA 12, 542 AR 68.

Liberal Party of Canada. "Liberals Announce Reconciliation Plan for the Métis Nation." 29 September 2015. online: https://www.liberal.ca/liberals-announce-reconciliation-plan-for-the-metis-nation/.

Library and Archives Canada. "Métis Scrip Records." Updated 1 March 2012. https://www.collectionscanada.gc.ca/metis-scrip/005005-3200-e.html.

———. "Use of the Term 'Half Breed.'" Updated 27 November 2013. http://www.bac-lac.gc.ca/eng/discover/aboriginal-heritage/metis/metis-scrip-records/Pages/term-half-breed.aspx.

Linden, Amanda. "The Advocate's Archive: Walter Rudnicki and the Fight for Indigenous Rights in Canada, 1955–2010." MA thesis, University of Manitoba/University of Winnipeg, 2016.

Louis Riel. Ottawa: Société Historique du Canada, 1992.

Luo, Shiyu C., Alexander Valencia, Jinglan Zhang, Ni-Chung Lee, Jesse Slone, Baoheng Gui, Xinjian Wang, Zhuo Li, Sarah Dell, Jenice Brown, Stella Maris Chen, Yin-Hsiu Chien, Wuh-Liang Hwu, Pi-Chuan Fan, Lee-Jun Wong, Paldeep S. Atwal, and Taosheng Huang. "Biparental Inheritance of Mitochondrial DNA in Humans." *PNAS* 115 (2018): 13039–44.

Lutz, Hartmut, Murray Hamilton, and Donna Heimbecker. *Howard Adams: Otapamy! The Life of a Métis Leader in His Own Words and in Those of His Contemporaries*. Saskatoon: Gabriel Dumont Institute, 2005.

Mabo and Others v. Queensland (No. 2), (1992) 175 CLR 1.

Macdougall, Brenda. *One of the Family: Metis Culture in Nineteenth-Century Northwestern Saskatchewan*. Vancouver: UBC Press, 2011.

———. "The Power of Legal and Historical Fiction(s): The *Daniels* Decision and the Enduring Influence of Colonial Ideology." *International Indigenous Policy Journal* 7, no. 3 (2016): 1–6.

———. "Space and Place within Aboriginal Epistemological Traditions: Recent Trends in Historical Scholarship." *Canadian Historical Review* 98, no.1 (2017): 64–82.

———. "Wahkootowin: Family and Cultural Identity in Northwestern Saskatchewan Metis Communities." *Canadian Historical Review* 86, no. 3 (2006): 431–62.

Macdougall, Brenda, and Nicole St-Onge. "Rooted in Mobility: Metis Buffalo Hunting Brigades." *Manitoba History* 71 (2013): 21–32.

Madden, Jason. "*Daniels v. Canada*: Understanding the Inkblot from a Métis Nation Perspective." in *Key Developments in Aboriginal Law 2019*, edited by Thomas Isaac, 85-114. Toronto: Thomson Reuters, 2019.

Madden, Jason, Zachary Davis, and Megan Strachan. "Recent Legal Developments on Métis Consultation in Alberta—A Case Summary of *MNA Local #125 v. Alberta*." Pape Salter Teillet LLP. 7 March 2017. http://albertametis.com/

wp-content/uploads/2017/03/PST-LLP-Summary-MNA-125-Local-v-
Alberta-Feb-2017-2.pdf.

Madden, Jason, Nuri Frame, Zachary Davis, and Megan Strachan. "'Another
Chapter in the Pursuit of Reconciliation and Redress . . .' A Summary of
Daniels v. Canada at the Supreme Court of Canada." Pape Salter Teillet LLP.
19 April 2016. http://www.metisnation.org/media/652855/pst-llp-summary-
daniels-v-canada-scc-april-19-2016.pdf.

Magnet, Joseph. "*Daniels v. Canada*: Origins, Intentions, Futures." *aboriginal
policy studies* 6, no. 2 (2017): 26–47.

Malette, Sébastien. "L'identité métisse au Québec: Le fil du fléché retrouvé." *Policy
Options Politiques*, 2 November 2014.

Manitoba Act, 1870, RSC 1985, App II, No 8, s. 31.

Manitoba Metis Federation. "Manitoba Metis Federation and Government of Canada
announce joint action plan on Advancing Reconciliation." 22 September 2018.
https://www.newswire.ca/news-releases/manitoba-metis-federation-and-
government-of-canada-announce-joint-action-plan-on-advancing-reconciliation-
694047101.html.

Manitoba Metis Federation Inc. v. Canada (Attorney General) et al., [2008] 2
C.N.L.R. 52.

Manitoba Metis Federation Inc. v. Canada (Attorney General), 2013 SCC 14,
[2013] 1 SCR 623.

Marcotte, Guillaume. "Un 'tracé d'une grande valeur': La carte indienne de
Cameron et son potentiel ethnohistorique associé à l'Outaouais supérieure,
1760–1870." *Recherches amérindiennes au Québec* 45, no. 2–3 (2015): 77–91.

Martel, Gilles. *Le messianisme de Louis Riel*. Waterloo: Wilfrid Laurier University
Press, 1984.

McCann, Michael. "How Does Law Matter for Social Movements?" In *How Does
Law Matter?* edited by Bryant Garth and Austin Sarat, 76–108. Evanston, IL:
Northwestern University Press, 1998.

McIvor, Bruce. "The Downside of Tsilhqot'in Decision." *First Peoples Law*, 19
October 2016. https://www.firstpeopleslaw.com/index/articles/286.php%3E.

McLean, Donald. "1885: Métis Rebellion or Government Conspiracy." In *1885
and After: Native Society in Transition*. Edited by F. Laurie Barron and James B.
Waldram, 79–104. Regina: Canadian Plains Research Center, 1986.

McLean, John. *John McLean's Notes of a Twenty-Five Years' Service in the Hudson's
Bay Territory*. Toronto: Champlain Society, 1932.

Medley, Mark. "Boyden Admits to Mistakes, Backs Down as Indigenous Spokesperson." *Globe and Mail*, 11 January 2017.

Meili, Dianne. "Sinclair Put Métis in Canada's Constitution." *Windspeaker* 30, no. 10 (2013): 26–27.

Métis Act, S.S. 2001, c M-14.01.

Métis Association of Alberta Fonds. Glenbow Library and Archives, Calgary, AB.

Métis Nation. "Métis Nation Citizenship." http://www.metisnation.ca/index. php/who-are-the-metis/citizenship (accessed 14 March 2018).

Métis Nation. "Supreme Court of Canada Affirms Canada has a Constitutional and Jurisdictional Responsibility to Deal with the Métis Nation." 14 April 2016. https://www.metisnation.ca/index.php/news/supreme-court-of-canada-affirms-canada-has-a-constitutional-and-jurisdictional-responsibility-to-deal-with-the-metis-nation.

Métis Nation Accord, 1992 (accessed 18 May 2018). http://www.metismuseum. ca/media/document.php/148925. Worsley77.pdf.

Métis Nation of Alberta. "After 90 years, Métis Nation Within Alberta Achieves Federal Recognition of its Self-Government—Métis Nation of Alberta and Canada Sign Historic Agreement in Ottawa." 27 June 2019. http:// albertametis.com/wp-content/uploads/2019/07/MNA-MGRSA-FAQ-DOCUMENT-V7.pdf.

———. "Bylaws." http://albertametis.com/governance/bylaws/ (accessed 23 January 2018).

———. "Governance." http://albertametis.com/governance.

Métis Nation of Alberta–Canada Framework Agreement for Advancing Reconciliation. 16 November 2017. http://albertametis.com/wp-content/ uploads/2017/02/MNA-GOC-Framework-Advancing-Reconciliation_ SIGNED.pdf.

Métis Nation of Ontario. "Métis Nation of Ontario and Canada Sign Breakthrough Agreement on Self-Government." 27 June 2019. http://www. metisnation.org/media/655331/2019-06-27-metis-government-recognition-and-self-government-agreement.pdf.

Métis Nation of Saskatchewan. "Métis Nation-Saskatchewan Signs Historic Self-Governance Agreement with the Government of Canada." 27 June 2019. MNS: https://metisnationsk.com/wp-content/uploads/2019/06/ M%C3%A9tis-Government-Recognition-and-Self-Government-Agreement-. pdf.

Métis Settlements Accord Implementation Act, SA 1990, c M-14.5.

Métis Settlements Act, RSA 2000, c M-14.

Métis Settlements General Council. Framework Agreement for Advancing Reconciliation between MSGC and Canada. http://msgcweb.ca/wp-content/uploads/2019/01/FRAMEWORK-AGREEMENT_001missingPP.pdf (accessed 22 October 2019).

Métis Settlements Lands Protection Act, SA 1990, c M-14.8.

Metis Settlements of Alberta, "Engaging with Canada."

Michaux, Émmanuel. "Ni Amérindiens ni Eurocanadiens: Une approche néomoderne du culturalisme métis au Canada." PhD diss., Université Laval, 2014.

Miranda, L. "Uploading the Local: Assessing the Contemporary Relationship between Indigenous People's Land Tenure Systems and International Human Rights Law Regarding the Allocation of Traditional Lands and Resources in Latin America." *Oregon Review of International Law* 10, no. 2 (2008): 419–52.

Mitchell v. Minister of National Revenue, 2001 SCC 33, [2001] 1 SCR 911.

Mohawks of the Bay of Quinte v. the Minister of Indian Affairs and Northern Development, 2013 FC 669.

Moreton-Robinson, Aileen. *The White Possessive: Property, Power, and Indigenous Sovereignty*. Minneapolis: University of Minnesota Press, 2015.

Morin, Gail. *Métis Families: A Genealogical Compendium*. 11 vols. Self-published, 2016 editions.

Morris, Alexander. *The Treaties of Canada with the Indians of Manitoba and the North-West Territories*. Toronto: Belfords, Clarke, 1880.

Morton, W.L. "Pierre-Guillaume Sayer." *Dictionary of Canadian Biography Online*. http://www.biographi.ca/en/bio/sayer_pierre_guillaume_7E.html (accessed 30 January 2018).

Musqueam Indian Band v. Musqueam Indian Band (Board of Review), 2016 SCC 36, [2016] 2 SCR 3.

Narine, Shari. "Métis Council, CAP May Tussle on Daniels." *Windspeaker* 34, no. 3 (2016). https://ammsa.com/publications/windspeaker/m%C3%A9tis-council-cap-may-tussle-daniels.

Nash, Catherine. *Genetic Geographies: The Trouble with Ancestry*. Minneapolis: University of Minnesota Press, 2015.

———. "Genetic Kinship." *Cultural Studies* 18 (2004): 1–33.

Native Council of Canada. Brief presented to the Honourable Gerard Pelletier, Secretary of State, by Native Council of Canada and its member associations, June 6, 1972 (Ottawa: Native Council of Canada, 1972), AMICUS No. 56078.

Native Council of Canada (with commentary by Harry Daniels). *Declaration of Métis and Indian Rights*. Ottawa: Native Council of Canada, 1979.

Native Women's Assn. of Canada v. Canada, [1994] 3 SCR 627, 119 DLR (4th) 224.

Nelson, Alondra. "Genetic Genealogy Testing and the Pursuit of African Ancestry." *Social Studies of Science* 38 (2008): 759–83.

Nuechterlein, Donald E. "The Demise of Canada's Confederation." *Political Science Quarterly* 96, no. 2 (1981): 225–40.

Opening statement of Prime Minister Trudeau at the First Ministers Conference on Aboriginal Constitutional Matters. Ottawa, 8–9 March 1983.

Organization of American States (OAS). "Inter-American Commission on Human Rights, Indigenous and Tribal Peoples' Rights Over Their Ancestral Lands and Natural Resources: Norms and Jurisprudence of the Inter-American Human Rights System." OEA/Ser.L/V/II. Doc. 56/09. 2009.

Osler, Edmund B., and Rossel Vien. *Louis Riel: Un homme à pendre*. Montréal: Éditions du Jour, 1964.

O'Toole, Darren. "A Legal Look at the Métis of Chibougamau." *The Nation: First Nation Cree Newspaper Serving Aboriginal Canada*, 3 March 2017. http://www.nationnews.ca/legal-look-metis-chibougamau/.

———. "Y a-t-il des communautés métisses au Québec?: Une perspective juridique." *Nouveaux cahiers du socialisme*, no. 18 (2017): 29–36.

Owram, Doug. "Conspiracy and Treason: The Red River Resistance From an Expansionist Perspective." *Prairie Forum* 3, no. 2 (1978): 157–74.

Palmater, Pamela. "Don't Partake in Celebrations over New Supreme Court Ruling on Métis Just Yet." *Rabble.ca* (blog), 15 April 2016. http://rabble.ca/blogs/bloggers/pamela-palmater/2016/04/dont-partake-celebrations-over-new-supreme-court-ruling-on-m%C3%A9.

Palmer, Brian. *Canada's 1960s: The Ironies of Identity in a Rebellious Era*. Toronto: University of Toronto Press, 2009.

Patterson, Stephen E. "Eighteenth-Century Treaties." *Native Studies Review* 18, no. 1 (2009): 25–52.

———. "Land Grants for Loyalists: A Report Prepared for the Department of Justice Canada." File no. CI 81-01-01010. Winnipeg, 31 October 2005.

Paulette et al. v. The Queen, [1977] 2 SCR 628, 72 DLR (3d) 161.

Payment, Diane. "Batoche after 1885, A Society in Transition." In *1885 and After: Native Society in Transition,* edited by F. Laurie Barron and James B. Waldram, 173–87. Regina: Canadian Plains Research Center, 1986.

———. *The Free People—Li Gens Libres: A History of the Metis Community of Batoche, Saskatchewan.* Calgary: University of Calgary Press, 2009.

———. *"The Free People—Otipemisiwak": Batoche, Saskatchewan, 1870–1930.* Ottawa: Canadian Parks Service, 1990.

———. "Une femme en vaut deux—'Strong Like Two People': Marie Fisher Gaudet of Fort Good Hope, Northwest Territories." In *Contours of a People: Metis Family, Mobility, and History,* edited by Nicole St-Onge, Carolyn Podruchny, and Brenda Macdougall, 265–99. Norman: University of Oklahoma Press, 2012.

Pelta, Anne. "La judiciarisation de l'identité métisse ou l'éveil des Métis au Québec." PhD diss., Université Laval, 2015.

"The People of the Red River." *Harper's New Monthly Magazine,* January 1859.

Perego, Ugo A., Norman Angerhofer, Maria Pala, Anna Olivieri, Hovirag Lancioni, Baharak Hooshiar Kashani, Valeria Carossa, Jayne E. Ekins, Alberto Gómez-Carballa, Gabriela Huber, Bettina Zimmermann, Daniel Corach, Nora Babudri, Fausto Panara, Natalie M. Myres, Walther Parson, Ornella Semino, Antonio Salas, Scott R. Woodward, Alessandro Achilli and Antonio Torroni. "The Initial Peopling of the Americas: A Growing Number of Founding Mitochondrial Genomes from Beringia." *Genome Research* 20 (2010): 1174–9.

Peters, Evelyn, Matthew Stock, and Adrian Werner. *Rooster Town: The History of an Urban Métis Community, 1901–1961.* Winnipeg: University of Manitoba Press, 2019.

Peterson, Jacqueline. "Gathering at the River: the Métis Peopling of the Northern Plains." In *The Fur Trade in North Dakota,* edited by Virginia Heidenreich, 47–70. Bismark: State Historical Society of North Dakota, 1990.

———. "Red River Redux: Métis Ethnogenesis and the Great Lakes Region." In *Contours of a People: Metis Family, Mobility, and History,* edited by Nicole St-Onge, Carolyn Podruchny, and Brenda Macdougall, 22–58. Norman: University of Oklahoma Press, 2012.

Peterson, Jaqueline, and Jennifer Brown. *The New Peoples: Being and Becoming Métis in North America*. Winnipeg: University of Manitoba Press, 1985.

Petten, Cheryl. "Friends Say Goodbye to Harry Daniels." *Alberta Sweetgrass* 1, no. 10 (2004): 2.

Pigeon, Émilie. "Au om du Bon Dieu et du Buffalo: Metis Lived Catholicism on the Northern Plains." PhD diss., York University, 2017.

———. "Lost in Translation: The Michif French Diaries of William Davis." *Champlain Society*, 2017. http://champlainsociety.utpjournals.press/findings-trouvailles/the-michif-french-diaries-of-william-davis (accessed 26 November 2017).

Podruchny, Carolyn, Jesse Thistle, and Elizabeth Jameson. "Women on the Margins of Imperial Plots: Farming on Borrowed Land." *Journal of the Canadian Historical Association* 29, no. 1 (2018): 158–81.

Préfontaine, Darren. *Gabriel Dumont: Li Chef Michif in Images and Words*. Saskatoon: Gabriel Dumont Institute, 2011.

Provincial Archives of Manitoba. District of Assiniboia Court Records. 17 May 1849, 151.

Pulla, Siomonn P. "Regional Nationalisms or National Mobilization." In *Métis in Canada: History, Identity, Law, and Politics*, edited by Christopher Adams, Gregg Dahl, and Ian Peach, 397–432. Edmonton: University of Alberta Press, 2013.

R. v. Badger, [1996] 1 SCR 771, 133 DLR (4th) 324.

R v. Belhumeur, 2007 SKPC 11.

R. v. Bernard, 2005 SCC 43.

R. v. Blais, [2003] 2 S.C.R. 236, 2003 SCC 44 (CanLII).

R. v. Côté, [1996] 3 SCR 139, 1996 CanLII 170 (SCC).

R. v. Gladstone, [1996] 2 SCR 723, 137 DLR (4th) 648.

R. v. Hirsekorn, 2011 ABQB 682, 520 AR 60.

R. v. Kapp, 2008 SCC 41, [2008] 2 SCR 483.

R. v. Kelley, 2007 ABCA 41, 413 AR 269.

R. v. Marshall, [1999] 3 S.C.R. 456.

R. v. Marshall, 2005 SCC 43, [2005] 2 SCR 220.

R. v. Nikal, [1996] 1 S.C.R. 1013.

R. v. Pamajewon, [1996] 2 S.C.R. 821.

R. v. Powley, 196 DLR (4th) 221 (Ont CA), 2003 SCC 43, 2 SCR 207.

R. v. Powley, 2003 SCC 43, [2003] 2 SCR 207.

R. v. Sparrow, [1990] 1 SCR 1075, 70 DLR (4th) 385.

R. v. Tronson, [1931], 57 C.C.C. 383, (1932).

R. v. Van der Peet, [1996] 2 SCR 507, 137 DLR (4th) 289.

Rasmussen, Morten, Martin Sikora, Anders Albrechtsen, Thorfinn Sand Korneliussen, J. Víctor Moreno-Mayar, G. David Poznik, Christoph P. E. Zollikofer, Marcia S. Ponce de León, Morten E. Allentoft, Ida Moltke, Hákon Jónsson, Cristina Valdiosera, Ripan S. Malhi, Ludovic Orlando, Carlos D. Bustamante, Thomas W. Stafford Jr, David J. Meltzer, Rasmus Nielsen and Eske Willerslev. "The Ancestry and Affiliations of Kennewick Man." *Nature* 523 (2015): 455–58.

Ray, Arthur J. *Telling It to the Judge: Taking Native History to Court*. Montreal: McGill-Queen's University Press, 2012.

Re Paulette et al. and Registrar of Titles (No.2), 42 D.L.R. (3d) 8, [1973] 6W.W.R. 115 (N.W.T.S.C.)

Reardon, Jenny, and Kim TallBear. "'Your DNA Is *Our* History': Genomics, Anthropology, and the Construction of Whiteness as Property." *Current Anthropology* 53 (2012): S233–45.

Reference as to whether "Indians" in s. 91(24) of the BNA Act Includes Eskimo Inhabitants of the Province of Quebec, [1939] SCR 104, 1939 CanLII 22 (SCC).

Reference re: British North America Act, 1867 (UK), s. 91, [1939] SCR 104.

Reference re Same-Sex Marriage, [2004] 3 S.C.R. 698, 2004 SCC 79.

Reference re: Secession of Quebec, [1998] 2 SCR 217.

Reid, Jennifer. *Louis Riel and the Creation of Modern Canada*. Santa Fe: University of New Mexico Press, 2008.

Relethford, John H., and Deborah A. Bolnick. *Reflections of Our Past: How Human History Is Revealed in Our Genes*. Boulder, CO: Westview Press, 2017.

Rex v. Syliboy, [1929] 1 D.L.R. 307.

Rhéaume, Gene. *Housing for Native People: A Low Income Housing Policy for 1971*. Ottawa: CMHC Policy Planning Group, 1970.

Riel, Louis. *The Collected Writings of Louis Riel/Les écrits complets de Louis Riel,* Vol. 3 ed. Thomas Flanagan et al. (Edmonton: University of Alberta 1985)

Riel to Dubuc, May 27, 1874. Exhibit 1–1001 as cited in *Manitoba Metis Federation Inc. v. Canada (Attorney General) et al.* [2008] 2 C.N.L.R. 52, File No.: CI 81-01-01010. Manitoba Metis Federation, Plaintiff's Final Argument, 1026.

Rindisbacher, Peter. *A Halfcast and His Two Wives.* 1825–26. Watercolour on wove paper, 26.8 X 21.3 cm. Library and Archives Canada, Acc. No. 1973-84-1. https://www.bac-lac.gc.ca/eng/CollectionSearch/Pages/record.aspx?app=FonAndCol&IdNumber=2835810.

Rio Tinto Alcan Inc. v. Carrier Sekani Tribal Council, 2010 SCC 43, [2010] 2 SCR 650.

Rivard, Étienne. "The Indefensible In-Betweenness or the Spatio-Legal Arbitrariness of the Métis Fact in Quebec." *Justice sociale /Spatial Justice* 11 (2017): 1–16.

———. "Prairie and Quebec Metis Territoriality: "Interstices territoriales" and the Cartography of In-Between Identity." PhD diss., University of British Columbia, 2004.

———. "Trajectoires cartographiques et métisses de la Franco-Amérique." In *Franco-Amérique,* edited by Dean Louder and Éric Waddell, 313–34. Québec: Septentrion, 2017.

Rose, Nikolas, and Marianna Valverde. "Governed by Law?," *Social and Legal Studies* 7, no. 4 (1998): 541–51.

Ross, Alexander. *The Red River Settlement: Its Rise, Progress, and Present State. With Some Account of the Native Races and Its General History to the Present Day.* London: Smith, Elder and Co., 1856.

Ross, Shane. "Native Council of P.E.I. Applauds Supreme Court Ruling." *CBC News,* 14 April 2016. https://www.cbc.ca/news/canada/prince-edward-island/pei-native-council-indian-status-court-ruling-1.3535674.

Rousseau, Louis-Philippe. "Ni tout l'un, ni tout l'autre." PhD diss., Université Laval, 2012.

Royal, Charmaine D., John Novembre, Stephanie M. Fullerton, David B. Goldstein, Jeffrey C. Long, Michael J. Bamshad, and Andrew G. Clark. "Inferring Genetic Ancestry: Opportunities, Challenges, and Implications." *American Journal of Human Genetics* 86 (2010): 661–73.

Royal Commission on Aboriginal Peoples. *Restructuring the Relationship,* Part 1. Vol. 2 of *Report of the Royal Commission on Aboriginal Peoples.* Ottawa: Communication Group, 1996.

———. *Perspectives and Realities.* Vol. 4 of *Report of the Royal Commission on Aboriginal Peoples.* Ottawa: Libraxus, 1997.

Rupertsland Centre for Métis Research. "Métis Scrip in Alberta." Edmonton: Rupertsland Centre for Métis Research and Métis Nation of Alberta, 2018.

Ryan, William. *Blaming the Victim.* Revised ed. New York: Vintage Books, 1976.

Salée, Daniel, and Carole Lévesque. "Representing Aboriginal Self-Government and First Nations/State Relations: Political Agency and the Management of the Boreal Forest in Eeyou Istchee." *International Journal of Canadian Studies,* 41 (2010): 99–135.

Sanders, Ronald. *Lost Tribes and Promised Lands: The Origins of American Racism.* Boston: Little, Brown and Company, 1978.

Sarat, Austin, and Thomas Kearns. "The Cultural Lives of Law." In *Law in the Domains of Culture,* edited by Austin Sarat and Thomas Kearns, 1–20. Ann Arbor: University of Michigan Press, 1998.

Saul, John Ralston. *A Fair Country: Telling Truths about Canada.* Toronto: Viking Canada, 2008.

Saunders, Kelly L. "No Other Weapon: Métis Political Organization and Governance in Canada." In *Métis in Canada: History, Identity, Law, and Politics,* edited by Christopher Adams, Gregg Dahl, and Ian Peach, 339–96. Edmonton: University of Alberta Press, 2013.

Saunders, Kelly L., and Janique Dubois. *Métis Politics and Governance in Canada.* Vancouver: UBC Press, 2019.

Schroeder, Kari Bitt, Theodore Schurr, Jeffrey C. Long, N.A. Rosenberg, Michael H. Crawford, L.A. Tarskaia, Ludmila Osipova, S.I. Zhadanov, and D.G. Smith. "A Private Allele Ubiquitous in the Americas." *Biology Letters* 3 (2007): 218–23.

Sealey, D. Bruce, and Antoine S. Lussier. *The Métis: Canada's Forgotten People.* Manitoba Metis Federation, 1975.

Senate of Canada. "'The People Who Own Themselves': Recognition of Métis Identity in Canada." Ottawa: Government of Canada, 2013.

———. "Proceedings of the Standing Senate Committee on Aboriginal Peoples, Issue no 25." 23 October 2012 and 24 October 2012, 25:26–25:27, 25:29.

Sga'nism Sim'augit (Chief Mountain) v. Canada (AG), 2013 BCCA 49.

Shanks, Signa A. Daum. "Commentary: The Wastelander Life: Living Before and After the Release of *Daniels v. Canada.*" *Osgoode Hall Law Journal* 54 (2017): 1341–58.

Siggins, Maggie. *Marie-Anne: The Extraordinary Life of Louis Riel's Grandmother.* Toronto: McClelland and Stewart, 2008.

———. *Riel: A Life of Revolution.* Toronto: HarperCollins, 1994.

Simeon, Richard. "An Overview of the Trudeau Constitutional Proposals." *Alberta Law Review* 19, no. 3 (1981): 391–400.

Simmons, Deborah. "In Tribute to Howard Adams." *Studies in Political Economy* 68 (2002): 5–12.

Simon, Cheryl, and Judy Clark. "Exploring Inequities under the Indian Act." *University of New Brunswick Law Journal* 64 (2013): 103–22.

Simpson, Leanne Betasamosake, ed. *Lighting the Eighth Fire: The Liberation, Resurgence, and Protection of Indigenous Nations.* Winnipeg: Arbeiter Ring Publishing, 2008.

Skutnabb-Kangas, Tove, and Robert Phillipson. "Submersion Education and the Killing of Languages in Canada: Linguistic Human Rights and Language Revitalization in the USA and Canada." In *Language Rights*, vol. 3, *Language Endangerment and Revitalisation; Language Rights Charters and Declarations*, edited by Tove Skutnabb-Kangas and Robert Phillipson. London and New York: Routledge, 2017.

Slattery, Brian. *Canadian Native Law Cases.* Vol. 1, 1763–1869. Saskatoon: Native Law Centre, 1980.

———. *Canadian Native Law Cases.* Vol. 2, 1870–1890. Saskatoon: Native Law Centre, 1981.

Slattery, Brian, and Linda Charlton. *Canadian Native Law Cases.* Vol. 3, 1891–1910. Saskatoon: Native Law Centre, 1985.

Sleeper-Smith, Susan. *Indian Women and French Men: Rethinking Cultural Encounter in the Western Great Lakes.* Amherst: University of Massachusetts Press, 2001.

Snyder, Charles R., and Carol E. Ford. *Coping with Negative Life Events: Clinical and Social Psychological Perspectives.* New York: Springer Science, 2013.

Sprague, Douglas. *Canada and the Métis, 1869–1885.* Waterloo, ON: Wilfrid Laurier University Press, 1988.

Sprague, Doug N. "The Manitoba Land Question, 1870–1882." *Journal of Canadian Studies/Revue d'études canadiennes* 15, no. 3 (1980): 74–84.

Sprague, Douglas N., and R.P. Frye. *The Genealogy of the First Metis Nation: The Development and Dispersal of the Red River Settlement, 1820–1900.* Winnipeg: Pemmican Publications, 1983.

Spry, Graham. "Canada: Notes on Two Ideas of Nation in Confrontation." *Journal of Contemporary History* 6, no. 1 (1971): 173–96.

Spry, Irene M. "The Métis and Mixed-Bloods of Rupert's Land before 1870." In *The New Peoples*, edited by Jacqueline Peterson and Jennifer S.H. Brown, 95–118. Winnipeg: University of Manitoba Press, 1981.

Stanley, George. *Louis Riel.* Toronto: Ryerson Press, 1963.

Statistics Canada. "Aboriginal Peoples in Canada: Key Results from the 2016 Census." http://www.statcan.gc.ca/daily-quotidien/171025/dq171025a-eng.htm (accessed 8 January 2018).

St. Catherine's Milling and Lumber Company v. The Queen, (1888), 14 A.C. 46 (P.C.)

Stevenson, Mark. "Section 91(24) and Canada's Legislative Jurisdiction with Respect to the Métis." *Indigenous Law Journal*, no. 1 (2002): 237–62.

Stewart, Sharon. *Louis Riel: Firebrand.* Montreal: XYZ Publishing, 2007.

Stone, Lawrence. "Prosopography." *Daedalus* 100, no. 1 (1971): 46–79.

St-Onge, Nicole. *Saint-Laurent, Manitoba: Evolving Métis Identities, 1850–1914.* Regina: University of Regina Press, 2004.

———. Voyageur Contracts Database. Centre du patrimonie. http://shsb.mb.ca/en/Voyageurs_database.

St-Onge, Nicole, Mike Evans, Chris Andersen, Ramon Lawrence, and Brenda Macdougall. Digital Archives Database (DAD) Project. http://dadp.ok.ubc.ca.

St-Onge, Nicole, Carolyn Podruchny, and Brenda Macdougall, eds. *Contours of a People: Metis Family, Mobility, and History.* Norman: University of Oklahoma Press, 2012.

Sturm, Circe. *Becoming Indian: The Struggle over Cherokee Identity in the Twenty-first Century.* Santa Fe: School for Advanced Research Press, 2010.

Sussman, Robert Wald. *The Myth of Race: The Troubling Persistence of an Unscientific Idea.* Boston: Harvard University Press, 2016.

TallBear, Kim. "Genomic Articulations of Indigeneity." *Social Studies of Science* 3 (2013b): 509–33.

————. "Molecular Death and Redface Reincarnation: Indigenous Appropriations in the U.S. and Canada." Keynote address, "*Daniels*: In and Beyond the Law" conference, hosted by the Rupertsland Centre for Métis Research, University of Alberta, Edmonton, 26–28 January 2017.

————. "Narratives of Race and Indigeneity in the Genographic Project." *Journal of Law, Medicine, and Ethics* 35 (2007): 412–24.

————. *Native American DNA: Tribal Belonging and the False Promise of Genetic Science*. Minneapolis: University of Minnesota Press, 2013.

————. "Who Owns the Ancient One?" *Buzzfeed News*, 23 July 2015. https://goo.gl/fHZchd.

Tamarkin, Noah. "Genetic Diaspora: Producing Knowledge of Genes and Jews in Rural South Africa." *Cultural Anthropology* 29 (2014): 552–74.

Tamm, Erika, Toomas Kivisild, Maere Reidla, Mait Metspalu, David Glenn Smith, Connie J. Mulligan, Claudio M. Bravi, Olga Rickards, Cristina Martinez-Labarga, Elsa K. Khusnutdinova, Sardana A. Fedorova, Maria V. Golubenko, Vadim A. Stepanov, Marina A. Gubina, Sergey I. Zhadanov, Ludmila P. Ossipova, Larisa Damba, Mikhail I. Voevoda, Jose E. Dipierri, Richard Villems, and Ripan S. Malhi. "Beringian Standstill and Spread of Native American Founders." *PLoS One* 2, no. 9 (2007): e829.

Taylor, Charles. *Reconciling the Solitudes: Essays on Canadian Federalism and Nationalism*. Montreal: McGill-Queen's University Press, 1993.

Teillet, Jean. *Métis Law in Canada*. Vancouver: Pape Salter Teillet, 2013.

————. *The Northwest Is Our Mother: The Story of Louis Riel's People, the Métis Nation*. Toronto: HarperCollins Publishers, 2019.

Teillet, Jean, and Carly Teillet. "Devoid of Principle: The Federal Court Determination That Section 91(24) of the Constitution Act, 1867 Is a Race-Based Provision." *Indigenous Law Journal* 13, no. 1 (2016): 12.

Thomas, Lewis H. "Louis Riel." *Dictionary of Canadian Biography Online*. http://www.biographi.ca/en/bio/riel_louis_1844_85_11E.html (accessed 1 January 2016).

Thorne, Tanis C. *The Many Hands of My Relations: French and Indian on the Lower Missouri*. Columbia: University of Missouri Press, 1996.

Tobler, Ray, Adam Rohrlach, Julien Soubrier, Pere Bover, Bastien Llamas, Jonathan Tuke, Nigel Bean, Ali Abdullah-Highfold, Shane Agius, Amy O'Donoghue, Isabel O'Loughlin, Peter Sutton, Fran Zilio, Keryn Walshe, Alan N Williams, Chris SM Turney, Matthew Williams, Stephen M Richards, Robert J Mitchell,

Emma Kowal, John R, Stephen, Lesley Williams, Wolfgang Haak and Alan Cooper. "Ancestral Mitogenomes Reveal 50,000 Years of Regionalism in Australia." *Nature* 544 (2017): 180–84.

Todd, Zoe. "From a Fishy Place: Examining Canadian State Law Applied in the Daniels Decision from the Perspective of Métis Legal Orders." *TOPIA: Canadian Journal of Cultural Studies* 36 (2016): 43–57.

Tough, Frank J. Métis Archival Project. MNC Historical Online Database. http://metisnationdatabase.ualberta.ca/MNC/about.jsp.

Tough, Frank J., and Kathleen Dimmer. "'Great Frauds and Abuses': Institutional Innovation at the Colonial Frontier of Private Property: Case Studies of the Individualization of Maori, Indian and Métis Lands." In *Settler Economies in World History*, edited by C. Lloyd, J. Metzer and R. Sutch, 205–49. Leiden: Brill, 2013.

Tough, Frank, and Erin McGregor. "'The Right to the Land May be Transferred': Archival Records as Colonial Text—A Narrative of Métis Scrip." In *Natives and Settlers, Now and Then: Historical Issues and Current Perspectives on Treaties and Land Claims in Canada*, edited by Paul W. DePasquale, 33–63. Edmonton: University of Alberta Press, 2007.

Tremblay, Guy. "Création d'une première communauté métisse dans le Nord du Québec." *La Sentinelle*, 31 January 2017. http://www.lasentinelle.ca/creation-dune-premiere-communaute-metisse-nord-quebec/.

Troupe, Cheryl. "Métis Women: Social Structure, Urbanization, and Political Activism, 1850–1980." MA thesis, University of Saskatchewan, 2010.

Trudeau, Justin, Prime Minister. Mandate letter to Dr. Carolyn Bennett, Minister of Indigenous and Northern Affairs. 2015. Last modified 12 November 2015. https://pm.gc.ca/eng/minister-indigenous-and-northern-affairs-mandate-letter_2015.

Truth and Reconciliation Commission of Canada. *Calls to Action*. Truth and Reconciliation Commission of Canada, 2012. www.trc.ca.

———. *Final Report of the Truth and Reconciliation Commission of Canada*. Truth and Reconciliation Commission of Canada, 2015. www.trc.ca.

Tsilhqot'in Nation v. British Columbia, 2014 SCC 44, [2014] 2 SCR 257.

Tsilhqot'in Nation v. British Columbia, [2014] SCC 44 at Supreme Court of Canada (website) "Webcast of the Hearing on 2013-11-07" Case number 34986 https://www.scc-csc.ca/case-dossier/info/webcastview-webdiffusionvue-eng.aspx?cas=34986&id=2013/2013-11-07--34986&date=2013-11-07&fp=n&audio=n.

Turner, Dale. *This Is Not a Peace Pipe: Towards a Critical Indigenous Philosophy.*
Toronto: University of Toronto Press, 2006.

Turpel, Mary Ellen. "Home/Land." *Canadian Journal of Family Law* 10, no. 1
(1991): 17–40.

United Nations Commission on Human Rights, Sub-Commission on the
Promotion and Protection of Human Rights. Commentary on the Norms
on the Responsibilities of Transnational Corporations and Other Business
Enterprises with Regard to Human Rights, 55th Sess, 2003, UN Doc. E/
CN.4/Sub.2/2003/38/Rev.2.

United Nations Committee on Economic, Social and Cultural Rights. *Concluding
Observations of the Committee on Economic, Social and Cultural Rights.* 4
September 2006. Morocco, UN Doc. E/C.12/MAR/CO/3.

United Nations Declaration on the Rights of Indigenous Peoples. GA Res 61/295,
UNGAOR, 61st Sess, 2007. UN Doc A/RES/61/295.

United Nations Declaration on the Rights of Indigenous Peoples. Indian and
Northern Affairs Canada. Last modified 3 August 2017. http://www.aadnc-
aandc.gc.ca/eng/1309374407406/1309374458958.

United Nations Educational, Scientific and Cultural Organization (UNESCO),
February 1990. Final Report and Recommendations of an International
Meeting of Experts on the Further Study of the Concept of the Right of
People for UNESCO. UN Doc SHS-89/Conf 602/7.

United Nations General Assembly. Resolution 61/295: Declaration on the Rights
of Indigenous Peoples. 13 September 2007. UN Doc. A/61/67, Annex.

United Nations Human Rights Committee. *Concluding Observations of the
Human Rights Committee: Canada.* 20 April 2006. UN Doc. CCPR/C/
CAN/CO/5.

United Nations Human Rights Council. UN Expert Mechanism on the Rights of
Indigenous Peoples. *Indigenous Peoples and the Right to Participate in Decision-
Making.* Advice No. 2 (2011). http://www.ohchr.org/Documents/Issues/
IPeoples/EMRIP/ Advice2_Oct2011.pdf.

United Nations Permanent Forum on Indigenous Issues. Report of the
International Workshop on "Methodologies Regarding Free, Prior and
Informed Consent and Indigenous Peoples." UNESCOR, 4th Sess., 2005.
UN Doc. E/C.19/2005/1.

Vago, Steven, and Adie Nelson. *Law and Society.* Toronto: Pearson Prentice Hall,
2003.

Van Kirk, Sylvia. *Many Tender Ties: Women in Fur Trade Society in Western Canada, 1670–1870*. Winnipeg: Watson and Dwyer, 1980.

Vermette, D'Arcy. "Beyond Doctrines of Dominance: Conceptualizing a Path to Legal Recognition and Affirmation of the Manitoba Métis Treaty." PhD diss., University of Ottawa, 2012.

———. "Colonialism and the Process of Defining Aboriginal People." *Dalhousie Law Journal* 31, no. 1 (2008): 211–46.

———. "Dizzying Dialogue: Canadian Courts and the Continuing Justification of the Dispossession of Aboriginal Peoples." *Windsor Yearbook of Access to Justice* 29, no. 1 (2011): 55–72.

———. "Rejecting the Standard Discourse on the Dispossession of Métis Lands in Manitoba." *aboriginal policy studies* 6, no. 2 (2017): 87–119.

Virtual Museum of Métis Culture and History. Gabriel Dumont Institute. http://www.metismuseum.ca.

Vowel, Chelsea, and Darryl Leroux. "White Settler Antipathy and the Daniels Decision." *TOPIA: Canadian Journal of Cultural Studies* 36 (2016): 30–42.

Vrooman, Nicholas C.P. "*The Whole Country Was . . . 'One Robe'": The Little Shell Tribe's America*. Helena, MT: Drumlummon Institute, 2012.

Wagner, Vit. "Northern Roots Still Fuel Joseph Boyden's Fiction." *Toronto Star*. 20 September 2008. https://www.thestar.com/entertainment/books/2008/09/20/northern_roots_still_fuel_joseph_boydens_fiction.html.

Wailoo, Keith, Alondra Nelson, and Catherine Lee. *Genetics and the Unsettled Past: The Collision of DNA, Race, and History*. New Brunswick, NJ: Rutgers University Press, 2012.

Waiser, Bill. "History Matters: Round Prairie Métis Made Saskatoon Their Home in Early 20th Century." *Saskatoon Star Phoenix*. 25 April 2017. https://thestarphoenix.com/opinion/columnists/history-matters-round-prairie-metis-made-saskatoon-their-home-in-early-20th-century.

Walker, Alexa, Brian Egan, and George Nicholas, eds. *DNA and Indigeneity: The Changing Role of Genetics in Indigenous Rights, Tribal Belonging, and Repatriation*. Symposium Proceedings, Simon Fraser University, 2016.

Walker, Ryan. "Aboriginal Self-Determination and Social Housing in Urban Canada: A Story of Convergence and Divergence." *Urban Studies* 45, no. 1 (2008): 185–205.

————. "Engaging the Urban Aboriginal Population in Low-Cost Housing Initiatives: Lessons from Winnipeg." *Canadian Journal of Urban Research* 12, no. 1 (2003): 99–118.

————. "Social Housing and the Role of Aboriginal Organizations in Canadian Cities." *IRPP Choices* 14, no. 4 (2008): 1–18.

Ward, Rachel. "Nova Scotia Indigenous Groups Welcome 'Landmark' Supreme Court Ruling." *CBC News*, 14 April 2016. https://www.cbc.ca/news/canada/nova-scotia/nova-scotia-metis-non-status-supreme-court-1.3536001.

Ward, T. "The Right to Free, Prior, and Informed Consent: Indigenous Peoples' Participation Rights within International Law." *Northwest Journal of International Human Rights* 10, no. 2 (2011): 54–84.

Watson, Bruce McIntyre. *Lives Lived West of the Divide: A Biographical Dictionary of Fur Traders Working West of the Rockies, 1793–1858.* 3 vols. Kelowna: Centre for Social, Spatial and Economic Justice, University of British Columbia Okanagan, 2010.

Webber, Jeremy. "Relations of Force and Relations of Justice: The Emergence of Normative Community between Colonists and Aboriginal Peoples." *Osgoode Hall Law Journal* 33 (1995): 623–60.

Weekes, Mary. *The Last Buffalo Hunter.* Saskatoon: Fifth House Publishers, 1994.

Weinstein, John. *Quiet Revolution West: The Rebirth of Metis Nationalism.* Saskatoon: Fifth House Publishers, 2007.

Wilkins, Kerry. "*R. v. Morris*: A Shot in the Dark and Its Repercussions." *Indigenous Law Journal* 7, no. 1 (2008): 31–32.

Williams, Robert A., Jr. *The American Indian in Western Legal Thought: The Discourses of Conquest.* New York: Oxford University Press, 1990.

Woodcock, George. *Gabriel Dumont.* Montréal: Lidec, 1979.

WPIG. UN Commission on Human Rights, Sub-commission on Prevention of Discrimination and Protection of Minorities, Working Group on Indigenous Populations. 10 June 1996. *Working Paper by the Chairperson-Rapporteur, Mrs. Erica-Irene A. Daes, on the Concept of 'Indigenous People.'* 14th Sess, 1996. UN Doc E/CN.4/Sub.2/AC.4/1996/.

Zelig, Ken, and Victoria Zelig. *Ste. Madeleine: Community without a Town: Metis Elders in Interview.* Winnipeg: Pemmican Publications, 1987.

Contributors

CHRIS ANDERSEN is Métis, originally from the Parkland region of Saskatchewan. He received his PhD in 2005 from the Department of Sociology at the University of Alberta and became a faculty member of that university's Faculty of Native Studies in 2000. In 2014, he was appointed Full Professor. He is the former Director of the Rupertsland Centre for Métis Research and is currently Dean of the Faculty. Andersen is the author of *"Métis": Race, Recognition and the Struggle for Indigenous Peoplehood* (UBC Press, 2014). In 2015, *"Métis"* was awarded the 2014 Prize for Best Subsequent Book in Native American and Indigenous Studies by the Native American and Indigenous Studies Association, and in 2016, it was shortlisted for the 2015 Canada Prize. Andersen is a founding member of the Native American and Indigenous Studies Association Executive Council and editor of the journal *aboriginal policy studies*. In 2014, he was named a member of the inaugural class of the Royal Society of Canada's College of New Scholars, Artists and Scientists.

TONY BELCOURT was born in the historic Métis community of Lac Ste. Anne, Alberta, and has had a long and distinguished career as a Métis leader and activist. Since being elected Vice-President of the Métis Association of Alberta in 1970, Belcourt has played a key role in establishing a national voice for Canada's Métis and non–Status Indians. In 1971 he moved to Ottawa to take up the role of the Founding President of the Native Council of Canada. His efforts to build a Canada-wide organization that established a national profile for Métis contributed to the recognition of the Métis in the Constitution Act, 1982 as one of the Aboriginal peoples of Canada. In the 1980s and '90s he also served as an advisor to the Métis National Council and the Inuit Committee on National Issues in the First Ministers' Conferences on the rights of Aboriginal peoples in the Constitution, the Meech Lake Accord, and the Charlottetown Accord in 1992. Most recently, he served as President of the Métis Nation of Ontario, an organization that he founded in 1993 and led to prominence until his retirement in May 2008. Recognized internationally for representation of the Métis Nation at the United Nations (UN) and the Organization of American States (OAS), Tony is a champion of access to, and the appropriate use of, ICT's by Indigenous people. He is Past Co-Chair of the Aboriginal Education Council at OCAD University. Tony Belcourt received the National Aboriginal Achievement Award for Public Service in 2006; received an Honorary Doctorate of Laws from Lakehead University in 2010 and was appointed an Officer of the Order of Canada, 2013. He has been carried by the Pipe since 2004. Now regarded as a Métis elder, Tony Belcourt is often invited to present on Indigenous culture, history and traditions.

CATHERINE BELL is Professor of Law at the University of Alberta, specializing in Indigenous legal issues, cultural heritage law, and interdisciplinary community-based legal research. She has been a visiting professor and scholar at various national and international universities and has helped develop and deliver Indigenous legal education programs, including the Program of Legal Studies for Native People (University of Saskatchewan), the Akitsiraq Law School for Inuit students (Nunavut), and the Banff Centre for Management Aboriginal Leadership and Self-Government Program. Professor Bell has published widely on Aboriginal constitutional rights and has worked in collaboration with Métis, First Nation, Inuit, federal, provincial, and international government bodies and organizations. She is the author of *Contemporary Métis Justice: The Settlement Way*; *Alberta Métis Settlements Legislation: An Overview of Ownership and Management of Settlement Lands*; and numerous articles on Métis constitutional rights. Other books include *Intercultural Dispute*

Resolution in Aboriginal Contexts (with D. Kahane); *First Nations' Cultural Heritage and Law: Case Studies, Voices and Perspectives* (with V. Napoleon); and *First Nations' Cultural Heritage and Law: Reconciliation and Reform* (with R.K. Paterson). In 2012 she was honoured with the CBA Ramon John Hnatyshyn Governor General's Gold Medal for outstanding contributions to the development of law and legal education in Canada. Her current research includes issues of jurisdiction and honour of the Crown in implementing modern constitutional and other solemn promises to Métis, and the intersection of Canadian property law, Indigenous law, and ethics in museum and collaborative research contexts.

DEBORAH A. BOLNICK is an anthropological geneticist and biological anthropologist who explores how socio-political forces, historical events, and social inequalities shape human genomic and epigenomic diversity, as well as human biology more broadly. In her research, Bolnick analyzes DNA from ancient and contemporary peoples, in conjunction with other lines of evidence, to help reconstruct population histories in the Americas. She received her PhD in anthropology from the University of California at Davis and is a past president of the American Association of Anthropological Genetics. She is also the co-author (with John Relethford) of *Reflections of Our Past: How Human History Is Revealed in Our Genes* and a co-organizer of the Summer internship for INdigenous peoples in Genomics (SING) program. Bolnick is currently working closely with Indigenous partners to assess the genetic and epigenetic impacts of settler colonialism in the southern United States and central Mexico. She is also interested in the ethical, legal, and social implications of genomic research, and she studies the methods and applications of genetic ancestry testing, investigating how ancestry tests influence and are influenced by contemporary understandings of race, ethnicity, gender, and identity. Through her work, Bolnick strives to help integrate more critical, intersectional, historically marginalized, and decolonial perspectives into science.

BRENDA L. GUNN is Associate Professor at Robson Hall Faculty of Law, University of Manitoba. She has a BA from the University of Manitoba and a JD from the University of Toronto. She completed her LLM in Indigenous Peoples Law and Policy at the University of Arizona. She articled with Sierra Legal Defence Fund (now Ecojustice Canada) and has also

worked at a community legal clinic in Rabinal, Guatemala, on a case of
genocide submitted to the Inter-American Commission of Human Rights,
and with First Nations on Aboriginal and treaty rights issues in Manitoba.
As a proud Metis woman, she continues to combine her academic research
with activism, pushing for greater recognition of Indigenous peoples'
inherent rights as determined by their own legal traditions. Gunn continues to be actively involved in the international Indigenous peoples'
movement, regularly attending international meetings. She developed a
handbook on understanding and implementing the UN Declaration that
is quickly becoming one of the main resources in Canada and has delivered workshops on the UN Declaration across Canada and internationally.
In 2013, she participated in the UNITAR Training Programme to Enhance
the Conflict Prevention and Peacemaking Capacities of Indigenous
Peoples' Representatives, which continues to influence her research.

AREND J.A. HOEKSTRA is an associate at Cassels Brock and Blackwell
LLP and also a Chartered Professional Accountant. Hoekstra advises
government, industry, and Indigenous clients across Canada on the
Crown's duty to consult, project development, regulatory processes, litigation strategy, and benefit agreements. His previous experience includes
acting as a senior advisor for one of Canada's largest mines and acting as
a controller for a large helicopter services company serving the mineral
exploration and mining industry in the Northwest Territories.

THOMAS ISAAC is a nationally recognized authority in the area of
Aboriginal law and leads Cassels Brock and Blackwell LLP's National
Aboriginal Law Practice. Isaac has served as a mediator in complex
multi-jurisdictional Aboriginal-related disputes and has appeared before
courts and regulatory bodies across Canada, including the Supreme
Court of Canada. He has published fourteen books and monographs on
Aboriginal law, including the fifth edition of his text *Aboriginal Law*. His
publications on Aboriginal law have been cited with approval by Canadian
courts, including the Supreme Court of Canada and the Federal Court
of Appeal. Isaac was former Chief Treaty Negotiator for the Government
of British Columbia, former Assistant Deputy Minister responsible for
establishing Nunavut for the Government of the Northwest Territories,
and previously served in a senior capacity with the Government of

Saskatchewan, dealing with Aboriginal issues. In 2015 Isaac was appointed by Canada as the Minister's Special Representative to the Minister of Crown-Indigenous Relations regarding Section 35 Métis Rights and Reconciliation. His report—"A Matter of National and Constitutional Import: Section 35 Métis Rights and the *Manitoba Metis Federation* Decision"—was released in 2016. Isaac also served as the Minister's Special Representative to the Minister of Crown-Indigenous Relations and the Premier of the Northwest Territories regarding the Southeast Northwest Territories Region and the Akaitcho Dene and the Northwest Territories Métis Nation negotiations. His report—"A Path to Reconciliation"— was released in 2017. He presently serves as the Minister's Special Representative for the Minister of Crown-Indigenous Relations to conduct exploratory discussions regarding the Gottfriedson class action lawsuit against Canada relating to residential schools' day students. Isaac is a member of the law societies of British Columbia, Alberta, Northwest Territories, Nunavut, and Yukon. He holds BA (Hons.), MA, LLB, and LLM degrees, and was named in 2018 as one of the "Top 25 Most Influential Lawyers" in Canada by *Canadian Lawyer*.

NATHALIE KERMOAL is a Breton (a people whose territory is situated on the west coast of France). She holds a PhD in history from the University of Ottawa and is Full Professor in the Faculty of Native Studies at the University of Alberta. Kermoal has published three books and numerous articles in academic journals and collected volumes. Her areas of research are Métis issues, Aboriginal constitutional issues, urban Indigenous history, and Indigenous women's issues. In 2011–12, she served as Interim Dean of the Faculty of Native Studies at the University of Alberta, and in 2013–14, she was special advisor on Aboriginal academic programs with the Provost's office. Since 2009, Kermoal has been Associate Dean Academic of the Faculty of Native Studies, and as of January 2016, she has also been Director of the Rupertsland Centre for Métis Research at the Faculty of Native Studies.

DARRYL LEROUX is Associate Professor in the Department of Social Justice and Community Studies at Saint Mary's University in Kjipuktuk (Halifax), in unceded Mi'kmaw territory. He is a white settler whose Norman, Poitevin, Breton, and Parisian ancestors were among the first

Europeans to colonize the St. Lawrence River Valley. His interest in exposing current efforts by French descendants to claim Indigenous identities
comes from his engagement with anti-colonial thinkers and activists. His
book *Distorted Descent: White Claims to Indigenous Identity* was published
by UMP in 2019.

BRENDA MACDOUGALL is University Research Chair in Metis Family
and Community Traditions at the University of Ottawa. Macdougall's
research centres on Metis family and culture, and she has worked extensively with Metis communities in Saskatchewan to document their history.
She is the author of several articles and a book, *One of the Family: Metis
Culture in Nineteenth-Century Northwestern Saskatchewan* (2010). In her
role at the University of Ottawa, Macdougall is engaged in a number of
research projects related to the history of Metis communities, including the
Digital Archives Database (DAD) Project, an online resource comprised of
transcribed archival material.

JASON MADDEN is co-managing partner of the law firm Pape Salter
Teillet LLP with offices in Toronto and Vancouver. He is a graduate of
Osgoode Hall Law School and called to the bar in Ontario, Manitoba,
Alberta, the Northwest Territories, and the Yukon. He is recognized by
Lexpert, *BestLawyers,* and *Chambers and Partners* as a leading lawyer in
the area of Aboriginal law and was named one of the 25 Most Influential
Lawyers in Canada by *Canadian Lawyer* in 2014. Madden is also recognized as being at the forefront in the advancement of Métis law in Canada.
He has appeared before the Supreme Court of Canada in all of the cases
dealing with Métis legal issues over the last seventeen years and has been
counsel in much of the Métis rights litigation advanced from Ontario
westward. He is a recipient of the Queen's Diamond Jubilee Medal (2012),
the Dianne Martin Medal for Social Justice Through Law (2015), and
a Lexpert Zenith Award (2018) for his work on the advancement of
Indigenous rights. Madden is a citizen of the Métis Nation and a descendant of the "Halfbreeds of Rainy Lake and River" who collectively adhered
to Treaty 3 in 1875.

AUSTIN W. REYNOLDS is currently an Assistant Professor in the
Department of Anthropology at Baylor University. As a human geneticist,

his primary research focus is to collect large genomic datasets in collaboration with diverse populations to answer questions about human population history and health. This research leverages expertise in applying computational and statistical tools to modern and ancient genomic datasets to reconstruct demographic history, identify local genetic adaptations, and understand the genetic risk factors for disease in populations historically underrepresented in genomics research. Reynolds has ongoing research collaborations with several communities in North America and southern Africa.

RICK W. A. SMITH is an Assistant Professor in the Department of Sociology and Anthropology at George Mason University. Smith is also affiliated with the Indigenous Science, Technology, and Society (STS) Lab in the Faculty of Native Studies at the University of Alberta and is part of the core organizing faculty for the Summer internship for INdigenous peoples in Genomics in Canada (SING Canada). As a biocultural anthropologist, Smith's work merges genomics and epigenomics with feminist, queer, and Indigenous science studies to trace how imperialism is felt on the molecular level.

LAUREN SPRINGS is a bioarcheologist and PhD candidate at the University of Texas at Austin. Her work integrates archeological, ethnohistorical, and genomic methodologies to investigate how historic populations have interacted with, and responded to, European colonial projects in the past and present. Springs is currently involved in multiple research collaborations in Central America and the Southeast United States.

D'ARCY VERMETTE (BA, LLB, LLM, LLD) is a citizen of the Métis Nation of Alberta and an Associate Professor in the Faculty of Native Studies at the University of Alberta. Prior to joining the Faculty of Native Studies, Vermette served as director of the Native Studies program at St. Thomas University.

Index

A

Abella, Rosalie: and defining Métis, 152; reasons for denying federal fiduciary obligation to Métis, 99–100; and writing of *Daniels* decision, 44, 59, 60, 109, 179, 180

Aboriginal law, 70n4

Aboriginal peoples, 64–65, 80. *See also* Indigenous Peoples; Inuit, Métis

Aboriginal rights, 83

Aboriginal title, 83

Acadia, 195

Adams, Howard, 16, 25, 27–28

Alberta, Government of, 25–26, 56, 99, 115n69

Alliance laurentienne des Métis et Indiens, 204n3

Assiniboine, Josephte, 251

Association des Métis d'Alberta et des Territories du Nord-Ouest, 25

Attorney General of Canada v. Canard, 60

Aubin, Claude, 191

B

Barrera, Jorge, 234

Battle of Grand Coteau, 257

Battle of Seven Oaks, 22

Belcourt, Tony, 29

Belhumeur, Marguerite Monet dit, 250

Bennett, Carolyn, 150, 181

Berger, Pierre, 258

Black Power Movement, 29

Borrows, John, 132

Boucher, Marguerite, 241

Boyden, Joseph, 234–35, 237

Brady, Jim, 25

Bruneau, Jean Baptiste, 251

C

Calder v. British Columbia, 144n47

Campbell v. British Columbia (AG), 73n36, 137, 146n109

Canada, Government of: agency of used by SCC as means of including Métis in s. 91(24), 131, 132–33; aim of opening west in 19th century, 23; appeals *Daniels v. Canada* decision, 56–58; attempt to delay *Daniels v. Canada,* 46; avoids dealing with Métis, 1–2, 6, 19, 26, 33–34; awareness of Métis poverty by, 2; colonial policies of, 153; commitment to UNDRIP, 150; dealings with Métis in 19th century, 23–24; and definition of Métis, 235; and division of powers in s. 91(24), 53–55; and duty to negotiate as responsibility of, 62–64; effect of *Daniels* decision on, 36; endorses UNDRIP, 110–11, 150; fiduciary responsibility to Métis, 99–100; framework agreements with Métis communities, 4, 67, 76n120, 104, 111, 114n44, 182; funding Métis programs, 19; implicated in *Daniels v. Canada* trial decision, 3–4, 55–56; and Manitoba Act, 100–101; and *MMF v. Canada,* 3; multiculturalism policy, 30–31; NCC lobbying of, 16–18; obligations of reconciliation on, 86; patriation of Constitution, 32–33; practical implications of *Daniels* case on, 64–65, 65–69; RCAP recommends it take responsibility for Métis, 2–3; reaction to *Daniels* decision, 181; and redress, 89; refusal to recognize s. 91(24), 34; role in declarations sought in *Daniels v. Canada,* 47–48; signs Canada-Métis Nation Accord, 36, 68–69; and White Paper, 30

Canada-Métis Nation Accord, 36, 68–69

Canadian Constitution: Aboriginal peoples defined in, 80; defining of Métis for, 49, 50; Métis mentioned in, 19; patriation, 32–33. *See also* Constitution Act; s. 35 of Constitutional Act; s. 91(24) of Constitutional Act

Canadian Human Rights Tribunal, 104

Charlottetown Accord, 2, 35

Chartier, Clement, 181

Cherokee Nation v. Georgia, 125–26

Chippewas of the Thames First Nation v. Enbridge Pipelines Inc., 91, 92, 93, 94

Chrétien, Jean, 17, 19

Christie, Gordon, 140

Clyde River (Hamlet) v. Petroleum Geo-Services Inc., 91, 92, 93

colonialism, 25, 27, 65, 119, 123, 200, 201, 211. *See also* racism

Communauté Autochtone Chibougamau-Chapais Eeyou Istchee, 205n6

Communauté Mikinak de la Montérégie, 151–52

Congress on Aboriginal Peoples (CAP): and *Daniels v. Canada,* 36, 46; and FCA, 103; and right to be consulted and negotiated with, 105, 108; split with MNC over control of Métis, 50–51, 181

Conrad, Grace, 181

Constitution Act, 21, 33. *See also* section 35 of Constitutional Act; section 91(24) of Constitutional Act

courts: acceptance of international human rights law by, 158; defining Métis for Canada's constitution, 49, 50; litigation of Métis rights and claims in, 51; and Métis fight for federal recognition, 36; and Métis right of representative authority, 109–10; *R. v. Tronson,* 127–30; studying internal logic of legal decisions, 118–20, 141n4; and weakness of legal histories, 117–18. *See also* Federal Court (FC); Federal Court of Appeal (FAC); Supreme Court of Canada (SCC)

D

Daniels, Gabriel, 46

Daniels, Harry: background, 40n60; and
  Daniels v. Canada, 46; as fieldwork
  organizer, 15; fight against government
  buck-passing, 30; fight for Métis under
  91(24), 35–36; on Métis-as-mixed,
  43n111; and patriation of Constitution,
  19, 32–33, 272; political development
  of, 29; as president of NCC, 19; views of
  Métis as founding nation of Canada, 32;
  views of multiculturalism, 31

Daniels, Stan, 16

Daniels v. Canada: circumstances leading
  to, 19; compared to *Tronson,* 140;
  conclusions on legal effectiveness of,
  90–91; criticized for missing opportunity to allow Métis to self-define, 159;
  decision in, 3, 21, 44, 55–56, 171; definition of Métis in, 80, 171, 175–76,
  178–80; effect on federal government,
  36; in Federal Court of Appeal, 56–61;
  and *Final Report of TRC,* 89–90; and
  genetic claims of Indigenous belonging, 211–12; how court contrasted s. 35
  from s. 91(24) in, 79; how it conflicts
  with UNDRIP, 110–11; importance
  of context in how it's understood, 273;
  importance of evolving language in, 79;
  incorrect assumptions about, 44–45;
  increase in self-identification after,
  149, 151–52, 233; intervenors in, 180;
  issues that have arisen since decision
  in, 151–54; legacy of, 91–92, 93–94;
  legal implications of, 61–65; main issues
  of, 179; and Métis self-government,
  160–61; Métis-as-mixed definition
  from, 4, 52, 63, 131, 175; mixing use of
  Aboriginal and Indigenous in, 82; and
  MNC-CAP battle for control of Métis,
  50–51; plaintiffs in, 46; practical implications of, 4, 65–69, 149, 163, 170–71,
  183–84; questions regarding redress in,
  84–85, 87–89, 90; racism of, 130; reaction to decision in, 180–83; resolves
  dispute over jurisdictional responsibility for Métis, 148–49; SCC avoids

recognition of Métis peoplehood in,
  136, 138–39; SCC rejects fiduciary
  duty in, 102–3; SCC rejects Métis right
  to choose representation, 109; and
  Supreme Court's use of term Indigenous,
  81–82; three declarations sought in,
  47–48, 98–99; as transformative case,
  3–4, 6; trial phase, 46–47

Delgamuukw v. British Columbia, 85, 99

discrimination, 226. *See also* colonialism;
  racism, 228

Dumont, Gabriel, 250–60

Dumont, Isadore, 250

Dumont, Jean Baptiste, 250–51

Durant, Paul, 251

E

Eastern Métis: anti-Indigenous viewpoint of,
  197–98, 201, 203; claims for their existence, 189–95, 203; French-English
  nationalist impulse of, 195–97, 202–3,
  204; ignores presence of Indigenous in
  Quebec, 201–2; rejection of Indigenous
  roots of Métis, 193, 195, 198–201, 204

Eastern Woodland Métis Nation of Nova
  Scotia (EWMNNS), 156

ethnic mobility, 233

F

Federal Court (FC), 136–37, 138

Federal Court of Appeal (FCA), 56–58, 63,
  100, 103, 113n32

*Final Report of the Truth and Reconciliation
  Commission,* 79, 89–90

First Nations, 199, 200

The Forgotten People (tabloid), 17

Fort Chipewyan Métis Nation of
  Alberta, 109–10

free, prior, and informed consent, 162–63

G

Gaboury, Marie-Anne, 265n31

Gagnon, Denis, 191–92, 193, 195, 196, 197–98, 199–200

Gardner, Leah, 36, 46

Gariepy, Joseph, 258

genealogies, 237, 239, 241

genetic ancestry tests: four reference group test of, 220–22; how they work and limitations of, 216–20; inability of to determine who is Indigenous, 224–25; lack of ability to link people to discrete groups or places, 222, 224; popularity of, 213–14; and proliferation of self-identification, 210–13; two stories of, 225–30; types of commercially available, 214–16

Grant, Cuthbert, 22, 265n33

H

Haida Nation v. BC, 61, 64, 92, 107

Hampton, Fred, 29

Hellyer report, 2, 39n41

historical literacy: and context, 273; importance to Métis, 259–60; lack of in Métis self-indentification, 234, 236–37

honour of the Crown: and duty to negotiate, 106; and MGRSAs, 68; other contexts for, 112n19; and s. 91(24), 104; and Supreme Court of Canada, 100, 101, 103

Hudson's Bay Company (HBC), 22–23, 246

I

Île à la Crosse mission, 248–49

Indian Act: colonial legacy of, 53–54; and *Daniels* decision, 44, 56; definition of Indians in, 49–50; plan to abolish, 30; and *R. v. Tronson,* 127, 129

Indigenous Peoples: definition of in international law, 154; DNA sequences common in, 219–20; Eastern Métis narrative as rejection of, 193, 195, 198–201, 204; inability of gene tests to determine, 224–25; international criteria for identifying, 155; international rights of, 158–63; land rights as key part of definition of, 161; legislation defining, 34–35; Supreme Court use of this term, 81–82, 91–93; as synonym for Aboriginal peoples, 80, 92–93. *See also* Métis; United Nations Declaration on the Rights of Indigenous Peoples (UNDRIP)

Innu, 197

Inter American Commission on Human Rights (IACHR), 156–57

International Covenant on Civil and Political Rights (ICCPR), 159–60

International Covenant on Economic, Social and Cultural Rights (ICESCR), 159–60

Inuit: in Canadian Constitution, 19, 21, 80; federal government agreements with, 71n19; and federal government definition of Indian, 35; federal government responsibility for, 15, 47; and MGRSAs, 68

Isaac, Thomas, 36, 66

J

Joudrey, Terry, 46, 149

juridical fields, 172–75

K

King Jr., Martin Luther, 28

kinscapes: defined, 236; and L. Riel's place in, 248, 249; and multiple connections between families, 242, 245–46, 250, 254, 257, 258

L

Lachapelle, Claude Riel, 192–93

Laframboise, Louise, 250, 254

Lagimodiere, Jean Baptiste, 265n31

Lagimodiere, Julie, 246, 247–48

Lake Nipigon Métis Association, 27

land claims, 35, 68, 77n124, 104

Lavallee, Harry, 16

Lépine, Maxine, 27

M

Macdonald, John A., 138

Magnet, Joseph, 2, 3–4

Malaterre, Isabelle, 245

Malcolm X, 28

Malette, Sébastien, 193–94, 197, 201

Manitoba Act of 1870: conditions of, 100–101, 146n109; evidence of Métis peoplehood from, 133–34; as roots of Métis identity, 31, 32; use of by SCC in *R. v. Blais,* 138; writing of, 23

Manitoba Métis Federation (MMF): in *Daniels v. Canada,* 101, 136; established, 27; framework for negotiations with federal government, 104; and interim reconciliation plan, 67; promises land base for Métis people, 161; recent agreements with federal government, 66–69; represent Métis in scrip claims case, 109. See also *MMF v. Canada*

Marshall, John, 125–26

Métis: accessing funds for programs, 19; agreements with provincial governments, 99; belief in their role as partner in Confederation, 31, 32; and Black Power Movement, 29; brief to federal government in 1972, 17–18; as buffalo hunters, 246–47, 251, 257; definition of in *Daniels,* 56, 72n30, 175–76; definition of in *Daniels* appeal, 57–58, 59; denied representative authority in *Daniels,* 109–10; development as distinct people, 48–49, 212–13, 236, 257–58; development of political movement, 22–24, 25–27, 31–32, 260; 156; effect of broadening definition of in *Powley,* 95n20; effect of denial of their peoplehood, 139–40; and failure of Charlottetown Accord, 2; failure of *Daniels* to delineate Métis from non-Status Indians, 153; federal government avoids dealing with, 1–2, 6, 19, 26, 33–34; feelings about multiculturalism policy, 30–31; fight against White Paper, 30; fight for inclusion in 91(24), 21, 34–36; and framework agreements with federal government, 4; as French-language adjective, 235–36; historical evidence of their peoplehood, 131–32, 133–34, 136–37; importance of historical literacy to, 238–39, 240, 259–60; and intergenerational relationships between families, 242, 245; international rights of, 158–61, 162, 163; and judge's decision in *Daniels v. Canada,* 55–56; L. Riel's prosopography, 241–50; lack of their perspective in *R. v. Blais,* 123–24; and Manitoba Act, 101; mentioned in Constitution, 19; and patriation of Constitution, 32–33; RCAP on, 2–3; and scrip, 15, 24, 30, 101, 109, 138; settlements, 15, 20n2, 25; settler society lack of awareness of, 16; Supreme Court avoids recognition of their peoplehood, 131–32, 133–35, 136, 138–39, 140; three creation stories of, 176–78; variety in origins and professions of, 264n28; and view of Métis-as-mixed narrative, 131; women-centred family networks of, 199. See also *Daniels v. Canada*

Métis and Non-Status Indian Constitutional Review Commission, 32–33, 35, 41n67

Métis Federation of Canada (MFC), 182

Métis Government Recognition and Self-Government Agreement (MGRSA), 67–68, 77n124

Métis Nation: creation story of, 177–78; entitled to human rights, 163; historical development of, 48–49; how it defines Métis, 49; and Louis Riel, 190; meeting WGIP criteria as Indigenous, 155–56; reaction to *Daniels* decision through MNC, 181; rejection of Métis-as-mixed, 52, 59; and the right to self-define, 159; self-declared Métis groups not accepted by, 156; signs Accord with Canada, 36, 68–69; who determines citizenship in, 49–50

Métis Nation Accord, 2, 35

Métis Nation of Alberta (MNA): agreement with Alberta government, 115n69; and framework agreement with federal government, 67–68, 76n123, 111, 114n44, 182; issue of representative authority, 109–10, 115n69; and scrip, 76n119

Métis Nation of Ontario (MNO), 51, 56, 68, 76n119, 176

Métis National Council (MNC): agreements with federal government, 66–69, 182; definition of Métis, 159, 180; formed, 35, 50; reaction to *Daniels* decision, 181; signs Canada-Métis Nation Accord, 36; split with CAP over control of Métis, 50–51, 181; tie to Métis Nation, 178

Métis Population Betterment Act, 25

Métis self-identification: Alliance laurentienne des Métis et Indiens, 204n3; and claims for Eastern Métis existence, 189–95; effect of *Daniels v. Canada* on, 69, 149, 151–52, 180; failure to meet WGIP criteria as Indigenous, 156; genetic ancestry tests boost to, 210–13; growth in literature on since *Powley*, 189, 272–73; IACHR criteria for, 156–57; increase in, 188, 204n2,

233–34, 272; and J. Boyden, 234–35; lack of historical literacy of, 234, 236–37; as part of Métis creation story, 176; use of genealogies for, 239. *See also* genetic ancestry tests; Métis-as-mixed

Métis Settlements General Council (MSGC), 66, 67, 115n69, 182

Métis Society of Saskatchewan, 27

Métis-as-mixed: creation stories of, 176–77; definition of Métis from *Daniels v. Canada*, 4, 52, 63, 131, 175; failure to meet international standards as a people, 156, 157, 158; and genetic claims of belonging, 212; H. Daniels view of, 43n111; and J. Boyden, 234–35; lack of place-specific connection, 163; Métis leaders view of, 31, 159; represents popular understanding of Métis, 176, 259; and section 35 of Constitutional Act, 152; supporters reaction to *Daniels* decision, 182–83; Supreme Court's changing position on, 57, 152–53. *See also* Métis self–identification

métissage, 192, 194, 196, 203

Michaux, Émmanuel, 190, 191, 194, 195, 196–97, 198

Mitch (pseudonym), 225, 228–29

MMF v. Canada: to advance section 35 rights, 51; and Crown's duty to negotiate, 108; and fiduciary relationship between Canada and Métis, 99, 100; findings of, 3; and Isaacs report, 66; SCC downplaying Métis agency in, 139

Monroe, John, 33

Morrow, William G., 125, 143n44

N

Nation Métis du Québec (NMQ), 190, 191

Native Council of Canada (NCC): accessing funds for programs by, 19; and Declaration of Métis and Indian Rights (1979), 31; establishing of, 6, 15–16, 27, 40n49; lobbying federal government, 16–18; and MNC, 35; and patriation of Constitution, 32–33

Native Housing Task Force, 26, 40n42

Natural Resource Transfer Agreements (NRTAs), 123

Neyihaw Pwat (Iron Alliance), 178

non-Status Indians, 57, 153

Norris, Malcom, 25

Northern Halfbreed Association, 26

Northwest Rebellion, 24, 27

O

Ontario Métis and Non-Status Indian Association, 27

P

patriation of Constitution, 32–33

Patterson, George, 124

Pearce, W. (government agent), 24

Pelletier, Gérard, 17

Pemmican Proclamation, 22

peoplehood, 144n67, 158

Phelan, Michael L., 46, 55–56, 56–58, 100

Pillard, Catherine, 234

Poitras, Gabriel, 245, 250

Prison of Grass: Canada from a Native Point of View (Adams), 27

prosopography: described, 240–41; of G. Dumont, 250–60; of L. Riel, 241–50

provincial governments: and agreements with Métis, 99, 112n8; and ARDA agreements, 19; federal government laying off responsibility to Métis on, 33–34; and federal obligations for child welfare services, 104; inability to act without federal cooperation, 1, 111; lack of action on Métis housing, 26; powers granted in s. 91(24), 52–53. *See also* Alberta, Government of

Q

Quebec, 31–32

R

R. v. Blais, 60, 74n87, 123–24, 137–38

R. v. Powley: attempt to advance s. 35 rights and claims, 51, 60, 61; and Crown's duty to negotiate, 108; implications of, 4; increase in self-identification after, 233; referred to in *Daniels v. Canada* definition of Métis, 179–80; and self-identification literature, 189, 272–73; and test for determining who is Métis, 3, 63–64, 80, 83–84, 95n20, 183

R. v. Sparrow, 85, 141n6

R. v. Tronson, 127–30, 140

R. v. Van der Peet, 64, 83

racial shifting, 233

racism: and cases of legal identity, 122–24; of *Daniels v. Canada,* 130; of denial of Métis peoplehood, 139–40; examples of structural racism in law, 125–26; overt v. structural, 124; in *R. v. Tronson,* 127–30. *See also* colonialism

Re Paulette et al. and Registrar of Titles, 125, 126

reconciliation, 64–65, 67, 85–86

redress: and concern with past harms, 90; in *Daniels v. Canada,* 84–85, 86–89; and

legacy of *Daniels v. Canada,* 93–94; role
of *Final Report of TRC* in, 89–90

Reference Re Eskimo, 15, 60, 122–23

residential schools, 87, 88, 94

Rex v. Syliboy, 124

Rhéaume, Gene, 26

Riel, Jean-Louis, 246–47

Riel, Louis: and 1885 Rebellion, 24, 138;
connection with G. Dumont, 258–59;
on Manitoba Act, 133; and Métis
Nation, 190; prosopography of, 241–50;
and provisional government, 23

Riel, Sara, 248

Riel Rebellion, 23

*Rio Tinto Alcan Inc. v. Carrier Sekani Tribal
Council,* 92

Rivard, Étienne, 190–91, 196, 197, 200

Royal Commission on Aboriginal Peoples
(RCAP), 2–3, 23, 48–49

S

Sarah (pseudonym), 225, 226–27

Sarcee, Josette, 251, 254

Saskatchewan Métis Association, 26

Saskatchewan Métis Society, 26

Saul, John Ralston, 235

Sayer, Pierre-Guillaume, 22, 155, 246–47

section 35 of Constitutional Act: attempt
to advance claims through *Powley,* 51,
60, 61; definition of Aboriginal peoples,
80; and duty of the Crown to negotiate,
106–8; how court contrasted s. 35 with
s. 91(24) in *Daniels,* 79; and Métis-as-
mixed definition, 152; and Powley test
for Métis rights, 83–84; and provincial
agreements with Métis, 99; and reconciliation, 85–86; role in legal implications
of *Daniels v. Canada,* 64, 65; supercedes
s. 91(24) in courts, 51; Supreme Court
ruling on in appeal, 59–60

section 91(24) of Constitutional Act: and
amended Powley test for, 84; *Daniels*
judge rules on, 55–56; explanation
of, 52–55; Federal Court of Appeal
ruling on, 56–58; federal government's
refusal to recognize, 34; framework
for provided by *Daniels,* 90–91; and
honour of the Crown principle, 104;
limits of argued in *Daniels v. Canada,*
47; Métis fight to be included in, 16, 18,
35–36; mixing use of terms Aboriginal
and Indigenous in, 82, 93; and modified definition of Métis for in *Daniels,*
80; practical implications of Métis
inclusion in, 103; RCAP on, 2–3; and
redress, 84–85, 86–89; reduced significance of, 72n32; Supreme Court rules
Métis Indians under, 21; Supreme Court
ruling on in *Daniels* appeal, 58–61; used
in arguments before Human Rights
Tribunal, 104

self-determination, 159–60

self-government, 67–68, 69, 77n124,
111, 160–61

self-Indigenization, 229. *See also* Métis
self-identification

settler colonialism, 211

settler nativism, 152

Simpson, George, 265n33

Sinclair, Jim, 16

Smitheram, Butch, 16

Spence, Angus, 16

Stanbury, Bob, 17

Supreme Court of Canada (SCC): approach
to s. 91(24), 54–55; avoids recognition
of Métis peoplehood, 131–32, 133–35,
136, 138–39, 140; conflating fiduciary
obligations with fiduciary relationships,
101–2; definition of Métis in *Daniels v.
Canada,* 152–53, 159, 175–76, 178–79,
179–80; denies two declarations of
Daniels v. Canada, 99, 102–3, 105–8,
109, 113n32; evidence it does not see
Aboriginal people as self-determining,
135–36; evolving language of, 78–79;

examples of downplaying Métis agency, 137–39; how it contrasts s. 35 from s. 91(24) in *Daniels,* 79; how its decisions are written, 172; importance of interveners in cases of, 185; judgement in *Daniels v. Canada,* 21, 44; legal implications of its ruling on *Daniels v. Canada,* 61–65; and Métis-as-mixed definition, 57, 152–53, 175; mixing use of terms Aboriginal and Indigenous by, 81–82, 91–93; modification of Powley test for Métis rights, 83; and *Paulette,* 125; political and social ramifications of its decisions, 4–5; and principle of honour of the Crown, 100, 101, 103; and *R. v. Blais,* 123–24; refractive and generative nature of its decisions, 5, 172–75, 184–85, 273; role in defining Métis rights, 2, 3–4; rules Métis as Indians under s. 91(24), 21, 131, 132–33, 145n87; rules on *Daniels v. Canada* on appeal, 58–61; and *Tsilhqot'in Nation v. BC,* 135; and use of redress in *Daniels,* 84–85, 86–90; view of Aboriginal rights, 83; view of reconciliation, 64–65, 85–86. See also *Daniels v. Canada*

Truth and Reconciliation Commission, 150. See also *Final Report of the Truth and Reconciliation Commission*

Tsilhqot' in Nation v. BC, 54, 61, 108, 113n39, 135, 141n9

U

UN Expert Mechanism on the Rights of Indigenous Peoples (EMRIP), 162

Unama'ki Voyageurs Métis Nation, 183

Union Est-Ouest, 197

Union nationale métisse Saint-Joseph du Manitoba, 197, 260

United Nations Declaration on the Rights of Indigenous Peoples (UNDRIP): adopted by UN General Assembly, 150; Canada's voting history on, 150; and federal government's commitment to, 110–11; future Métis governments obligated to rights in, 164; Indigenous rights recognized by, 149–50, 158–59, 160, 162; Métis involvement with, 156

T

Tomkins, Peter, 25

Treaty 3 Adhesion, 136, 137

Trottier, Charles, 254

Trudeau, Justin, 66, 150

Trudeau, Pierre E., 17, 29–30, 33

W

White Paper, 29–30

Wilkie, Cecilia, 258

Wilkie, Jean Baptiste, 257

Wilkie, Judith, 258

Wilkie, Madeleine, 257–58

Working Group on Indigenous Populations (WGIP), 155